MICROSOFT® OFFICE

Publisher 2003

**Complete Concepts
and Techniques**

Gary B. Shelly

Thomas J. Cashman

Joy L. Starks

THOMSON
COURSE TECHNOLOGY

COURSE TECHNOLOGY
25 THOMSON PLACE
BOSTON MA 02210

SHELLY
CASHMAN
SERIES®

Australia • Canada • Denmark • Japan • Mexico • New Zealand • Philippines • Puerto Rico • Singapore
South Africa • Spain • United Kingdom • United States

THOMSON

COURSE TECHNOLOGY

Microsoft Office Publisher 2003
Complete Concepts and Techniques

Gary B. Shelly
Thomas J. Cashman
Joy L. Starks

Executive Editor:
Cheryl Costantini

Senior Acquisitions Editor:
Dana Merk

Senior Product Manager:
Alexandra Arnold

Associate Product Manager:
Reed Cotter

Editorial Assistant:
Selena Coppock

Print Buyer:
Laura Burns

Signing Representative:
Cheryl Costantini

Series Consulting Editor:
Jim Quasney

Director of Production:
Becky Herrington

Production Editor:
Deb Masi

Production Assistant:
Jennifer Quiambao

Development Editor:
Lyn Markowicz

Copy Editor:
Lyn Markowicz

Proofreader:
Nancy Lamm

Interior Designer:
Becky Herrington

Cover Designers:
Ken Russo
Richard Herrera

Illustrators:
Richard Herrera
Andrew Bartel

Compositors:
Jeanne Black
Andrew Bartel
Kellee LaVars

Indexer:
Cristina Haley

Printer:
Banta Menasha

MICROSOFT® OFFICE

Publisher 2003

Complete Concepts and Techniques

Contents

Microsoft Office
Publisher 2003

Project Five

Creating Business Forms and Tables

Project Six

Creating an E-Commerce Web Site

Preface

The Shelly Cashman Series® offers the finest textbooks in computer education. We are proud of the fact that our series of Microsoft Office 4.3, Microsoft Office 95, Microsoft Office 97, Microsoft Office 2000, and Microsoft Office XP textbooks have been the most widely used books in education. With each new edition of our Office books, we have made significant improvements based on the software and comments made by the instructors and students. The *Microsoft Office Publisher 2003* books continue with the innovation, quality, and reliability that you have come to expect from the Shelly Cashman Series.

In this *Microsoft Office Publisher 2003* book, you will find an educationally sound, highly visual, and easy-to-follow pedagogy that combines a vastly improved step-by-step approach with corresponding screens. All projects and exercises in this book are designed to take full advantage of the Publisher 2003 enhancements. The project material is developed to ensure that students will see the importance of learning Publisher for future coursework. The popular Other Ways and More About features offer in-depth knowledge of Publisher 2003, and the new Q&A feature offers students a way to solidify important desktop publishing concepts. The Learn It Online page presents a wealth of additional exercises to ensure your students have all the reinforcement they need.

Objectives of This Textbook

Microsoft Office Publisher 2003: Complete Concepts and Techniques is intended for a two-unit course or a major portion of a full semester desktop-publishing course that uses Microsoft Office Publisher 2003 to create publications. No experience with a computer is assumed, and no mathematics beyond the high school freshman level is required. The objectives of this book are:

- To teach the fundamentals of Microsoft Office Publisher
- To acquaint students with the proper procedures to design and create professional quality publications suitable for course work, professional purposes, and personal use
- To expose students to practical examples of the computer as a useful desktop publishing tool
- To create a Web site using Microsoft Office Publisher
- To develop an exercise-oriented approach that allows learning by doing
- To introduce students to new input technologies
- To encourage independent study and help those who are working alone

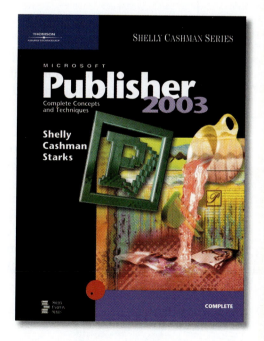

The Shelly Cashman Approach

Features of the Shelly Cashman Series *Microsoft Office Publisher 2003* books include:

- **Project Orientation:** Each project in the book presents a practical problem and complete solution using an easy-to-understand methodology.
- **Step-by-Step, Screen-by-Screen Instructions:** Each of the tasks required to complete a project is identified throughout the project. Full-color screens accompany the steps.
- **Thoroughly Tested Projects:** Unparalleled quality is ensured because every screen in the book is produced by the author only after performing a step, and then each project must pass Course Technology's award-winning Quality Assurance program.
- **Other Ways Boxes and Quick Reference Summary:** The Other Ways boxes displayed at the end of many of the step-by-step sequences specify the other ways to perform the task completed in the steps. Thus, the steps and the Other Ways box make a comprehensive reference unit.
- **More About and Q&A Features:** These marginal annotations provide background information, tips, and answers to common questions that complement the topics covered, adding depth and perspective to the learning process.
- **Integration of the World Wide Web:** The World Wide Web is integrated into the Publisher 2003 learning experience by (1) More About annotations that send students to Web sites for up-to-date information and alternative approaches to tasks; (2) a Publisher 2003 Quick Reference Summary Web page that summarizes the ways to complete tasks (mouse, menu, shortcut menu, and keyboard); and (3) the Learn It Online page at the end of each project, which has project reinforcement exercises, learning games, and other types of student activities.

Organization of This Textbook

Microsoft Office Publisher 2003: Complete Concepts and Techniques provides basic instruction on how to use Publisher 2003. The material is divided into six projects, an E-Mail Letter feature, and Integration feature, four appendices, and a Quick Reference Summary.

Project 1 — Creating and Editing a Publication In Project 1, students are introduced to Publisher terminology and the Publisher screen by preparing an advertising flyer with tear-offs. Topics include starting and quitting Publisher; using the New Publication task pane for color and font decisions; editing text and synchronized objects; using Publisher's zoom features; editing graphics; using the Clip Art task pane; creating bulleted lists; formatting, printing, and saving a publication; opening and modifying a publication; deleting objects; and converting a print publication to a Web publication.

Other Ways

1. Right-click coupon, click Format AutoShape, click BorderArt
2. In Voice Command mode, say "Format, AutoShape, BorderArt"

More About

Digital Signatures

Several companies provide authenticated, certified digital signatures via the Web. When you attach a digital signature to a macro project, Publisher will display the digital signature when the user of the file is asked to enable macros.

Q&A

Q: Can I make a transparent shadow?

A: To change the shadow color so you can see through it, click the Shadow Style button on the Formatting toolbar, and then click Shadow Settings. When the Shadow Settings toolbar is displayed, click the Shadow Color button arrow and then click Semitransparent Shadow.

Project 2 — Designing a Newsletter   In Project 2, students create a two-page newsletter using a Publisher-designed template. Topics include identifying the advantages of the newsletter medium and the steps in the design process; editing typical newsletter features including mastheads, multi-column articles, sidebars, pull quotes, and graphics; using the Page Navigation control and pagination; importing text and graphic files; using Microsoft Word as an editor; formatting personal information components and attention getters; using WordArt; and moving between foreground and background elements. Finally, students check the publication for spelling, use the Design Checker, and then print the newsletter double-sided.

Project 3 — Preparing a Tri-Fold Brochure   In Project 3, students prepare a tri-fold brochure with three panels displaying text, shapes, graphics, an order form, a price list, and a personalized logo. Topics include the proper use of graphics; inserting a photograph from a file; creating a composite logo using custom shapes; deleting and inserting text boxes; using Smart Tags; grouping, rotating, and overlapping objects; editing form components; and preparing the publication for outside printing by choosing appropriate printing services, paper, and color libraries. This project also illustrates Publisher's Pack and Go feature.

E-Mail Feature — Creating an E-Mail Letter Using Publisher   In the E-Mail Letter feature, students are introduced to a new publication type in Publisher 2003, as they create an e-mail letter. Topics include the advantages and disadvantages of sending a publication as an e-mail message versus an attachment; using an e-mail letter design template; editing e-mail letter objects; selecting a logo design; editing logo text; previewing an e-mail letter; using an e-mail address as a hyperlink; and using Publisher's Send E-mail command.

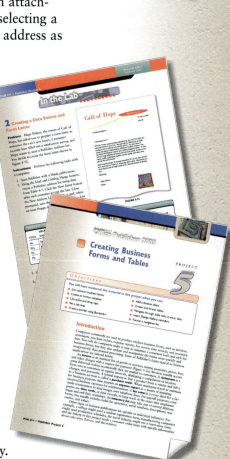

Project 4 — Personalizing and Customizing Publications with Information Sets   In Project 4, students learn how to use information sets to create a letterhead for a bakery and then apply the fields, graphic, and design scheme to a business card, an envelope, mailing labels, and a Web page. Topics include using layout and ruler guides to assist with design and margins; editing information sets and inserting the components; creating a letterhead with background effects such as tints, shades, patterns, and gradients; inserting and cropping a graphic; formatting line borders, inserting a system date, and using the Measurement toolbar to format character spacing and placement. The project creates an address list and demonstrates how to merge using field codes in a main publication. Finally, Publisher's Easy Web Site builder is used to create a Web page with information components and a background sound.

Project 5 — Creating Business Forms and Tables   In Project 5, students learn how to use Publisher to create common business forms including an invoice, a coupon, an order form and a calendar on a Web page. Topics include creating an invoice template; creating styles to maintain consistency across publications; using font effects and decorative borders; formatting drop caps, tabs, and margins; creating, formatting, and navigating in a table; creating custom size publications; and shadowed text boxes. Finally, the project shows how to create a two-page Web site with a formatted calendar and navigation bar from the Publisher Design Gallery.

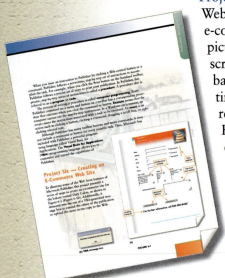

Project 6 — Creating an E-Commerce Web Site   Students are introduced to Web form controls in this project, used to create an electronic order form for e-commerce complete with text fields, option buttons, check boxes, list boxes, picture hyperlinks, and submit buttons. Topics include creating a Web page from scratch; setting a description and keywords for search engines; inserting textured backgrounds; aligning and distributing objects; inserting form controls and setting form control properties; creating alternate text for graphics; working with return data labels for submission to Web databases; and setting security levels. Finally, students are shown how to write a VBA macro procedure to create an event-driven message box.

Integration Feature — Linking a Publisher Publication to an Excel Worksheet   In the Integration Feature, students are introduced to linking a publication to an Excel worksheet. Topics include a discussion of the differences among copying and pasting, copying and embedding, and copying and linking; opening multiple applications; editing, printing and saving a publication with a linked worksheet; and embedding a worksheet within a publication.

Appendices   The book includes four appendices. Appendix A presents an introduction to the Microsoft Publisher Help system. Appendix B describes how to use Publisher's speech and handwriting recognition and speech playback capabilities. Appendix C explains how to publish Web pages to a Web server. Appendix D shows how to change the screen resolution and reset the Publisher toolbars and menus.

Quick Reference Summary   In Publisher 2003, you can accomplish a task in a number of ways, such as using the mouse, menu, shortcut menu, and keyboard. The Quick Reference Summary at the back of the book provides a quick reference to each task presented.

End-of-Project Student Activities

A notable strength of the Shelly Cashman Series *Microsoft Office Publisher 2003* books is the extensive student activities at the end of each project. Well-structured student activities can make the difference between students merely participating in a class and students retaining the information they learn. The activities in the Shelly Cashman Series *Microsoft Office Publisher 2003* books include the following.

- **What You Should Know**   A listing of the tasks completed within a project together with the pages on which the step-by-step, screen-by-screen explanations appear.
- **Learn It Online**   Every project features a Learn It Online page that contains 12 exercises. These exercises include True/False, Multiple Choice, Short Answer, Flash Cards, Practice Test, Learning Games, Tips and Tricks, Newsgroup usage, Expanding Your Horizons, Search Sleuth, Office Online Training, and Office Marketplace.
- **Apply Your Knowledge**   This exercise usually requires students to open and manipulate a file on the Data Disk that parallels the activities learned in the project. To obtain a copy of the Data Disk, follow the instructions on the inside back cover of this textbook.

- **In the Lab** Three in-depth assignments per project require students to utilize the project concepts and techniques to solve problems on a computer.
- **Cases and Places** Five unique real-world case-study situations, including one small-group activity.

Instructor Resources CD-ROM

The Shelly Cashman Series is dedicated to providing you with all of the tools you need to make your class a success. Information on all supplementary materials is available through your Course Technology representative or by calling one of the following telephone numbers: Colleges and Universities, 1-800-648-7450; High Schools, 1-800-824-5179; Private Career Colleges, 1-800-347-7707; Canada, 1-800-268-2222; Corporations with IT Training Centers, 1-800-648-7450; and Government Agencies, Health-Care Organizations, and Correctional Facilities, 1-800-477-3692.

The Instructor Resources for this textbook include both teaching and testing aids. The contents of each item on the Instructor Resources CD-ROM (ISBN 0-619-20051-0) are described below.

INSTRUCTOR'S MANUAL The Instructor's Manual is made up of Microsoft Word files, which include detailed lesson plans with page number references, lecture notes, teaching tips, classroom activities, discussion topics, projects to assign, and transparency references. The transparencies are available through the Figure Files described below.

LECTURE SUCCESS SYSTEM The Lecture Success System consists of intermediate files that correspond to certain figures in the book, allowing you to step through the creation of an application in a project during a lecture without entering large amounts of data.

SYLLABUS Sample syllabi, which can be customized easily to a course, are included. The syllabi cover policies, class and lab assignments and exams, and procedural information.

FIGURE FILES Illustrations for every figure in the textbook are available in electronic form. Use this ancillary to present a slide show in lecture or to print transparencies for use in lecture with an overhead projector. If you have a personal computer and LCD device, this ancillary can be an effective tool for presenting lectures.

POWERPOINT PRESENTATIONS PowerPoint Presentations is a multimedia lecture presentation system that provides slides for each project. Presentations are based on project objectives. Use this presentation system to present well-organized lectures that are both interesting and knowledge based. PowerPoint Presentations provides consistent coverage at schools that use multiple lecturers.

SOLUTIONS TO EXERCISES Solutions are included for the end-of-project exercises, as well as the Project Reinforcement exercises.

TEST BANK & TEST ENGINE The ExamView test bank includes 110 questions for every project (25 multiple choice, 50 true/false, and 35 completion) with page number references and, when appropriate, figure references. A version of the test bank you can print also is included. The test bank comes with a copy of the test engine, ExamView, the ultimate tool for your objective-based testing needs. ExamView is a state-of-the-art test builder that is easy to use. ExamView enables you to create paper-, LAN-, or Web-based tests from test banks designed specifically for your Course Technology textbook. Utilize the ultra-efficient QuickTest Wizard to create tests in less than five minutes by taking advantage of Course Technology's question banks, or customize your own exams from scratch.

DATA FILES FOR STUDENTS All the files that are required by students to complete the exercises are included. You can distribute the files on the Instructor Resources CD-ROM to your students over a network, or you can have them follow the instructions on the inside back cover of this book to obtain a copy of the Data Disk.

ADDITIONAL ACTIVITIES FOR STUDENTS These additional activities consist of Project Reinforcement Exercises, which are true/false, multiple choice, and short answer questions that help students gain confidence in the material learned.

Online Content

Course Technology offers textbook-based content for Blackboard, WebCT, and MyCourse 2.1.

BLACKBOARD AND WEBCT As the leading provider of IT content for the Blackboard and WebCT platforms, Course Technology delivers rich content that enhances your textbook to give your students a unique learning experience.

MYCOURSE 2.1 MyCourse 2.1 is Course Technology's powerful online course management and content delivery system. MyCourse 2.1 allows nontechnical users to create, customize, and deliver Web-based courses; post content and assignments; manage student enrollment; administer exams; track results in the online grade book; and more.

Acknowledgments

The Shelly Cashman Series would not be the leading computer education series without the contributions of outstanding publishing professionals. First, and foremost, among them is Becky Herrington, director of production and book designer. She is the heart and soul of the Shelly Cashman Series, and it is only through her leadership, dedication, and tireless efforts that superior products are made possible.

Under Becky's direction, the following individuals made significant contributions to these books: Deb Masi, production editor; Jennifer Quiambao, production assistant; Ken Russo, senior Web and graphic designer; Richard Herrera, cover designer; Kellee LaVars, Andrew Bartel, Phillip Hajjar, and Kenny Tran, graphic artists; Michelle French, Jeanne Black, Andrew Bartel, and Kellee LaVars, QuarkXPress compositors; Lyn Markowicz, copy editor; Nancy Lamm, proofreader; and Cristina Haley, indexer.

We also would like to thank Kristen Duerr, executive vice president and publisher; Cheryl Costantini, executive editor; Alexandra Arnold, senior product manager; Dana Merk, senior acquisitions editor; Jim Quasney, series consulting editor; Marc Ouellette and Heather McKinstry, online product managers; Reed Cotter, product manager; and Selena Coppock, editorial assistant.

Gary B. Shelly
Thomas J. Cashman
Joy L. Starks

To the Student... Getting the Most Out of Your Book

Welcome to *Microsoft Office Publisher 2003: Complete Concepts and Techniques*. You can save yourself a lot of time and gain a better understanding of Microsoft Office Publisher 2003 if you spend a few minutes reviewing the figures and callouts in this section.

1 Project Orientation

Each project presents a practical problem and shows the solution in the first figure of the project. The project orientation lets you see firsthand how problems are solved from start to finish using application software and computers.

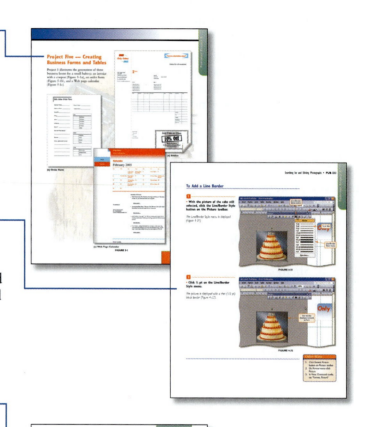

2 Consistent Step-by-Step, Screen-by-Screen Presentation

Project solutions are built using a step-by-step, screen-by-screen approach. This pedagogy allows you to build the solution on a computer as you read through the project. Generally, each step is followed by an italic explanation that indicates the result of the step.

3 More Than Just Step-by-Step

More About and Q&A annotations in the margins of the book and substantive text in the paragraphs provide background information, tips, and answers to common questions that complement the topics covered, adding depth and perspective. When you finish with this book, you will be ready to use Publisher to solve problems on your own.

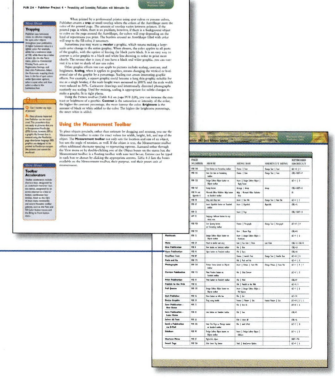

4 Other Ways Boxes and Quick Reference Summary

Other Ways boxes that follow many of the step sequences and a Quick Reference Summary at the back of the book explain the other ways to complete the task presented, such as using the mouse, menu, shortcut menu, and keyboard.

5 Emphasis on Getting Help When You Need It

The first project of each application and Appendix A show you how to use all the elements of the Publisher Help system. Being able to answer your own questions will increase your productivity and reduce your frustrations by minimizing the time it takes to learn how to complete a task.

6 Review

After you successfully step through a project, a section titled What You Should Know summarizes the project tasks with which you should be familiar. Terms you should know for test purposes are bold in the text.

7 Reinforcement and Extension

The Learn It Online page at the end of each project offers reinforcement in the form of review questions, learning games, and practice tests. Also included are Web-based exercises that require you to extend your learning beyond the book.

8 Laboratory Exercises

If you really want to learn how to use the applications, then you must design and implement solutions to problems on your own. Every project concludes with several carefully developed laboratory assignments that increase in complexity.

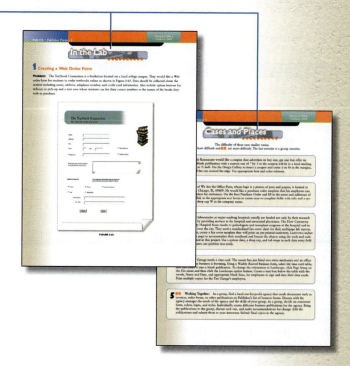

Shelly Cashman Series – Traditionally Bound Textbooks

The Shelly Cashman Series presents the following computer subjects in a variety of traditionally bound textbooks. For more information, see your Course Technology representative or call 1-800-648-7450. For Shelly Cashman Series information, visit Shelly Cashman Online at **scseries.com**

COMPUTERS	
Computers	Discovering Computers 2005: A Gateway to Information, Web Enhanced, Complete Edition
	Discovering Computers 2005: A Gateway to Information, Web Enhanced, Introductory Edition
	Discovering Computers 2005: A Gateway to Information, Web Enhanced, Brief Edition
	Discovering Computers 2005: Fundamentals Edition
	Teachers Discovering Computers: Integrating Technology in the Classroom 3e
	Exploring Computers: A Record of Discovery 4e
	Study Guide for Discovering Computers 2005: A Gateway to Information, Web Enhanced
	Essential Introduction to Computers 5e (40-page)

WINDOWS APPLICATIONS	
Microsoft Office	Microsoft Office 2003: Essential Concepts and Techniques (5 projects)
	Microsoft Office 2003: Brief Concepts and Techniques (9 projects)
	Microsoft Office 2003: Introductory Concepts and Techniques (15 projects)
	Microsoft Office 2003: Advanced Concepts and Techniques (12 projects)
	Microsoft Office 2003: Post Advanced Concepts and Techniques (11 projects)
	Microsoft Office XP: Essential Concepts and Techniques (5 projects)
	Microsoft Office XP: Brief Concepts and Techniques (9 projects)
	Microsoft Office XP: Introductory Concepts and Techniques, Windows XP Edition
	Microsoft Office XP: Introductory Concepts and Techniques, Enhanced Edition (15 projects)[1]
	Microsoft Office XP: Advanced Concepts and Techniques (11 projects)
	Microsoft Office XP: Post Advanced Concepts and Techniques (11 projects)
Integration	Integrating Microsoft Office XP Applications and the World Wide Web: Essential Concepts and Techniques
PIM	Microsoft Office Outlook 2003: Introductory Concepts and Techniques • Microsoft Outlook 2002: Essential Concepts and Techniques
Microsoft Works	Microsoft Works 6: Complete Concepts and Techniques[2] • Microsoft Works 2000: Complete Concepts and Techniques[2]
Microsoft Windows	Microsoft Windows XP: Complete Concepts and Techniques[3]
	Microsoft Windows XP: Brief Concepts and Techniques
	Microsoft Windows 2000: Complete Concepts and Techniques (6 projects)[3]
	Microsoft Windows 2000: Brief Concepts and Techniques (2 projects)
	Microsoft Windows 98: Essential Concepts and Techniques (2 projects)
	Microsoft Windows 98: Complete Concepts and Techniques (6 projects)[3]
	Introduction to Microsoft Windows NT Workstation 4
Word Processing	Microsoft Office Word 2003[3] • Microsoft Word 2002[3]
Spreadsheets	Microsoft Office Excel 2003[3] • Microsoft Excel 2002[3]
Database	Microsoft Office Access 2003[3] • Microsoft Access 2002[3]
Presentation Graphics	Microsoft Office PowerPoint 2003[3] • Microsoft PowerPoint 2002[3]
Desktop Publishing	Microsoft Office Publisher 2003[2] • Microsoft Publisher 2002[2]

PROGRAMMING	
Programming	Microsoft Visual Basic.NET: Complete Concepts and Techniques[3] • Microsoft Visual Basic 6: Complete Concepts and Techniques[2]
	Programming in QBasic • Java Programming 2e: Complete Concepts and Techniques[3] • Structured COBOL Programming 2e

INTERNET	
Concepts	Discovering the Internet: Complete Concepts & Techniques[2]
Browser	Microsoft Internet Explorer 6: Introductory Concepts and Techniques • Microsoft Internet Explorer 5: An Introduction • Netscape Navigator 6: An Introduction
Web Page Creation and Design	Web Design: Introductory Concepts and Techniques • HTML: Complete Concepts and Techniques 2e[3]
	Microsoft Office FrontPage 2003[3] • Microsoft FrontPage 2002[3] • Microsoft FrontPage 2002: Essential Concepts and Techniques
	Java Programming: Complete Concepts and Techniques 2e[3] • JavaScript: Complete Concepts and Techniques 2e[2] • Macromedia Dreamweaver MX: Complete Concepts and Techniques[3]

SYSTEMS ANALYSIS	
Systems Analysis	Systems Analysis and Design 5e

DATA COMMUNICATIONS	
Data Communications	Business Data Communications: Introductory Concepts and Techniques 4e

[1] Available running under Windows XP or running under Windows 2000.

[2] Also available as an Introductory Edition, which is a shortened version of the complete book.

[3] Also available as an Introductory Edition, which is a shortened version of the complete book and also as a Comprehensive Edition, which is an extended version of the complete book.

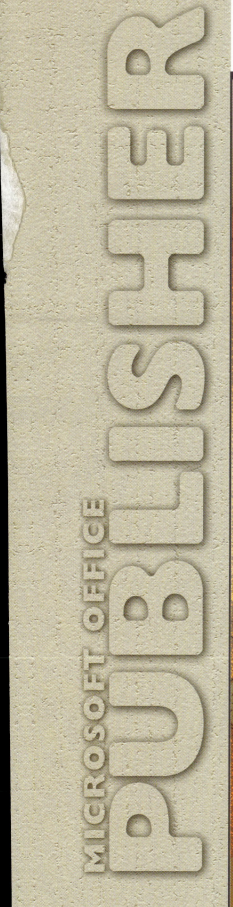

MICROSOFT

Office Publisher 2003

PROJECT 1

Creating and Editi
Racing fans every
in the most exhila
Formula One Grand
a variety of countr
Germany, Italy, Sp
of each event, driv
sions begin on the
pate in a drivers' p
One Grand Prix rac
miles, Formula One
pit-box.
When the Formula
reports begin takin
is a senior travel a
employed as a sun
the guidelines for
ing classes and ha
announcing Space
title. To attract att
include a large gra
approves the conc
businesses for dist
fronts.
As you read throu
Word to create, sp
image.

Creating and Editing a Publication

PROJECT

1

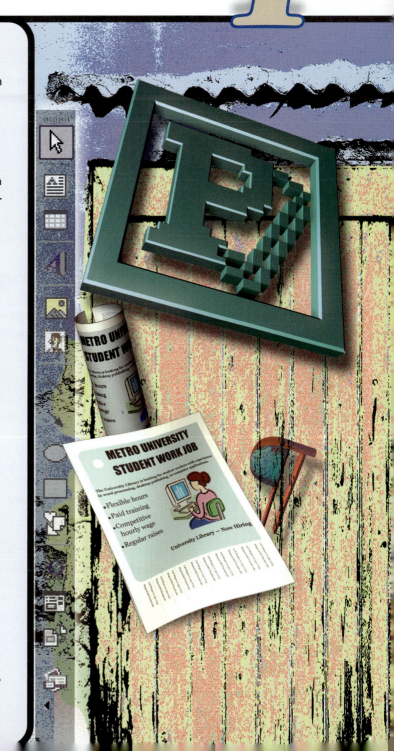

CASE PERSPECTIVE

Metro University is an urban university with more than 20,000 students. It is located in the heart of the city, close to numerous businesses and Metro High School. Its population is diverse, and its campus is modern, including the latest technology and software and wireless Internet access on campus. The university services traditional students matriculating directly from the high school, students transferring from area community colleges, and others, including older students who are returning to school to finish a degree or those who desire to further their education by taking a few classes. Megan Rivera works in the financial aid office at Metro University. She is in charge of hiring student workers on campus. Megan matches the various departments that need help with students who want part-time work, usually 10 to 15 hours a week.

Megan knows of your interest in Microsoft Publisher and has asked you to design a flyer to advertise openings at the University Library. The library needs student workers with experience in word processing, desktop publishing, and office applications. She would like you to design a flyer that she can post around campus on bulletin boards, in the dormitories, and at the library.

Because of your experience with desktop publishing and the Web, you suggest to Megan that she also might want to post the flyer on the school's electronic bulletin board or send it to the student LISTSERV. Megan agrees. Together, you decide to use a Microsoft Publisher Sale Flyer with a strong bold heading, descriptive text, a sharp graphic, and tear-offs. Megan decides on a color scheme that uses one of Metro's school colors, light blue.

As you read through this project, you will learn how to use Publisher to create, save, and print a publication that includes text, a bulleted list, a graphic, and tear-offs.

Office Publisher 2003

Creating and Editing a Publication

Objectives

You will have mastered the material in this project when you can:

- Start and quit Publisher
- Describe the Publisher window
- Edit text and graphics
- Use the Best Fit feature to adjust font size
- Edit a synchronized object
- Replace a picture
- Resize and delete objects

- Correct spelling errors
- Save and print a publication
- Open a publication
- Convert to a Web publication and publish
- Use the Publisher Help system to answer questions

What Is Microsoft Office Publisher 2003?

Microsoft Office Publisher 2003 is a powerful desktop publishing (DTP) program that assists you in designing and producing professional, quality documents that combine text, graphics, illustrations, and photographs. DTP software provides additional tools over and above those typically found in word processing packages, including design templates, graphic manipulation tools, color schemes or libraries, advanced layout and printing tools, and multiple templates. For large jobs, businesses use DTP software to design publications that are camera ready, which means the files are suitable for outside commercial printing.

The publishing industry has undergone tremendous change in the past few years due to advancements in hardware and software technology. Books, magazines, and brochures used to be created by slower, more expensive methods such as typesetting — a process that had not changed fundamentally since the days of Gutenberg and his *Bible*. With desktop publishing software, you can create professional looking documents on your own computer and produce work that previously could be achieved only by graphic artists. Both cost and time are significantly decreased. Microsoft Publisher is becoming the choice of people who regularly produce high-quality color publications such as newsletters, flyers, logos, signs, and forms. Saving publications as Web pages or complete Web sites is a powerful feature in Publisher. All publications can be saved in a format that easily is viewed and manipulated using a browser. Some examples of these publications are shown in Figure 1-1.

PUB 4 • Publisher Project 1

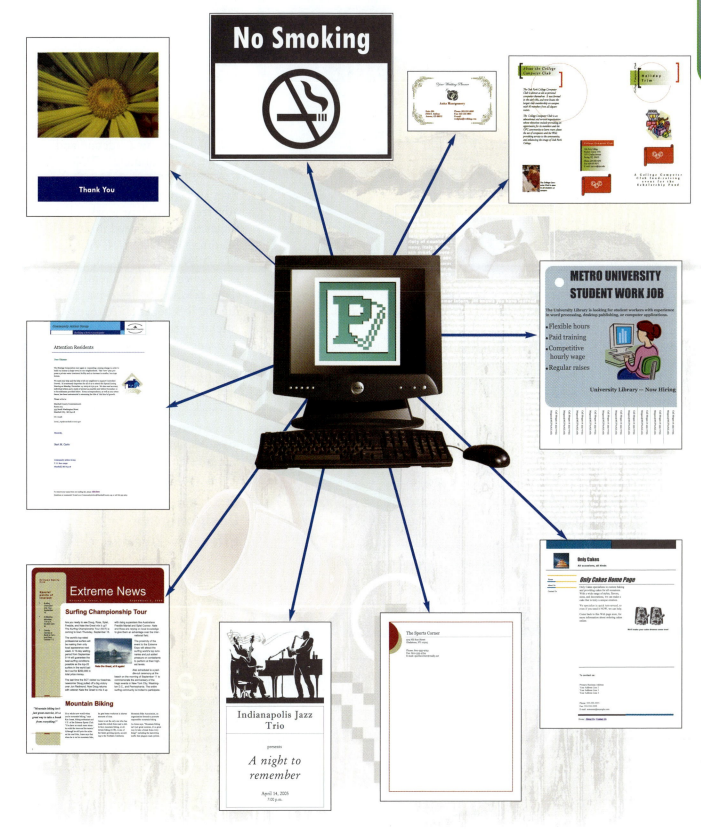

FIGURE 1-1

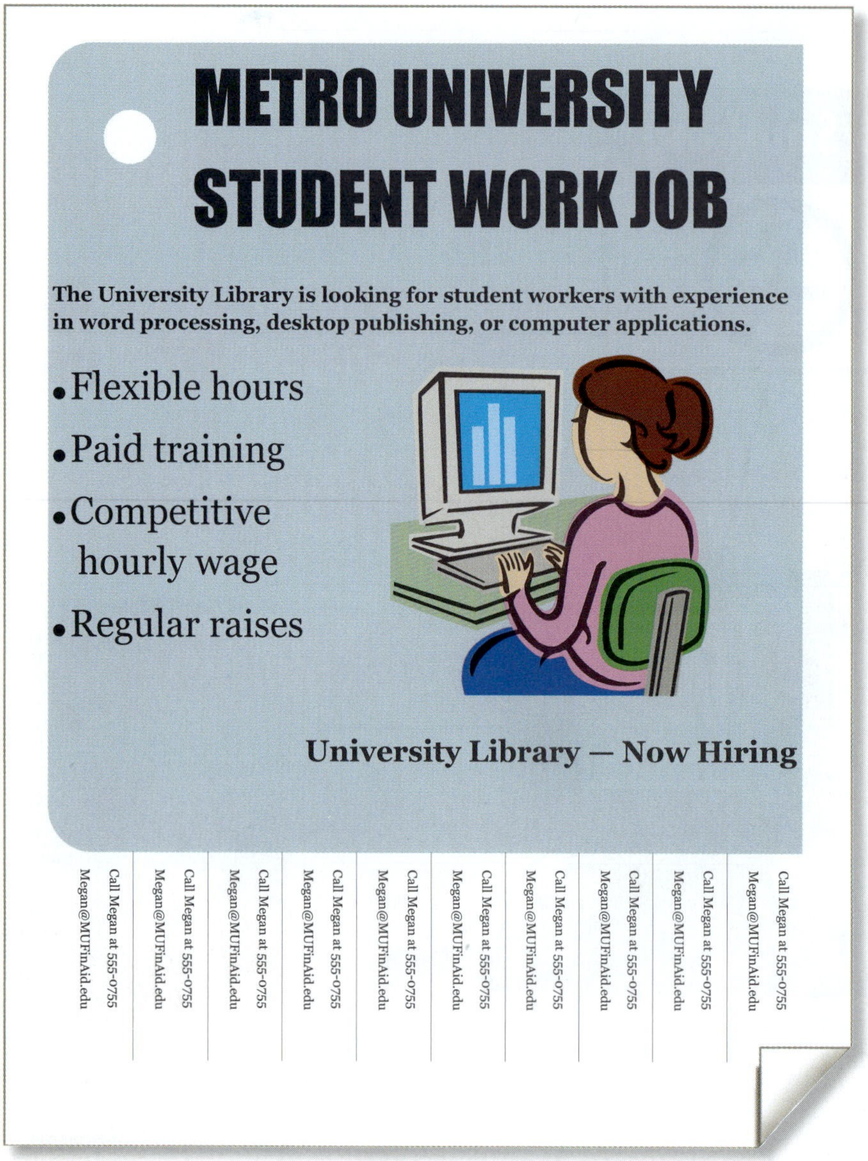

METRO UNIVERSITY STUDENT WORK JOB

The University Library is looking for student workers with experience in word processing, desktop publishing, or computer applications.

- Flexible hours
- Paid training
- Competitive hourly wage
- Regular raises

University Library — Now Hiring

Call Megan at 555-0755 Megan@MUFinAid.edu

FIGURE 1-2

Project One — Student Work Job Flyer

To illustrate the features of Microsoft Publisher 2003, this book presents a series of projects that use Publisher to create publications similar to those you will encounter in academic and business environments. Project 1 uses Publisher to produce the flyer shown in Figure 1-2. The flyer advertises a student work job opening at the University Library. The heading, METRO UNIVERSITY STUDENT WORK JOB, is designed to draw attention to the flyer, as is the bulleted list describing the job benefits. An eye-catching graphic of a person working at a computer is on the right. Text below the heading explains where the job is located and what kind of experience applicants should have. Finally, in the lower portion of the flyer, is a set of tear-offs with a contact person's name, telephone number, and e-mail address.

Designing an Effective Flyer

A good flyer, or any publication, must deliver a message in the clearest, most attractive, and effective way possible. You must clarify your purpose and know your target audience. You need to gather ideas and plan for the printing of the flyer. Finally, you must edit, proofread, and then publish your flyer.

Table 1-1 outlines the issues to consider during the design process and their application to flyers.

Table 1-1	Design Process
DESIGN ISSUE	**FLYER APPLICATION**
Purpose	To communicate a single concept, notion, or product in a quick, easy-to read format
Audience	Wide, non-specific audience
Gather data	Content for heading, bulleted list, tear-offs, other text boxes
Plan for printing	Color or black and white; number of copies varies greatly
Layout	Single page with perforated tear-offs
Synthesis	Edit, proofread, and publish both print and Web publications

Starting and Customizing Publisher

If you are stepping through this project on a computer and you want your screen to match the figures in this book, then you should change your computer's resolution to 800 × 600. For more information about how to change the resolution on your computer, read Appendix D.

To start Publisher, Windows must be running. The following steps show how to start Publisher. You may need to ask your instructor how to start Publisher on your system.

More About

Publisher 2003

For more information about the features of Microsoft 2003, visit the Publisher 2003 More About Web page (scsite.com/ pub2003/more) and click Microsoft Publisher 2003 Features.

To Start Publisher

1

• **Click the Start button on the Windows taskbar, point to All Programs on the Start menu, point to Microsoft Office on the All Programs submenu, and then point to Microsoft Office Publisher 2003 on the Microsoft Office submenu.**

Windows displays the commands on the Start menu above the Start button and displays the All Programs and Microsoft Office submenus (Figure 1-3).

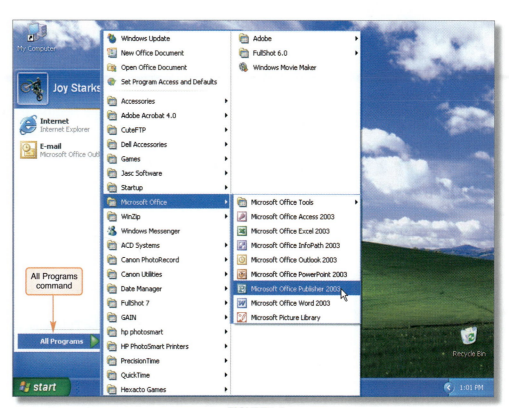

FIGURE 1-3

2

• **Click Microsoft Office Publisher 2003.**

Publisher starts. After a few moments, Publisher displays the Start window and the New Publication task pane (Figure 1-4). The Windows taskbar displays the Publisher program button, indicating Publisher is running.

3

• **If the Publisher window is not maximized, double-click its title bar to maximize it.**

• **If your system displays a different task pane, click the Other Task Panes button and click New Publication in the list.**

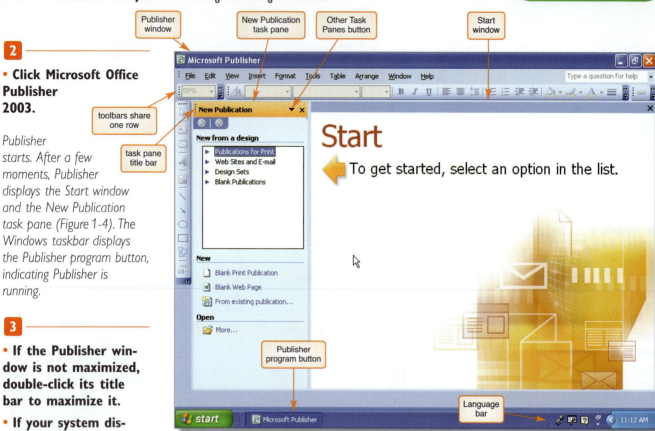

FIGURE 1-4

The screen in Figure 1-4 shows how the Publisher window looks the first time you start Publisher after installation on most computers. As shown, Publisher displays a task pane on the left side of the screen. A **task pane** is a separate window that enables users to carry out some Publisher tasks more efficiently. When you start Publisher, it displays the New Publication task pane, which provides commonly used links and commands that allow you to open new files from design templates, create new files, or open previously created publications.

If the Office Speech Recognition software is installed and active on your computer, the Language bar is displayed on the screen when you start Publisher. The **Language bar** allows you to speak commands and dictate text. It usually is located on the right side of the Windows taskbar next to the notification area, and changes to include the speech recognition functions available in Publisher. In this book, the Language bar is closed because it takes up computer resources. Also, with the Language bar active, the microphone can be turned on accidentally, which can cause your computer to act in an unstable manner. For additional information about the Language bar, see page PUB 21 and Appendix B.

At startup, Publisher sometimes displays multiple toolbars on a single row. Other toolbars also may be displayed. To allow for more efficient use of the buttons, the most commonly used toolbars should be displayed on two separate rows, instead of sharing a single row. The following steps show how to close the Language bar, close extra toolbars, and instruct Publisher to display the commonly used toolbars on two separate rows.

To Customize the Publisher Window

1

• **If the Language bar shows and it indicates that the microphone is on, click the Microphone button to turn it off.**

• **To close the Language bar, right-click it to display a list of commands.**

The Language bar shortcut menu is displayed (Figure 1-5).

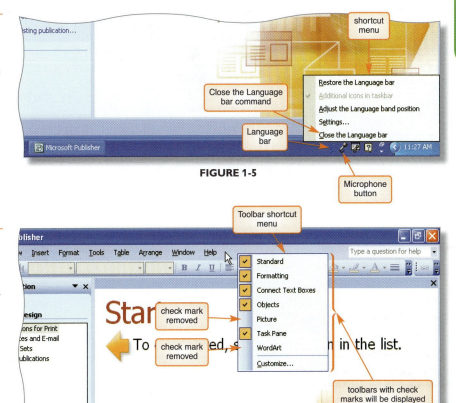

FIGURE 1-5

2

• **Click Close the Language bar.**

• **If Publisher displays a Language Bar dialog box, click its OK button.**

• **Right-click any of the toolbars.**

• **When Publisher displays the shortcut menu, if the Picture command displays a check mark, click Picture.**

• **If the WordArt command displays a check mark, click WordArt.**

The Language bar no longer is displayed. Check marks indicate which toolbars will be displayed in the Publisher window (Figure 1-6).

FIGURE 1-6

3

• **If the toolbars are positioned on the same row, click the Toolbar Options button. If your installation of Publisher already displays the toolbars on two rows, you may skip Steps 3 and 4.**

Publisher displays the Toolbar Options list showing the buttons that do not fit on the toolbars when toolbars are positioned on one row (Figure 1-7).

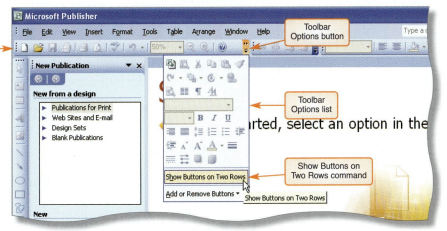

FIGURE 1-7

Microsoft Office
Publisher 2003

4

• **Click Show Buttons on Two Rows.**

Publisher displays the toolbars on two separate rows (Figure 1-8).

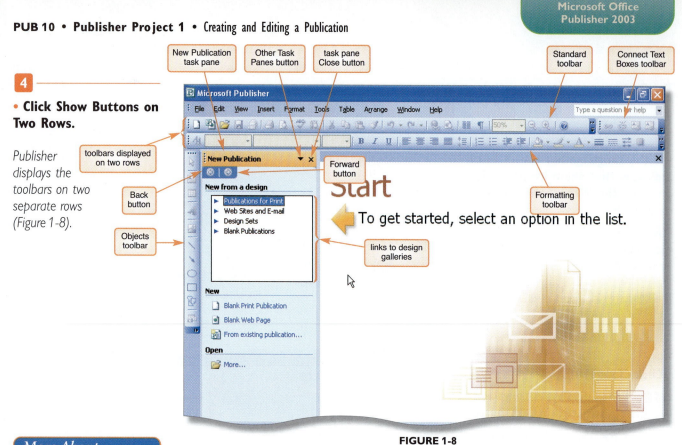

FIGURE 1-8

As an alternative to Steps 3 and 4 above, you can point to the left edge of the second toolbar, and when the mouse pointer changes to a four-headed arrow, drag the toolbar down to create two rows of toolbars.

Each time you start Publisher, the Publisher window is displayed the same way it was the last time you used Publisher. If the toolbar buttons are displayed on one row, then they will be displayed on one row the next time you start Publisher. Typically, three toolbars are displayed on two rows when you first install Publisher: the Standard toolbar, the Connect Text Boxes toolbar, and the Formatting toolbar. These toolbars are discussed later in this project. The Objects toolbar is displayed on the left. You can display or hide toolbars by right-clicking any toolbar and clicking the appropriate check boxes, or by clicking Toolbars on the View menu.

As you work through creating a publication, you will find that other toolbars will be displayed automatically as they are needed in order to edit particular types of objects in Publisher.

When you first start Publisher, the New Publication task pane usually is displayed (Figure 1-8). If it is not displayed, click Options on the Tools menu, and then click Use New Publication task pane at startup in the General sheet.

Additionally, certain Publisher operations will cause other task panes to be displayed. Publisher provides more than 20 additional task panes, in addition to the New Publication task pane shown in Figure 1-8. Some of the more important ones are the Help, Publication Designs, Clipboard, and Clip Art task panes. Throughout the book, these task panes are discussed when they are used.

At any point while working with Publisher, you can open or close a task pane by clicking the Task Pane command on the View menu. You can activate additional task panes by clicking the Other Task Panes button to the left of the Close button on the task pane title bar (Figure 1-8) and then selecting a task pane in the Other Task Panes list. The Back and Forward buttons below the task pane title bar allow you to switch between task panes that you opened during a session.

Creating a Publication

Publisher provides many ways to begin the process of creating a publication. You can:

- Create a new publication from a design
- Create a new publication from a blank publication or Web page
- Create a new publication based on an existing one
- Open an existing publication

Choosing the appropriate method depends upon your experience with desktop publishing and how you have used Publisher in the past. In this first project, as you are beginning to learn about the features of Publisher, a series of steps is presented to create a publication using a design template.

Because composing and designing from scratch is a difficult process for many people, Publisher provides templates to assist in publication preparation. Publisher has more than 2,000 templates to create professionally designed and unique publications. A **template** is a tool that helps you through the design process by offering you publication options and changing your publication accordingly. A template is similar to a blueprint you can use over and over, filling in the blanks, replacing prewritten text as necessary, and changing the art to fit your needs.

Using the New Publication Task Pane

The New Publication task pane displays links to four design galleries in the New from a design area (Figure 1-8):

- Publications for Print
- Web Sites and E-mail
- Design Sets
- Blank Publications

A **gallery** is a collection of publication templates organized by type. As you click a design gallery link in the task pane, the list of publication types expands, and **previews** of the templates are displayed on the right side of the Publisher window, alphabetically (Figure 1-9 on the next page). The gallery previews change based on your choices in the task pane.

Once you choose a publication from the gallery, the task pane will allow you to make choices about the color and font schemes. A **color scheme** is a defined set of colors that complement each other when used in the same publication. Each Publisher color scheme provides a main color and four accent colors. A **font scheme** is a defined set of fonts associated with a publication. A **font**, or typeface, defines the appearance and shape of the letters, numbers, and special characters. For example, a font scheme might be made up of one font for headings, one for body text, and another for captions. Font schemes make it easy to change all the fonts in a publication to give it a new look. Within each font scheme, both a major font and a minor font are specified. Generally, a major font is used for titles and headings, and a minor font is used for body text.

The steps on the next page show how to create a publication using a template from the design gallery.

More About

Templates

For more information about templates, visit the Publisher 2003 More About Web page (scsite.com/pub2003/more) and click Templates.

More About

Maximizing the Publisher Window

The number of previews you see in the gallery (Figure 1-9) may vary depending on the resolution and the size of your window. To make sure you see as many previews as possible, maximize the Publisher window by double-clicking the title bar, or by clicking the Maximize button on the title bar.

To Create a Publication Using a Template

1

• **In the New Publication task pane, click Publications for Print.**

The Quick Publications gallery is displayed on the right (Figure 1-9).

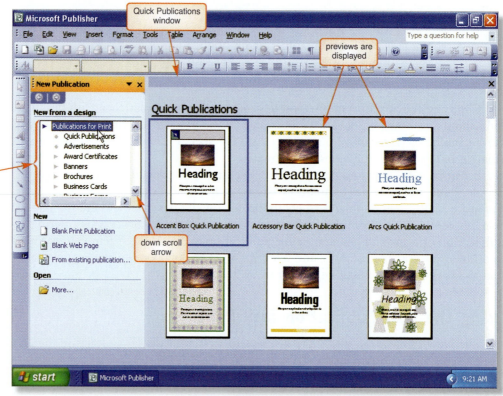

FIGURE 1-9

2

• **Click the down scroll arrow in the New from a design list until Flyers is displayed in the list.**

• **Click Flyers.**

• **When the types of Flyers are displayed, click Sale in the list.**

Publisher displays the Sale Flyers gallery on the right (Figure 1-10). Each category of publication type displays a unique publication gallery.

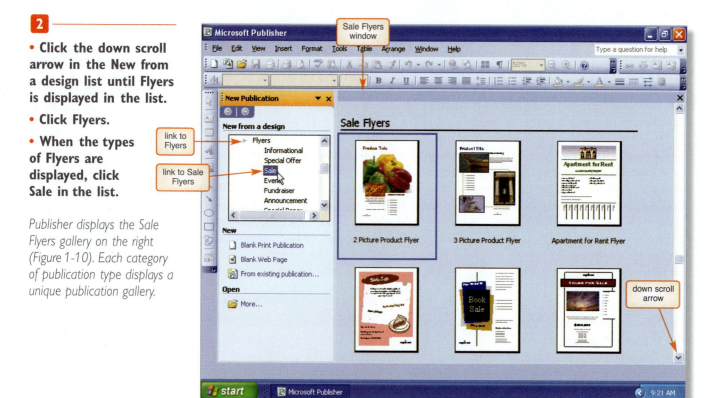

FIGURE 1-10

3

• **Click the down scroll arrow in the gallery until For Sale Flyer 2 is displayed.**

• **Point to the For Sale Flyer 2 preview.**

The For Sale Flyer 2 is displayed (Figure 1-11). Publisher displays a blue box around the flyer as you point to it.

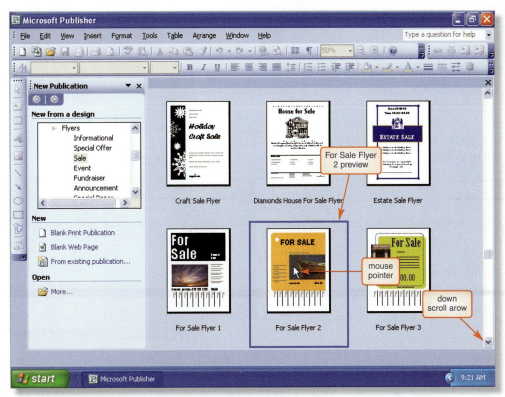

FIGURE 1-11

4

• **Click the For Sale Flyer 2.**

• **If Publisher displays a Personal Information dialog box, click its Close button.**

The gallery window closes, and the flyer is displayed in the Publisher workspace (Figure 1-12). The task pane changes to reflect the current publication's options. The Flyer Options task pane displays links to Publication Designs, Color Schemes, and Font Schemes, as well as options to display the publication with and without a Graphic, a Customer address, and Tear-offs.

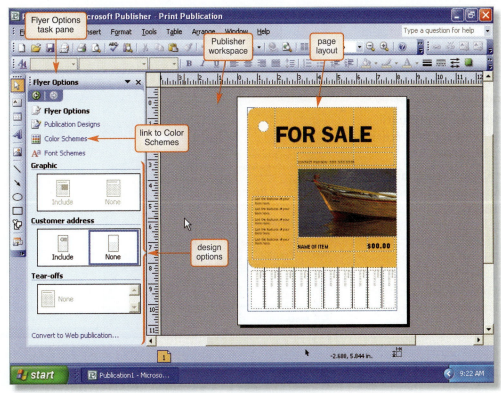

FIGURE 1-12

5

• **Click Color Schemes in the Flyer Options task pane.**

• **When the task pane changes to Color Schemes, click Aqua in the Apply a color scheme list.**

*The Color Schemes task pane appears with a list of color schemes (Figure 1-13). Each color scheme uses colors that complement one another. The **main color** is displayed to the left, and the four **accent colors** are displayed to its right. The Aqua color scheme is applied to the flyer.*

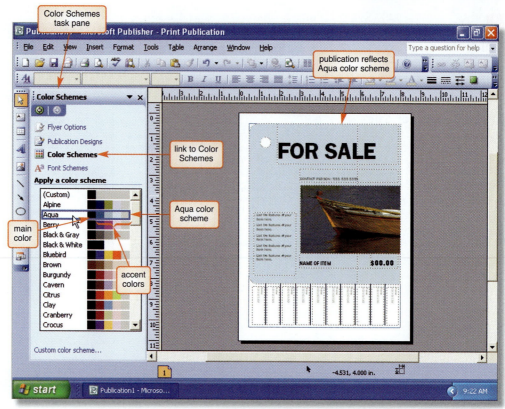

FIGURE 1-13

6

• **Click Font Schemes in the Color Schemes task pane.**

• **When the task pane changes to Font Schemes, scroll until the Impact font scheme is displayed.**

• **Click Impact in the Apply a font scheme list.**

A ScreenTip appears with the name of the scheme, as well as the names of the major and minor fonts used in the scheme (Figure 1-14). The Impact font scheme is applied to the flyer.

FIGURE 1-14

7

• **Click the Close button
in the Font Schemes
task pane.**

*The task pane closes, and
the publication, ready to edit,
is displayed in the Publisher
workspace (Figure 1-15).*

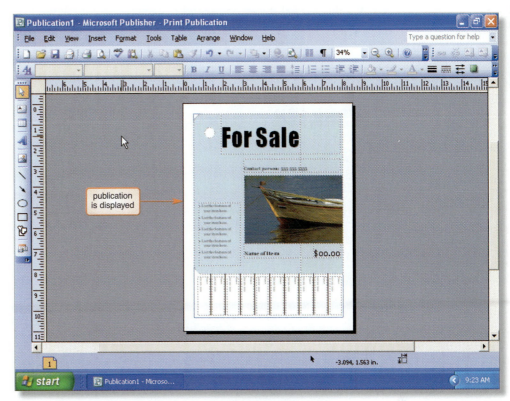

FIGURE 1-15

The **Flyer Options task pane** displays its option links in the upper portion of the
task pane and design choices in the lower portion (Figure 1-12 on page PUB 13).
Each publication design will differ slightly in its options. The Publication Designs
option offers you the ability to apply a different design from the gallery. Publication
options can be revisited at any time during the design process by clicking the option
in the task pane. If the task pane does not display, click Task Pane on the View
menu.

The Publisher Window

The Publisher window consists of a variety of components to make your work more
efficient and your publication more professional. The following sections discuss these
components, which are identified in either Figures 1-16 or 1-17 on the next page.

The Workspace

The **workspace** contains several elements similar to the document windows in
other applications, as well as some elements unique to Publisher. As you create a
publication, the page layout, rulers, scroll bars, guides and boundaries, and objects
are displayed in the gray workspace (Figure 1-16).

PAGE LAYOUT   The **page layout** contains a view of the publication, all the objects
contained therein, plus the guides and boundaries for the page and its objects. The
page layout can be changed to accommodate multi-page spreads. You also can use

the Special Paper command to view your page layout, as it will be printed on special paper, or see the final copy after preparing your publication for a printing service.

RULERS   Two rulers outline the workspace at the top and left. A **ruler** is used to measure and place objects on the page. Although the vertical and horizontal rulers display at the left and top of the work-space, they can be moved and placed any-where you need them. You use the rulers to measure and align objects on the page, set tab stops, adjust text frames, and change margins. Additionally, the rulers can be hidden to show more of the workspace. You will learn more about rulers in a later project.

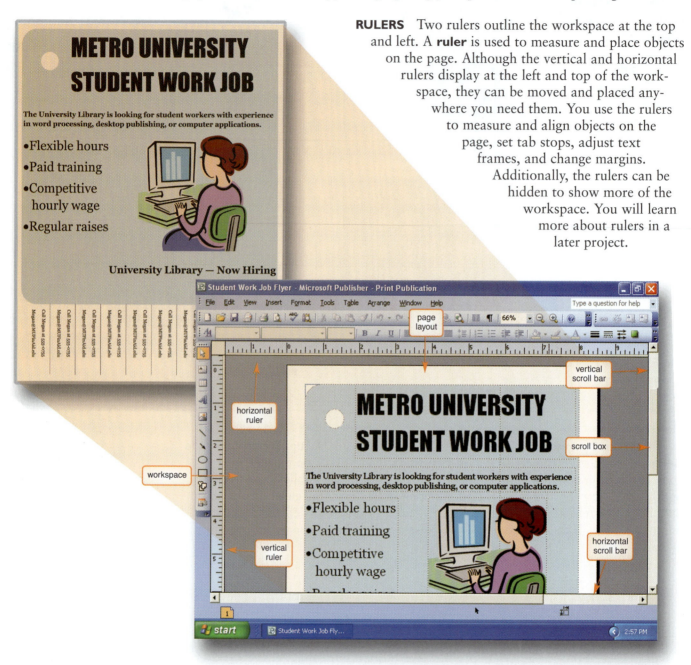

FIGURE 1-16

More About

The Rulers

If the rulers are not displayed on your screen, click View on the menu bar and click Rulers. To hide the rulers, also click View on the menu bar and click Rulers.

SCROLL BARS   By using **scroll bars**, you display different portions of your publication in the workspace. At the right edge of the publication window is a vertical scroll bar. At the bottom of the publication window is a horizontal scroll bar. On both the vertical and horizontal scroll bars, the position of the **scroll box** reflects the location of the portion of the publication that is displayed in the publication window.

BOUNDARIES AND GUIDES   Publisher's page layout displays the boundaries and guides of the page and its objects. Aligning design elements in relation to each other, both vertically and horizontally, is a tedious task. **Layout guides** create a grid that repeats on each page of a publication (Figure 1-17). They define sections of the page and help you align elements with precision. Page **margin guides** are displayed in pink. **Grid guides**, which are displayed in blue, assist you in organizing text pictures and objects into columns and rows to give a consistent look to your publication.

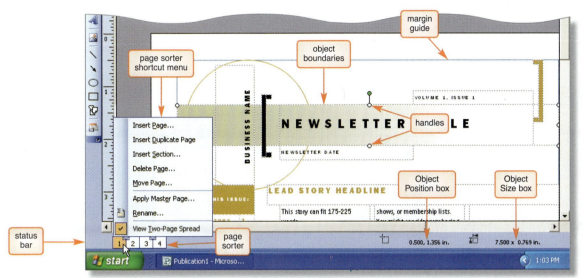

FIGURE 1-17

Boundaries are the gray lines surrounding an object. Boundaries are useful when you want to move or resize objects on the page. Boundaries and guides can be turned on and off using the View menu.

OBJECTS **Objects** include anything you want to place in your publication, such as text, WordArt, tear-offs, graphics, pictures, bullets, lines, and Web tools. You can choose objects from the Objects toolbar, from the Design Gallery, or insert them from original material. You click an object on the page to **select** it; selected objects are displayed with **handles**, at each corner and middle location of the object boundary. Many objects also display a green rotation handle connected to the top of the object or a yellow adjustment handle used to change the shape of some objects. A selected object can be resized, rotated, moved, deleted, or grouped as necessary. To select an object such as a picture, click the picture. The entire object is selected automatically. If you want to select a text box, however, you must click the boundary of the text box rather than the text inside. You will learn more about object manipulation later in the project.

STATUS BAR Immediately above the Windows taskbar at the bottom of the Publisher window is the status bar. In Publisher, the **status bar** contains the page sorter, the Object Position box, and the Object Size box (Figure 1-17). The **page sorter** displays a button for each page of your publication. The current page in a multi-page document will display selected in blue in the page sorter. You may click any page to display it in the workspace or right-click to display the page sorter shortcut menu.

As an alternative to using the rulers, you can use the **Object Position** and **Object Size** boxes as guidelines for lining up objects from the left and top margins. The exact position and size of a selected object is displayed in inches as you create or move it. You may choose to have the measurement displayed in pica, points, or centimeters. If no object is selected, the Object Position box displays the location of the mouse pointer. Double-clicking the status bar will display the Measurements toolbar. You will learn more about the Measurements toolbar in a future project.

Menu Bar and Toolbars

Publisher displays the menu bar at the top of the screen just below the title bar. The toolbars display below the menu bar and down the left side of the Publisher window (Figure 1-18).

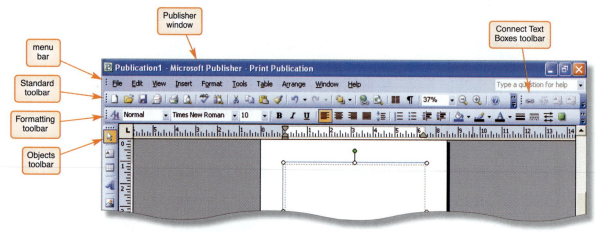

FIGURE 1-18

MENU BAR The **menu bar** is a special toolbar displaying at the top of the window, just below the Publisher title bar (Figure 1-18). The menu bar lists the menu names. When you point to a **menu name** on the menu bar, the area of the menu bar containing the name displays a button. Publisher shades selected buttons in light orange and surrounds them with a blue outline.

When you click a menu name, Publisher displays a menu. A **menu** contains a list of commands that you can use to retrieve, store, print, and manipulate data in the publication. To display a menu, such as the Edit menu, click the Edit menu name on the menu bar. If you point to a command with an arrow to its right, a **submenu** is displayed from which you can choose a command. An ellipsis (…) denotes that Publisher will display a dialog box when you click that menu command. **Keyboard shortcuts**, when available, are displayed to the right of menu commands.

When you click a menu name on the menu bar, Publisher displays a **short menu** listing the most recently used commands (Figure 1-19a). If you wait a few seconds or click the arrows at the bottom of the short menu, the full menu displays. The **full menu** lists all the commands associated with a menu (Figure 1-19b). You also can display a full menu immediately by double-clicking the menu name on the menu bar.

In this book, when you display a menu, always display the full menu using one of the following techniques.

1. Click the menu name on the menu bar and then wait a few seconds.
2. Click the menu name and then point to or click the arrows at the bottom of the short menu.
3. Double-click the menu name.
4. In Voice Command mode, say the name of the menu and then wait a few seconds.

Both short and full menus display some dimmed commands. A **dimmed command** displays gray, or dimmed, instead of black, which indicates it is not available for the current selection. A command with medium blue shading in the rectangle to the left of it on a full menu is called a **hidden command** because it does not display on a short menu. As you use Publisher, it automatically personalizes the short

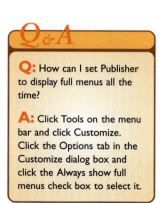

Q&A

Q: How can I set Publisher to display full menus all the time?

A: Click Tools on the menu bar and click Customize. Click the Options tab in the Customize dialog box and click the Always show full menus check box to select it.

menus for you based on how often you use commands. That is, as you use hidden commands on the full menu, Publisher unhides them and places them on the short menu. You can reset the menus to their original configuration by clicking Customize on the Tools menu, and then clicking the Reset My Usage Data button in the Options sheet. The process is described in greater detail in Appendix D.

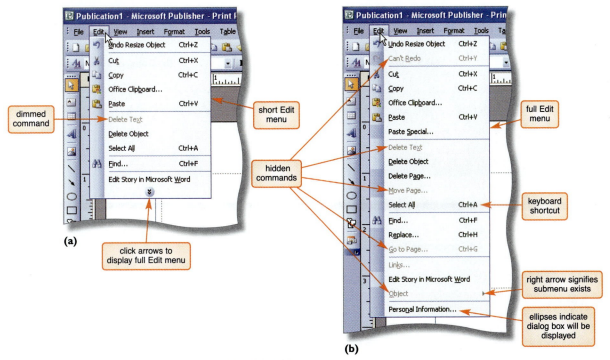

FIGURE 1-19

TOOLBARS **Toolbars** contain buttons and boxes that allow you to perform frequent tasks more quickly than when using the menu bar. For example, to print a publication, you can click the Print button on a toolbar instead of navigating through the File menu to reach the Print command.

Each button on a toolbar has a picture on its face that helps you remember its function. In addition, when you move the mouse pointer over a button or box, the name of the button or box displays below it in a **ScreenTip**. Each button and box is explained in detail as it is used in the projects.

The **Standard toolbar** (Figure 1-20a on the next page) is displayed just below the menu bar. The **Connect Text Boxes toolbar** (Figure 1-20b) is displayed to the right of the Standard toolbar. Immediately below the Standard toolbar is the **Formatting toolbar** (Figure 1-20c). The Formatting toolbar **enables,** or turns on, different buttons depending on the type of object you select. The toolbar changes when you click the object. For instance, in Figure 1-18, the selected text box displays a Formatting toolbar with font options, whereas a graphic object, such as a picture, will not. The **Objects toolbar** (Figure 1-20d) displays on the left edge of the Publisher window and contains buttons for each category of objects you can add to a publication. Additional toolbars, such as the Measurements toolbar, the Picture toolbar, and WordArt toolbar are object-specific, which means they are displayed only when you use that specific type of object. You will learn about other toolbars in future projects. If you do not see a toolbar in the window, click Toolbars on the View menu and then click the name of the toolbar you want to be displayed.

More About

Toolbar Buttons

If a toolbar cannot display all of its buttons because the window is not maximized, or the toolbar shares a row with another toolbar, the Toolbar Options button on the right side of the toolbar displays right-pointing arrows. You can access these hidden buttons by clicking the Toolbar Options button to display its menu and clicking the button. To add a new command button to a toolbar, click Customize on the Tools menu, and click the Commands tab. You then can drag a command from the Commands tab to the toolbar.

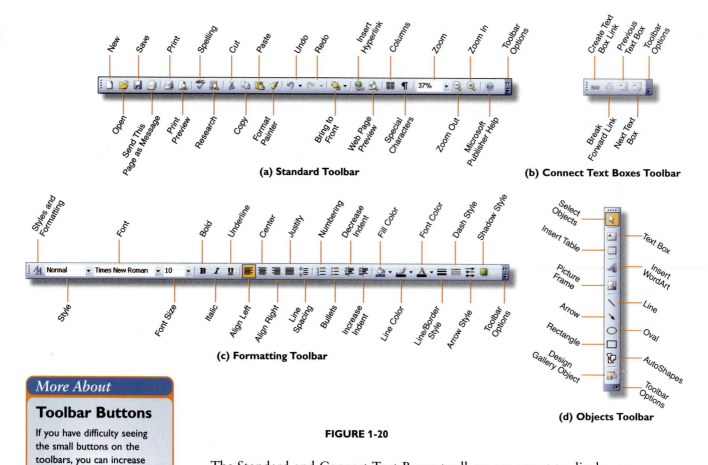

FIGURE 1-20

The Standard and Connect Text Boxes toolbars are preset to display on one row, immediately below the menu bar. The Formatting toolbar is displayed below that (Figure 1-18 on the previous page). Unless the resolution of your display device is greater than 800 × 600, some of the buttons that belong on these toolbars do not display. Use the **Toolbar Options button** to display these hidden buttons (Figure 1-21). If more than one toolbar is displayed on a single row, you can double-click the **move handle** on the left of each toolbar to display more buttons.

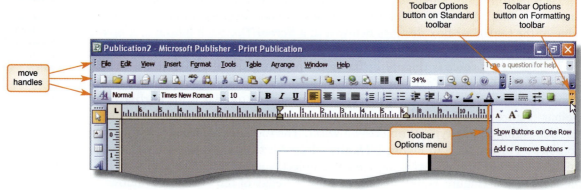

FIGURE 1-21

The toolbars initially are displayed **docked**, or attached, to the edge of the Publisher window. Additional toolbars may be displayed either stacked below the Formatting toolbar or floating in the Publisher window. A **floating toolbar** is not attached to an edge of the Publisher window. You can rearrange the order of **docked toolbars** and can move floating toolbars anywhere in the Publisher window by dragging the move handle to the desired location.

Resetting Menus and Toolbars

Each project in this book begins with the menus and toolbars displaying as they did at the initial installation of the software. If you are stepping through this project on a computer and you want your menus and toolbars to match the figures in this book, then you should reset your menus and toolbars. For more information about how to reset menus and toolbars, read Appendix D.

Speech Recognition

With the **Office Speech Recognition software** installed and a microphone, you can speak the names of toolbar buttons, menus, menu commands, list items, alerts, and dialog box controls, such as OK and Cancel. You also can dictate text and numeric entries. To indicate whether you want to speak commands or dictate entries, you use the Language bar.

The Language bar can be in one of four states: (1) **restored**, which means it is displayed somewhere in the Publisher window (Figure 1-22a); (2) **minimized**, which means it is displayed on the Windows taskbar (Figure 1-22b); (3) **hidden**, which means you do not see it on the screen but it will be displayed the next time you start your computer; (4) **closed**, which means it is hidden permanently until you enable it. If the Language bar is hidden or closed and you want it to be displayed, then do the following:

1. Right-click an open area on the Windows taskbar at the bottom of the screen.
2. Point to Toolbars and then click Language bar on the Toolbars submenu.

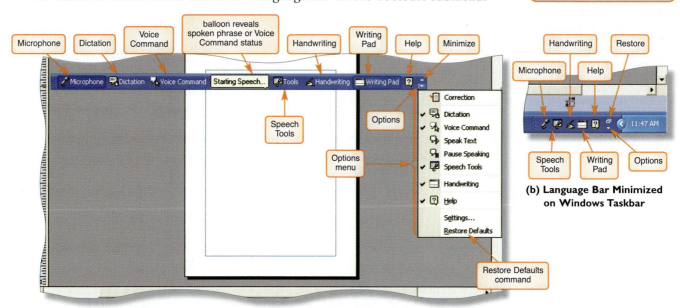

(a) Language Bar in Publisher Window with Microphone Enabled

(b) Language Bar Minimized on Windows Taskbar

FIGURE 1-22

If the Language bar command is dimmed on the Toolbars submenu or if the Speech command is dimmed on the Tools menu, the Office Speech Recognition software is not installed.

In this book, the Language bar is not displayed in the figures. If you want to close the Language bar so your screen is identical to what you see in the book, right-click the Language bar and then click Close the Language bar on the shortcut menu. Additional information on Office Speech Recognition is available in Appendix B.

Entering Text

More About

Entering Text

In the days of typewriters, the letter I was used for both the letter I and the numeral one. Keyboards, however, have both the letter I and the numeral one. Keyboards also have both the numeral zero and the letter o. Be careful to press the correct keyboard character when creating text in a publication.

Most of the templates in the design galleries come with text already inserted into text boxes. A **text box** is an object in a publication designed to hold text in a specific shape, size, and style. Text boxes also can be drawn on the page using the **Text Box button** on the Objects toolbar. Text boxes can be formatted from the menu, on the Formatting toolbar, or on the shortcut menu displayed by right-clicking the text box.

To enter text into a text box you can type on the keyboard or speak into the microphone. To replace **placeholder text**, or text supplied by the template, you click the placeholder text and then enter the new text.

A text box has changeable properties. A **property** is an attribute or characteristic of an object. Within text boxes, you can **edit**, or make changes to, the following properties: font, spacing, alignment, fill color, and margins, among others.

Zooming

Sometimes the size of the text box or other Publisher object is small and, therefore, difficult to edit. Publisher provides several ways to **zoom in**, or increase the magnification of an object, to facilitate viewing and editing.

Table 1-2 shows several zoom methods.

More About

Zooming Pictures

If you want to zoom in and out of pictures or graphics more quickly, click View on the menu bar, and click Pictures. When the Pictures dialog box is displayed, click the Fast resize and zoom option button.

Editing small areas of text is easier if you use zooming techniques to enlarge the view of the publication. When viewing an entire printed page, 8½-by-11 inches, the magnification is approximately 34%, which makes reading the small text difficult. You may press the F9 key to enlarge selected objects to 100% magnification. Pressing the F9 key a second time returns the layout to its previous magnification. Publisher also allows you to zoom using the **Zoom box** on the Standard toolbar (Figure 1-23). Clicking the Zoom box arrow displays a list of magnifications, such as Whole Page, Page Width, and various magnifications. Whole Page displays the complete page layout at approximately 34%. Page Width displays at approximately 86%, filling the workspace. Additionally, the **Zoom In button** on the Standard toolbar allows you to increase magnification. If you click an object before zooming in, Publisher displays the selected object magnified, in the center of the workspace, when you zoom.

More About

Zooming

If text is too small to read on the screen, you can zoom the publication by clicking View on the menu bar, clicking Zoom, selecting the desired percentage, and then clicking the OK button. Changing the zoom percent has no effect on the printed publication.

Table 1-2	Zoom Methods	
NUMBER	**METHOD**	**RESULT**
1	Press the F9 key on the keyboard.	Selected object is displayed centered in the workspace at 100% magnification.
2	Click the Zoom box arrow on the Standard toolbar. Click desired magnification.	Objects are displayed at selected magnification.
3	Click the Zoom In button on the Standard toolbar.	Objects display at increased magnification.
4	Right-click object, point to Zoom on shortcut menu, click desired magnification.	Objects display at selected magnification.
5	On View menu, point to Zoom, click desired magnification.	Objects display at selected magnification.
6	Using a microphone, say "Zoom in."	Objects display at increased magnification.

Editing Publisher Text Boxes

The next series of steps show how to edit the placeholder text in the heading, sub-heading, the bulleted list, the tear-offs, and other text boxes. Flyers typically display a **heading**, or title, in the upper portion of the page layout using the major font from the font scheme. A heading is designed to identify, with just a few words, the purpose of the flyer and to draw attention to the flyer.

Each text entry in a bulleted list is preceded by a **bullet** which is a dot or other symbol that is placed before the text to add emphasis. A bulleted list identifies key elements related to the publication in an easy to read format. When editing a bulleted list, each time you press the ENTER key, a bullet displays at the beginning of the next line or paragraph.

Tear-offs are small, ready-to-be scored text boxes with some combination of name, telephone, fax, e-mail, or address. Designed for customer use, tear-offs typically are perforated so a person walking by can tear off a tab to keep, rather than having to stop, find a pen and paper, and write down the name and telephone number. Traditionally, small businesses or individuals wanting to advertise something locally used tear-offs; but more recently, large companies are mass-producing advertising flyers with tear-offs to post at shopping centers, display in offices, and advertise on college campuses. Publisher tear-offs are **synchronized**, which means when you finish editing one of the tear-off text boxes, the others change to match it automatically. You may undo synchronization by clicking the Undo button on the Standard toolbar.

The following steps illustrate how to edit placeholder text.

To Edit Placeholder Text

1

• **Click For Sale in the heading of the flyer.**

• **If your page layout is not centered in the workspace, you may drag the horizontal scroll box at the bottom of the workspace.**

The text box is displayed with its text selected (Figure 1-23). Handles indicate the object can be resized. Publisher displays a ScreenTip immediately below the object.

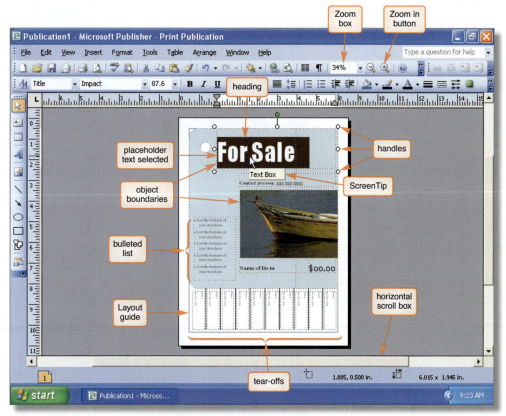

FIGURE 1-23

2

• **Type** METRO UNIVERSITY STUDENT WORK JOB **in the text box.**

The selected text is replaced automatically (Figure 1-24). Publisher automatically resizes the text so it fits into the allotted amount of space. The Impact major font from the font scheme is used for the text. The font size has been reduced to accommodate the new, longer phrase.

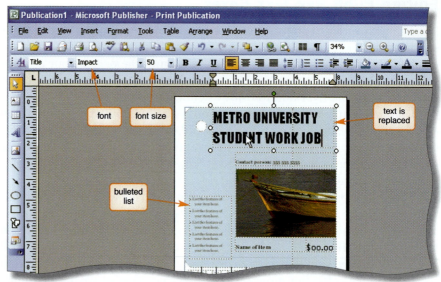

FIGURE 1-24

3

• **Click the bulleted list on the left side of the flyer to select it and then press the F9 key to zoom in on the object.**

The selected bulleted list is displayed at 100% magnification in the middle of the screen (Figure 1-25).

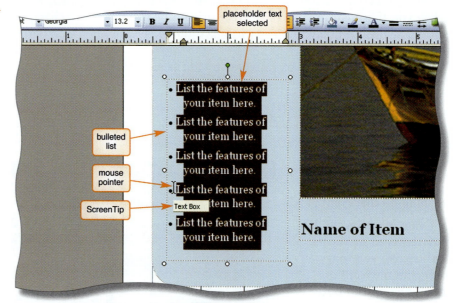

FIGURE 1-25

4

• **Type** Flexible hours **in the text box.**

The new text displays in a bulleted format (Figure 1-26). The minor font displays in the Font box on the Formatting toolbar.

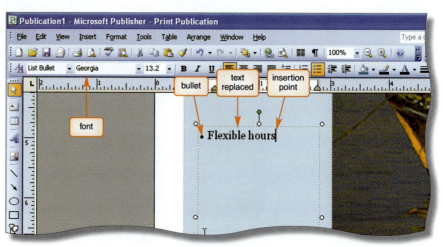

FIGURE 1-26

5

• **Press the ENTER key.**

• **Enter the remaining lines of text from Figure 1-27.**

The bulleted list is complete.

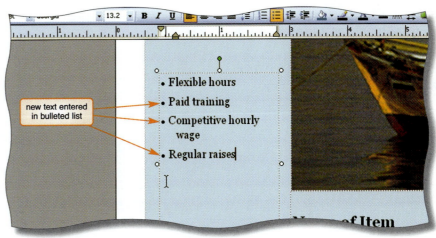

new text entered in bulleted list

• Flexible hours
• Paid training
• Competitive hourly wage
• Regular raises

FIGURE 1-27

6

• **Click the Zoom box arrow on the Standard toolbar.**

The Zoom list is displayed (Figure 1-28).

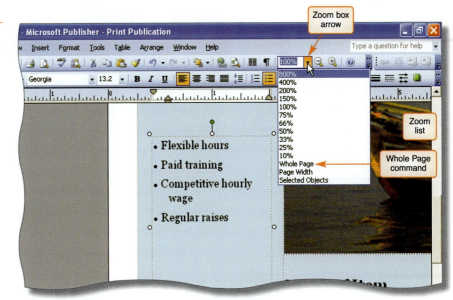

Zoom box arrow

Zoom list

Whole Page command

FIGURE 1-28

7

• **Click Whole Page in the Zoom list.**

• **Click the text in the first tear-off text box on the left to select it.**

The placeholder text in the tear-off is selected (Figure 1-29).

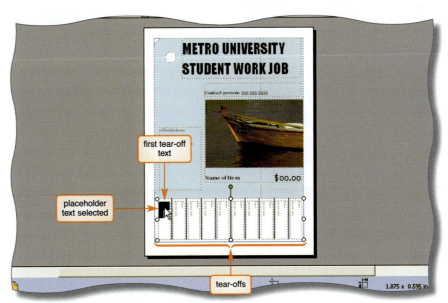

METRO UNIVERSITY STUDENT WORK JOB

first tear-off text

placeholder text selected

tear-offs

FIGURE 1-29

Microsoft Office
Publisher 2003

8

• **Press the F9 key to increase the magnification.**

• **Type** Call Megan at 555-0755 **and then press the ENTER key.**

• **Type** Megan@MUFinAid.edu **to enter the e-mail address.**

The new text appears in the first tear-off (Figure 1-30).

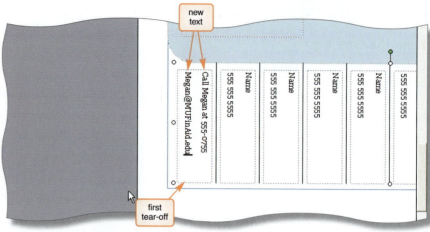

FIGURE 1-30

9

• **Click the gray workspace area, outside of the tear-offs.**

The other tear-off text boxes synchronize and display the newly edited text (Figure 1-31).

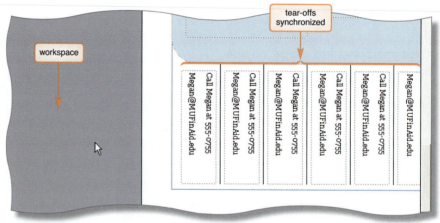

FIGURE 1-31

In Figure 1-24 on page PUB 24, the font size is 50. **Font size** specifies the size of the characters and is determined by a measurement system called points. A single **point** is about 1/72 of one inch in height. Thus, a character with a font size of 12 is about 12/72 or 1/6 of one inch in height.

As you type to replace placeholder text, Publisher will change the font size and wrap the text. **Wordwrap** allows you to type words continually without pressing the ENTER key at the end of each line. When the insertion point reaches the right side of the text box, Publisher automatically positions the insertion point at the beginning of the next line. As you type, if a word extends beyond the right margin, Publisher also automatically positions that word on the next line with the insertion point.

Deleting Objects

Recall that a Publisher object includes anything you want to place in your publication, such as text boxes, graphics, or shapes. Sometimes you may want to **delete**, or permanently remove, an object. In order to delete an object, the object must be selected.

Publisher provides four different ways to delete an object:

- Right-click the object and click Delete Object on the shortcut menu.
- Select the object and click Delete Object on the Edit menu.

- Select the object (not the text inside) and press the DELETE key.
- Select the object and click the Cut button on the Standard toolbar.

Deleting Objects in the Flyer

The text box below the graphic that displays a dollar amount is unnecessary in this flyer. Therefore, you will delete it.

The following steps show how to delete an object using the shortcut menu.

Q&A

Q: How do I delete multiple objects?

A: Click an object, SHIFT-click subsequent objects, and then press the DELETE key.

To Delete an Object

1

• **Right-click anywhere in the Publisher workspace and then point to Zoom on the shortcut menu.**

The Zoom submenu appears with magnification choices (Figure 1-32).

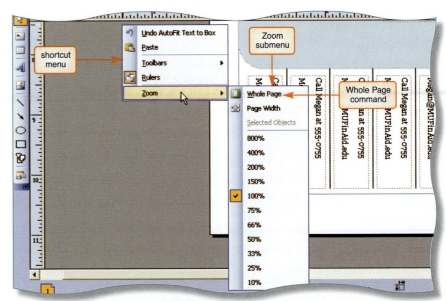

FIGURE 1-32

2

• **Click Whole Page on the Zoom submenu.**

• **When the entire page layout is displayed, right-click the dollar amount text box below the graphic.**

A shortcut menu appropriate for text box editing is displayed (Figure 1-33). Shortcut menus vary depending upon the selected object.

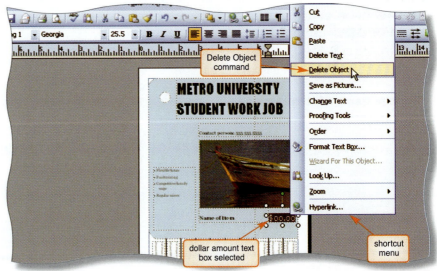

FIGURE 1-33

3

• **Click Delete Object on the shortcut menu.**

The text box is deleted.

Other Ways

1. On Edit menu, click Delete Object
2. Press DELETE key
3. On Standard toolbar, click Cut button

If you delete an object accidentally, you can click the Undo button on the Standard toolbar to retrieve it. Or, if you used the Cut button, you can click the Paste button to retrieve the deleted object.

You delete text in a similar manner to deleting an object. First you select the text, and then you can use the Delete Text command on a menu, the DELETE key on the keyboard, or the Cut button on the Standard toolbar.

Checking Spelling as You Type

As you type text in a publication, Publisher checks your typing for possible spelling and grammar errors. If a word you type is not in the dictionary, a red wavy underline is displayed below the word. Similarly, if text you type contains a possible grammar error, a green wavy underline is displayed below the text. Although you can check the entire document for spelling and grammar errors at once, you also can check these flagged errors immediately.

To verify that the Check spelling as you type feature is enabled, point to Spelling on the Tools menu, then click Spelling Options on the Spelling submenu. If a check mark does not display beside Check spelling as you type, click the check box.

When a word is flagged with a red wavy underline, it is not in Publisher's dictionary. To display a list of suggested corrections for a flagged word, you right-click the word. A flagged word, however, is not necessarily misspelled. For example, many names, abbreviations, and specialized terms are not in Publisher's main dictionary. In these cases, you tell Publisher to ignore the flagged word. As you type, Publisher also detects duplicate words. For example, if your document contains the phrase, to the the store, Publisher places a red wavy underline below the second occurrence of the word, the.

In the following example, the word, library, has been misspelled intentionally as libray to illustrate Publisher's Check spelling as you type feature. If you are completing this project on a personal computer, your flyer may contain different misspelled words, depending on the accuracy of your typing. The following steps illustrate how to check spelling as you type.

To Check Spelling as You Type

1

• **Click the Name of Item text box below the graphic.**

The text is displayed selected (Figure 1-34).

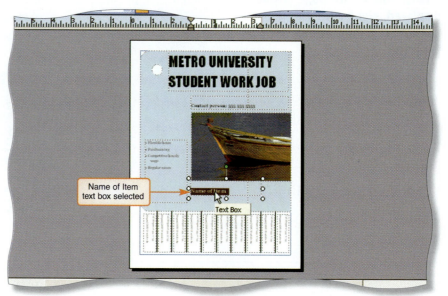

FIGURE 1-34

2

- **Press the F9 key.**
- **Type** University Libray **and then press the SPACEBAR.**
- **Right-click the flagged word, Libray.**

Publisher flags the misspelled word, Libray, by placing a red wavy underline below it (Figure 1-35). The shortcut menu lists suggested spelling corrections for the flagged word.

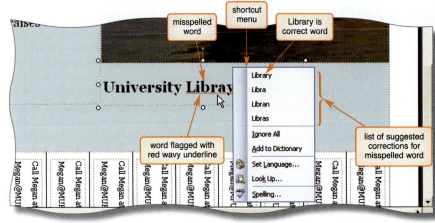

FIGURE 1-35

3

- **Click Library on the shortcut menu.**

Publisher replaces the misspelled word with the word selected on the shortcut menu and removes the red wavy underline (Figure 1-36).

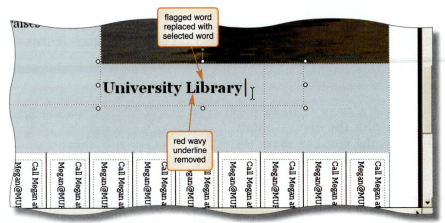

FIGURE 1-36

If a flagged word actually is spelled correctly and, for example, is a proper name, you can right-click it and then click Ignore All on the shortcut menu (Figure 1-35). If when you right-click the misspelled word, your desired correction is not in the list on the shortcut menu, you can click outside the shortcut menu to close the menu and then retype the correct word, or you can click Spelling on the shortcut menu to display the Spelling dialog box. You will learn more about the Spelling dialog box in a later project.

The next step is to type the remainder of text in the text box, as described in the following steps.

Other Ways

1. Double-click wavy line, press F7, click correctly spelled word, click Change
2. Double-click wavy line, on Tools menu point to Spelling, on Spelling submenu click Spelling, click correctly spelled word, click Change button

To Enter More Text

1 **Press the END key to move the insertion point to the end of the line.**

2 **Type** - Now Hiring **as the rest of the entry.**

The text box is complete (Figure 1-37).

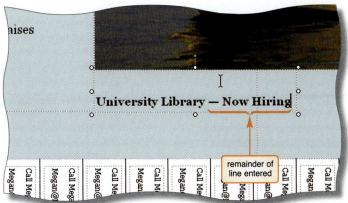

FIGURE 1-37

Table 1-3 Selecting Text	
TYPE OF SELECTION	**ACTIONS**
Character	Drag through character or press SHIFT+RIGHT ARROW
Word	Drag through word or double-click word
Line	Press SHIFT+END or SHIFT+DOWN ARROW
Paragraph	Drag through paragraph or triple-click paragraph
Placeholder text	Click
Multiple placeholder text items	Click first item, SHIFT-click second item
All text in text box	Press CTRL+A

Selecting Text

The final text box to edit in the flyer contains two occurrences of placeholder text in the same text box. To replace the text, you could click and delete each, one at a time, or you can select both and then type. Publisher provides ways to select portions of text, as shown in Table 1-3.

The following steps illustrate using the SHIFT key to make multiple selections of the placeholder text items and then insert new text.

To Select and Replace Multiple Placeholder Text Items

1

• **If necessary, zoom to whole page and then click the words, Contact person, in the text box above the graphic to select the placeholder text.**

• **Press the F9 key.**

The first placeholder text is displayed selected (Figure 1-38).

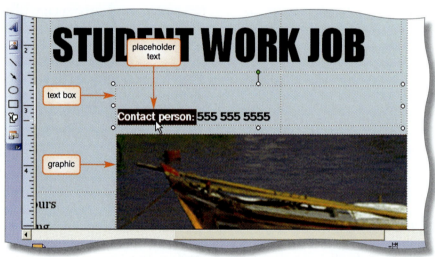

FIGURE 1-38

2

• **SHIFT-click the phone number, 555 555 5555.**

Both placeholder text items are selected (Figure 1-39).

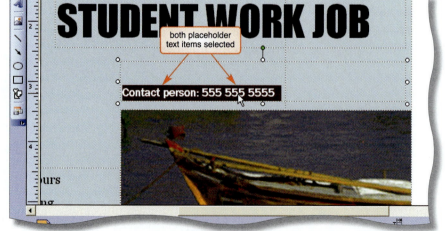

FIGURE 1-39

Other Ways

1. Select text box, press CTRL+A
2. On Edit menu, click Select All, press DELETE key

To select multiple areas of text that are not next to each other, make your first selection, hold down CTRL, and then select any other items you want.

Fitting Text

The Contact person text box above the graphic does not adjust the font size automatically to fit new text. Because this box will hold many words in the flyer, you need to change the way Publisher will fit text in the text box. The Format menu contains an AutoFit Text command. When you point to the AutoFit Text command, the AutoFit Text submenu displays three choices, Do Not Autofit, Best Fit, and Shrink Text On Overflow. **Do Not Autofit** will retain the font size, even if you type more words than will fit in the text box. Publisher stores the extra text in **overflow**, meaning that the text is hidden until it can be formatted to a smaller font size, flowed into a new text box, or until the text box itself is enlarged. **Best Fit** allows Publisher to change the font size so all text will fit in the text box. Sometimes that means reducing the font size, but it also might mean increasing short text to a very large font to create the best fit. An additional feature of Best Fit resizes the font whenever the text box itself changes in size. **Shrink Text On Overflow** means that Publisher will change the font only if necessary to display all of the text.

You will select Best Fit to allow for more words in the Contact person text box, as shown in the following steps. Additionally, you will choose the Best Fit option for the text box containing the bulleted list and the University Library – Now Hiring text box.

To Use Best Fit

1

• **With both of the placeholder text items still selected, click Format on the menu bar and then point to AutoFit Text.**

The AutoFit Text submenu displays the three options (Figure 1-40).

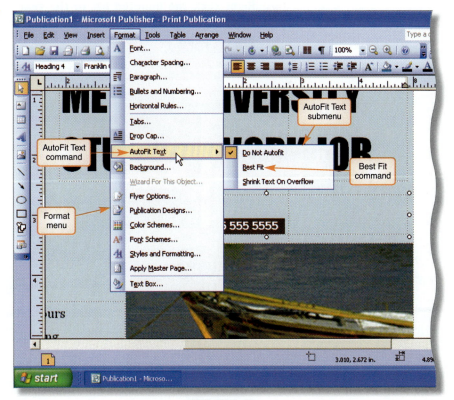

FIGURE 1-40

2

• **Click Best Fit on the AutoFit Text submenu.**

• **Type** The University Library is looking for student workers with experience in word processing, desktop publishing, or computer applications.

As you type, the font size reduces to allow all of the text to be displayed (Figure 1-41).

FIGURE 1-41

Alternately, you can right-click a text box to display a shortcut menu with a Change Text command. The Change Text submenu displays an AutoFit Text command with the three fit options.

The final step in editing text is to choose Best Fit for the bulleted list and the University Library – Now Hiring text boxes.

To AutoFit Other Text Boxes

1 Press the F9 key to display the whole page.

2 Right-click the bulleted list in the text box to the left of the graphic. Point to Change Text on the shortcut menu. When the Change Text submenu is displayed, point to AutoFit Text.

The three AutoFit Text options are displayed on the AutoFit Text submenu (Figure 1-42).

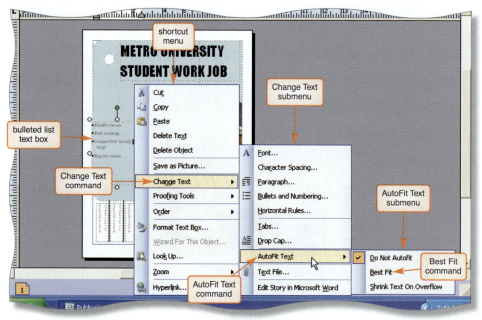

FIGURE 1-42

3 Click Best Fit on the AutoFit Text submenu.

4 Right-click the University Library – Now Hiring text box below the graphic. Point to Change Text on the shortcut menu. When the Change Text submenu is displayed, point to AutoFit Text. When the AutoFit Text menu is displayed, click Best Fit.

The text now is sized as large as possible for the size of the text box.

Using Best Fit allows you to change the size of the text box at a later time without worrying about changing the size of the font.

Saving a New Publication

The text changes in your publication now are complete. Because you have made so many changes, now is a good time to save a copy of your work. You may click either the Yes button or the No button when Publisher reminds you to save. The next series of steps illustrates how to save a publication on a floppy disk inserted in drive A using the Save button on the Standard toolbar.

More About

Saving

When you save a publication, you should create readable and meaningful file names. A file name can include up to 255 characters, including spaces. The only invalid characters are backslash (\), slash (/), colon (:), asterisk (*), question mark (?), quotation mark ("), less than symbol (<), greater than symbol (>), and vertical bar (|).

To Save a New Publication

1

• **With a formatted floppy disk in drive A, click the Save button on the Standard toolbar.**

Publisher displays the Save As dialog box (Figure 1-43). Publisher uses a default file name on unsaved publications. Your default file name may differ. With this file name selected, you can change it by immediately typing the new file name.

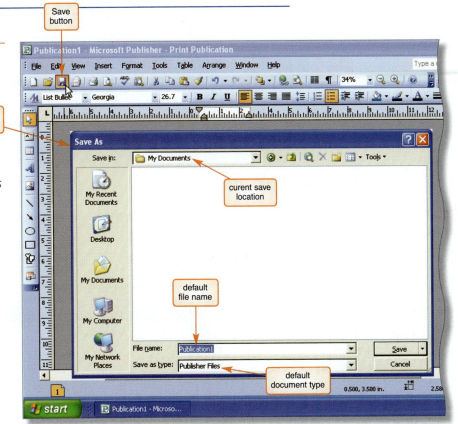

FIGURE 1-43

2

• **With the default file name selected, type the file name** Student Work Job Flyer **in the File name text box.**

• **Do not press the ENTER key after typing the file name.**

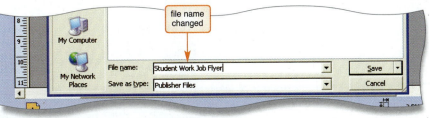

FIGURE 1-44

*The file name, Student Work Job Flyer, replaces the text in the File name text box (Figure 1-44). Notice that the current save location is the My Documents folder (Figure 1-43). A **folder** is a specific location on a disk. To change to a different save location, you use the Save in box.*

3

• **Click the Save in box arrow.**

The Save in list displays the available save locations (Figure 1-45). Your list may differ depending on your system configuration.

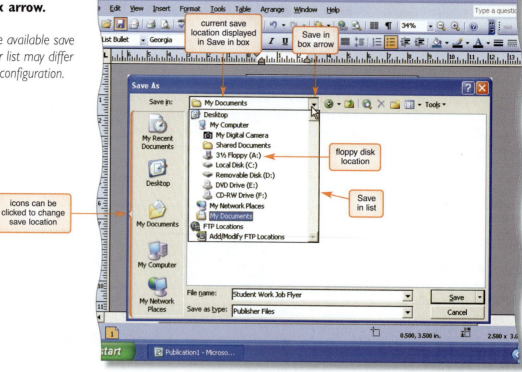

FIGURE 1-45

4

• **Click 3½ Floppy (A:) in the Save in list.**

The 3½ Floppy (A:) drive becomes the selected location (Figure 1-46). The names of existing files that are stored on the floppy disk in drive A are displayed. In Figure 1-46, no files currently are stored on the floppy disk. Your list may differ.

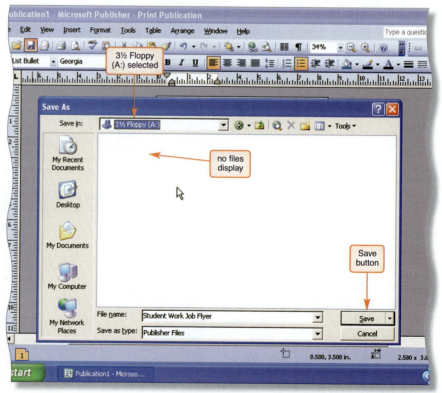

FIGURE 1-46

5

• **Click the Save button in the Save As dialog box.**

The saved publication displays the new file name, Student Work Job Flyer, on the title bar and on the taskbar (Figure 1-47). Although the publication is saved on a floppy disk, it also remains in memory and is displayed in the workspace.

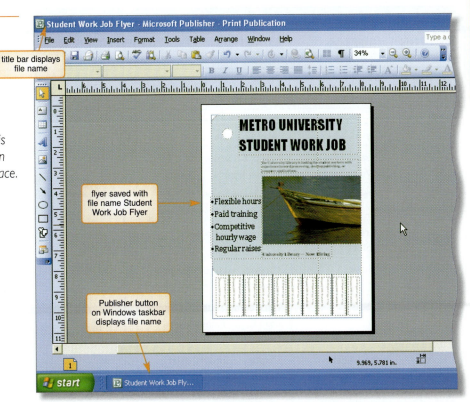

FIGURE 1-47

You can use the seven buttons at the top of the Save As dialog box (Figure 1-45) and the five icons along the left edge to change the save location and other tasks. Table 1-4 on the next page lists the function of the buttons and icons in the Save As dialog box.

When you click the **Tools button** in the Save As dialog box, a list is displayed. The **General Options command** in the list allows you to save a backup copy of the publication, create a password to limit access to the publication, and carry out other functions that are discussed later. Saving a backup publication means that each time you save a publication, Publisher copies the current version of the publication on disk to a file with the same name, but with the words, Backup of, appended to the front of the file name. In the case of a power failure or some other problem, use the backup version to restore your work.

You also can use the General Options command on the Tools list to assign a **password** to a workbook so others cannot open it. A password is case-sensitive and can be up to 15 characters long. **Case-sensitive** means Publisher can differentiate between uppercase and lowercase letters. If you assign a password and forget the password, you cannot access the publication.

The five buttons on the left of the Save As dialog box in Figure 1-43 on page PUB 33 allow you to select often used folders. The My Recent Documents button displays a list of shortcuts to the most recently used files in a folder titled Recent. You cannot save publications to the Recent folder.

When creating file names, you should make them as meaningful as possible. A **file name** can contain up to 255 characters and can include spaces.

Other Ways

1. On File menu click Save As
2. In Voice Command mode, say "File, Save As"

Q&A

Q: How can I help prevent wrist injury while working on a computer?

A: Typical computer users frequently switch between the keyboard and the mouse during a word processing session, an action that strains the wrist. To help prevent wrist injury, minimize switching. If your fingers already are on the keyboard, use keyboard keys to scroll. If your hand already is on the mouse, use the mouse to scroll.

Table 1-4   Save As Dialog Box Toolbar Buttons

BUTTON	BUTTON NAME	FUNCTION
	Default File Location	Displays contents of default file location
	Up One Level	Displays contents of next level up folder
	Search the Web	Starts browser and displays search engine
	Delete	Deletes selected file or folder
	Create New Folder	Creates new folder
	Views	Changes view of files and folders
Tools	Tools	Lists commands to print or modify file names and folders
My Recent Documents	My Recent Documents	Displays contents of My Recent Documents in Save in list (you cannot save to this location)

Table 1-4   Save As Dialog Box Toolbar Buttons

BUTTON	BUTTON NAME	FUNCTION
Desktop	Desktop	Displays contents of Windows desktop folder in Save in list to save quickly to the Windows desktop
My Documents	My Documents	Displays contents of My Documents in Save in list to save quickly to the My Documents folder
My Computer	My Computer	Displays contents of My Computer in Save in list to save quickly to another drive on the computer
My Network Places	My Network Places	Displays contents of My Network Places in Save in List to save quickly to My Network Places

Using Graphics

Files containing graphical images, also called **graphics**, are available from a variety of sources. Publisher includes a series of predefined graphics such as drawings, photographs, sounds, videos, and other media files called clips. A **clip** is a single media file, including art, sound, animation, or movies, that you can insert and use in print publications, Web publications, and other Microsoft Office documents.

You can find, add, and organize media clips by displaying the **Clip Art Task Pane** (Figure 1-48). **Clip art** is an inclusive term given to a variety of predefined graphics such as images, artwork, and draw-type images that are created from a set of instructions (also called object-based or vector graphics). You can search for clip art based on descriptive keywords, file name, file format, or clip collection. The **clip collection** is a hierarchical organization of media clips. You can create your own clip collections; import clip collections; or add, move, or copy clips from one collection to another. The Search in box arrow displays three areas in which to search: My Collections, Office Collections, and Web Collections. The Results should be box arrow displays four types of media to include the search results: Clip Art, Photographs, Movies, and Sounds. More information on graphics, animation, and sound is presented in later projects.

At the bottom of the Clip Art task pane is a link to Organize clips, which opens the Microsoft Clip Organizer. You can use the **Clip Organizer** to browse through clip collections, add clips, or catalog clips in ways that make sense to you. For example, you can create a collection to group the clips you use most frequently, or let Clip Organizer automatically add and catalog clips on your hard disk.

If you have an Internet connection established, clip art search results automatically will include content from the Microsoft Office Online Web site. Or, you can visit the site yourself by clicking the **Clip art on Office Online** link at the bottom of the Clip Art task pane.

Using the Clip Art Task Pane

Because this flyer is advertising for a computer-related job, it is more appropriate to choose a graphic related to computers and workers rather than the picture of the boat supplied by the template. A graphic should enhance the message of the publication.

The following steps illustrate how to retrieve an appropriate graphic using the Clip Art task pane to replace the supplied graphic. If you cannot access the graphic described, choose a suitable replacement from your system's clip art.

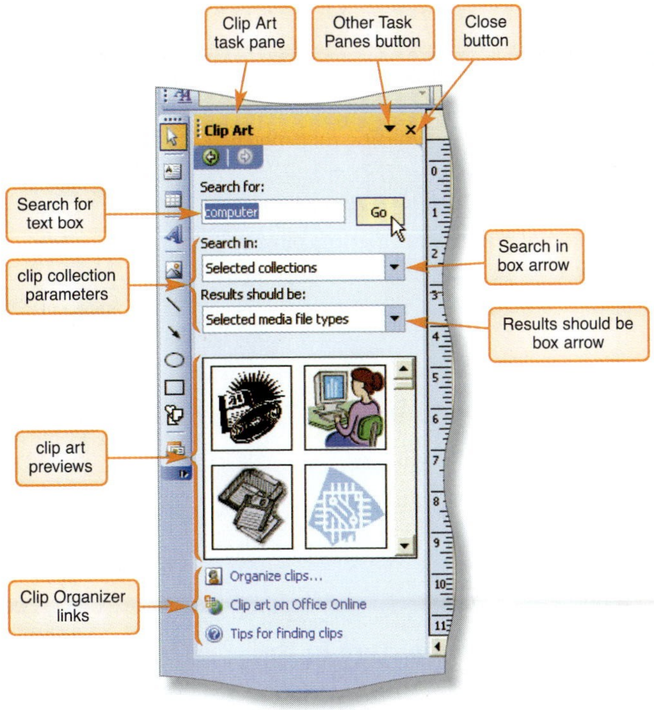

FIGURE 1-48

To Replace a Graphic Using the Clip Art Task Pane

1

• **If necessary to view the whole page, click the Zoom box arrow, and then click Whole Page in the Zoom list.**

• **Double-click the graphic of the boat.**

• **When the Clip Art task pane is displayed, if the Search for text box contains text, drag through the text to select it.**

• **Type** computer **in the Search for text box.**

Publisher displays the Clip Art task pane at the left edge of the Publisher window (Figure 1-49). Recall that a task pane is a separate window that enables you to carry out some Publisher tasks more efficiently. When you enter a description of the desired graphic in the Search for text box and click the Go button, Publisher searches the clip collection for clips that match the description. Publisher also may display the Picture toolbar.

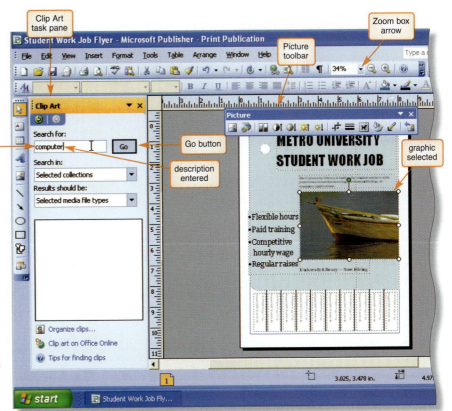

FIGURE 1-49

2

• **Click the Go button.**

Publisher displays a list of clips that match the description, computer (Figure 1-50). Your pictures may vary depending on the installation of Publisher or the files on your network. Choose an appropriate image from your clip collection.

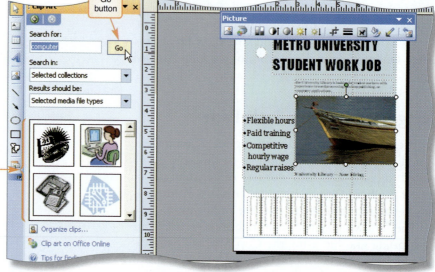
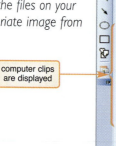

FIGURE 1-50

3

• **Click the desired picture in the task pane.**

Publisher inserts the clip art into the publication (Figure 1-51). The new image replaces the previous boat picture. The size of your graphic may differ.

4

• **Close the Clip Art task pane by clicking its Close button.**

• **Close the Picture toolbar by clicking its Close button.**

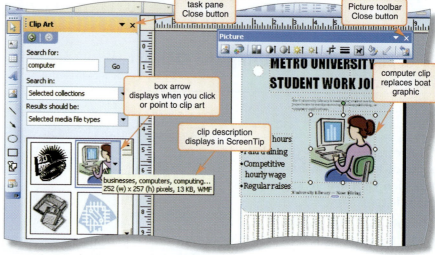

FIGURE 1-51

A graphic is any object in Publisher other than a text box. Graphics may include objects from the clip collection, imported images and pictures, drawings, tables, WordArt, shapes, lines, and arrows. A full installation of Publisher copies thousands of graphics including clip art, pictures, sounds, video clips, and animation to the computer's hard disk. For network installations, ask your instructor for the location of the graphic files.

Graphic files also are available from a variety of other sources. If you have a scanner or digital camera attached to your system, Publisher can insert the graphic directly from the scanner or camera. Alternatively, you can save the graphic in a file and then insert it into the publication at a later time. Some users purchase photographs from local software retailers, have their film developed on a CD-ROM, or locate pictures on the Web.

You can use the Clip collection to organize your clips by category or keyword so that finding the one you want is made easier. Some graphics are more suitable for display on the Web, while others print better on color printers. Future projects discuss the various types of graphics files in detail, including their advantages and disadvantages.

Moving and Resizing Objects

A key feature of desktop publishing software is its capability to move objects around and resize them on the page layout. You **move** an object by dragging its boundary to a new location. You **resize**, or change the width and height of an object, by dragging one of its handles.

Moving an Object

In general, moving an object requires you to select it and then drag it to the desired position. Unless a specific effect is desired, you usually move objects to a blank portion of the page layout. While you drag an object, the mouse pointer changes to a four-headed arrow, as shown in the following steps.

To Move an Object

1

• **If necessary, click the Zoom box arrow on the Standard toolbar and then click Whole Page in the Zoom list.**

• **Click the bulleted list text box and then point to its boundary.**

The mouse pointer changes to a four-headed arrow (Figure 1-52).

2

• **Drag the text box up so that its top boundary is approximately even with the top boundary of the graphic.**

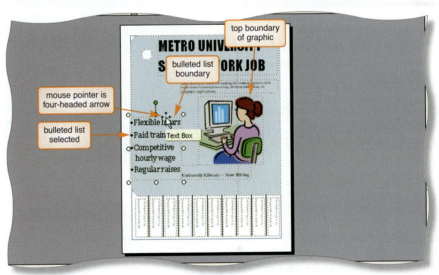

FIGURE 1-52

Publisher has a special feature called **snapping**, which adjusts the placement of an object automatically so it aligns to rulers, boundaries, or guides. You may turn on and off the snapping feature by pointing to Snap on the Arrange menu, and then clicking the appropriate choice. If you want objects moved close to but not adjacent to other objects, you should turn off the snapping feature. You will learn more about snapping in a later project.

Resizing Objects

You easily can change the size of objects to fit your needs. Resizing includes both enlarging and reducing the size of an object. You can reshape an object by clicking a handle and dragging. Recall that a handle is one of several small shapes displayed around an object when the object is selected.

Two text boxes are resized in the steps on the next page. In a later project, you will learn how to resize objects in other ways.

To Resize an Object

 1

• **Click the University Library – Now Hiring text box.**

• **Point to the middle handle on the right side of the text box.**

Publisher selects the text box, which displays with eight small circle handles in its boundary at each corner and middle location (Figure 1-53). The mouse pointer shape changes to a two-headed arrow when it is positioned over a handle.

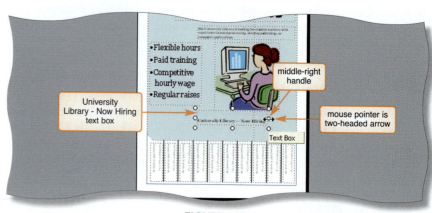

FIGURE 1-53

 2

• **Drag the middle-right handle to the right until the dotted boundary is even with the right guide of the page layout.**

The text box is resized, and the text automatically resizes to Best Fit (Figure 1-54). Publisher displays a dotted line while you are resizing.

FIGURE 1-54

 3

• **Select the text box above the graphic that begins with the phrase, The University Library is looking for student workers.**

• **Drag the middle-left handle to the left guide of the page layout.**

The text box is resized, and the text automatically resizes to Best Fit (Figure 1-55).

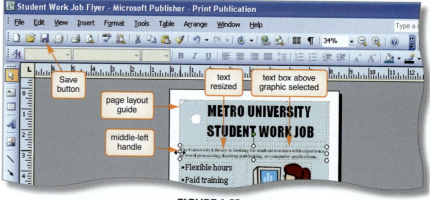

FIGURE 1-55

Other Ways

1. On Format menu click Text Box, click Size tab, enter desired height and width, click OK button
2. On shortcut menu, click Format Text Box, click Size tab, enter desired height and width, click OK button
3. Double-click status bar, on Measurements toolbar, enter desired height and width

When you drag a corner handle instead of a middle handle, you can change both the width and height of the object. Special care should be taken if the object is a graphic, because dragging the middle handle sometimes may cause the graphic to look distorted.

Instead of resizing a selected object by dragging with the mouse, you also can use the Size sheet displayed by clicking the object's Format command on the Format menu. Later, you also will learn how to resize an object using the Measurements toolbar. Either way, you can enter exact height and width measurements.

Saving an Existing Publication with the Same File Name

The print version of the flyer now is complete. To transfer the formatting and graphic changes to your floppy disk in drive A, you must save the publication again. When you saved the publication the first time, you assigned the file name, Student Work Job Flyer. Publisher assigns this same file name automatically to the publication each time you subsequently save it, if you use the following procedure. The following step saves the publication using the same file name.

To Save an Existing Publication with the Same File Name

1 **Click the Save button on the Standard toolbar.**

Publisher saves the publication on a floppy disk inserted in drive A using the current file name, Student Work Job Flyer. The publication remains in memory and is displayed on the screen.

If for some reason, you want to save an existing publication with a different file name, click Save As on the File menu to display the Save As dialog box. Then, fill in the Save As dialog box as discussed in Steps 2 through 5 on pages PUB 33 through PUB 35 using a different file name in the File name text box.

Other Ways

1. On File menu click Save
2. Press CTRL+S
3. In Voice Command mode, say "Save"

Printing a Publication

Once you have created a publication and saved it, you might want to print it. A printed version of the publication is called a **hard copy** or printout. The following steps print the publication created in Project 1.

Other Ways

1. On File menu click Print, click OK button
2. Press CTRL+P, click OK button
3. In Voice Command mode, say "Print"

To Print a Publication

1

• **Ready the printer according to the printer instructions.**

• **Click the Print button on the Standard toolbar.**

A dialog box briefly appears indicating it is preparing to print the publication. A few moments later, the publication begins printing on the printer. The tray status area displays a printer icon while the publication is printing (Figure 1-56).

2

• **When the printer stops, retrieve the printout.**

FIGURE 1-56

More About

**Healthy
Computing**

For more information about
healthy computing, visit the
Publisher 2003 More About
Web page (scsite.com/
pub2003/more) and click
Healthy Computing.

When you use the Print button to print a publication, Publisher prints the entire publication automatically. You then may distribute the hard copy or keep it as a permanent record of the publication.

If you want to cancel a job that is printing or waiting to be printed, double-click the printer icon in the tray status area (Figure 1-56 on the previous page). In the Print dialog box, right-click the job to be canceled and then click Cancel Printing on the shortcut menu.

Quitting Publisher

After you create, save, and print the publication, you are ready to quit Publisher and return control to Windows. The following step shows how to quit Publisher.

To Quit Publisher

1 Click the Close button in the upper-right corner on the title bar (Figure 1-56 on the previous page). If a Microsoft Office Publisher dialog box is displayed asking if you want to save the changes, click the No button.

Other Ways

1. On File menu, click Exit
2. Press ALT+F4
3. In Voice Command mode, say "File, Exit"

If you made changes to the publication since the last save, Publisher displays a dialog box asking if you want to save the changes. Clicking the Yes button saves changes; clicking the No button ignores the changes; and clicking the Cancel button returns to the publication. If you did not make any changes since you saved the publication, this dialog box does not display.

Closing a publication is different from quitting Publisher. Closing a publication, by clicking Close on the File menu, leaves any other Publisher publications open and Publisher running. If no other publication was open, the Close command displays the New Publication task pane.

As you created the flyer, you edited the template, resized text boxes and changed the way they fit text, inserted a picture from the clip collection, printed the publication, and saved it. You might decide, however, to change the publication at a later date. To do this, you must start Publisher again and then retrieve your publication from the floppy disk in drive A.

More About

Opening Files

In Publisher, you can open a
recently used file by clicking
File on the menu bar and
clicking the file name on
the File menu. To instruct
Publisher to show the
recently used publications on
the File menu, click Tools on
the menu bar, click Options,
click the General tab, click
Recently used file list to place
a check mark in the check
box, and click the OK button.

Opening a Publication

Once you have created and saved a publication, you often will have reason to retrieve it from disk. For example, you might want to revise the publication or print it again. Earlier, you saved the publication created in this project on a floppy disk using the file name, Student Work Job Flyer. The following steps illustrate how to open the file from a floppy disk in drive A, and make changes to the Publication to prepare it for publishing on the Web.

To Open a Publication

1

• **With your floppy disk in drive A, click the Start button on the Windows taskbar, point to All Programs on the Start menu, point to Microsoft Office on the All Programs submenu, and then click Microsoft Office Publisher 2003 on the Microsoft Office submenu.**

Publisher starts. The Open area of the New Publication task pane lists up to four of the most recently used files (Figure 1-57).

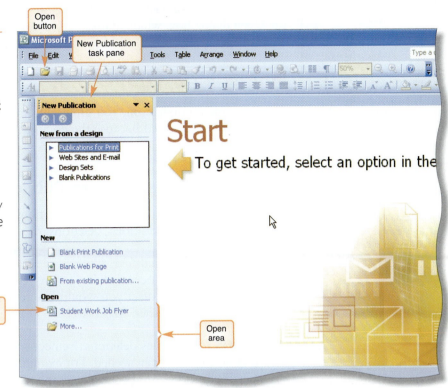

FIGURE 1-57

2

• **Click Student Work Job Flyer in the New Publication task pane.**

Publisher opens the document, Student Work Job Flyer, from the floppy disk in drive A and displays it in the Publisher window (Figure 1-58).

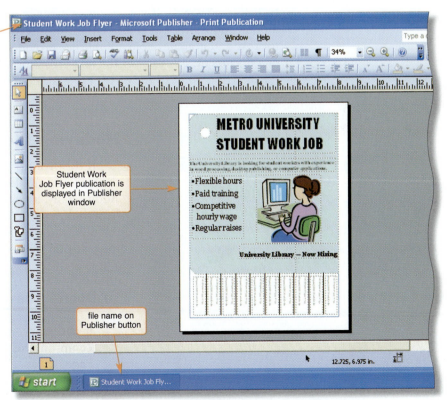

FIGURE 1-58

If you want to open a publication other than one of the four most recently opened ones, click the Open button on the Standard toolbar or the More link at the bottom of the New Publication task pane. Clicking the Open button or the More link displays the Open dialog box, which allows you to navigate to a document stored on disk.

Modifying a Publication

After creating a publication, you often will find that you must make changes to it. Changes can be required because the document contains an error or because of new circumstances.

Types of Changes Made to Publications

The types of changes made to publications normally fall into one of the three following categories: additions, deletions, or modifications.

ADDITIONS Additional text, objects, or formatting may be required in the publication. Additions occur when you are required to add items to a publication. For example, in this project you would like to insert a text box that will display when the flyer is published to the Web.

DELETIONS Sometimes deletions are necessary in a publication because objects are incorrect or are no longer needed. For example, to place this advertising flyer on the electronic bulletin board at the college, the tear-offs no longer are needed. In that case, you would delete them from the page layout.

MODIFICATIONS If you make an error in a document or want to make other modifications, normal combinations of inserting, deleting, and editing techniques for text and graphics apply. Publisher provides several methods for correcting errors in a document. For each of the text error correction techniques, you first must move the insertion point to the error. For graphic modification, the object first must be selected.

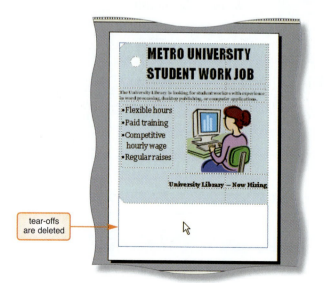

tear-offs are deleted

FIGURE 1-59

Modifying the Flyer

If this flyer displays on an electronic bulletin board, the tear-offs are unnecessary and should be deleted. Additionally, a new text box should be inserted, with a hyperlink, in preparation for creating a Web version of the publication. The following steps show how to delete the tear-offs.

To Delete the Tear-Offs

1. If necessary, right-click the workspace. Point to Zoom on the shortcut menu and then click Whole Page.

2. Right-click any of the tear-offs, and then click Delete Object on the shortcut menu.

The tear-offs are deleted (Figure 1-59).

If you delete an object accidentally, you can restore it by clicking the Undo button on the Standard toolbar. If you want to cancel your undo, you can use the Redo button. Some actions, such as saving or printing a document, cannot be undone or redone.

Inserting a Text Box

The final step in modifying the flyer is to create a new text box. Recall that the Objects toolbar contains buttons for many different kinds of objects that you can insert into publications. In the case of a text box, you click the Text Box button and then drag in the publication to create the text box. Once it is created, you can type in the text box just as you did with those created by the template. You will use a font from the font scheme of the publication, as well as the Best Fit option.

The following steps illustrate how to insert a text box in the publication.

To Insert a Text Box

1

• **Click the Text Box button on the Objects toolbar and then move the mouse to the lower portion of the flyer where the tear-offs were located.**

• **Drag a rectangle approximately 5.5 inches wide and 1.5 inches tall.**

The empty text box is inserted (Figure 1-60). The width and height are displayed on the status bar as you drag. The mouse pointer changes to a cross hair.

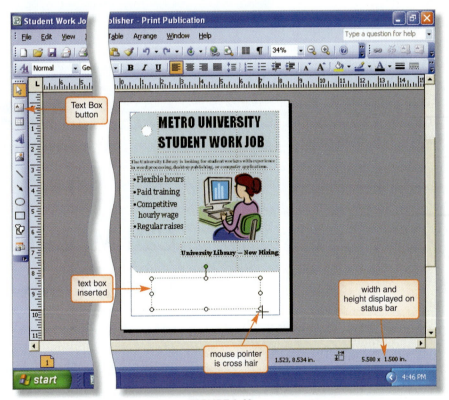

FIGURE 1-60

2

• **Press the F9 key to zoom in.**

• **Type** Call Megan at 555-0755 **and then press the ENTER key.**

• **Type** Megan@MUFinAid.edu **to complete the text box.**

• **Right-click the text box. On the shortcut menu, point to Change Text.**

• **Point to AutoFit Text on the Change Text submenu.**

The AutoFit Text submenu displays three choices (Figure 1-61).

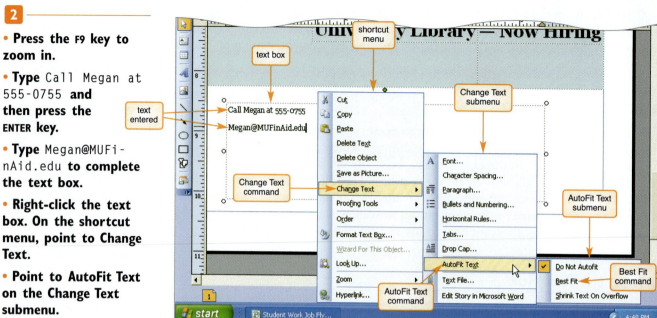

FIGURE 1-61

3

• **Click Best Fit on the AutoFit Text submenu.**

Publisher increases the font size of the text to fill the text box (Figure 1-62).

FIGURE 1-62

Inserting a Hyperlink

The final modification in preparation for converting this publication to a Web publication is inserting a hyperlink. A **hyperlink** is colored and underlined text or a graphic that you click to go to a file, a location in a file, a Web page, or an e-mail address. When you insert a hyperlink, you select the text or object and then click the Insert Hyperlink button on the Standard toolbar. The **Insert Hyperlink dialog box** allows you to select options and enter Web addresses, as shown in the following steps.

To Insert a Hyperlink

1

• **Select the text, Megan@MUFinAid.edu, by dragging through it in the text box.**

Publisher displays the e-mail address selected (Figure 1-63).

FIGURE 1-63

2

• **Click the Insert Hyperlink button on the Standard toolbar.**

*The Insert Hyperlink dialog box is displayed (Figure 1-64). Publisher displays Link to locations on the **Link to bar** on the left.*

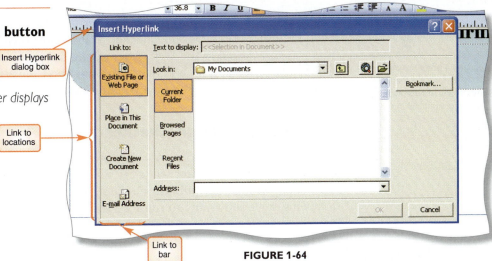

FIGURE 1-64

3

• **Click E-mail Address on the Link to bar in the Insert Hyperlink dialog box.**

• **Type** Megan@MUFinAid.edu **in the E-mail address text box. Press the TAB key.**

• **Type** Student Work Job Web Flyer Inquiry **in the Subject text box.**

The mailto: prefix automatically is placed before the e-mail address (Figure 1-65). The Subject text box entry will be entered as the e-mail subject line when users click the link.

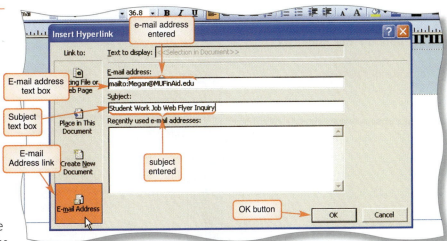

FIGURE 1-65

Microsoft Office
Publisher 2003

4

• **Click the OK button.**

The Insert Hyperlink dialog box closes, and the e-mail address is displayed as a hyperlink (Figure 1-66).

e-mail address hyperlink

FIGURE 1-66

The Link to bar in the Insert Hyperlink dialog box displays links to an Existing File or Web Page, Place in This Document, Create New Document, and E-mail Address. When you click one of these links on the Link to bar, the dialog box displays text boxes and information unique to the type of link. The **E-mail Address link** allows you to edit the e-mail address and provides a subject line to be inserted in the resulting e-mail message. It also displays a list of recently used e-mail addresses (Figure 1-65 on the previous page).

More About

Creating Web Pages

For more information about the creating Web pages in Publisher, visit the Publisher 2003 More About Web page (scsite.com/pub2003/more) and click Creating Web Pages.

Creating a Web Page from a Publication

Publisher can create a Web page from your publication. It is a three-step process. First, Publisher uses a **Design Checker** to look for potential problems if the publication was transferred to the Web. After saving the publication with a new file name, it will be converted to a Web Publication using the Convert to Web Publication command on the File menu. Finally, Publisher publishes the Web page.

Running the Design Checker

If your publication contains a layout that is not appropriate, such as overlapping objects, the Design Checker will alert you. If you use links or hot spots to other Web pages within your publication, Design Checker will verify the addresses. The following steps show how to run the Design Checker.

To Run the Design Checker

1

• **Click Tools on the menu bar.**

The Tools menu is displayed (Figure 1-67).

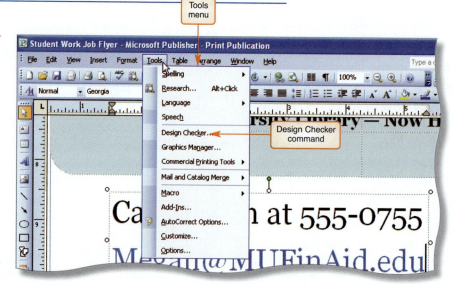

Tools menu

Design Checker command

FIGURE 1-67

2

- **Click Design Checker.**
- **When Publisher displays the Design Checker task pane, if any problems are listed in the Select an item to fix text box, click the problem.**
- **When Publisher selects the object, fix the error.**
- **When no design errors exist, Publisher displays a message, indicating there are no problems in the publication.**

A progress bar appears as the Design Checker checks the publication (Figure 1-68).

3

- **Click the Close Design Checker button in the Design Checker task pane.**

The task pane closes.

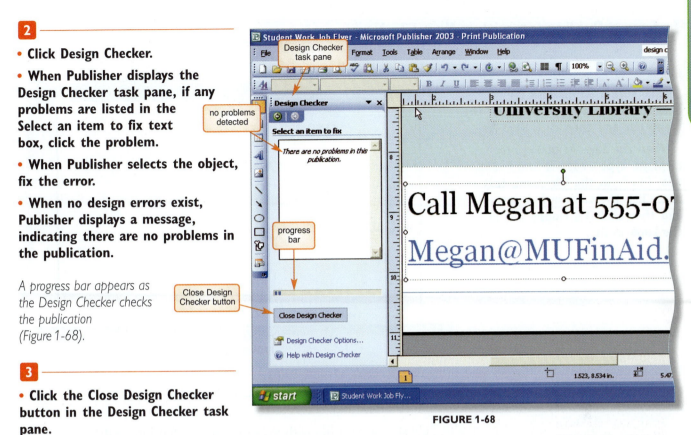

FIGURE 1-68

If your publication had problems or contained design errors, you would have been given the option to go to the error, ignore, continue, or obtain more information about the problems. The Design Checker looks for appropriate layouts. If text overlaps an object, the Design Checker offers to convert the text box to a graphic so it will display properly. The Design Checker looks at all graphics and may display suggestions on those that load slowly. More about the Design Checker and information on types of graphics will be covered in future projects.

Saving a Publication with a New File Name

The steps on the next page illustrate how to save the publication with a new file name in preparation for converting it to a Web publication. It is important to save the publication before converting it to a Web publication so you can make changes at a later time, if necessary.

To Save a Publication with a New File Name

1

• **Make sure a floppy disk is inserted in drive A. Click File on the menu bar and then click Save As.**

• **When the Save As dialog box displays, type** Student Work Job Web Flyer **in the File name text box. Click the Look in box arrow and then click 3½ Floppy (A:) in the Look in list.**

The Save As dialog box is displayed (Figure 1-69).

2

• **Click the Save button.**

The saved file is stored with a new file name on the disk in drive A.

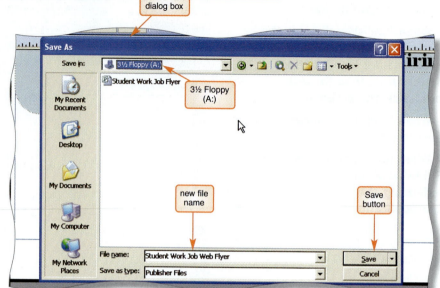

FIGURE 1-69

Normally, Publisher saves a file with the three-letter extension, .pub. The **.pub extension** allows Publisher easily to open your formatted file and assign a recognizable icon to the shortcut on your disk.

Converting a Print Publication to a Web Publication

You can create two types of publications with Microsoft Publisher: print publications and Web publications. A **Web publication** is one suitable for publishing to the Web with certain objects, formatting options, hyperlinks, and other features specific to Web pages.

A command on Publisher's File menu converts publications from one type to another. Up to now, you have worked on a print publication as noted in the title bar (Figure 1-68 on the previous page). Once you convert the file, you work in **Web mode**. The options available to you in Web mode are tailored specifically to Web publications so you can create a publication that is optimized for display in a Web browser. A **browser** is a piece of software that interprets and formats files into Web pages and displays them. A Web browser, such as Microsoft Internet Explorer, can follow hyperlinks, transfer files, and play sound or video files that are embedded in Web pages. You always can determine which publication mode you are in by looking at the title bar of your open publication, which will display either Print Publication or Web Publication, depending on the publication type.

When you convert a publication from one type to the other, Publisher copies the text and graphics from your original publication into the new publication type. Because certain print features are not available in Web mode, and certain Web features are not available in Print mode, your publication may undergo formatting changes when you convert it from one publication type to the other.

The following steps illustrate how to convert a print publication to a Web publication. A two-step wizard helps you through the conversion process. A **wizard** is a series of dialog boxes and questions to help you make choices and format publications based on your responses.

To Convert a Print Publication to a Web Publication

1

• **Click File on the menu bar.**

Publisher displays the File menu (Figure 1-70).

FIGURE 1-70

2

• **Click Convert to Web Publication.**

• **When Publisher displays the Convert to Web Publication dialog box with the Save Your Current Print Publication step, click the No option button to select it.**

The first dialog box reminds you to save the publication (Figure 1-71). Because you previously saved the file, you will choose not to save the file again.

FIGURE 1-71

3

• **Click the Next button. When Publisher displays the Add a Navigation Bar step, click the No option button to select it.**

This single page Web page will not use a navigation bar (Figure 1-72). If Publisher displays the Web Tools toolbar, click its Close button.

4

• **Click the Finish Button.**

FIGURE 1-72

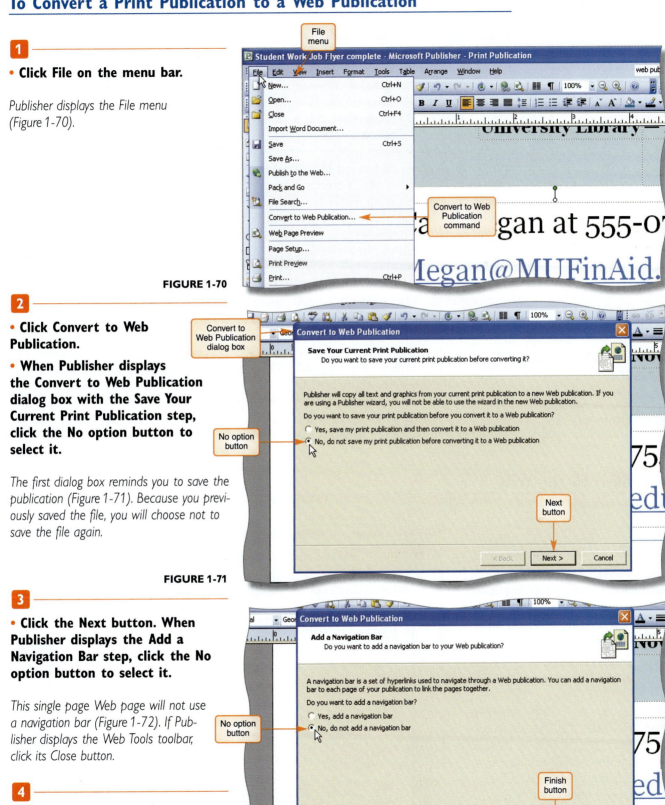

More About

HTML

For more information about HTML, visit the HTML Web page (scsite.com/html) and click More About.

Publishing to the Web

The final step in preparing the flyer's Web presence is to publish it to the Web. **Publishing to the Web** is the process of making Web pages available to others, for example on the World Wide Web or on a company's intranet. Files intended for use on the Web, however, need a different format. A **Hypertext Markup Language** (**HTML**) file is a file capable of being stored and transferred electronically on a file server in order to display on the Web. When you publish, Publisher can save your file in a **filtered HTML format** that is smaller than regular HTML files. It can be published to, and downloaded from, the Internet quickly.

In Publisher, you can publish to the Web using a wizard accessed through the File menu, which creates a filtered HTML file; or, you can save a publication as a Web page to a Web folder, which creates a traditional HTML file. Either way, Publisher creates an accompanying folder for each separate publication intended for the Web. A **folder** is a logical portion of a disk created to group and store similar documents. Inside this folder, Publisher will include copies of the associated graphics. Once created, your publication can be viewed by a Web browser, such as Microsoft Internet Explorer.

The concept of a Web folder facilitates integration of Publisher with other members of the Microsoft Office 2003 Suite and Windows. With Windows, you can choose to use Web style folders on your desktop, which means that the desktop is interactive, and all your folders look like Web pages. Publisher also will take care of uploading, or transferring, your files to the Web, if you are connected to an Internet service provider or host. See Appendix C for more information on Web folders.

The following steps show how to use the Publish to the Web command on the File menu to create a Web site from your publication. Because not all systems are connected to the Internet and not all users subscribe to a Web hosting service, the following steps store the resulting Web files on the floppy disk.

More About

Using Web Folders

For more information about publishing to the Web using a Web folder, see Appendix C.

To Publish to the Web

1

• **Click File on the menu bar.**

• **Click Publish to the Web on the File menu. If a Microsoft Publisher dialog box displays reminding you about Web hosting services, click its OK button.**

• **Type** Student Work Job Web Flyer **in the File name text box.**

Publisher displays the Publish to the Web dialog box (Figure 1-73). The Save in location, file name, and file type are displayed. You will save the publication in the same location and with the same file name; the Save as type box will change the publication's file name extension.

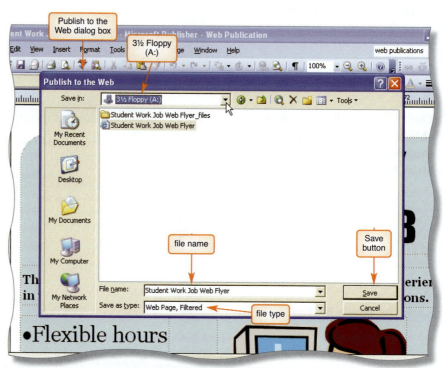

FIGURE 1-73

2

• **Click the Save button in the Save As dialog box.**

Publisher displays a Microsoft Office Publisher dialog box describing filtered HTML files (Figure 1-74).

3

• **Click the OK button.**

The saved files are ready to send to the Web.

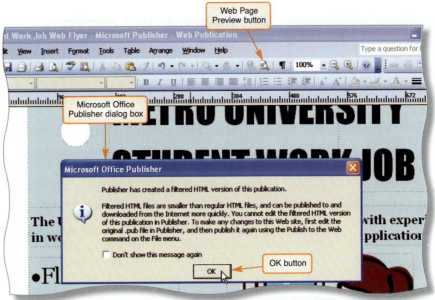

FIGURE 1-74

To preview what the Web publication looks like, you can click the Web Page Preview button on the Standard toolbar, as shown in the following step.

To Preview the Web Publication in a Browser

1 Click the Web Page Preview button on the Standard toolbar. When the browser window opens, if necessary, maximize it by clicking the Maximize button on the title bar.

2 Click the Close button on the browser title bar.

Microsoft Internet Explorer displays the Publisher Web publication (Figure 1-75). Your browser may be different.

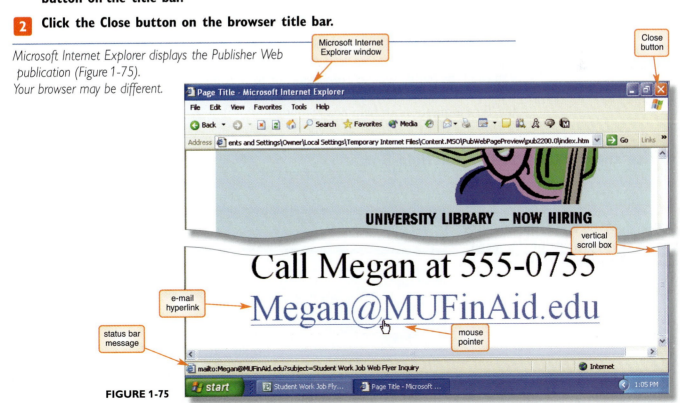

FIGURE 1-75

Closing the Entire Publication

Sometimes, everything goes wrong. If this happens, you may want to close the publication entirely and start over. You also may want to close a publication when you are finished with it so you can begin your next publication.

To Close the Entire Publication and Start Over

1 Click File on the menu bar and then click Close.

2 If Publisher displays a dialog box, click the No button to ignore the changes since the last time you saved the publication.

3 Click the Blank Print Publication link on the New Publication task pane.

You also can begin a new publication by clicking the New button on the Standard toolbar.

More About

The Quick Reference

For a table that lists how to complete the tasks covered in this book using the mouse, menu, shortcut menu, and keyboard, see the Quick Reference Summary at the back of this book, or visit the Publisher 2003 Quick Reference Web page (scsite.com/pub2003/qr).

More About

The Publisher Help System

The best way to become familiar with the Publisher Help system is to use it. Appendix A includes detailed information on the Publisher Help system and exercises that will help you gain confidence in using it.

Publisher Help System

At any time while you are using Publisher, you can get answers to questions by using the **Publisher Help system**. You activate the Publisher Help system by using the Type a question for help box on the menu bar, the Microsoft Publisher Help button on the Standard toolbar, or the Help menu. Used properly, this form of interactive assistance can increase your productivity and reduce your frustrations by minimizing the time you spend learning how to use Publisher.

The following section shows how to get answers to your questions using the Type a question for help box. Additional information about using the Publisher Help system is available in Appendix A.

Using the Type a Question for Help Box

Through the Type a question for help box on the right side of the menu bar, you type free-form questions, such as *how do I save* or *how do I create a Web page*, or you can type terms, such as *copy*, *save*, or *formatting*. Publisher responds by displaying a list of topics related to what you entered. The following steps show how to use the Type a question for help box to obtain information on color schemes.

To Use the Type a Question for Help Box

1

• Click the Type a question for help box on the right side of the menu bar and then type color schemes (Figure 1-76).

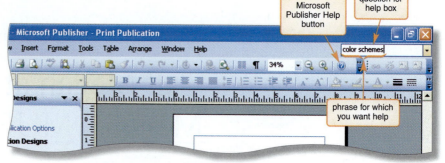

FIGURE 1-76

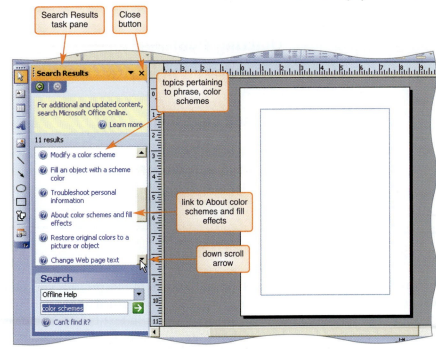

2

- **Press the ENTER key.**
- **When Publisher displays the Search Results task pane, scroll to display the topic, About color schemes and fill effects.**

Publisher displays the Search Results task pane with a list of topics relating to the phrase, color schemes (Figure 1-77).

FIGURE 1-77

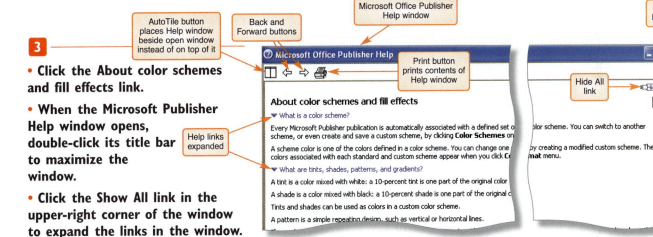

3

- **Click the About color schemes and fill effects link.**
- **When the Microsoft Publisher Help window opens, double-click its title bar to maximize the window.**
- **Click the Show All link in the upper-right corner of the window to expand the links in the window.**

Publisher opens a Microsoft Publisher Help window that provides information about color schemes (Figure 1-78). The Show All link becomes the Hide All link.

FIGURE 1-78

4

- **Click the Close button on the Microsoft Publisher Help window title bar.**
- **Click the Close button in the Search Results task pane.**

Publisher closes the Microsoft Publisher Help window. The Publisher window again is active.

Use the buttons in the upper-left corner of the Microsoft Publisher Help window (Figure 1-78) to navigate through the Help system, change the display, and print the contents of the window.

You can use the Type a question for help box to search for Help about any topic concerning Publisher. As you enter questions and terms in the Type a question for help box, Publisher adds them to the Type a question for help list. Thus, if you click the Type a question for help box arrow, Publisher displays a list of previously asked questions and terms.

Quitting Publisher

The final step in this project is to quit Publisher, as shown in the following step.

To Quit Publisher

1 **Click the Close button on the title bar (Figure 1-78 on the previous page). If a Microsoft Office Publisher dialog box is displayed, click the No button.**

The Publisher window closes, and the Windows desktop is displayed.

Project Summary

In creating the Student Work Job Flyer publication in this project, you gained a broad knowledge of Publisher. First you were introduced to starting Publisher. You learned about the Publisher workspace. You chose a flyer publication and replaced the template-supplied text in text boxes. You deleted objects, resized objects, moved objects, and changed how the text fit within the text box.

Once you saved the print publication, you learned how to replace a graphic using the Clip Art task pane. You deleted the tear-offs at the bottom of the flyer and inserted a text box with a hyperlink. You used the Design Checker to check the publication for potential errors. You then saved the flyer as a Web publication and published it on the Web. Finally, you learned how to use the Publisher Help system to answer questions.

What You Should Know

Having completed this project, you should be able to perform the tasks below. The tasks are listed in the same order they were presented in this project. For a list of the buttons, menus, toolbars, and commands introduced in this project, see the Quick Reference Summary at the back of this book and refer to the Page Number column.

1. Start Publisher   (PUB 7)
2. Customize the Publisher Window   (PUB 9)
3. Create a Publication Using a Template   (PUB 12)
4. Edit Placeholder Text   (PUB 23)
5. Delete an Object   (PUB 27)
6. Check Spelling as You Type   (PUB 28)
7. Enter More Text   (PUB 29)
8. Select and Replace Multiple Placeholder Text Items   (PUB 30)
9. Use Best Fit   (PUB 31)
10. AutoFit Other Text Boxes   (PUB 32)
11. Save a New Publication   (PUB 33)
12. Replace a Graphic Using the Clip Art Task Pane (PUB 37)
13. Move an Object   (PUB 39)
14. Resize an Object   (PUB 40)
15. Save an Existing Publication with the Same File Name   (PUB 41)
16. Print a Publication   (PUB 41)
17. Quit Publisher   (PUB 42)
18. Open a Publication   (PUB 43)
19. Delete the Tear-Offs   (PUB 44)
20. Insert a Text Box   (PUB 45)
21. Insert a Hyperlink   (PUB 47)
22. Run the Design Checker   (PUB 48)
23. Save a Publication with a New File Name (PUB 50)
24. Convert a Print Publication to a Web Publication (PUB 51)
25. Publish to the Web   (PUB 52)
26. Preview the Web Publication in a Browser (PUB 53)
27. Close the Entire Publication and Start Over (PUB 54)
28. Use the Type a question for help Box   (PUB 54)
29. Quit Publisher   (PUB 56)

Learn It Online

Instructions: To complete the Learn It Online exercises, start your browser, click the Address bar, and then enter the Web address scsite.com/pub2003/learn. When the Publisher 2003 Learn It Online page is displayed, follow the instructions in the exercises below. Each exercise has instructions for printing your results, either for your own records or for submission to your instructor.

1 Project Reinforcement TF, MC, and SA

Below Publisher Project 1, click the Project Reinforcement link. Print the quiz by clicking Print on the File menu for each page. Answer each question.

2 Flash Cards

Below Publisher Project 1, click the Flash Cards link and read the instructions. Type 20 (or a number specified by your instructor) in the Number of playing cards text box, type your name in the Enter your Name text box, and then click the Flip Card button. When the flash card is displayed, read the question and then click the ANSWER box arrow to select an answer. Flip through Flash Cards. If your score is 15 (75%) correct or greater, click Print on the File menu to print your results. If your score is less than 15 (75%) correct, then redo this exercise by clicking the Replay button.

3 Practice Test

Below Publisher Project 1, click the Practice Test link. Answer each question, enter your first and last name at the bottom of the page, and then click the Grade Test button. When the graded practice test is displayed on your screen, click Print on the File menu to print a hard copy. Continue to take practice tests until you score 80% or better.

4 Who Wants To Be a Computer Genius?

Below Publisher Project 1, click the Computer Genius link. Read the instructions, enter your first and last name at the bottom of the page, and then click the PLAY button. When your score is displayed, click the PRINT RESULTS link to print a hard copy.

5 Wheel of Terms

Below Publisher Project 1, click the Wheel of Terms link. Read the instructions, and then enter your first and last name and your school name. Click the PLAY button. When your score is displayed, right-click the score and then click Print on the shortcut menu to print a hard copy.

6 Crossword Puzzle Challenge

Below Publisher Project 1, click the Crossword Puzzle Challenge link. Read the instructions, and then enter your first and last name. Click the SUBMIT button. Work the crossword puzzle. When you are finished, click the Submit button. When the crossword puzzle is redisplayed, click the Print Puzzle button to print a hard copy.

7 Tips and Tricks

Below Publisher Project 1, click the Tips and Tricks link. Click a topic that pertains to Project 1. Right-click the information and then click Print on the shortcut menu. Construct a brief example of what the information relates to in Publisher to confirm you understand how to use the tip or trick.

8 Newsgroups

Below Publisher Project 1, click the Newsgroups link. Click a topic that pertains to Project 1. Print three comments.

9 Expanding Your Horizons

Below Publisher Project 1, click the Expanding Your Horizons link. Click a topic that pertains to Project 1. Print the information. Construct a brief example of what the information relates to in Publisher to confirm you understand the contents of the article.

10 Search Sleuth

Below Publisher Project 1, click the Search Sleuth link. To search for a term that pertains to this project, select a term below the Project 1 title and then use the Google search engine at google.com (or any major search engine) to display and print two Web pages that present information on the term.

11 Publisher Online Training

Below Publisher Project 1, click the Publisher Online Training link. When your browser displays the Microsoft Office Online Web page, click the Publisher link. Click one of the Publisher courses that covers one or more of the objectives listed at the beginning of the project on page PUB 4. Print the first page of the course before stepping through it.

12 Office Marketplace

Below Publisher Project 1, click the Office Marketplace link. When your browser displays the Microsoft Office Online Web page, click the Office Marketplace link. Click a topic that relates to Publisher. Print the first page.

1 Editing a Publication

Instructions: Start Publisher. Open the publication, Apply 1-1 Music Lessons Flyer, on the Data Disk. See the inside back cover of this book for instruction for downloading the Data Disk or see your instructor for information about accessing files required in this book.

The publication on the Data Disk is a flyer that contains some template text, a graphic that needs to be replaced, and spelling errors. You are to fix the spelling mistake, replace the template text, use the Best Fit option on the information text box, resize the information text box, and change the font and color scheme so that it looks like Figure 1-79.

1. Correct each spelling error by right-clicking the flagged word and then clicking the appropriate correction on the shortcut menu, so the flyer text matches Figure 1-79. The flyer contains three spelling errors (indicated by a red wavy underline).

2. If the task pane is not displayed, click View on the menu bar and then click Task Pane. Click the Other Task Panes button in the task pane title bar (see Figure 1-8 on page PUB 10 for the location of the Other Task Panes button). Select Font Schemes from the list. Scroll to and then select the Versatile font scheme.

3. Click the Other Task Panes button again and select Color Schemes from the list. Scroll to and then select the Clay color scheme.

4. Double-click the graphic. When the Clip Art task pane is displayed, type `piano` in the Search for text box. Click the Go button. When the clip selections display, scroll to find a photograph of a piano similar to the one in Figure 1-79.

5. Close the task pane by clicking the Close button in the task pane title bar.

6. Right-click the information text box that displays to the left of the graphic. On the shortcut menu, point to Change Text, then point to AutoFit Text, and then click Best Fit on the AutoFit Text submenu.

7. Drag the middle-right handle of the information text box so the right boundary is positioned closer to the graphic.

8. Click the Contact person placeholder text and type `Contact Joy at` to replace the text.

9. Click the phone number placeholder text and type `(555) 436-1217` to replace the text.

Piano Lessons

I am a graduate student at the conservatory of music, majoring in music education. I teach both adults and children at all levels of proficiency.

Individual lessons are 45 minutes and include both theory and hands-on instruction.

Contact Joy at (555) 436-1217

Contact Joy at (555) 436-1217

FIGURE 1-79

Apply Your Knowledge

10. Click the text in any one tear-off and type `Contact Joy` at and then press the ENTER key. Type `(555) 436-1217` and then click outside the tear-offs to synchronize them all.

11. Fix any other spelling errors you might have made while typing the text. Right-click any words with red wavy underlines below them and then choose a correct spelling on the shortcut menu. Run the Design Checker and fix any errors that Publisher displays.

12. Click File on the menu bar and then click Save As. Save the publication using Apply 1-1 Music Lessons Flyer Revised as the file name.

13. Print the revised publication.

In the Lab

1 Creating a Flyer with Tear-Offs

Problem: A friend of yours would like to get some part-time work as a tutor for mathematics courses. He has asked you to create a flyer advertising his services. He would like his name, e-mail, and telephone number on tear-offs at the bottom, along with an eye-catching graphic. A big, bold heading should attract passers-by.

You prepare the publication shown in Figure 1-80. *Hint:* Remember, if you make a mistake while editing the publication, you can click the Undo button on the Standard toolbar to undo your last action.

1. Start Publisher.
2. In the New Publication task pane, click Publications for Print, click Flyers, click Sale. When the previews are displayed, scroll to and then click For Sale Flyer 1.
3. When the correct flyer is displayed, click the Close button on the Flyer Options task pane.

FIGURE 1-80

(continued)

In the Lab

Creating a Flyer with Tear-Offs *(continued)*

4. Click the heading, For Sale. Type `Need a Math Tutor?` to replace the placeholder text.
5. Click the text in the Name of Item text box. Type `All Math Courses` to replace the placeholder text.
6. Click the bulleted list to the right of the graphic. Type the following list:
   - `Senior math major`
   - `Tutoring experience`
   - `Flexible hours`
   - `Meet at the library`
   - `Algebra`
   - `Trigonometry`
   - `Calculus`
7. Click the placeholder text, Contact person. Type `Call Mike at:` to replace the text. Click the phone number placeholder text. Type `(555) 852-7226` to replace the phone number.
8. Click the dollar amount text box. Type `$10/hour` to replace the text.
9. Click the text in one of the tear-offs. Type `Mike (555) 852-7226` and press the ENTER key. Type `mike@mathtutor.com` to complete the text.
10. Double-click the graphic. When Publisher displays the Clip Art task pane, type `math` in the Search for text box. Click the Go button.
11. Scroll through the available clips and choose a graphic that is similar to the one in Figure 1-80 on the previous page. Click the clip in the Clip Art task pane to replace the graphic in the publication. Click the Close button in the Clip Art task pane.
12. Fix any spelling errors you might have made while typing the text. Right-click any words with a red wavy underline below them and then choose the correct spelling on the shortcut menu. Run the Design Checker and fix any errors that Publisher displays.
13. Click File on the menu bar and then click Save As. Save the publication with the file name, Lab 1-1 Math Tutor Flyer.
14. Print the publication.

2 Planning and Creating a Flyer Using Font and Color Schemes

Problem: You have taken a part-time job as an intern at the Ponderosa Realty company. Your first assignment is to create a flyer about a special piece of land that the realty company is trying to sell. Your boss has given you the details about the acreage.

You prepare the publication shown in Figure 1-81. **Hint:** Remember, if you make a mistake while editing the publication, you can click the Undo button on the Standard toolbar to undo your last action.

1. On a piece of paper, fill in the following table to plan for the publication (Table 1-5). See page PUB 6 for information about each of the design issues.
2. Start Publisher.
3. In the New Publication task pane, click Publications for Print, click Flyers, click Sale. When the previews are displayed, click Borders House For Sale Flyer.
4. In the Flyer Options task pane, click Color Schemes. Click Tuscany in the list of color schemes.

In the Lab

5. In the Color Schemes task pane, click Font Schemes. Click Online in the list of font schemes.

6. Right-click the Organization logo at the top of the publication and then click Delete Object on the shortcut menu.

7. Replace the placeholder text in the heading with the words, Land for Sale as the new heading.

8. Replace the other text boxes with the text shown in Figure 1-81.

9. Double-click the graphic. When the Clip Art task pane displays, type scenery in the Search for text box. Click the Go button. Choose an appropriate graphic, similar to the one in Figure 1-81.

10. If you choose a graphic that is different from the one in Figure 1-81, choose a complementary color scheme by clicking the Other Task Panes button on the Clip Art task pane title bar. Click Color Schemes in the list. Choose a color scheme whose second accent color closely matches one of the colors in the graphic.

11. Fix any spelling errors you might have made while typing the text. Right-click each word with a red wavy underline below it and then choose the correct spelling on the shortcut menu. Run the Design Checker and fix any errors that Publisher displays.

12. Click File on the menu bar and then click Save As. Save the publication with the file name, Lab 1-2 Land For Sale Flyer.

13. Print the publication. On the back of the printout, list five places that you might post the flyer in your community if you actually were trying to sell the land. Turn in the planning table and the printout to your instructor.

Land for Sale

- 5 acres
- 8 miles from schools and shopping
- Zoned residential and/or farm
- Horses OK
- Well on property
- Lush vegetation

A beautiful, five-acre setting with mountains on the horizon.

$125,000

Call Chandra at 555 903-8642

Ponderosa Realty

9753 Smiley Lane
Gilbert, CA 94558

Phone: (555) 903-8642
Fox (555) 903-8643
E-mail: Chandra@ponderosarealty.com

FIGURE 1-81

Table 1-5 Planning a Flyer	
DESIGN ISSUE	**REALTY FLYER PUBLICATION**
Purpose	
Audience	
Gather data	
Plan for printing	
Layout	
Synthesis	

In the Lab

3 Creating a Flyer and Converting it to a Web Publication

Problem: As the resident assistant (RA) in your dormitory, you have been approached by a tour company hoping to schedule a kayak trip for an upcoming weekend. You decide to use your Publisher skills to create a flyer to hang on the bulletin boards in each of the dorms. You also want to post the flyer on the school's electronic bulletin board in hopes of getting 10 people to go, thereby receiving a discount.

Instructions Part 1:   Perform the following tasks to create the publication shown in Figure 1-82a:

1. Start Publisher.
2. In the New Publication task pane, click Publications for Print, click Flyers, click Announcement, and then click Baby-Sitting Announcement Flyer.
3. In the Flyer Options task pane, click Color Schemes. Click Sapphire in the list of color schemes.
4. One at a time double-click each of the two graphics. When the Clip Art task pane displays, type `kayak` in the Search for text box. Click the Go button. When the clips are displayed, click a clip that closely matches the one in Figure 1-82a.
5. Close the Clip Art task pane.
6. Click the heading, Baby-Sitting. Type `Kayak Trip` to replace the text.
7. Click the text in the description text box. Type `Kayak the New River!` and then press the ENTER key. Type `With 10 students, we can get a discounted rate. Call or e-mail today!` to complete the description.
8. Click the text in the hourly rate text box. Type `October 23-24, 2004` to replace the text.
9. Click the Contact person placeholder text. SHIFT-click the telephone number placeholder text so both are selected. Type `Contact Katie at (555) 501-1603` and then press the ENTER key. Type `Or e-mail Katie@kayaktrip.org` to complete the contact information.

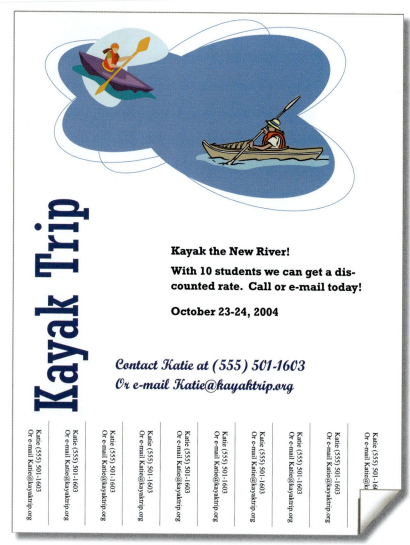

FIGURE 1-82a

In the Lab

10. Click the text in any one of the tear-offs. Type Katie (555) 501-1603 and then press the ENTER key. Type Or e-mail Katie@ kayaktrip.org as the entry.

11. Fix any spelling errors you might have made while typing the text. Run the Design Checker, and fix any errors that Publisher displays.

12. Save the publication on your floppy disk with the file name, Lab 1-3 Kayak Trip Flyer.

13. Print the print publication.

Instructions Part 2: Perform the following tasks to convert the flyer to a Web publication shown in Figure 1-82a:

1. When Publisher displays the Kayak Trip Flyer, right-click the tear-offs and then click Delete Object on the shortcut menu.

2. In the contact information text box, select the text, Katie@ kayaktrip.org, by dragging through it. Click the Insert Hyperlink button on the Standard toolbar. When the Insert Hyperlink dialog box is displayed, click

Kayak the New River!

With 10 students, we can get a discounted rate. Call or e-mail today!

October 23-24, 2004

Contact Katie at (555) 501-1603
Or e-mail <u>*Katie@kayaktrip.org*</u>

FIGURE 1-82b

E-mail Address on the Link to bar. Type Katie@kayaktrip.org in the E-mail address text box. Press the TAB key. Type Kayak Trip Web Flyer Inquiry in the Subject text box. Click the OK button.

3. Run the Design Checker and fix any errors that Publisher displays.

4. Click Save As on the File menu and save the file on your floppy disk with the file name, Lab 1-3 Kayak Trip Web Flyer.

5. Click File on the menu bar and then click Convert to Web Publication. When Publisher displays the Saves Your Current Print Publication step, click the No option button to select it. When Publisher displays the Add a Navigation Bar step, click the No option button to select it. Click the Finish button.

6. Click File on the menu bar and then click Publish to the Web. If a Microsoft Office Publisher dialog box is displayed, click its OK button. Save the file as, Lab 1-3 Kayak Trip Web Flyer.

7. When the Publish to the Web dialog box is displayed, click the Save button. When the Microsoft Office Publisher dialog box that describes filtered HTML files is displayed, click the OK button.

8. Preview the Web Flyer by clicking the Web Page Preview button on the Standard toolbar. When you are done previewing, click the browser's Close button. Print the Web publication.

Cases and Places

The difficulty of these case studies varies:
■ are the least difficult and ■■ are more difficult. The last exercise is a group exercise.

1 ■ Use the Flyers Fundraiser template titled Car Wash Fundraiser Flyer 2 to create a flyer for your club's upcoming 5K walk-a-thon for charity. Select the Crocus color scheme and the Casual font scheme in the Flyer Options task pane. The walk-a-thon is Saturday, September 18 from 10:00 a.m. to 2:00 p.m. Use the name of your own school and address in the appropriate areas. The starting location is the College Library parking lot.

2 ■ Your high school has asked you to create a flyer for the upcoming 10-year class reunion. Create a table similar to Table 1-1 on page PUB 6. Once you are satisfied with your planning, create the flyer with information from your high school. Be sure to include at least two bulleted items in a list, and insert an appropriate graphic from the Media Gallery or the Web.

3 ■■ Start the Play Announcement Flyer template to create a flyer for a local dramatic production. Use the Cranberry color scheme and the Fusion font scheme. Look through a local newspaper to find a community theater production. Use the techniques in Project 1 to edit the flyer with the local information. Include the name of the play, the author, the dates, the time, the location, and the ticket prices. Choose an appropriate graphic from the Clip Art task pane. Delete any unused or unnecessary objects.

4 ■■ Many communities offer free Web page hosting for religious organizations. Using a Flyers template, create a flyer for a local house of worship. Include the name, address, telephone, worship and education hours, as well as the name of a contact person. If possible, include a photo of the building. Run the publication through the Design Checker and then save it as a Web publication.

5 ■■ Your Internet service provider maintains an electronic bulletin board where customers may post one-page business announcements. Create an advertising flyer for the place where you work or want to work. You may use one of Publisher's templates, or design the flyer from scratch. Use color and graphics to attract attention. Use a bulleted list to describe your company's services. Instead of tear-offs, use a text box that includes the company's e-mail address as a hyperlink. Use words in your text boxes that will produce many hits during Web searches. Save the flyer as a Web publication.

6 ■■ **Working Together** Schools, churches, libraries, grocery stores, and other public places have bulletin boards for flyers and other postings. Often, these bulletin boards have so many flyers that some go unnoticed. Look at a local bulletin board and find a posted flyer that you think might be overlooked. Copy the text from the announcement and distribute it to each team member. Each member then independently should use this text to create an announcement that would be more likely to catch a reader's eye. Be sure to check the spelling and run the Design Checker. As a group, critique each flyer and have each member redesign his or her flyer based on the group's recommendations. Hand in printouts of each team member's original and final flyer.

MICROSOFT
Office Publisher 2003

Designing a Newsletter

PROJECT

2

CASE PERSPECTIVE

Extreme Sports Club is a student organization at Ventana State College. The club's membership includes students who are interested in playing, watching, and learning more about extreme sports. The members meet once each month and plan extreme activities such as gravity games, bungee jumping, and various forms of biking, skating, and board sports. The campus is close to the beach, so many of the club's members are interested in surfing, as well. Extreme Sports Club has 30 members, both male and female, from freshmen to seniors, who represent many different academic majors on campus. Ventana State College provides student organizations, such as Extreme Sports Club, with a place to meet and a faculty sponsor.

Each month, the club sends a newsletter via e-mail to its members, other interested students, and people who subscribe to the athletics listserv. It also distributes a printed version on paper around campus. Several students submit monthly articles for the newsletter after they are approved by the faculty sponsor, Mr. Sullivan. Some of the members are graduating, so the club needs help with the publication of the newsletter.

Because you are both a member of Extreme Sports Club and a computer and information technology major, Mr. Sullivan has asked you to use Publisher to create the newsletter this year. You agree, as your assignments for your desktop publishing class include similar projects. Together, you and Mr. Sullivan decide on a color scheme and font that matches the flair and personality of this club. Because the club does not have a large budget, the newsletter will be just two pages, printed front and back.

As you read through this project, you will learn how to use Publisher to create, save, and print a newsletter that includes a masthead, imported text and graphics, a pull quote, and WordArt.

 Office Publisher 2003

Designing a Newsletter

Objectives

You will have mastered the material in this project when you can:

- Describe the advantages of using a newsletter medium and identify the steps in its design process
- Edit a newsletter template
- Insert, delete, and navigate pages in a newsletter
- Edit a masthead
- Import text files and graphics
- Edit personal information components, design sets, attention getters, styles, and sidebars
- Insert a WordArt object and pull quote
- Add page numbers to the master page
- Identify foreground and background elements
- Check a newsletter for spelling and design errors
- Print a two-sided page

Introduction

Desktop publishing is becoming the most popular way for businesses of all sizes to produce their printed publications. The desktop aspects of design and production make it easy and inexpensive to produce high-quality documents in a short time. **Desktop** implies doing everything from a desk, including the planning, designing, writing, layout, cutting, and pasting, as well as printing, collating, and distributing. With a personal computer and a software program such as Publisher, you can create a professional document from your computer without the cost and time of sending it to a professional publisher.

Project Two — Designing a Newsletter

Project 2 uses a Publisher Newsletter template to produce *Extreme News*, the newsletter shown in Figures 2-1a and 2-1b. This semi-monthly publication informs a college community about events sponsored by the Extreme Sports Club on campus. The club's two-page newsletter contains articles, features, event dates, and graphics.

Special points of interest:

- Surfing Championship Tour, September 15
- X-Meeting Mondays, 7:00 p.m. Student Center
- Gravity Games at Back to Campus Days, October 1-2

Extreme News

Volume 3, Issue 1   September 2, 2005

Surfing Championship Tour

Are you ready to see Doug, Ross, Spiel, Freddie, and Nate the Great mix it up? The Surfing Championship Tour (SCT) is coming to town Thursday, September 15.

The world's top-rated professional surfers will be making their only local appearance next week. A 10-day waiting period from September 5-14 will guarantee the best surfing conditions possible as the top-25 surfers in the world battle it out for $250,000 in total prize money.

Nate the

The last time the SCT visited our bea newcomer Doug pulled off a big victo over Jon Redmond. Now Doug retur with veteran Nate the Great to mix it

with rising superstars like Australians Freddie Mantel and Spiel Connor. Nate and Ross are relying on local knowledge to give them an advantage over the international field.

The proximity of the event to the Extreme Expo will attract the surfing world's top luminaries and put added pressure on contestants to perform at their high-

Mountain Bik

"Mountain biking isn't just great exercise, it's a great way to take a break from everything!"

It's a whole new world when you're mountain biking," says Ken Jones, biking enthusiast and V.P. of the Extreme Sports Club. "You have so much more stimulus with the trees and the terrain." Although he still puts the miles on his road bike, Jones says that when he is on his mountain bike,

he gets amoun

Jones i made t In fact, terrain the fast ing to t

1

Extreme Sports Club

Campus Student Union
Ventana State College
Big Sur, California

Phone: 831-555-1234
Fax: 831-555-1235
E-mail: extremesports@vsc.edu

Everything Extreme!

Do you march to the beat of a different drummer? Do you push the boundaries? Are you an adrenaline junkie?

In the Extreme Sports Club, we understand your passion for that tingling feeling. We understand why you ignore that faint voice in your head that asks, "Why am I doing this?" We know what it is like to have folks shake their heads in bewilderment.

Breathe deeply. You are now among friends. Whether it is battling gravity on the side of a rock, punching through life's less than peaceful waters, or wheeling over a poorly maintained trail, just choose an extreme and go! In the Extreme Sports Club, we will keep you up-to-date with awesome information, cool locations, local accommodations, and just plain nonsensical verbiage. After all, life is WAY too short to be normal.

Mondays, Student Center, 7 p.m.

Up for Gravity Games?

The 2005 Campus Gravity Games will be held October 1-2, at the Campus Arena during the annual Back to Campus days. The campus TV station will broadcast this year's games.

The Campus Gravity Games competitions will be held in the following categories: Inline Vert, Bike Vert, Bike Street, Skateboarding Street, and Skateboarding Vert.

In general, gravity games include any kind of extreme sport in which participants leave the ground, such as skateboarding or trick biking, although recently it has started to include wakeboarding and wake skating.

Last year, more than 250 people participated in the games, which drew a huge crowd from students, the community, and parents who were on campus for Back to Campus days.

The Campus Gravity Games are both invitational (some of the

Skateboarding tricks thrill the audience at last year's event.

local stars will compete) and open for rookie qualifiers. You can pick up an application at the Student Union. All participants need to supply their own helmets, as well as knee and elbow pads, which are required.

Qualification rounds begin at 8:00 a.m. Music, food, and fun begin at 10:00 a.m. Several local bands are scheduled to perform.

Tickets are $5.00 for students and children and $8.00 for adults. After defraying the cost of the arena and judges, all proceeds from this year's Campus Gravity Games will benefit the Extreme Sports Club on campus.

2

FIGURE 2-1

Starting Publisher

To start Publisher, Windows must be running. The following steps explain how to start Publisher.

More About

Desktop Publishing

Desktop publishing, or electronic publishing, is an extremely marketable skill in today's information-intensive workplace. For more information about desktop publishing software, visit the Publisher 2003 More About Web page (scsite.com/pub2003/more) and click Desktop Publishing Software.

To Start Publisher

1 Click the Start button on the Windows taskbar, point to All Programs on the Start menu, point to Microsoft Office on the All Programs submenu, and then click Microsoft Office Publisher 2003 on the Microsoft Office submenu.

2 If the Publisher window is not maximized, double-click its title bar to maximize it.

3 If Publisher does not display the New Publication task pane, click View on the menu bar and then click Task Pane. If the Publication Designs task pane is displayed, click the Other Task Panes button in the task pane title bar, and then click New Publication.

4 If the Language bar displays, click its Minimize button.

You may recall that Publisher's New Publication task pane displays publication types, commands to begin new publications, and the names of previously opened publications on your computer.

More About

Newsletters

Many newsletters are published regularly on the Web. To look at some samples and for more information on newsletter content, visit the Publisher 2003 More About Web page (scsite.com/pub2003/more) and click Newsletters.

The Newsletter Medium

Newsletters are a popular way for offices, businesses, and other organizations to distribute information to their clientele. A **newsletter** usually is a double-sided multipage publication with newspaper features such as columns and a masthead, and the added eye appeal of sidebars, pictures, and other graphics.

Newsletters have several advantages over other publication media. They are easy to produce. **Brochures**, designed to be in circulation longer as a type of advertising, usually are published in greater quantities and on more expensive paper than newsletters and are, therefore, more costly. Additionally, newsletters differ from brochures in that they commonly have a shorter shelf life, making newsletters a perfect forum for dated information.

Newsletters are narrower and more focused in scope than newspapers; their eye appeal is more distinctive. Many organizations and companies distribute newsletters inexpensively to interested audiences, although that is beginning to change. Newsletters are becoming an integral part of many marketing plans because they offer a legitimate medium by which to communicate services, successes, and issues.

Table 2-1 lists some benefits and advantages of using the newsletter medium.

Table 2-1	Benefits and Advantages of Using a Newsletter Medium
AREA	**BENEFITS AND ADVANTAGES**
Exposure	An easily distributed publication — office mail, bulk mail, electronically A pass-along document for other interested parties A coffee table reading item in reception areas
Education	An opportunity to inform in a nonrestrictive environment A directed education forum for clientele An increased, focused feedback — unavailable in most advertising
Contacts	A form of legitimized contact A source of free information to build credibility An easier way to expand a contact database than other marketing tools
Communication	An effective medium to highlight the inner workings of a company A way to create a discussion forum A method to disseminate more information than a brochure
Cost	An easily designed medium using desktop publishing software An inexpensive method of mass production A reusable design

Designing a Newsletter

Designing an effective newsletter involves a great deal of planning. A good newsletter, or any publication, must deliver a message in the clearest, most attractive, and effective way possible. You must clarify your purpose and know your target audience. You need to gather ideas and plan for the printing of the newsletter. Finally, you must determine the best layout for eye appeal and reliable dissemination of content.

Table 2-2	Design Process Issues
DESIGN ISSUE	**NEWSLETTER APPLICATION**
Purpose	To communicate and to educate readers about the organization
Audience	Local interested clientele or patrons, both present and future
Gather data	Articles, pictures, dates, figures, tables, discussion threads
Plan for printing	Usually mass-produced, collated, and stapled
Layout	Consistent look and feel; simple, eye-catching graphics
Synthesis	Edit, proofread, and publish

Table 2-2 outlines the issues to consider during the design process and their application to newsletters.

Creating a Newsletter Template Using a Template

You can type a newsletter from scratch by choosing a blank publication from the task pane, or you can use a template that Publisher preformats with appropriate headings, graphics, and spacing. You can customize the resulting newsletter by filling in the blanks, and selecting and replacing objects.

Many design planning features are built into Publisher, including 65 different newsletter templates from which you may choose, each with its own set of design, color, font, and layout schemes. The Newsletter Options task pane provides options for double-sided printing and customer address, color and font schemes links, and page content design choices.

The steps on the next page illustrate how to choose a newsletter template and make design choices.

To Choose a Newsletter Template and Change Options

1

• **In the New Publication task pane, click Publications for Print in the New from a design area. When the types of publications are displayed, scroll as necessary to display Newsletters.**

• **Click Newletters.**

• **Scroll to display the Banded Newsletter preview.**

Publisher displays the New Publication task pane on the left and the previews on the right in the Newsletters pane (Figure 2-2). The list of previews may display differently on your computer. The Banded Newsletter preview displays a blue box around it when you point to it.

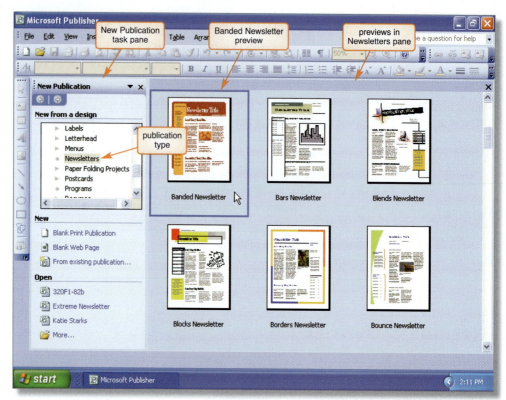

FIGURE 2-2

2

• **Click the Banded Newsletter preview. If Publisher displays a Personal Information dialog box, click its Cancel button.**

The Newsletter Options task pane is displayed on the left. In the workspace, page 1 of the Banded Newsletter displays (Figure 2-3). Newsletter options include both the choice of one- or two-sided printing and whether or not to include a customer address.

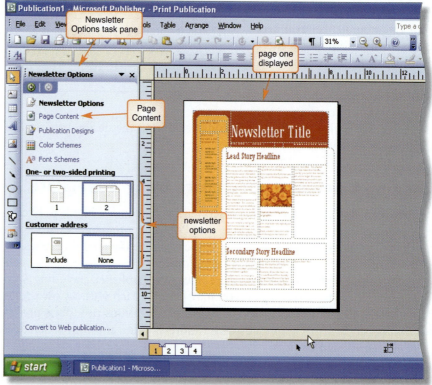

FIGURE 2-3

3

• **In the Newsletter Options task pane, click Page Content. When the Page Content task pane is displayed, click Mixed in the Columns area.**

*The page content of the newsletter will display a **mixed** variety of 1, 2, and 3 columns of text (Figure 2-4).*

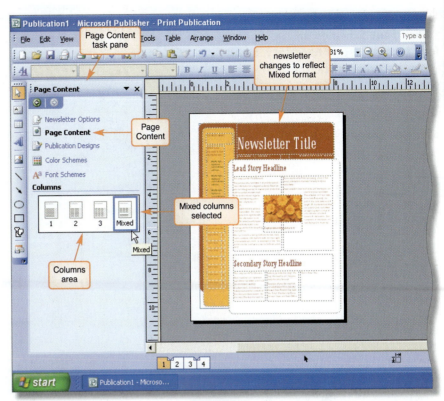

FIGURE 2-4

4

• **Click Color Schemes. In the Apply a color scheme list, click Cranberry.**

The newsletter is displayed with the Cranberry color scheme (Figure 2-5).

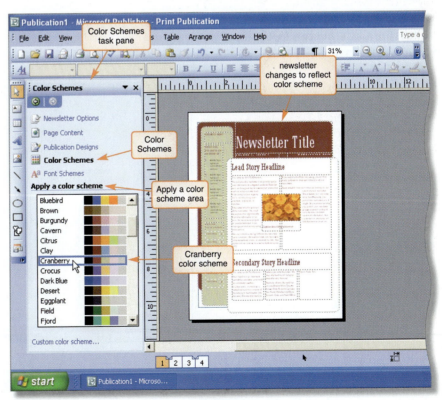

FIGURE 2-5

5

• **Click Font Schemes. In the Apply a font scheme list, if necessary, scroll down and then click the Basis font scheme.**

Publisher displays the newsletter with the Basis font scheme (Figure 2-6).

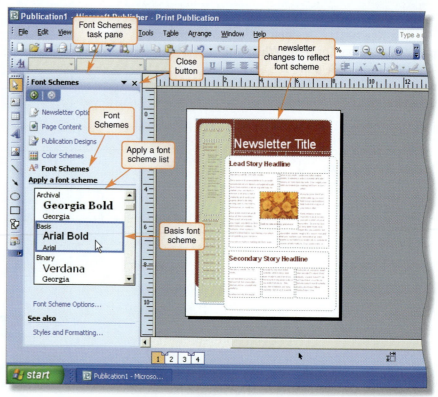

FIGURE 2-6

6

• **Click the Close button in the Font Schemes task pane.**

The publication displays the options, content layout, color, and font choices selected from the task panes (Figure 2-7).

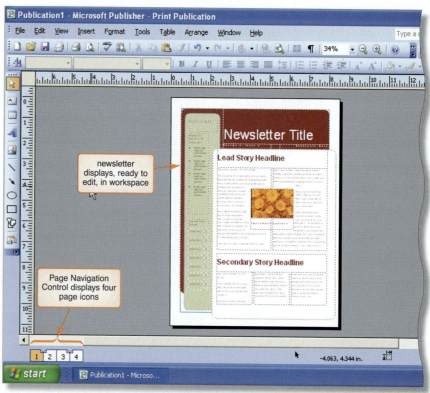

FIGURE 2-7

You can revisit newsletter options to make changes by clicking View on the menu bar and then clicking Task Pane.

Any publication you choose in the Publications list is a Publisher-designed publication. You may use these publications, of course, as part of Publisher's licensing agreement. Using proven design strategies, Publisher places text and graphics in the publication at appropriate places for a professional looking newsletter.

Editing the Newsletter Template

As the first step in the design process, the purpose of a newsletter is to communicate and educate its readers. Publisher places the lead story in a prominent position on the page and uses a discussion of purpose and audience as the default text.

The following pages discuss how to edit various articles and objects in the newsletter.

Pagination

Publisher's Newsletter template creates four pages of text and graphics. This template is appropriate for some applications, but the Extreme Sports Club wants to print a single sheet, two-sided newsletter. Page 4 of the newsletter contains objects typically used on the back page, so you will delete pages 2 and 3. The following steps show how to change and delete pages.

To Change and Delete Pages in a Newsletter

1

• **Click the Page 2 icon on the Page Navigation Control.**

Pages 2 and 3 are displayed in the workspace (Figure 2-8). The Page Navigation Control displays the selected pages in light orange on the status bar.

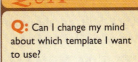

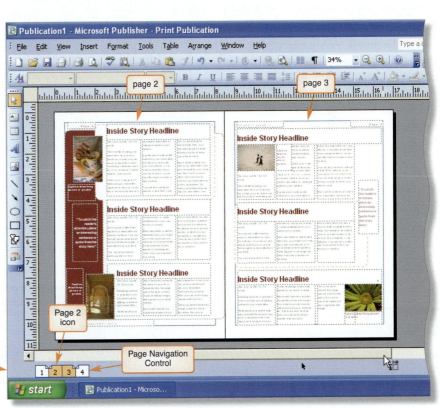

FIGURE 2-8

2

• **Click Edit on the menu bar and then click Delete Page.**

• **When the Delete Page dialog box is displayed, if necessary, click Both pages to select it.**

Publisher displays a dialog box with options for deleting either or both pages (Figure 2-9).

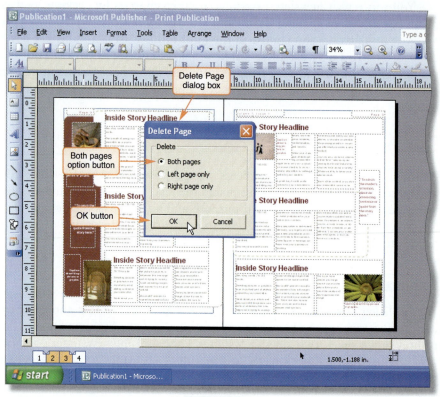

FIGURE 2-9

3

• **Click the OK button in the Delete Page dialog box.**

• **If a Microsoft Publisher dialog box displays to confirm deleting all the objects, click the OK button.**

Publisher deletes pages 2 and 3 and displays the back page as the new page 2 (Figure 2-10).

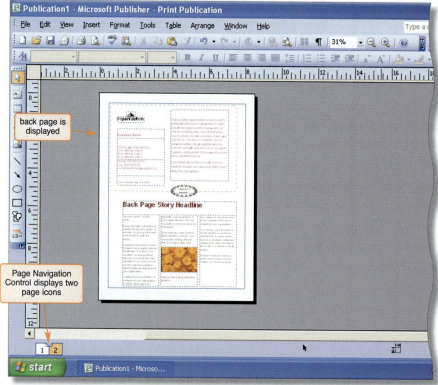

FIGURE 2-10

Inserting pages in a newsletter is just as easy as deleting them. The Page command on the Insert menu provides the option of inserting a left- or right-hand page, as well as choices in the types of objects to display on the page. When you choose to insert or delete, when working on the first or last page, Publisher will warn you of pagination problems and will offer you a confirmation dialog box.

With the newsletter containing two pages, you are ready to edit the masthead, graphics, and articles.

Editing the Masthead

Most newsletters and brochures contain a masthead similar to those used in newspapers. A **masthead** is a box or section printed in each issue that lists information, such as the name, publisher, location, volume, and date. The Publisher-designed masthead, included in the Banded Newsletter template, contains several text boxes and color-filled shapes that create an attractive, eye-catching graphic that complements the Banded Newsletter design set. You need to edit the text boxes, however, to convey appropriate messages.

Publisher incorporates three text boxes in the Banded Newsletter masthead (Figure 2-11 on the next page). The newsletter title is displayed in a text box layered on top of a rectangle. Two text boxes are displayed in the lower portion of the masthead for the volume/issue and date.

Editing Techniques

Recall that Publisher uses text-editing techniques similar to most word processing programs. To insert text, position the insertion point and type the new text. Publisher always inserts the text to the left of the insertion point. The text to the right of the insertion point moves to the right and downward to accommodate the new text.

The BACKSPACE key deletes text to the left of the insertion point. To delete or change more than a few characters, however, you should select the text. Publisher handles selecting text in a slightly different manner than word processing programs. In Publisher, you select unedited default text, such as placeholder titles and articles in the newsletters, with a single click. To select large amounts of text, click the text and then press CTRL+A to select all the text in the text box, or drag through the text. To select individual words, double-click the word, as you would in word processing.

The steps on the next page demonstrate some of these techniques as text is selected and edited.

More About

Design Issues

The steps in good design and attractive layout are similar to the steps in designing any new product, program, or presentation. For more information on design, visit the Publisher 2003 More About Web page (scsite.com/pub2003/more) and click Design Issues.

More About

Design Sets

Each Publisher-designed newsletter is part of a design set, which is a collection of related publication types that share a consistent color scheme, design, and look. For example, a master set includes a business card, a company letterhead, and a company brochure, each with a matching design. To view design sets and their elements, click the Design Gallery Object button, and then click the Objects by Design tab.

More About

Deleting

Whether to delete using the BACKSPACE key or the DELETE key is debated in word processing circles. It really depends on the location of the insertion point in the publication. If the insertion point already is positioned left of the character you want to delete, it makes more sense to press the DELETE key rather than reposition the insertion point just to use the BACKSPACE key.

To Edit the Masthead

1

• **Click the Page 1 icon on the Page Navigation Control.**

• **Click the text, Newsletter Title. Press the F9 key to view the masthead more closely.**

Publisher enlarges the masthead and selects the entire title's text because it is placeholder text (Figure 2-11).

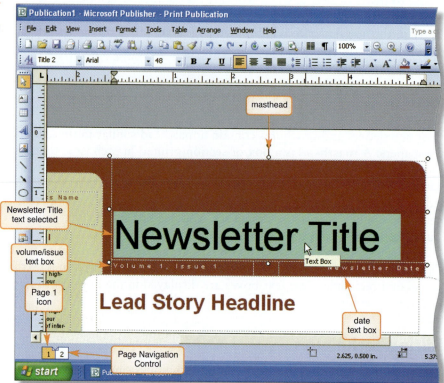

FIGURE 2-11

2

• **Type** Extreme News **in the text box.**

• **Click the placeholder text in the volume/issue text box.**

Publisher replaces the selected text using the font from the design set (Figure 2-12). Because fonts sometimes are printer-dependent, your font may differ from the one shown. Publisher selects the placeholder text in the volume/issue text box.

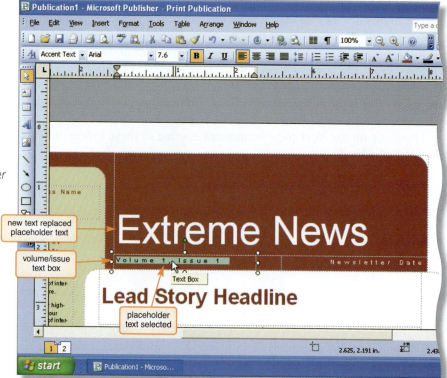

FIGURE 2-12

3

• **Type** Volume 3, Issue 1 **to replace the selected text.**

• **Click the placeholder text, Newsletter Date.**

Publisher selects the entire date because it is placeholder text, designed to be replaced (Figure 2-13). The new volume and issue information is entered.

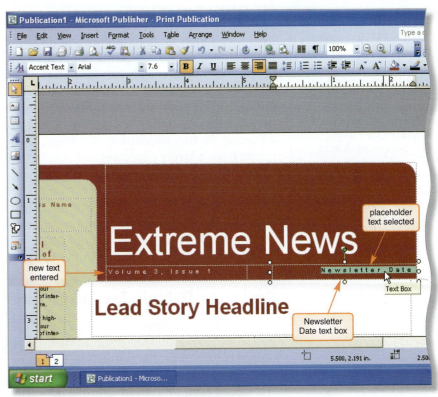

FIGURE 2-13

4

• **Type** September 2, 2005 **in the text box.**

The masthead edits are complete (Figure 2-14).

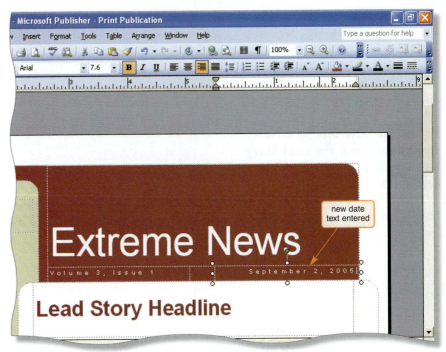

FIGURE 2-14

Different newsletter templates may include other shapes and text boxes in their mastheads, such as a text box that displays the organization name.

Importing Files

More About

Importing Files

In order to import all manner of word processing documents, you must have chosen to perform a full installation of Microsoft Publisher. Publisher will remind you to reinsert the Publisher CD-ROM if it needs more information about the type of file you are trying to import.

Publisher allows users to import text and graphics from many sources into its publications. Publisher accepts imported objects from a variety of different programs and in many different file formats. Gathering data of interest to the readers is an important phase in the design process. The stories for the newsletter are provided on the Data Disk associated with this textbook. See the inside back cover for instructions for downloading the Data Disk or see your instructor for information on accessing the files required in this book. **Downloading** means moving data or programs from a larger computer to a smaller one. Publisher uses the term **importing** to describe inserting text or objects from any other source into the Publisher workspace.

Publisher uses the term, **story**, to mean text that is contained within a single text box or a chain of linked text boxes. Each newsletter template provides **linked text boxes**, or text boxes whose text flows from one to another. In the templates, two or three text boxes may be linked automatically; however, if a story is too long to fit in the linked text boxes, Publisher will offer to link even more text boxes for easy reading.

Replacing Default Text Using an Imported File

Publisher suggests that 175 to 225 words will fit in the space allocated for the lead story. This Publisher-designed newsletter uses a two-column text format that **connects**, or wraps, the running text from one linked text box to the next.

This edition of *Extreme News* has three stories that previously have been typed and stored using Microsoft Word. The stories, stored on the Data Disk that accompanies this textbook, are ready to be used in the newsletter.

The following steps first edit the Lead Story Headline placeholder text and then import a text file from a floppy disk to replace the Publisher-supplied default text.

To Edit a Headline and Import a Text File

1

• **With the Data Disk in drive A, scroll down until the Lead Story Headline is displayed. Click the headline text to select it.**

The placeholder text is selected (Figure 2-15).

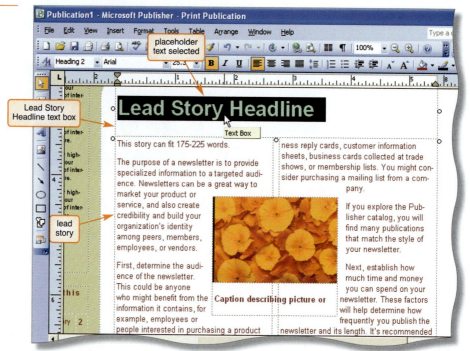

FIGURE 2-15

2

• **Type** Surfing Championship Tour **to replace the selected placeholder text.**

• **Click the story below the headline. Read the story.**

Publisher displays the new headline and selects the entire story (Figure 2-16). Reading the story will provide you with valuable suggestions about the design process of newsletter publications.

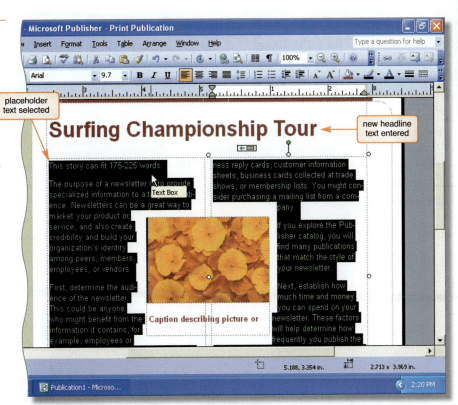

FIGURE 2-16

3

• **Click Insert on the menu bar.**

Publisher displays the Insert menu (Figure 2-17).

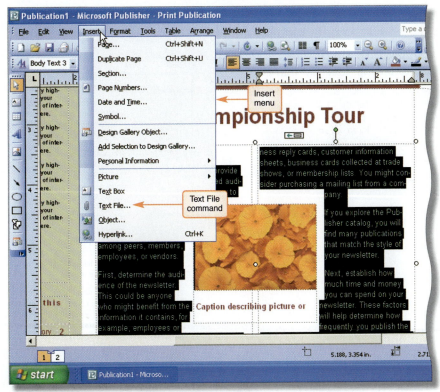

FIGURE 2-17

4

- **Click Text File. When the Insert Text dialog box is displayed, click the Look in box arrow, and then click 3½ Floppy (A:) in the Look in list.**

- **Double-click the Project 2 folder.**

The data files on the floppy disk are displayed below the Look in box (Figure 2-18). Your list of files may differ.

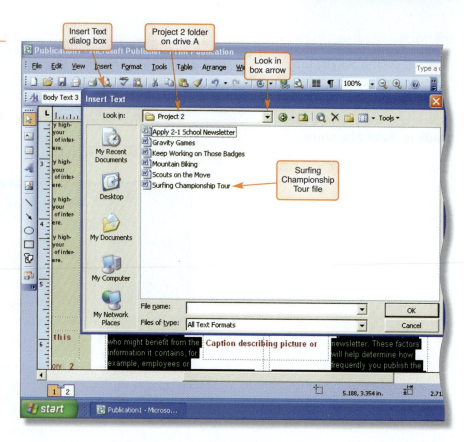

FIGURE 2-18

5

- **Double-click the Surfing Championship Tour file name.**

The story is inserted in the newsletter (Figure 2-19).

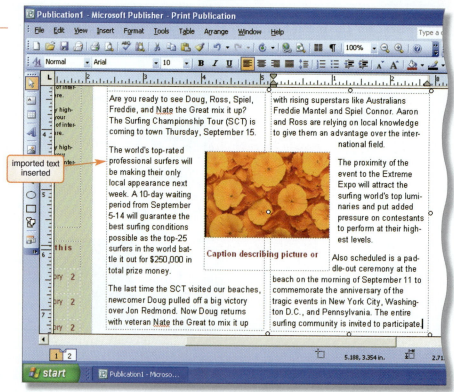

FIGURE 2-19

Other Ways

1. Right-click story, point to Change Text on shortcut menu, click Text File

Continuing a story across columns or text boxes is one of the features that Publisher performs for you. If the story contains more text than will fit in the default text box, Publisher displays a message to warn you. You then have the option of connecting to another box or continuing the story on another page. Publisher will add the continued notices, or **jump lines**, to guide readers through the story.

Recall that the **F9 function key** toggles between the current page view and 100% magnification. **Toggle** means the same key will alternate views, or turn a feature on and off. Editing text is much easier if you view the text box at 100% magnification or even larger. Page editing techniques, such as moving graphics, inserting new boxes, and aligning objects, more easily are performed in **whole page view**. Toggling back and forth with the F9 function key works well. You also may choose different magnifications and views by clicking the Zoom box arrow on the Standard toolbar.

Importing Text for the Secondary Story

The next step is to edit the secondary story headline and import the text for the story in the lower portion of page 1 of the newsletter as explained in the steps below.

More About

Zooming

To adjust the size of the characters on the screen, you can click the Zoom In or Zoom Out button, click the Zoom box arrow and then select the desired percentage or magnification style, or type a percentage of your choice in the Zoom box. To have the screen redraw even faster during the zooming, you can reduce the quality of the picture display by clicking Pictures on the View menu.

To Import More Text

1 Scroll to display the lower portion of page 1 and then click the Secondary Story Headline placeholder text to select it.

2 Type Mountain Biking to replace the selected headline.

3 Click the secondary story to select it.

4 Click Insert on the menu bar and then click Text File.

5 If not already selected, click 3½ Floppy (A:) in the Look in list.

6 Double-click the Mountain Biking file name.

The story is imported as shown in Figure 2-20. Your screen may differ slightly, depending on the fonts your computer uses.

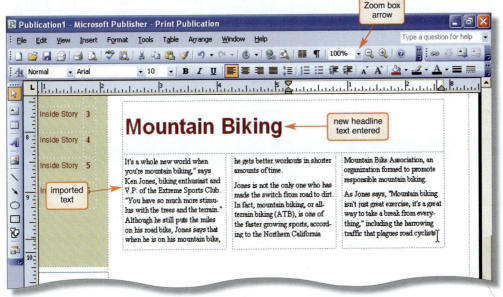

FIGURE 2-20

Importing Text on the Back Page

The final steps to finish the imported stories in the newsletter involve importing text for the back page story, as described in the following steps.

To Import the Back Page Story

1 **Click the Page 2 icon on the Page Navigation Control.**

2 **Click the Back Page Story Headline placeholder text.**

3 **Type** Up for Gravity Games? **to replace the selected text.**

4 **Click the back page story text below the headline to select it.**

5 **Click Insert on the menu bar and then click Text File.**

6 **If not already selected, click 3½ Floppy (A:) in the Look in list.**

7 **Double-click the Gravity Games file name.**

The imported story and headline are shown in Figure 2-21.

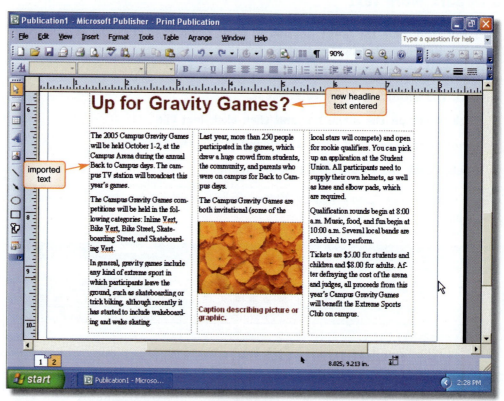

FIGURE 2-21

All the stories for the newsletter now are complete. Importing the stories instead of typing them saves time and adds the convenience of using word processing. Publisher accepts most file formats from popular word processing programs and text editors.

Saving an Intermediate Copy of the Newsletter

A good practice is to save intermediate copies of your work. That way, if your computer loses power or you make a serious mistake, you always can retrieve the latest copy from disk. Use the Save button on the Standard toolbar often, because you can save time later if the unexpected happens.

With the masthead and story headlines edited, and the text files imported, it now is a good time to save the entire newsletter before continuing. For the following steps, it is assumed you have a floppy disk in drive A.

To Save an Intermediate Copy of the Newsletter

1 Click the Save button on the Standard toolbar.

2 Type `Extreme Newsletter` in the File name text box. If necessary, click 3½ Floppy (A:) in the Save in list.

3 Click the Save button in the Save As dialog box.

Publisher saves the publication on a floppy disk in drive A using the file name, Extreme Newsletter (Figure 2-22). The new file name displays on the Publisher title bar and the Publisher button on the taskbar.

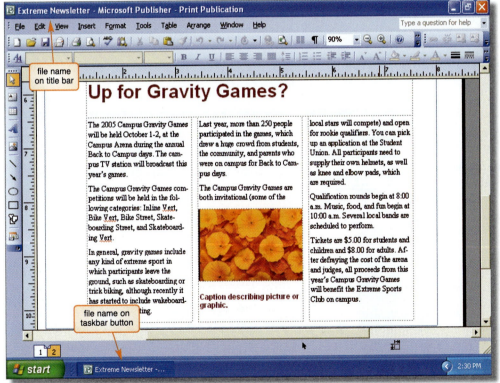

FIGURE 2-22

More About

Personal Information Sets

Publisher maintains four personal information sets: Primary Business, Secondary Business, Other Organization, and Home/Family. Every new publication has the Primary Business personal information set selected by default. You can apply a different personal information set to the publication, however. Simply click Personal Information on the Edit menu and then click the appropriate set.

Working with Personal Information Sets

Publisher permits you to store four unique sets of personal information for use at work and home. The name of the organization, the address, the telephone number, and other pieces of information such as tag lines and logos are stored in personal information sets. In **personal information sets**, Publisher can keep track of data about you, your business, an organization affiliation, or other personal information that you might use to create publications. In this newsletter, you will edit the text box for the organization name, address lines, phone, fax, and e-mail. You will learn more about permanently changing personal information components in a future project.

Editing the Personal Information Components

Both pages of the newsletter contain an Organization Name Text Box. Editing one of these text boxes automatically changes the other. Additionally, after typing the name of your organization, Publisher can reuse the text in other publications, if it is saved as a personal information component. A **personal information component** is a text box or logo that contains information about the organization from the Personal Information Set. This information can carry over from one publication to the next. For example, the name of the company might be displayed at the top of the newsletter, on the business cards, and on the letterhead stationery.

The following steps show how to edit personal information components for this publication only.

To Edit Personal Information Components

1

• **With page 2 still displayed, scroll if necessary, and drag through the placeholder text in the Organization Name Text Box in the upper-left corner.**

Your Personal Information Set may display a different organization name in the text box (Figure 2-23).

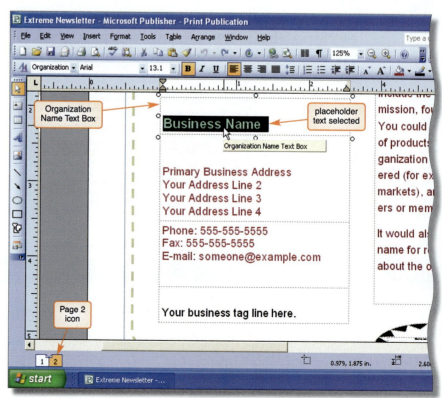

FIGURE 2-23

2

• **Type** Extreme Sports Club **to replace the text in the text box.**

The text, Extreme Sports Club, replaces the selected text (Figure 2-24). Because it is part of the personal information set, Publisher changed the Organization Name Text Box on both pages of the publication.

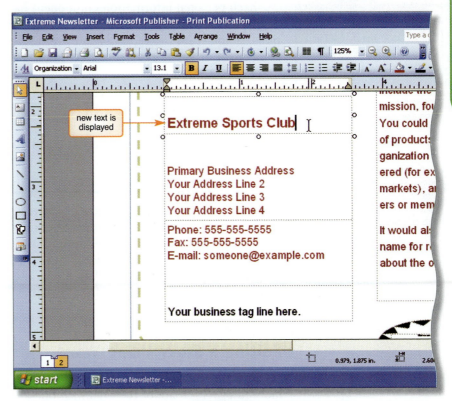

FIGURE 2-24

3

• **Repeat Step 2 to edit the text boxes for the address lines, phone, fax, and e-mail, and the Tag Line Text Box, as shown in Figure 2-25.**

• **As you type, press the ENTER key for new lines of text inside the text boxes when necessary.**

The edited personal information components are displayed in the newsletter (Figure 2-25).

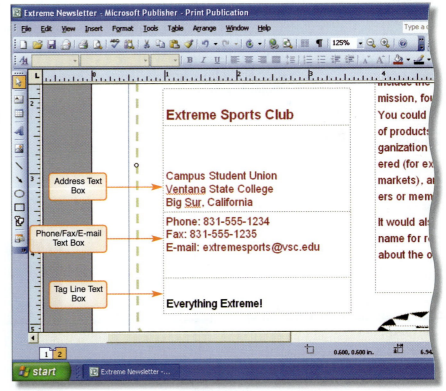

FIGURE 2-25

Other Ways

1. On Edit menu, click Personal Information

Q&A

Q: Which should I use for creating my text, Publisher or Word?

A: Microsoft recommends using the best tool for the job. For desktop publishing, Publisher offers more features and buttons related to the many kinds of objects desktop publishers need and use than does Word. For straight typing tasks, such as term papers and letters that need little or no graphics or advanced page layout and design, Word is a better tool.

Each personal information component has its own preset font, font size, and text alignment. If desired, you can make changes to the formatting for individual publications. If you want to keep Publisher from synchronizing, or repeating, the changed component on other pages, click Undo on the Edit menu.

Editing Stories in Microsoft Word

You have seen that you can edit text directly in Microsoft Publisher or import text from a previously stored file. A third way to edit text is to use Microsoft Word as your editor. Publisher provides an easy link between the two applications.

If you need to edit only a few words, it is faster to stay in Publisher. If you need to edit a longer story that appears on different pages in a publication or one that has not been stored previously, it might be easier to edit the story in Word. Many users are accustomed to working in Word and want to take advantage of available Word features, such as grammar checking and revision tracking. It sometimes is easier to drag and drop paragraphs in a Word window rather than performing the same task in a Publisher window, especially when it involves moving across pages in a larger Publisher publication.

Editing a Story Using Word

In the *Extreme News* newsletter, the back page contains a text box to display more information about the organization. The club's informational text has not been stored previously in a file for importing, so it must be typed.

Microsoft Word version 6.0 or later must be installed on your computer for this procedure to work. Occasionally, if you have many applications running, such as virus protection and other memory-taxing programs, Publisher may warn you that you are low on computer memory. In that case, close the other applications, and try editing the story in Word again.

The following steps illustrate how to use Microsoft Word in conjunction with Publisher to create the text.

To Edit a Story Using Word

• **If necessary, click the Page 2 icon on the Page Navigation Control. Scroll to display the text box in the upper-right portion of the page.**

• **Click any text in the text box and then press CTRL+A to select all of the text.**

The text is selected in the text box (Figure 2-26).

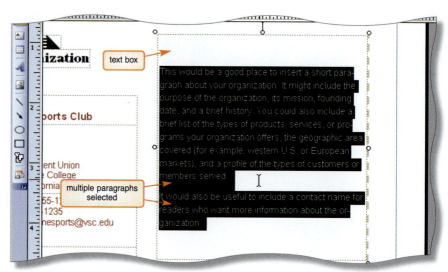

FIGURE 2-26

2

- **Press the DELETE key to delete the current story.**
- **Click Edit on the menu bar.**

Publisher displays the Edit menu (Figure 2-27).

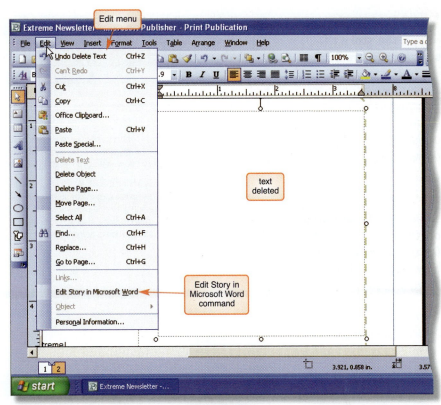

FIGURE 2-27

3

- **Click Edit Story in Microsoft Word.**

Microsoft Word starts in a new window (Figure 2-28).

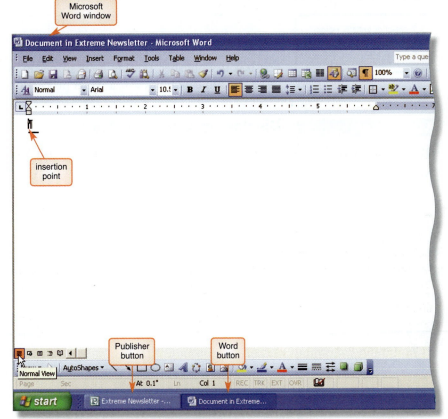

FIGURE 2-28

4

• **Type the story as shown in Figure 2-29.**

The text displays the same formatting as the previously deleted text in Publisher. Your display may differ depending on available fonts.

new text entered

5

• **Click the Close button on the title bar of the Document in Extreme Newsletter – Microsoft Word window.**

The edited story is displayed in the Publisher text box (see Figure 2-30 on the next page).

Close button

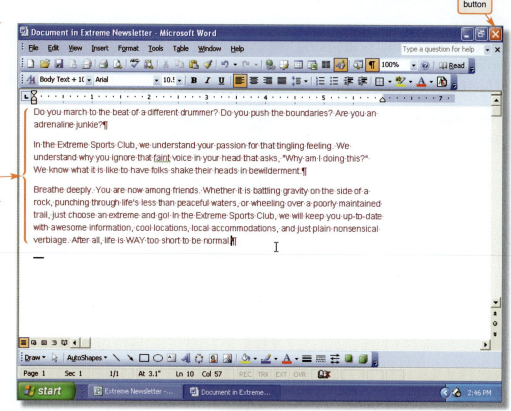

FIGURE 2-29

While you are working on a story in Word, you cannot edit the corresponding text box in Publisher. Editing your stories in Word allows you to manipulate the text using the full capabilities of a word processing program.

Displaying Overflow Text

Below the text box in Figure 2-30 is a **Text in Overflow indicator**, which means that there is more text than can fit in the current text box. The **overflow area** is an invisible storage location within your publication to hold extra text — similar to a clipboard, but saved with the publication. The overflow area is not electricity-dependent. You can move your text out of overflow and back into your publication by one of several means: fitting text automatically using the Best Fit option, enlarging the text font size, changing the text size, changing the margins within the text box, or deleting some of the text in the text box.

The following steps resize the text box to accommodate overflow text.

To Display Overflow Text

1

• **Point to the middle-right handle of the text box as shown in Figure 2-30.**

The mouse pointer changes to a double-headed arrow.

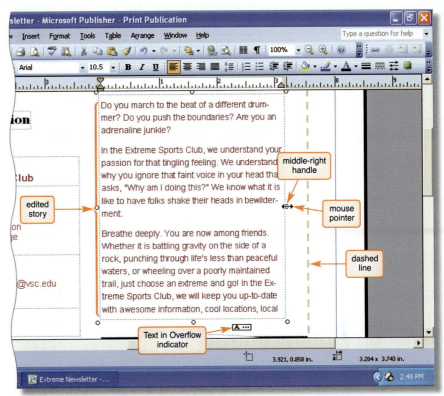

FIGURE 2-30

2

• **Drag the handle to the right until it aligns with the dashed line.**

• **Release the mouse button.**

The text box is resized (Figure 2-31). All of the text now fits inside the text box, and the Text in Overflow indicator no longer is displayed.

Other Ways

1. Right-click text, point to Change Text, point to AutoFit Text, click Shrink Text On Overflow
2. Select text, enter smaller number in Font Size box
3. Double-click status bar, increase Width and Height numbers

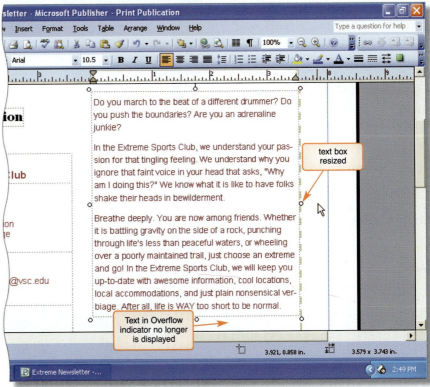

FIGURE 2-31

Editing the Design Set

Page 2 of the newsletter contains several objects that are part of the newsletter publication design set. A design set is specific to the type of publication and chosen template. Recall that an object in Publisher is any text box, shape, border, image, or table inserted in the publication. The Banded Newsletter design contains a logo and an attention getter on the back page, among other objects. In the following sections, you will learn how to change the design of the attention getter, format the text with a new style, and then delete the logo.

Editing an Attention Getter

Attention getters are eye-catching graphics and text that draw attention to a location on the page. They contain graphic boxes, text frames, geometric designs, and colors intended to draw attention to your publication. Publisher displays a small, nonprinting button just below attention getters that you can click to change their options and design.

The Banded Newsletter uses a starburst cutout attention getter which groups a starburst shape and a text box. You will change the design of the attention getter on the back page. It is located just above the Gravity Games story. The following steps illustrate how to change the design.

To Edit the Attention Getter Design

1

• **If necessary, scroll to display the attention getter above the Gravity Games headline on page 2 of the newsletter. Click the attention getter to select it.**

The attention getter is a starburst with a text box inside it (Figure 2-32). Publisher also displays an Options button. If the AutoFit text feature has been turned on, your attention getter may display more text.

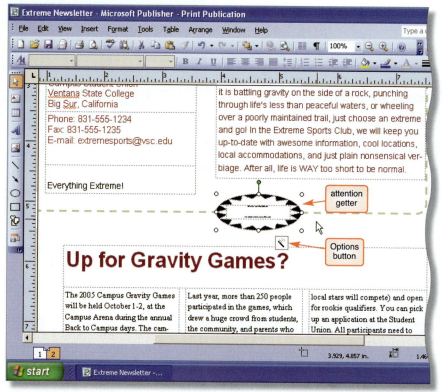

FIGURE 2-32

2

• **Click the Options button.**

• **When the Attention Getter Designs task pane appears, click the Side Curves Attention Getter preview.**

The Attention Getter Designs task pane displays a gallery of attention getters in the Apply a design area (Figure 2-33).

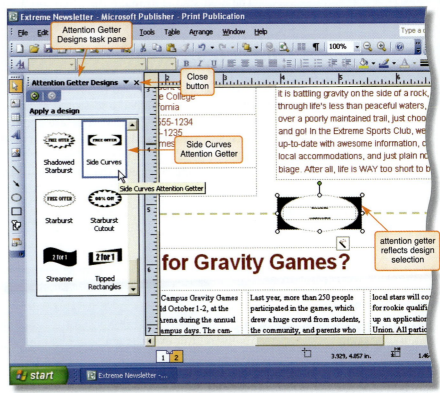

FIGURE 2-33

3

• **Click the Close button in the Attention Getter Designs task pane.**

• **Drag the middle-right handle of the attention getter to the right, until it aligns with the dashed line.**

The attention getter is resized (Figure 2-34).

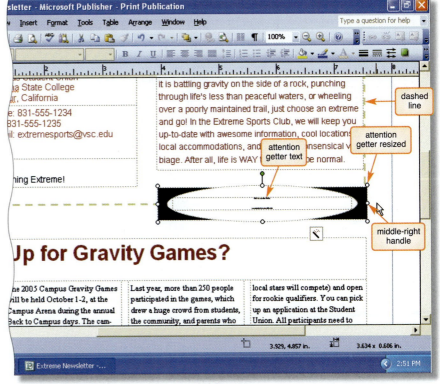

FIGURE 2-34

The next step is to make the attention getter text legible, by changing the font style.

Using Styles

A **style** is a combination of formatting characteristics, such as font, font size, and indentation that are named and stored as a set. When you apply a style, all of the formatting instructions in that style are applied at one time. To apply a style, you simply select the text and then select the style from the **Style list** on the Formatting toolbar.

The following steps edit the font style of the attention getter.

To Edit the Style

1

• **Click the text inside the attention getter's text box.**

• **Click the Style box arrow on the Formatting toolbar.**

The styles associated with the newsletter display (Figure 2-35).

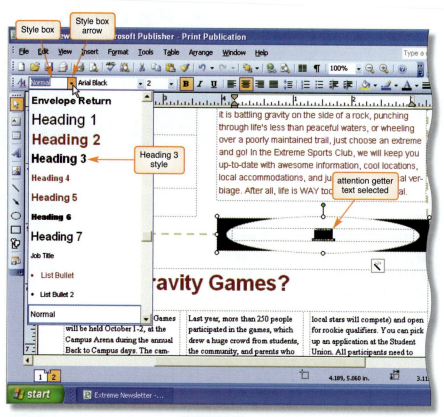

FIGURE 2-35

2

- **Click Heading 3 in the Style list.**
- **With the text still selected, type** Mondays, Student Center, 7 p.m.

The font style changes in the attention getter, and the style name displays in the Style box (Figure 2-36). The newly entered text is displayed with the new formatting.

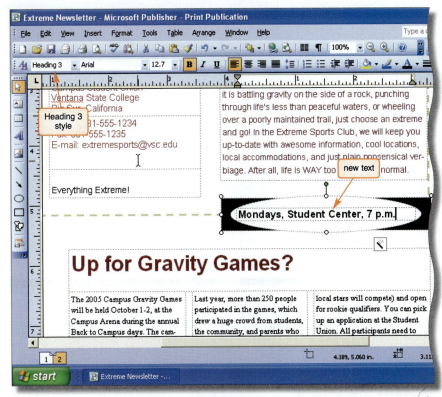

FIGURE 2-36

You can edit the text, text color, fill color, borders, and shadows of attention getters. Publisher's Design Gallery also has other styles and shapes from which you may choose.

Deleting the Logo

The Banded Newsletter design set displays an organization logo on the back page. A **logo** is a personal information component usually containing some combination of small graphics and words that identify or represent a company in a visual way. Publisher-supplied logos vary with each personal information set. Because the Extreme Sports Club has no logo, the following steps show how to delete the logo.

To Delete the Logo

1 Scroll to the top and left of page 2 in the Newsletter to display the logo as shown in Figure 2-37 on the next page.

2 Right-click the logo.

3 Click Delete Object on the shortcut menu.

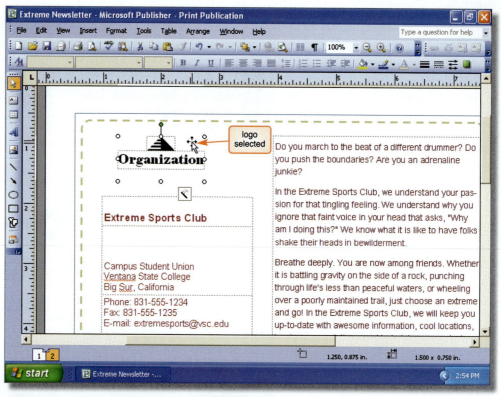

FIGURE 2-37

If you delete an object by accident, click the Undo button on the Standard toolbar. The Edit menu also contains a Delete Object and an Undo command.

WordArt

WordArt is a program that works with Publisher to create fancy text effects. A WordArt object actually is a graphic and not text at all. Publication designers typically use WordArt to create eye-catching headlines and banners. WordArt uses its own toolbar to add effects to the graphic.

Inserting a WordArt Object

The *Extreme News* newsletter will use a WordArt object as a heading in the upper-left corner of the back page. A heading can be text, formatted to draw attention, but using WordArt increases the number of special effect possibilities and options.

The following steps explain how to add a WordArt object as the headline for the back page of the newsletter.

To Insert a WordArt Object in the Newsletter

1

• **If necessary, scroll to the top and left of the back page of the newsletter.**

• **Click the Insert WordArt button on the Objects toolbar. When the WordArt Gallery dialog box is displayed, locate an appropriate style.**

The WordArt Gallery dialog box is displayed (Figure 2-38).

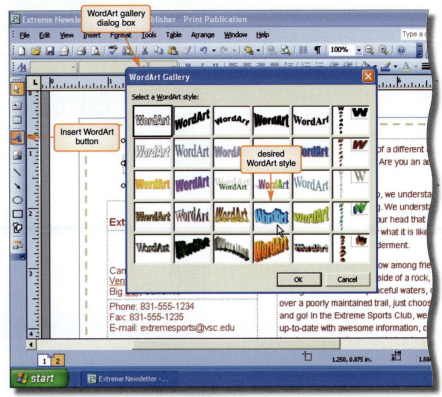

FIGURE 2-38

2

• **Double-click the style.**

Publisher displays the Edit WordArt Text dialog box (Figure 2-39).

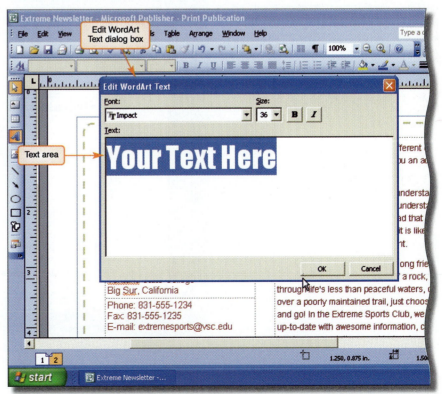

FIGURE 2-39

3

• **Type** Extreme **as the new text.**

The new text is displayed in the Text area (Figure 2-40).

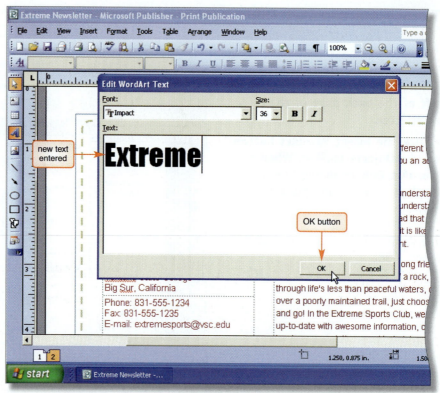

FIGURE 2-40

4

• **Click the OK button.**

Publisher displays the WordArt object and the WordArt toolbar (Figure 2-41).

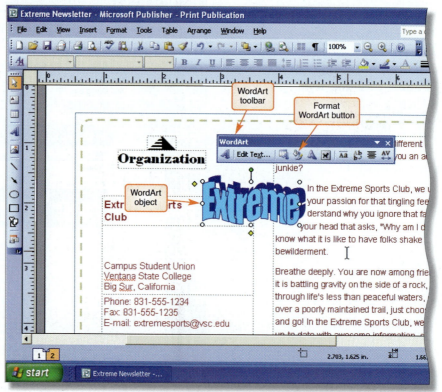

FIGURE 2-41

5

• **Click the Format WordArt button on the WordArt toolbar.**

• **When the Format WordArt dialog box is displayed, if necessary, click the Colors and Lines tab, and then click the Color box arrow in the Fill area.**

Publisher displays the Format WordArt dialog box (Figure 2-42). The Cranberry font scheme colors display in the color palette. Your colors may vary.

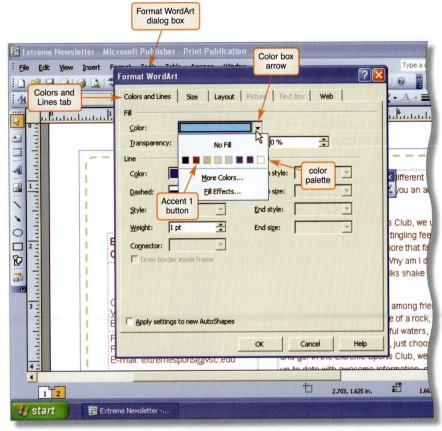

FIGURE 2-42

6

• **Click the Accent 1 button in the color palette.**

The new color is displayed in the Color box in the Fill area (Figure 2-43).

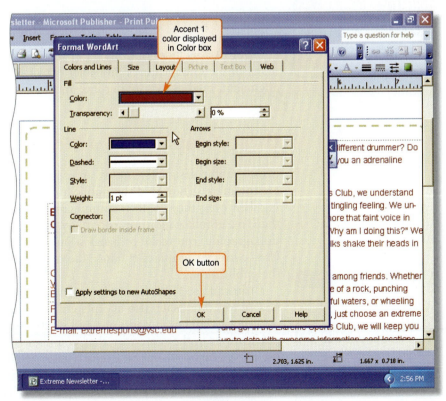

FIGURE 2-43

7

• **Click the OK button in the Format WordArt dialog box.**

• **Drag the WordArt object above the Organization Name Text Box so that it aligns approximately with its left border.**

• **If necessary, click the Close button on the WordArt toolbar to remove it from the screen.**

The WordArt Object, with its new color, is displayed in the newsletter (Figure 2-44).

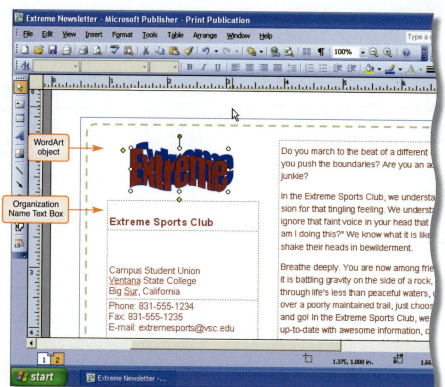

FIGURE 2-44

WordArt includes options for spacing, rotating, shadows, and borders, as well as many of the same features Publisher provides on its Formatting toolbar, such as alignment, bold, italics, underline, and fonts.

Using Graphics in a Newsletter

Most graphic designers employ an easy technique for deciding how many graphics are too many. They hold the publication at arm's length and glance at it. Then, closing their eyes, they count the number of things they remember. Remembering more than five graphics indicates too many, two or fewer indicates too few. Without question, graphics can make or break a publication. The world has come to expect them. Used correctly, graphics enhance the text, attract the eye, and brighten the look of the publication.

You can use Publisher's clip art images in any publication you create, including newsletters. Publisher also accepts graphics and pictures created by other programs, as well as scanned photographs and electronic images. You can import graphics into publications in the same way that you imported stories. In newsletters, you should use photographs when you desire true-to-life representations, such as pictures of employees and products. Graphics, on the other hand, can explain, draw, instruct, entertain, or represent images for which you have no picture. The careful use of graphics can add flair and distinction to your publication.

Graphics do not have to be images and pictures. They also can include tables, charts, shapes, lines, boxes, borders, pull quotes, and sidebars. A **sidebar** is a small piece of text, set off with a box or graphic, and placed beside an article. It contains text that is not vital to understanding the main text; it usually adds interest or additional information. Tables of contents and bulleted points of interest are examples of sidebars. A **pull quote** is an excerpt from the main article to highlight the ideas or to attract readers. As with other graphics, it adds interest to the page. Pull quotes, like sidebars, can be set off with a box or graphic.

The following sections illustrate how to import graphics from the Data Disk, edit the captions and sidebar text, delete a sidebar, and insert a pull quote.

More About

Graphics

For tips on using graphics effectively in a publication, visit the Publisher 2003 More About Web page (scsite.com/pub2003/more) and click Discovering Presentation.

Importing Graphics

Graphics can be imported from previously stored files, just as stories can. The following steps show how to import graphics from the Data Disk associated with this textbook.

To Import Graphics and Edit the Caption

1

• **On the back page of the newsletter, scroll to the Gravity Games article in the lower part of the page.**

• **Right-click the flower graphic. When the shortcut menu is displayed, point to Change Picture and then point to From File on the Change Picture submenu.**

Publisher displays the shortcut menu and the Change Picture submenu (Figure 2-45).

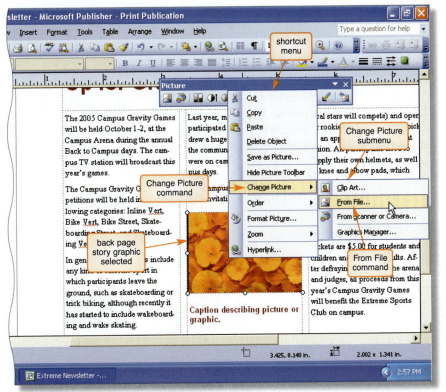

FIGURE 2-45

2

• **Click From File. When the Insert Picture dialog box is displayed, click the Look in box arrow, and then click 3½ Floppy (A:) in the Look in list.**

• **Click the Skateboarding picture.**

Publisher displays the graphics contained on the floppy disk in drive A (Figure 2-46).

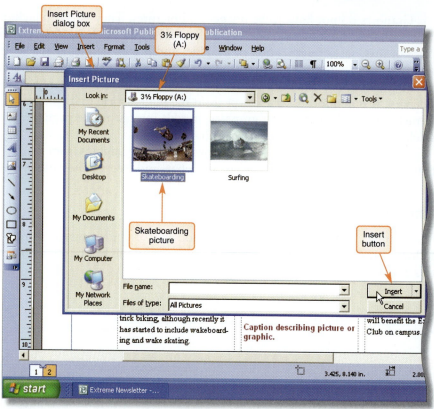

FIGURE 2-46

3

• **Click the Insert button in the Insert Picture dialog box. When the publication again is visible, click the text in the caption text box.**

The picture is inserted as the new graphic for the back page story (Figure 2-47). The text in the caption is selected.

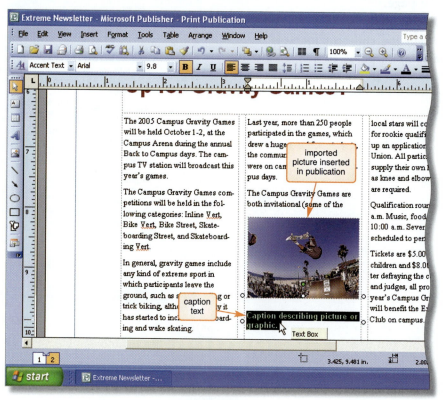

FIGURE 2-47

4

• **Type** Skateboarding tricks thrill the audience at last year's event. **to replace the selected placeholder text.**

Publisher displays the new caption (Figure 2-48).

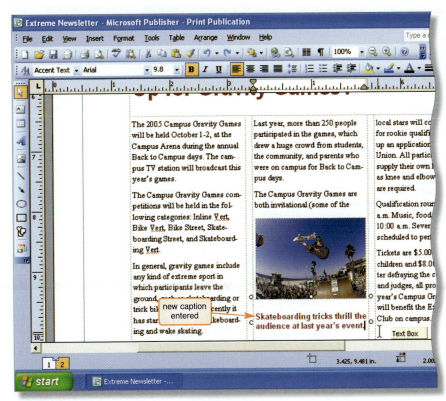

FIGURE 2-48

If necessary, imported graphics may be resized to better complement the stories. Publisher automatically wraps the text around the graphic regardless of its size.

The next step is to import a graphic for the lead story.

To Import a Graphic on Page 1

1 Click the Page 1 icon on the Page Navigation Control.

2 Right-click the graphic in the Surfing Championship Tour story. When the shortcut menu is displayed, point to Change Picture and then click From File on the Change Picture submenu.

3 When the Insert Picture dialog box is displayed, click the Look in box arrow, and then click 3½ Floppy (A:) in the Look in list. Click the Surfing picture (Figure 2-46).

4 Click the Insert button in the Insert Picture dialog box.

5 When the publication again is visible, click the text in the caption text box. Type Nate the Great, at it again! to replace the selected placeholder text.

Publisher displays the new graphic and caption (Figure 2-49 on the next page).

More About

Portrait and Landscape Orientation

The terms portrait and landscape are used to refer to more than just graphic orientation. Portrait also refers to printing a document so the short edge of the paper is the top of the page. Landscape printing assumes the long edge to be the top of the page.

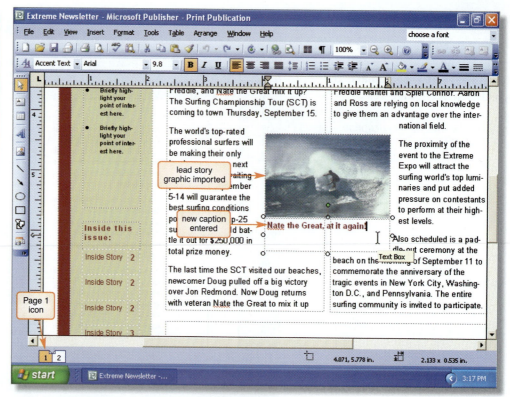

FIGURE 2-49

If you choose to include Publisher-supplied graphics, remember that graphics in the Clip Art Gallery are not all the same size. Some of the images and clip art will be displayed in **portrait** orientation, which means they are taller than they are wide. The opposite graphic orientation is **landscape**. When you change graphics, your choice may alter both the way the columns look and where the columns break. You may want to experiment with dragging the picture in small increments to make the columns symmetrical. The text automatically wraps around the graphic in the newsletter. The column breaks do not have to match the project newsletter exactly.

Graphics in the Clip Art Gallery are proportional, which means the height and width have been set in relation to each other, so as not to distort the picture. If you resize the graphic, be sure to hold down the SHIFT key while dragging a corner sizing handle as described in Project 1. Shift-dragging maintains the graphic's proportional height and width.

Editing a Sidebar

The Banded Newsletter template included two sidebars in the newsletter. The first is a bulleted list of special points of interest. The following steps edit that bulleted list.

More About

Sidebars

This More About box is an example of a sidebar. The Shelly Cashman Series textbooks use sidebars to offer more information about subjects in the text, as well as to direct readers to Web pages about the topic. The Other Ways feature in the book also is a sidebar.

To Edit a Sidebar

1

• **Scroll to display the Special points of interest sidebar in the upper-left part of page 1.**

• **Click the text of the bulleted list.**

Publisher highlights the entire bulleted list (Figure 2-50).

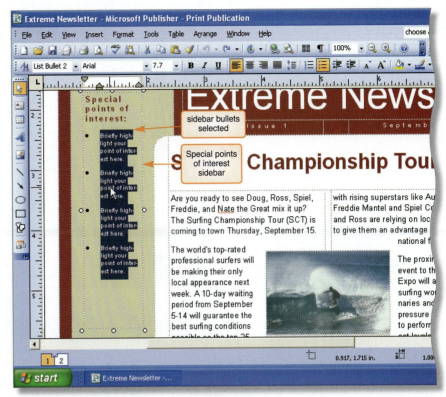

FIGURE 2-50

2

• **Type** Surfing Championship Tour, September 15 **as the first bullet.**

Publisher maintains the bulleted formatting and displays the new text (Figure 2-51).

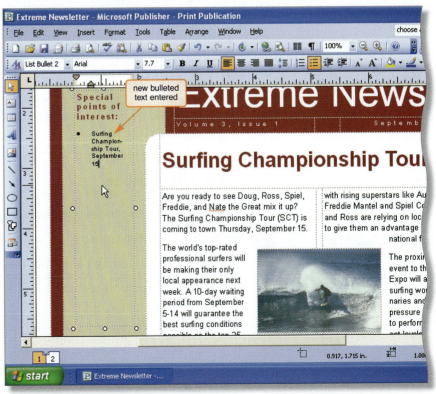

FIGURE 2-51

3

• **Press the ENTER key. Type**
X-Meeting Mondays, 7:00 p.m.
Student Center **and then press**
the ENTER key.

• **Type** Gravity Games at Back
to Campus Days, October 1-2
to finish the bullets.

The new bullets are entered (Figure 2-52).

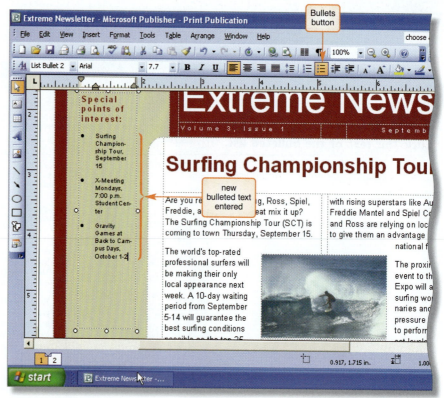

FIGURE 2-52

Recall that you can turn off bullets by clicking the Bullets button on the Formatting toolbar. You also can change the format of bullets by clicking Bullets and Numbering on the Format menu.

Deleting a Sidebar

The other sidebar in the Banded Newsletter is a table of contents. Because the newsletter now has only two pages, a table of contents is not necessary. The following steps delete the sidebar.

To Delete the Sidebar

1 Scroll to display the **Inside this issue** sidebar as shown in Figure 2-53.

2 Right-click the sidebar text.

3 Click **Delete Object** on the shortcut menu.

4 If a shaded background rectangle still is displayed, repeat Steps 2 and 3 to delete it also.

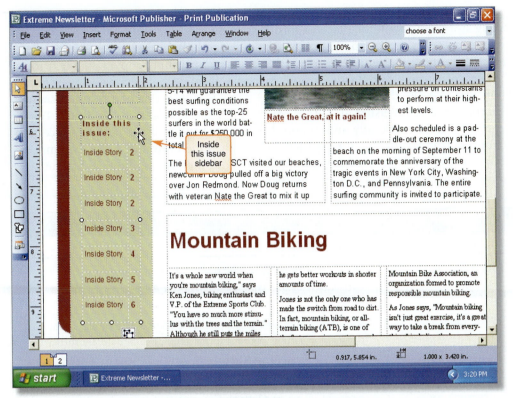

FIGURE 2-53

This table was an index used to locate articles in longer newsletters. Many newsletters have a table of contents, not only to reference and locate, but also to break up a long text page and attract readers to inside pages. Tables can be used for purposes other than displaying contents and page numbers. You will learn more about tables in a later project.

Inserting a Pull Quote

People often make reading decisions based on the size of the text. Using a pull quote brings a small portion of the text to their attention and invites readership. Pull quotes are especially useful for breaking the monotony of long columns of text. Desktop publishers also use pull quotes to add visual interest. Finally, pull quotes and sidebars are good multiple entry devices, offering readers many ways to digest information. Layout specialists stress that story titles and pull quotes should summarize the intended message.

The final step to complete page 1 of the newsletter is to create a pull quote using Publisher's Design Gallery. The **Design Gallery** is a group of objects that you can place in your publications, including sidebars, pull quotes, mastheads, and other individual objects not readily available on the Objects toolbar.

The pull quote graphic in this newsletter will contain a quote from the Mountain Biking story and should be placed appropriately on the page to draw the reader's attention. As you cut and paste text for the pull quote, Publisher will offer you the choice of keeping the source or original, formatting, or simply copying the text to the new formatting. The **Paste Options button** is displayed after a paste operation to allow you to make this choice. The Paste Options button is one of a series of smart tags contained in Publisher and other Microsoft Office applications. A **Smart Tag** is a button that automatically appears on the screen when Publisher performs a certain action, such as identifying a misspelled word. When the button displays, you may click it to display a menu of actions associated with the button. Table 2-3 summarizes the Smart Tags available in Publisher.

Table 2-3 Smart Tags in Publisher		
SMART TAG BUTTON		**MENU FUNCTION**
	AutoCorrect Options	Undoes an automatic correction, stops future automatic corrections of this type, or displays the AutoCorrect Options dialog box
	Paste Options	Specifies how moved or pasted items should display, e.g., with original formatting, without formatting, or with different formatting
	Smart Tag Actions	Displays a menu of actions related to names, dates, addresses, or places associated with Microsoft Outlook
	• Person's name	Adds this name to Outlook Contacts folder or schedules a meeting in Outlook Calendar with this person
	• Date or time	Schedules a meeting in Outlook Calendar at this date or time
	• Address	Adds this address to Outlook Contacts folder
	• Place	Adds this place to Outlook Contacts folder or schedules a meeting in Outlook Calendar at this location

With the Autocorrect Options button and the Smart Tag Actions button, Publisher notifies you that the smart tag is available by displaying a **Smart Tag indicator** on the screen. The smart tag indicator for AutoCorrect Options is a small blue box. The smart tag indicator for Smart Tag Actions is a purple dotted line. If you want to display the Smart Tag button, point to the Smart Tag indicator.

Clicking a Smart Tag Button displays a menu that contains commands relative to the action performed at the location of the smart tag. For example, if you want to add a name in your Publisher document to the Outlook Contacts folder, point to the purple dotted line below the name to display the Smart Tag Actions button. Then, click the Smart Tag Actions button to display the Smart Tag Actions menu. Finally, click Add to Contacts on the Smart Tag Actions menu to display the Contacts dialog box in Outlook.

A Paste Options button will be displayed in the following steps to add a pull quote to the publication and insert text.

To Add a Pull Quote

1

• **With the lower part of page 1 still displayed, click the Design Gallery Object button on the Objects toolbar. If necessary, click the Objects by Category tab.**

Publisher displays the Design Gallery dialog box (Figure 2-54).

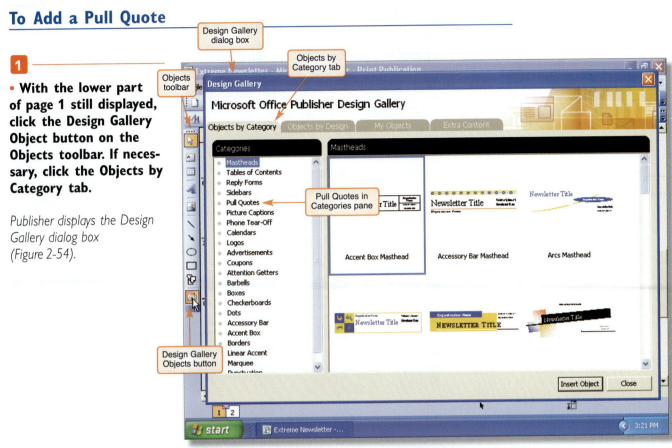

FIGURE 2-54

2

• **Click Pull Quotes in the Categories pane. Scroll to and then click the Punctuation Pull Quote preview shown in Figure 2-55.**

The previews display in alphabetical order in the Pull Quotes pane (Figure 2-55). The Punctuation Pull Quote is selected.

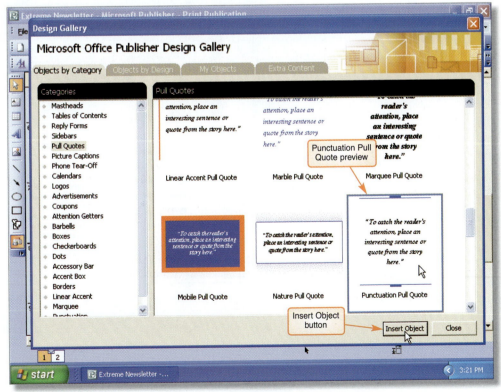

FIGURE 2-55

3

• **Click the Insert Object button.**

The pull quote is inserted in the publication (Figure 2-56).

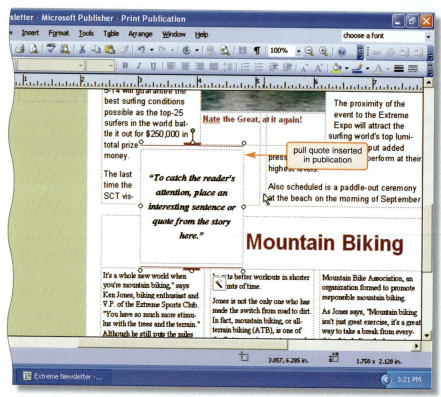

FIGURE 2-56

4

• **Drag the pull quote to the left margin below the Special points of interest sidebar and to the left of the Mountain Biking story.**

The pull quote is dragged to the left of the story (Figure 2-57).

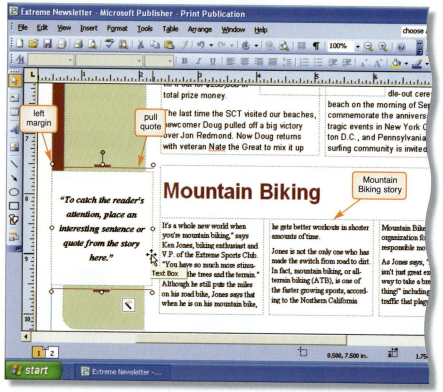

FIGURE 2-57

5

• **In the third column of the Mountain Biking story, select the quotation text as shown in Figure 2-58.**

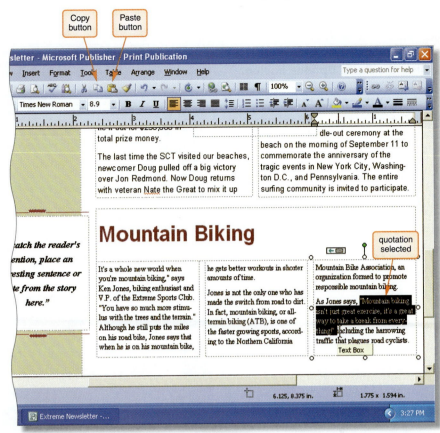

FIGURE 2-58

6

• **Click the Copy button on the Standard toolbar.**

• **Click the placeholder text in the pull quote to select it.**

• **Click the Paste button on the Standard toolbar.**

The new text replaces the placeholder text in the pull quote (Figure 2-59). The Paste Options button also is displayed.

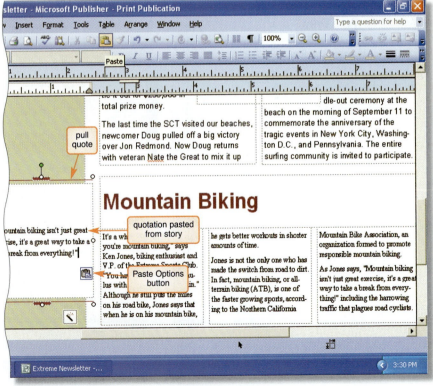

FIGURE 2-59

Microsoft Office
Publisher 2003

7

• **Click the Paste Options button.**

The Paste Options menu is displayed (Figure 2-60). The menu includes options to keep the source, or original, formatting, or to keep the text only and let the destination format preside.

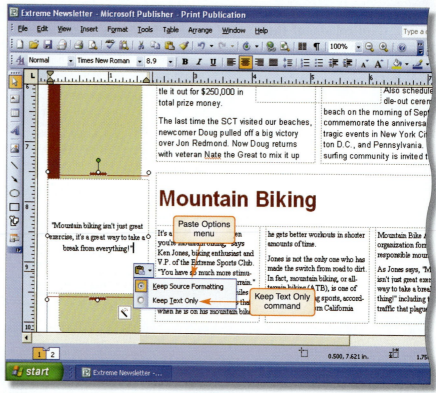

FIGURE 2-60

8

• **Click Keep Text Only.**

The font changes to match the pull quote's original, or source, formatting (Figure 2-61).

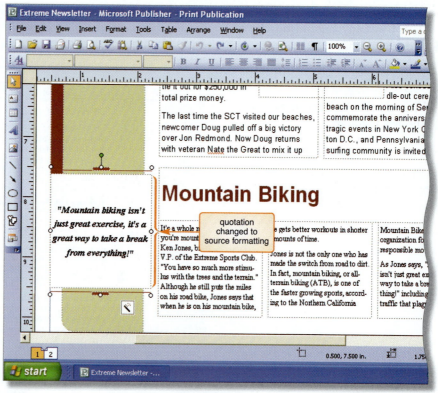

FIGURE 2-61

Other Ways

1. On Insert menu click Design Gallery Object

The Paste Options button, which enables you to specify the formatting of pasted text, appears at the bottom corner of your text as you paste it. You can choose not to display the Paste Options button by clicking Tools on the menu bar, clicking Options, and then clicking Edit.

Adding Page Numbers to the Master Page

Page numbering on a two-page newsletter probably is not as important as it is for longer publications. Many readers, however, reference articles and points by page numbers. Part of the design process is to provide a consistent look and feel to the layout, so page numbers can furnish a reference for the organization in designing future, perhaps longer, newsletters. Additionally, certain features always may appear on specific pages. Placing page numbers in prominent locations, or using fancy fonts and colors, can make page numbers a design element in and of themselves.

The next steps in this project describe how to add page numbers in the lower-left corner of each page of the newsletter by inserting a page number on the publication's master page. The **master page** is a blank sheet located behind your publication where you place objects that will display on every page, such as headers and footers, page numbers, and logos. Most publication objects, such as text and graphics, actually lie in front of the master page, allowing the format to display from behind. You can insert and edit these recurring objects in two ways. If you want an object to display on every page, you can move it to the master page, or you can go to master page view and create the object there.

Inserting Page Numbers on the Master Page

The following steps show how to display the master page and then insert the automatic page number so it will be displayed on all pages.

To Display the Master Page and Insert Automatic Page Numbering

1

• **Click View on the menu bar.**

Publisher displays the View menu (Figure 2-62).

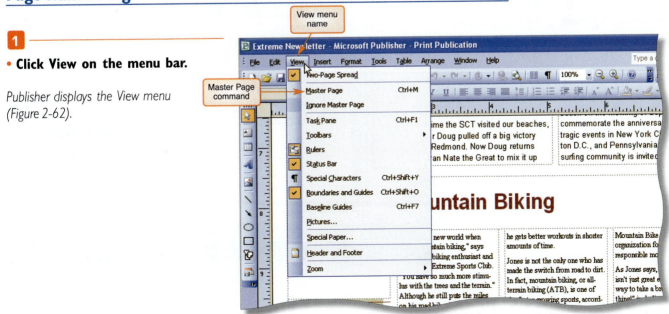

FIGURE 2-62

2

• **Click Master Page.**

• **When the master page is displayed, click Insert on the menu bar.**

The master page displays as a blank page on which you may insert objects that will appear on all pages of the publication (Figure 2-63). Publisher also displays the Edit Master Pages toolbar.

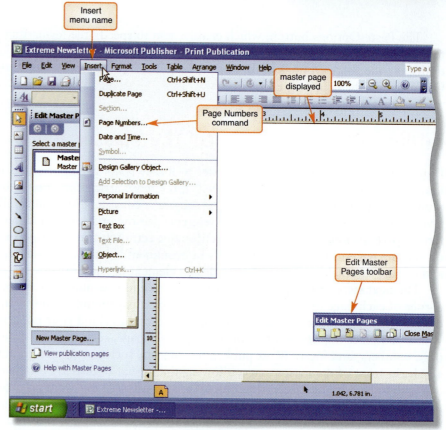

FIGURE 2-63

3

• **Click Page Numbers on the Insert menu. When the Page Numbers dialog box is displayed, click the Position box arrow and then click Bottom of page (Footer) in the list.**

The Page Numbers dialog box offers choices for Position, Alignment, and whether or not to show the page number on the first page (Figure 2-64).

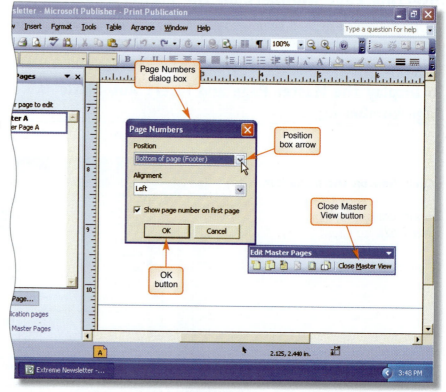

FIGURE 2-64

4

- **Click the OK button in the Page Numbers dialog box.**
- **Click the Close Master View button in the Edit Master Pages toolbar.**

The page number is placed in the publication (Figure 2-65). Publisher automatically reflects the current page number. The Apply Master Page task pane is displayed as well, which allows you to specify a range of pages or change master pages for facing pages.

5

- **Click the Close button in the Apply Master Page task pane.**

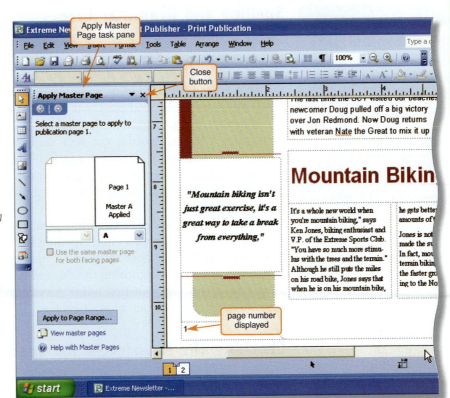

FIGURE 2-65

Logical choices for objects on a master page might include personal information, dates, times, headers and footers, and page numbers. Options on the Insert menu allow you to insert dates and times derived from the operating system that will update automatically when the publication is edited or printed.

Many newsletters have a master page texture or pattern on each page. As with watermarks, a master page pattern can provide additional interest and contrast. By creating a text box on the master page, you can use fill colors or gradient patterns from the color scheme to add interest and individuality to your newsletter.

If an object does not display when you insert it on the master page, it does not mean that it is gone; rather, it may be behind another object in the foreground. Typically, items in the foreground, or in the front, which partially cover an item in the master page, need to be transparent. The combination keystrokes of CTRL+T will convert selected objects into transparent ones. Should you change your mind, CTRL+T is a toggle; press it again to turn off transparency and make the object opaque again.

Other Ways

1. Click Insert Page Numbers button on Header and Footer toolbar

More About

Backgrounds on the Master Page

If you want the master page background not to display on a given page, such as a page number text box on page 1, click Ignore Master Page on the View menu.

Checking a Newsletter for Errors

The final phase of the design process is a synthesis involving editing, proofreading, and publishing. Publisher offers several methods to check for errors in your newsletter. None of these methods is a replacement for careful reading and proofreading. Similar to the spell checking programs in word processing applications, Publisher looks for misspelled words, grammatically incorrect sentences, punctuation problems, and mechanical errors in text boxes.

More About

Spelling Options

On the Tools menu, the Spelling command allows you to access Spelling Options for use in checking the spelling of the publication. Included in the Spelling Options dialog box are check boxes for checking the spelling as you type, flagging repeated words, and ignoring words in upper-case, among other options.

Spelling and Grammar Errors

As you type text in a text box, Publisher checks your typing for possible spelling and grammar errors. Recall that if a typed word is not in the dictionary, a red wavy underline is displayed below it. Likewise, if typed text contains possible grammar errors, a green wavy underline is displayed below the text. You can check the entire newsletter for spelling and grammar errors at once or as you are typing.

When a word is flagged with a red wavy underline, it is not in Publisher's dictionary. A flagged word is not necessarily misspelled, as many names, abbreviations, and specialized terms are not in Publisher's main dictionary. In these cases, instruct Publisher to ignore the flagged word. To display a list of suggested corrections for a flagged word, right-click it, and then click a replacement word on the shortcut menu.

When using imported text, as in the newsletter, it may be easier to check all the spelling at once. Publisher's check spelling feature looks through the selected text box for errors. Once errors are found, Publisher offers suggestions and provides the choice of correcting or ignoring the flagged word. If you are creating this project on a personal computer, your text boxes may contain different misspelled words, depending on the accuracy of your typing.

Checking the Newsletter for Spelling and Grammar Errors

The Spelling command is accessed through the Tools menu. The following steps illustrate how to check your newsletter for spelling and grammar errors. You may encounter spelling mistakes you have made while typing. Choose to correct those errors as necessary. The following steps check the newsletter for spelling and grammar errors.

To Check the Newsletter for Spelling and Grammar Errors

1

• **With page 1 of the Extreme Newsletter still displayed, click the Championship Surfing story text box. Click the Spelling button on the Standard toolbar.**

The Check Spelling dialog box is displayed (Figure 2-66). Publisher flags the name, Nate. Because this is a personal name and spelled correctly, you will ignore this flag.

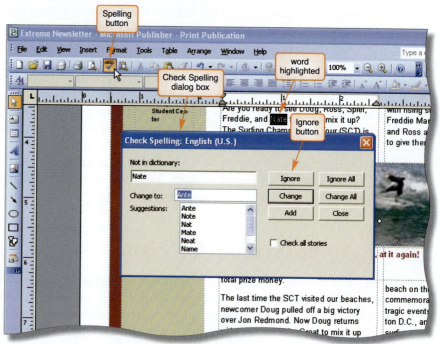

FIGURE 2-66

2

• **Click the Ignore button. Publisher continues to check the story. If you have other errors, correct them using the Check Spelling dialog box.**

Publisher did not find any more errors in the book review article. It displays a dialog box that asks if you want to check the rest of the publication (Figure 2-67).

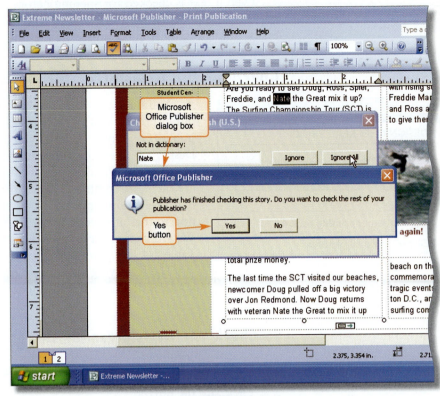

FIGURE 2-67

3

• **Click the Yes button. As Publisher displays more personal names, choose to ignore them. If you have other errors, choose the appropriate measure to fix or ignore them. When the check spelling process is complete, a dialog box will be displayed.**

Publisher displays a dialog box informing you that the process is complete (Figure 2-68).

4

• **Click the OK button.**

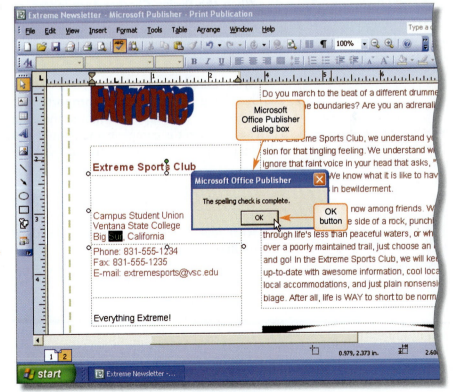

FIGURE 2-68

Other Ways

1. On Tools menu point to Spelling, click Spelling on Spelling submenu

Even if text is checked for spelling before it is imported, Publisher flags words, phrases, and punctuation not found in its dictionary. The process is worth the time it takes, but again, there is no substitute for proofreading the text yourself.

Checking the Newsletter for Design Errors

You now are ready to check the newsletter for design errors as you did in Project 1. The Design Checker can check single pages or entire publications for a specific type of error or all types of errors. The Design Checker looks for errors related to design issues and object interaction, providing comments and correction choices. Design errors are the most common type of problem when submitting a publication to a professional printer. In a later project, you will learn that, in addition to the interactive Design Checker, Publisher's Pack and Go Wizard checks for errors related to embedded fonts and graphics. Table 2-4 lists errors detected by the Design Checker.

The following steps show how to have Publisher check for all kinds of design errors throughout the newsletter.

Table 2-4   Design Checker Errors

DESIGN CHECKER ERRORS
Empty frames
Covered objects
Text in overflow area
Objects in nonprinting region
Disproportional pictures
Spacing between sentences

To Check the Newsletter for Design Errors

1 Click Tools on the menu bar and then click Design Checker.

2 Click the OK button.

3 If the Design Checker finds errors, choose to fix or ignore them as necessary. When the Design Checker terminates, click the OK button.

If you have made errors in placing graphics or WordArt objects, you may have to accept or ignore other Design Checker recommendations.

If you resized any graphic in the newsletter, Publisher's Design Checker will warn you that the graphic may not be proportionally correct. At that time, you may choose to resize the graphic or ignore the change.

The newsletter is complete and should be saved again before printing. The following step saves the newsletter using the same file name.

To Save an Existing Newsletter Using the Same File Name

1 With your floppy disk in drive A, click the Save button on the Standard toolbar.

Publisher saves the publication using the same file name, Extreme Newsletter, on the floppy disk in drive A.

More About

Hyphenation

You can change the number of hyphens that are added automatically to the text to achieve a more even right edge, to reduce white gaps in the text, or the number of hyphens and short syllables. On the Tools menu, point to Language, and then click Hyphenation. To achieve a different effect, change the number in the Hyphenation zone in one of the following ways: for a more even right edge and fewer white gaps in the text, reduce the number; or for fewer hyphens and fewer short syllables before or after hyphens, increase the number.

Printing a Two-Sided Page

Printing the two pages of the newsletter back to back is a process that is highly dependent upon the printer. Some printers can perform duplex printing, which prints both sides before ejecting the paper, while other printers require the user to reload the paper manually. If you are attached to a single-user printer, you must check the printer's documentation to see if it supports double-sided printing. If you are connected to a network printer, you probably will need to feed the paper through a second time manually.

The following steps illustrate how to print the first page and then manually feed the page through a second time. Adjust the steps as necessary for your printer.

To Print a Two-Sided Page

1

• **If necessary, click the Page 1 icon on the Page Navigation Control. Ready the printer according to the printer instructions. Click File on the menu bar and then click Print. When the Print dialog box displays, click Current page in the Print range area.**

The Print dialog box is displayed (Figure 2-69). Your dialog box may differ.

2

• **Click the OK button. When printing is complete, retrieve the printout.**

The printed newsletter is shown in Figures 2-1a and 2-1b on page PUB 67. Publications with many graphics and fonts take longer to print than plain text documents.

3

• **After retrieving the printout, wait a few seconds for it to dry. Reinsert the printout in the manual tray of the printer; usually blank side down, top first. Click the Page 2 icon on the Page Navigation Control. Click File on the menu bar and then click Print. When the Print dialog box is displayed, repeat Steps 1 and 2 to print page 2 of the newsletter.**

Retrieve the printout from the printer.

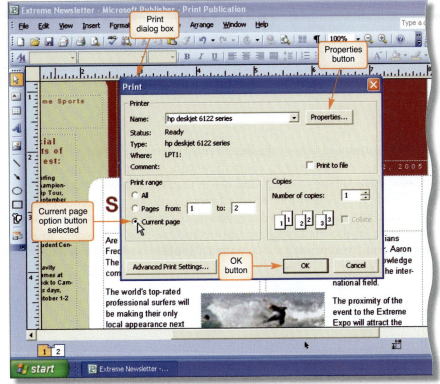

FIGURE 2-69

Other Ways

1. Press CTRL+P

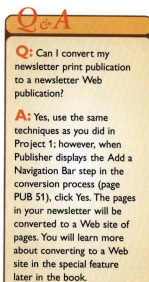

More About

Network Printing

If your network printer seems to lock up or prints only part of the page, it may not have enough memory to store the large print files that Publisher creates. Consider one of the following solutions: wait until other print jobs are complete; print in black and white instead of color; print lower-resolution graphics; or finally, print the text only and then send the paper through a second time for the graphics. The memory setting on your printer driver influences your printer's ability to reproduce your publication. If your printer driver's memory setting is too low, the publication may not appear complete when printed.

If you have an Options button, a Properties button, or an Advanced Print Settings button in your Print dialog box (Figure 2-69 on the previous page), you may be able to duplex print. Check your printer documentation, or click the button for more information.

If you are unsure how to load the paper, you can run a test page through the printer. Mark an X in the upper-right corner of a blank sheet and then insert the sheet into the printer, noting where the X is. If your printer has a Manual Feed button or Paper Source list, be sure to click Manual. Print the first page. Note where the X is in relation to the printed page and turn the paper over to print the other side accordingly. In a later project, you will learn more about types of paper best suited for printing on both sides, as well as how to prepare a publication for a printing service.

The newsletter is now complete. The following step quits Publisher.

To Quit Publisher

1 **Click the Close button on Publisher's title bar.**

Publisher closes, and the Windows desktop is displayed.

Project Summary

Project 2 introduced you to the design process and the newsletter medium. Using the Banded Newsletter template, you learned how to edit a masthead, import text from other sources, and add appropriate graphics. You also learned how to insert and delete pages in a newsletter and incorporate personal information components. With WordArt, you inserted a fancy headline with special text effects. You imported graphics and edited captions. Using the Design Gallery, you inserted an attention getter. After you added page numbers to the master page, you used the check spelling feature and the Design Checker to identify spelling, grammar, and design errors. Finally, you printed the newsletter double-sided and saved it on a floppy disk.

Q&A

Q: Can I convert my newsletter print publication to a newsletter Web publication?

A: Yes, use the same techniques as you did in Project 1; however, when Publisher displays the Add a Navigation Bar step in the conversion process (page PUB 51), click Yes. The pages in your newsletter will be converted to a Web site of pages. You will learn more about converting to a Web site in the special feature later in the book.

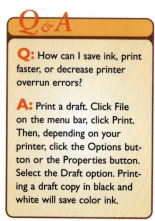

Q&A

Q: How can I save ink, print faster, or decrease printer overrun errors?

A: Print a draft. Click File on the menu bar, click Print. Then, depending on your printer, click the Options button or the Properties button. Select the Draft option. Printing a draft copy in black and white will save color ink.

More About

Folders

You can store publications in any folder on your hard disk, floppy disk, or on a network, but it is a good practice to store them together in a folder that you can find easily. The preset storage location for publications on a new installation of Publisher is in a folder named My Documents. My Documents can serve as a place to store the publications you use frequently. If you work with many different types of documents, you can organize them in subfolders within My Documents.

What You Should Know

Having completed this project, you now should be able to perform the tasks below. The tasks are listed in the same order they were presented in this project. For a list of the buttons, menus, toolbars, and commands introduced in this project, see the Quick Reference Summary at the back of this book and refer to the Page Number column.

1. Start Publisher   (PUB 68)
2. Choose a Newsletter Template and Change Options   (PUB 70)
3. Change and Delete Pages in a Newsletter (PUB 73)
4. Edit the Masthead   (PUB 76)
5. Edit a Headline and Import a Text File (PUB 78)
6. Import More Text   (PUB 81)
7. Import the Back Page Story   (PUB 82)
8. Save an Intermediate Copy of the Newsletter (PUB 83)
9. Edit Personal Information Components (PUB 84)
10. Edit a Story Using Word   (PUB 86)
11. Display Overflow Text   (PUB 89)
12. Edit the Attention Getter Design   (PUB 90)
13. Edit the Style   (PUB 92)
14. Delete the Logo   (PUB 93)
15. Insert a WordArt Object in the Newsletter (PUB 95)
16. Import Graphics and Edit the Caption   (PUB 99)
17. Import a Graphic on Page 1   (PUB 101)
18. Edit a Sidebar   (PUB 103)
19. Delete the Sidebar   (PUB 104)
20. Add a Pull Quote   (PUB 107)
21. Display the Master Page and Insert Automatic Page Numbering   (PUB 111)
22. Check the Newsletter for Spelling and Grammar Errors   (PUB 114)
23. Check the Newsletter for Design Errors (PUB 116)
24. Save an Existing Newsletter Using the Same File Name   (PUB 116)
25. Print a Two-Sided Page   (PUB 117)
26. Quit Publisher   (PUB 118)

Learn It Online

Instructions: To complete the Learn It Online exercises, start your browser, click the Address bar, and then enter the Web address scsite.com/pub2003/learn. When the Publisher 2003 Learn It Online page is displayed, follow the instructions in the exercises below. Each exercise has instructions for printing your results, either for your own records or for submission to your instructor.

1 Project Reinforcement TF, MC, and SA

Below Publisher Project 2, click the Project Reinforcement link. Print the quiz by clicking Print on the File menu for each page. Answer each question.

2 Flash Cards

Below Publisher Project 2, click the Flash Cards link and read the instructions. Type 20 (or a number specified by your instructor) in the Number of playing cards text box, type your name in the Enter your Name text box, and then click the Flip Card button. When the flash card is displayed, read the question and then click the ANSWER box arrow to select an answer. Flip through Flash Cards. If your score is 15 (75%) correct or greater, click Print on the File menu to print your results. If your score is less than 15 (75%) correct, then redo this exercise by clicking the Replay button.

3 Practice Test

Below Publisher Project 2, click the Practice Test link. Answer each question, enter your first and last name at the bottom of the page, and then click the Grade Test button. When the graded practice test is displayed on your screen, click Print on the File menu to print a hard copy. Continue to take practice tests until you score 80% or better.

4 Who Wants To Be a Computer Genius?

Below Publisher Project 2, click the Computer Genius link. Read the instructions, enter your first and last name at the bottom of the page, and then click the PLAY button. When your score is displayed, click the PRINT RESULTS link to print a hard copy.

5 Wheel of Terms

Below Publisher Project 2, click the Wheel of Terms link. Read the instructions, and then enter your first and last name and your school name. Click the PLAY button. When your score is displayed, right-click the score and then click Print on the shortcut menu to print a hard copy.

6 Crossword Puzzle Challenge

Below Publisher Project 2, click the Crossword Puzzle Challenge link. Read the instructions, and then enter your first and last name. Click the SUBMIT button. Work the crossword puzzle. When you are finished, click the Submit button. When the crossword puzzle is redisplayed, click the Print Puzzle button to print a hard copy.

7 Tips and Tricks

Below Publisher Project 2, click the Tips and Tricks link. Click a topic that pertains to Project 2. Right-click the information and then click Print on the shortcut menu. Construct a brief example of what the information relates to in Publisher to confirm you understand how to use the tip or trick.

8 Newsgroups

Below Publisher Project 2, click the Newsgroups link. Click a topic that pertains to Project 2. Print three comments.

9 Expanding Your Horizons

Below Publisher Project 2, click the Expanding Your Horizons link. Click a topic that pertains to Project 2. Print the information. Construct a brief example of what the information relates to in Publisher to confirm you understand the contents of the article.

10 Search Sleuth

Below Publisher Project 2, click the Search Sleuth link. To search for a term that pertains to this project, select a term below the Project 2 title and then use the Google search engine at google.com (or any major search engine) to display and print two Web pages that present information on the term.

11 Publisher Online Training

Below Publisher Project 2, click the Publisher Online Training link. When your browser displays the Microsoft Office Online Web page, click the Publisher link. Click one of the Publisher courses that covers one or more of the objectives listed at the beginning of the project on page PUB 66. Print the first page of the course before stepping through it.

12 Office Marketplace

Below Publisher Project 2, click the Office Marketplace link. When your browser displays the Microsoft Office Online Web page, click the Office Marketplace link. Click a topic that relates to Publisher. Print the first page.

Apply Your Knowledge

1 Editing a School Newsletter

Instructions: Start Publisher. Open the publication, Apply 2-1 School Newsletter, on the Data Disk. See the inside back cover of this book for instruction for downloading the Data Disk or see your instructor for information about accessing files required in this book.

The publication on the Data Disk is a newsletter from Jefferson Metro College, home of the Patriots. The newsletter contains some template text, a graphic that needs to be replaced, and sidebars that need to be edited. You are to change the following on page 1 of the newsletter: replace the template text, change the newsletter title, edit and move the graphic, delete a sidebar, and insert a pull quote. On page 2, you are to change the attention getter text, and edit the back page story and headline.

The edited page 1 is displayed in Figure 2-70.

FIGURE 2-70

(continued)

Apply Your Knowledge

Editing a School Newsletter *(continued)*

Perform the following tasks.

1. On page 1, highlight the text The Weekly Patriot in the masthead. Type `The Patriot Journal` to replace the text. In the upper-right corner of Page 1, replace the Newsletter Date placeholder text with your current date.

2. In the lower-left of the page, right-click the sidebar titled, Inside this Issue. Click Delete Object on the shortcut menu.

3. Click the Design Gallery Object button on the Objects toolbar and then click Pull Quotes in the Categories list. Insert the Straight Edge Pull Quote. Drag it to the empty space left by the deleted sidebar. With the pull quote still selected, press CTRL+T to make it transparent.

4. Select and copy the next to the last sentence of the article titled, Where to Live? Next, click the pull quote text to select it. Paste the sentence into the pull quote. When the Smart Tag displays, click the Paste Options button and then click Keep Text Only on the Paste Options menu.

5. Delete the picture of the student. Use the Clip Art task pane to find a different picture of students. Drag the picture to the end of the article.

6. Drag a corner handle to resize the picture proportionally until it fits in the third column.

7. Click the Organization Name Text Box located below the masthead. Replace the business name with the name of your school or business.

8. Edit the Special Points of Interest bullets to match those in Figure 2-70 on the previous page.

9. Click page 2 in the Page Navigation Control. Use the Edit menu to delete pages 2 and 3.

10. On the back page, click the attention getter text box at the top of the page. Zoom as necessary. Use your school or business Web page address (URL) in the attention getter.

11. Click the back page story in the lower part of page 2. On the Edit menu, click Edit Story in Microsoft Word. In the Word window, type a few paragraphs describing your first day at school in the current term or your first day on the job. When you are done, close the Word window. In Publisher, change the back page story headline to match your story.

12. Check your publication for spelling errors. Correct any errors.

13. Click File on the menu bar and then click Save As. Save the publication using Apply 2-1 School Newsletter Revised as the file name. Print the revised newsletter using double-sided printing.

In the Lab

1 Creating a Masthead

Problem: The human resources department of Nutshell and Associates has asked you to create a masthead for its newsletter. Mr. Nutshell wants you to incorporate the company logo and colors in the masthead.

Instructions: Perform the following tasks to create the masthead shown in Figure 2-71.

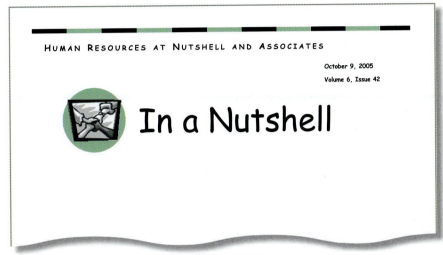

HUMAN RESOURCES AT NUTSHELL AND ASSOCIATES

October 9, 2005

Volume 6, Issue 42

In a Nutshell

FIGURE 2-71

1. Start Publisher. From the New Publication task pane, click Blank Print Publication. Close the Publication Designs task pane.
2. Click the Design Gallery Object button on the Objects toolbar. When the Design Gallery dialog box is displayed, click the Voyage Masthead and then click the Insert Object button.
3. When the masthead is inserted in the page layout, drag it to the top of the blank page.
4. Edit the text boxes to match Figure 2-71.
5. Double-click the star graphic to the left of the title. Using the Clip Art task pane, find a clip related to teamwork. Do not close the Clip Art task pane.
6. On the task pane title bar, click the Other Task Panes button and click Color Schemes in the list. Click Sagebrush in the Apply a Color Scheme list. Click Font Schemes in the task pane and then click Casual in the Apply a Font Scheme list.
7. Use the Design Checker to correct any errors in the publication.
8. Save the publication on your floppy disk using the file name, Lab 2-1 Nutshell Masthead.
9. Print a copy of the masthead.

In the Lab

2 Creating a Special-Purpose Newsletter

Problem: You are leader of a scout group for elementary school children. You thought the scouts and their parents might find a monthly newsletter interesting and informative. The scouts could write the articles concerning happenings in the troop, and you could include dates of future events and projects (Figure 2-72a). In addition, you would like to include a monthly feature called "Caught Being Good," a list of scouts who have gone out of their way to do something good and caring (Figure 2-72b). Using Publisher's Kid Stuff Newsletter template, create a two-page, double-sided newsletter with columns.

The articles for the two front page stories are included on the Data Disk that accompanies this book.

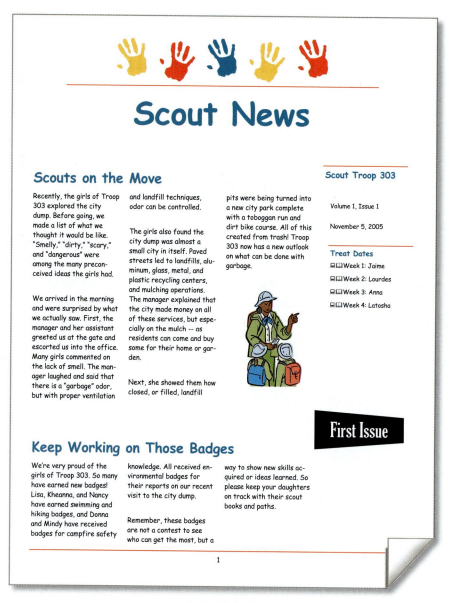

Scout News

Scouts on the Move

Recently, the girls of Troop 303 explored the city dump. Before going, we made a list of what we thought it would be like. "Smelly," "dirty," "scary," and "dangerous" were among the many preconceived ideas the girls had.

We arrived in the morning and were surprised by what we actually saw. First, the manager and her assistant greeted us at the gate and escorted us into the office. Many girls commented on the lack of smell. The manager laughed and said that there is a "garbage" odor, but with proper ventilation and landfill techniques, odor can be controlled.

The girls also found the city dump was almost a small city in itself. Paved streets led to landfills, aluminum, glass, metal, and plastic recycling centers, and mulching operations. The manager explained that the city made money on all of these services, but especially on the mulch -- as residents can come and buy some for their home or garden.

Next, she showed them how closed, or filled, landfill pits were being turned into a new city park complete with a toboggan run and dirt bike course. All of this created from trash! Troop 303 now has a new outlook on what can be done with garbage.

Scout Troop 303

Volume 1, Issue 1

November 5, 2005

Treat Dates

Week 1: Jaime

Week 2: Lourdes

Week 3: Anna

Week 4: Latosha

First Issue

Keep Working on Those Badges

We're very proud of the girls of Troop 303. So many have earned new badges! Lisa, Kheanna, and Nancy have earned swimming and hiking badges, and Donna and Mindy have received badges for campfire safety knowledge. All received environmental badges for their reports on our recent visit to the city dump.

Remember, these badges are not a contest to see who can get the most, but a way to show new skills acquired or ideas learned. So please keep your daughters on track with their scout books and paths.

1

FIGURE 2-72a

In the Lab

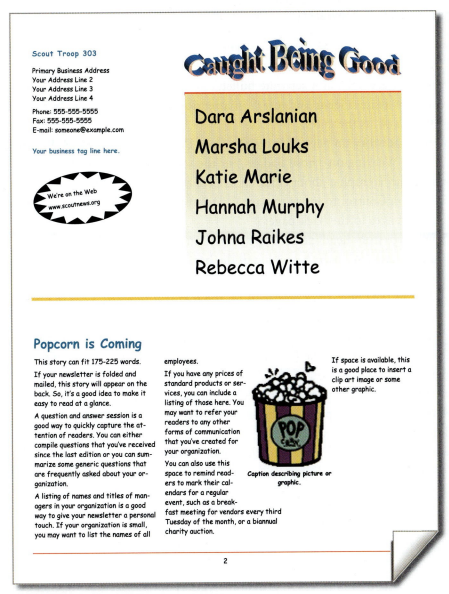

FIGURE 2-72b

Instructions: Perform the following tasks.

1. Start Publisher. In the New Publication task pane, click Publications for Print.
2. Click Newsletters in the list. Select the Kid Stuff Newsletter. Choose an appropriate color and font scheme in the task pane.
3. Make the following changes on page 1:
   a. Change the newsletter title to Scout News.
   b. Change the Lead Story Headline to Scouts on the Move.
   c. Change the Secondary Story Headline to Keep Working on Those Badges!
   d. Change the Organization name to Scout Troop 303.
   e. Change the date to your current date.

(continued)

Creating a Special-Purpose Newsletter *(continued)*

    f. In the bulleted list sidebar, change the title to `Treat Dates` and then in the list, type the following: `Week 1: Jaime, Week 2: Lourdes, Week 3: Anna, Week 4: Latosha,` pressing the ENTER key after each name so that each entry has a separate bullet.

    g. Delete the Inside this Issue sidebar and insert an attention getter in its place. In the attention getter text box, type `First Issue` as the entry.

4. Select the text in the lead story on page 1. From the Data Disk, import the story, Scouts on the Move. Import the story, Keep Working on Those Badges, for the secondary story on page 1.

5. Replace the graphic with a graphic about children. Delete the caption.

6. Use the Page Navigation Control to move to page 2. Delete pages 2 and 3.

7. Make the following changes to the back page:

    a. Change the back page story headline to, Popcorn is Coming.

    b. Use a keyword to locate and insert a graphic in the back page story about popcorn.

    c. Delete the logo on the back page.

    d. Click the text box in the upper-right corner. With the text still selected, type the following names: `Dara Arslanian, Marsha Louks, Katie Marie, Hannah Murphy, Johna Raikes, Rebecca Witte`, pressing the ENTER key after each to place each name on a separate line. Right-click the text box. On the shortcut menu, point to Change Text. On the Change Text submenu, point to AutoFit Text and then click Best Fit on the AutoFit Text submenu.

    e. Add a WordArt shape with the text, Caught Being Good, positioned above the list.

8. View the master page and insert a page number in the lower center of each page.

9. Spell check and design check the newsletter.

10. Save the newsletter on a floppy disk using the file name, Lab 2-2 Scout Newsletter, and print a copy.

3 Looking at Publisher's Newsletter Choices

Problem: You work in the public relations department of an advertising firm. Your supervisor wants to publish a weekly newsletter for customers and potential clients, but would like to see some samples first. You decide to use Publisher's newsletter templates to give him a variety from which he may choose.

Instructions: Using the techniques presented in this project, access the New Publication task pane, and choose five different newsletter templates. Choose templates you have not used before. Below are some general guidelines for each template.

1. Select the template and choose font and color schemes for each. Make a note of each scheme you choose.

2. Print page 1 of each newsletter. Write on the back the schemes you chose.

3. Identify the parts of the newsletter on the printout. Label things such as the masthead, design set, color scheme, personal information components, and all objects.

4. Pick your favorite of the five newsletters. For that one, print all the pages and identify any different components or objects. If possible, print double-sided.

5. Convert your favorite to a Web publication and print it. Note the differences between the print publication and the Web publication.

6. Let your instructor look at all the printouts.

Cases and Places

The difficulty of these case studies varies:
■ are the least difficult and ■■ are more difficult. The last exercise is a group exercise.

1 ■ Use the Newsletter template titled Bubbles Newsletter to create a letterhead for your personal use. Delete all the pages except page 1. Delete all the objects on page 1 except the masthead and the line graphic across the bottom. Put your name in the Newsletter Title and your address and telephone number in the volume and date text boxes.

2 ■ Use the Newsletter Template titled Voyage Newsletter, to create a two-page newsletter for the Seniors Abroad Club. This local club of senior citizens gets together to take group trips. For the newsletter title, type We're on the Road, and place today's date in the masthead. Include an article headline for the lead story, which concerns the club's most recent trip to Ontario (you may use the default text), and a secondary article headline that tells how to pack light for Europe. Add a list of dates for upcoming trips to Orlando, Paris, and Tokyo in the Special Points of Interest sidebar. Replace the graphics with suitable pictures from Publisher's clip art.

3 ■ Using Table 2-2 on page PUB 69 as an example, make a chart describing the newsletter created in Project 2. Describe the purpose, audience, how you gathered data, the plan for printing, layout, and synthesis.

4 ■■ Ask a local civic group for a sample of its newsletter. Try to recreate its style and format using a blank publication page in Publisher. Use Publisher's Design Gallery and personal information sets to customize the newsletter. Print your final product and compare the two.

5 ■■ Offer to create a newsletter for a department on campus or for a department within your company. Ask others to supply the content for the stories in a word processing file. Try to obtain pictures and graphics from the department. Choose colors and fonts that match the style of the office. Ask the department if they already have a logo. If so, try to obtain an electronic copy of the logo and use it in the newsletter. Use at least one example of a pull quote, WordArt, and an attention getter.

6 ■■ Create a blank print publication with a large text box that fills the page. Using the Edit Story in Microsoft Word feature, type an assignment, such as an essay or short report, for one of your classes. Print a copy. On the back, write three things you found easier to do in Publisher and three things you found easier to do in Word.

Cases and Places

7 ■■ **Working Together** Many clubs and organizations publish their newsletters on the Web. Browse the Web and look for examples of newsletters. Note how many pages, graphics, and articles they use. Look at their mastheads and logos. Choose a newsletter that you think displays good desktop publishing practices. Print the newsletter or copy its Web address to distribute to each team member. Discuss the newsletters and note which parts were most effective. Each member then independently should use the most effective newsletter ideas, together with the techniques presented in this project, to create a newsletter that would be likely to catch a reader's eye. Use a Publisher Newsletter template to create a newsletter for a club or organization with which you are affiliated. Include at least three articles, one sidebar or pull quote, a masthead, and several graphics. Be sure to check the spelling and run the Design Checker. As a group, critique each newsletter and have each member redesign his or her newsletter based on the group's recommendations. Hand in printouts of each team member's original and final newsletter.

Publishing a Tri-Fold Brochure

PROJECT

3

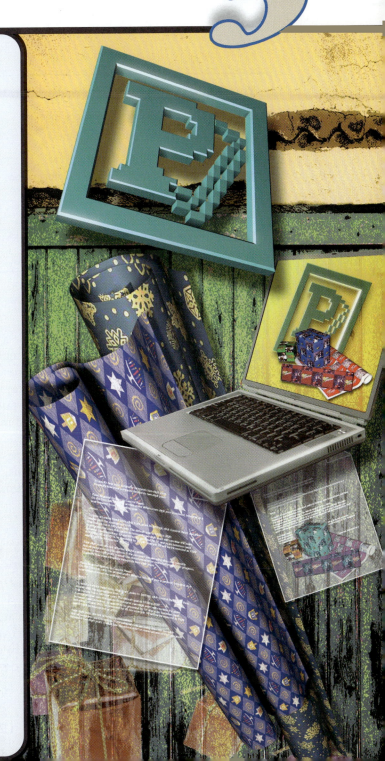

CASE PERSPECTIVE

The College Computer Club at Oak Park College (OPC) was formed in the early 1980s by a few students from the math and science departments. Now it boasts the largest membership on campus with 80 members from all departments. As both an educational and service organization, the club's objectives include providing an opportunity for its members and the OPC community to learn more about the use of computers and the Web; providing service to the community; and enhancing the image of OPC. The club sponsors and maintains Web pages for organizations and individuals desiring to publish pages on its server. It is the club's intent to provide service primarily to students, faculty, other organizations, and members of the OPC community, thus providing a wider opportunity to have a Web presence or obtain Web publishing experience.

The College Computer Club is sponsoring a fund-raiser for its scholarship fund. Club members voted to sell holiday wrapping paper and trim, contracting with a local supply company. To keep costs down and showcase the desktop publishing skills of some of its members, the club membership has decided to create its own brochures. As a member of the fund-raising committee, you have volunteered to design the brochure. The president of the club would like to see a sample at the first fall meeting.

The brochure should contain images and text that describe the gift wrap and trim items, information about the club, and an order form. You use a tri-fold brochure template in Publisher and customize it with your club's contact information and logo.

As you read through this project, you will learn how to use Publisher to create, save, and print a brochure that includes text, graphics, personal information, a logo, and an order form.

MICROSOFT
Office Publisher 2003

Publishing a Tri-Fold Brochure

PROJECT

Objectives

You will have mastered the material in this project when you can:

- Discuss advantages of the brochure medium
- Use the Brochure Options task pane
- Create a custom color scheme
- Edit placeholder text and personal information components
- Format fonts and paragraphs
- Describe the use of photographs versus images
- Insert a photograph from a file
- Create a logo from scratch using AutoShapes
- Create a composite object in the scratch area
- Group and ungroup objects
- Choose appropriate printing services, paper, and color libraries
- Prepare a publication for outside printing
- Use the Pack and Go Wizard

Introduction

Whether you want to advertise a service, event, or product, or merely want to inform the public about a current topic of interest, brochures are a popular type of promotional publication. A brochure, or pamphlet, usually is a high-quality document with lots of color and graphics, created for advertising purposes. Businesses that may not be able to reach potential clientele effectively through traditional advertising, such as newspapers and radio, can create a long-lasting advertisement with a well-designed brochure.

Brochures come in all shapes and sizes. Colleges and universities produce brochures about their programs. The travel industry uses brochures to entice tourists. Service industries and manufacturers display their products using this visual, hands-on medium.

Project Three — The Holiday Trim Brochure

Project 3 uses Publisher to illustrate the production of the two-page, tri-fold brochure shown in Figure 3-1. The brochure informs the public about a fund-raiser sponsored by a computer club at the local college. Each side of the brochure has three panels. Page 1 (Figure 3-1a) contains the front and back panels, as well as the inside fold. Page 2 (Figure 3-1b) contains a three-panel display that, when opened completely, provides the reader with more details about the items for sale and an order form.

inside fold

back panel

front panel

About the College Computer Club

College Computer Club

**H o l i d a y
T r i m**

The Oak Park College Computer Club is almost as old as personal computers themselves. It was formed in the early 80s, and now boasts the largest club membership on campus with 90 members from all departments.

story

The College Computer Club is an educational and service organization whose objectives include providing an opportunity for its members and the OPC community to learn more about the use of computers and the Web; providing service to the community; and enhancing the image of Oak Park College.

graphic

College Computer Club

Oak Park College
Student Union 1306
127 S. Jordan Avenue
Baring, NJ 08625

Phone: 609-555-9078
Fax: 609-555-9075
E-mail: opc.ccc@opc.edu

logo

image

The College Computer Club is open to all students on campus.

A College Computer Club fund-raising event for the Scholarship Fund

(a) Page 1 of Tri-Fold Brochure

Our Products

Our holiday wrapping paper and trim are provided by the College Fund-raiser Service, an East-Coast supplier providing fund-raising ideas and products for colleges and universities across the nation.

All items are made from the highest-quality paper and foils and are completely guaranteed.

Holiday bundles include everything you need to wrap six large boxes. Regular rolls are 48 by 60 inches. Ask your salesperson to see the samples.

price list

Price List

Holiday Bundle	**$14.00**
2 large rolls, 8 bows, and ribbon	
Birthday Delight	**$8.00**
1 roll, bow, and ribbon	
Evergreen/Winter Scene	**$8.00**
1 roll, bow, and ribbon	
Bright Red or Bright Green	**$6.00**
Large, 8' roll	
Bows Galore	**$6.00**
24 assorted colors and sizes	
Candle Holiday	**$12.00**
2 rolls, 2 bows, and ribbon	
Angels on High	**$6.00**
Large, 8' roll	
That Jolly Ol' Man	**$8.00**
1 roll, bow, and ribbon	

Holiday Bundles

order form

My Holiday Trim Order

Item #	Description	Qty.	Price	Subtotal

Order total:
Tax:
Shipping:
Total:

Name
Address

Phone

Method of Payment
☐ Check
☐ Bill Me
☐ Visa
☐ MasterCard
☐ American Express

Credit Card #   Exp. date

Signature

College Computer Club

Oak Park College
Student Union 1306
127 S. Jordan Avenue
Baring, NJ 08625

Phone: 609-555-9078
Fax: 609-555-9075
E-mail: opc.ccc@opc.edu

(b) Page 2 of Tri-Fold Brochure

FIGURE 3-1

On page 1, the front panel contains shapes, text boxes, and a graphic designed to draw the reader's attention and inform the reader of the intent of the brochure. The back panel, which displays in the middle of page 1, contains the name of the club and school, the address, telephone numbers, and the organization logo. The inside fold, on the left, contains an article about the club, with a colored background and graphic.

The three inside panels on page 2 contain more information about the supplier, a price list, and a form the reader may use to place an order.

The Brochure Medium

More About

Brochures

Many brochures are published regularly on the Web. To look at some samples and for information on brochure content, visit the Publisher 2003 More About Web page (scsite.com/pub2003/more) and then click Brochures.

Brochures are professionally printed on special paper to provide long-lasting documents and to enhance the graphics. The brochure medium is intentionally tactile. Brochures are meant to be touched, carried home, passed along, and looked at, again and again. Newspapers and fliers usually are produced for short-term readership on paper that soon will be thrown away or recycled. Brochures frequently use a heavier stock of paper so they can stand better in a display rack.

The content of a brochure needs to last longer, too. On occasion, the intent of a brochure is to educate, such as a brochure on health issues in a doctor's office. More commonly, though, the intent is to market a product or sell a service. Prices and dated materials that are subject to frequent change affect the usable life of a brochure.

Typically, brochures use a great deal of color, and they include actual photographs instead of drawings or graphic images. Photographs give a sense of realism to a publication and should be used to show people, places, or objects that are real, whereas images or drawings more appropriately are used to convey concepts or ideas.

Many brochures incorporate newspaper features such as columns and a masthead, and the added eye appeal of logos, sidebars, shapes, and graphics. Small brochures are separated into panels and folded. Larger brochures resemble small magazines, with multiple pages and a stapled binding.

Brochures, designed to be in circulation for longer periods as a type of advertising, ordinarily are published in greater quantities and on more expensive paper than newsletters and are, therefore, more costly. The cost, however, is less prohibitive when produced **in-house** using desktop publishing rather than hiring an outside service. The cost per copy sometimes is less than a newsletter, because brochures are produced in mass quantities.

Table 3-1 lists some benefits and advantages of using the brochure medium.

Table 3-1 Benefits and Advantages of Using the Brochure Medium	
AREA	**BENEFITS AND ADVANTAGES**
Exposure	An attention getter in displays
	A take-along document encouraging second looks
	A long-lasting publication due to paper and content
	An easily distributed publication — mass mailings, advertising sites
Information	Give readers an in-depth look at a product or service
	An opportunity to inform in a nonrestrictive environment
	An opportunity for focused feedback using tear-offs and forms
Audience	Interested clientele and retailers
Communication	An effective medium to highlight products and services
	A source of free information to build credibility
	An easier method to disseminate information than a magazine

Besides the intent and content of the brochure, you must consider the shape and size of the page when designing this type of publication. Publisher can incorporate a variety of paper sizes from the standard 8½-by-11-inch to 8½-by-24-inch. You also can design smaller brochures, such as those used as liner notes for CD jewel cases or inserts for videotapes. In addition, you need to think about how the brochure or pamphlet will be folded. Publisher's brochure templates can create three or four panels. Using the page setup options, you may create special folds, such as book or card folds.

Starting Publisher

To start Publisher, Windows must be running. The following steps explain how to start Publisher.

To Start Publisher

1 Click the Start button on the Windows taskbar, point to All Programs on the Start menu, point to Microsoft Office on the All Programs submenu, and then click Microsoft Office Publisher 2003 on the Microsoft Office submenu.

2 If the Publisher window is not maximized, double-click its title bar to maximize it.

3 If Publisher does not display the New Publication task pane, click View on the menu bar and then click Task Pane. If the Publication Designs task pane is displayed, click the Other Task Panes button in the task pane title bar, and then click New Publication.

4 If the Language bar displays, click its Minimize button.

You now are ready to use Publisher's New Publication task pane to create a tri-fold brochure.

More About

Starting Publisher

Microsoft Windows provides many ways to start Publisher. You have been using the All Programs submenu on the Start menu. If you have installed the Office toolbar, you may have a button on your desktop for Publisher. You can right-click the desktop, point to New on the shortcut menu, and then click Microsoft Office Publisher Document. Finally, you can open any Publisher file by double-clicking its icon.

Creating a Tri-Fold Brochure

Publisher-supplied templates use proven design strategies and combinations of objects, which are placed to attract attention and disseminate information effectively. The options for brochures differ from other publications in that they allow you to choose from page sizes, special kinds of forms, and panel/page layout options.

Making Choices in the Brochure Options Task Pane

For the Holiday Trim brochure, you will use the Axis Price List Brochure as a template, making changes to its page size, customer address, sign-up form, color scheme, and font scheme. **Page size** refers to the number of panels in the brochure. The **Customer address** selection offers choices to include or not to include the customer's address in the brochure. **Form** options, which display on page 2 of the brochure, include None, Order form, Response form, and Sign-up form. The **Order form** displays fields for the description of items ordered as well as types of payment information, including blank fields for entering items, quantities, and prices. The **Response form** displays check box choices and fields for comments, and blanks for up to four multiple-choice questions and a comment section. The **Sign-up form** displays check box choices, fields for time and price, as well as payment information.

All three forms are meant to be detached and mailed in as turnaround documents. Each form contains blanks for the name and address of prospective customers or clients. The company not only verifies the marketing power of its brochure, but also is able to create a customer database with the information.

Table 3-2 displays the task pane selections you will make in the following steps.

Table 3-2 Task Pane Selections	
BROCHURE OPTIONS TASK PANE	**SELECTION**
Page size (Panels)	3-panel (default value for Price List Brochures)
Customer address	None
Form	Order form
Color Scheme	Custom
Font Scheme	Modern

To Choose Brochure Options

1

• **Click Publication for Print in the New Publication task pane. Click Brochures in the list, then click Price List. If necessary, click the down scroll arrow in the previews pane until the Axis Price List Brochure preview is visible.**

Publisher displays the New Publication task pane on the left and the previews on the right in the Publisher window (Figure 3-2). The list of previews may display differently on your computer.

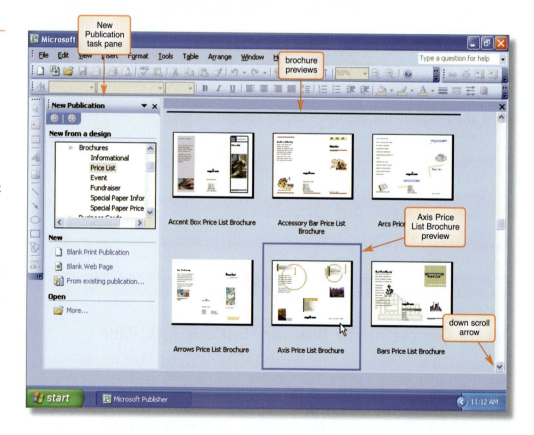

FIGURE 3-2

2

• **Click the Axis Price List Brochure preview. If Publisher displays the Personal Information dialog box, click its Close button.**

Publisher displays page one of the tri-fold brochure (Figure 3-3). The Brochure Options task pane replaces the New Publication task pane.

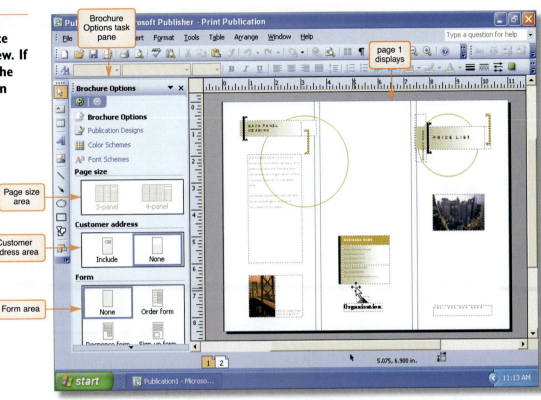

FIGURE 3-3

3

• **In the Brochure Options task pane, if necessary, click None in the Customer address area. In the Form area, click Order form.**

The selected brochure options for page size, customer address, and sign-up form are displayed (Figure 3-4). Publisher automatically moves to page 2 in the publication in order to display the Order form.

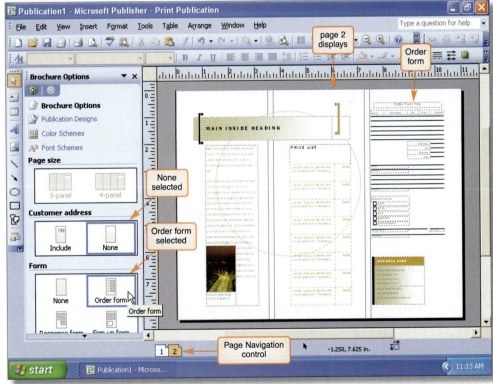

FIGURE 3-4

4

• **Click Page 1 in the Page Navigation control on the status bar. In the task pane, click Font Schemes. Scroll to and then click Modern in the Apply a font scheme list.**

The Modern font scheme includes the Tw Cen MT Bold major font and the Garamond minor font (Figure 3-5).

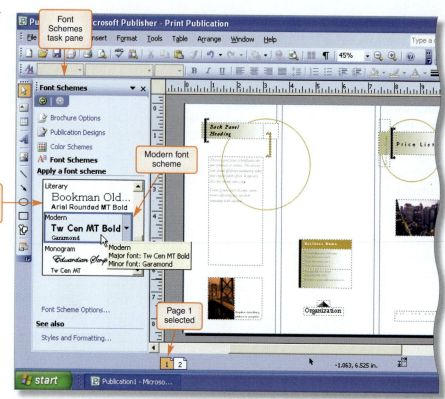

FIGURE 3-5

The changes you make in the Brochure Options task pane change how the publication looks in the workspace. To specifically look at the order form or other changes on page 2, click the Page 2 icon in the Page Navigation control on the Publisher status bar.

Custom Color Schemes

Recall that a color scheme is a predefined set of harmonized colors that you can apply to text and objects. Text and objects with an applied color scheme will change automatically when you switch to a new color scheme or modify the current color scheme. Publisher provides an option for users to create their own color schemes, rather then using one of the predefined sets. Creating a **custom color scheme** means choosing your own colors to use in a publication. You may choose one main color, five accent colors, a hyperlink color, and a followed hyperlink color. The **main color** commonly is used for text in major eye-catching areas of the publication. The first accent color is used for graphical lines, boxes, and separators. The second accent color typically is used as fill color in prominent publication shapes. Subsequent accent colors may be used in several ways, including shading, text effects, and alternate font color. The hyperlink color is used as the font color for hyperlink text. After a hyperlink is clicked, the color changes to show the user what path, or trail, they have clicked previously.

Q&A

Q: Can I create a multi-colored font?

A: The color scheme you create will apply to fonts as well as graphics, but only one color per font. Fonts themselves have no color. Software can cause text to display on screen or print out in certain colors, but the fonts themselves have no color. When you see multi-colored fonts displayed in a publication on the Web, such as red, white, and blue lettering, it usually is a graphic image created in a software program. You can apply two color fill effects to shapes.

Custom color schemes can be given a name that will appear in the Apply a color scheme list in the Color Schemes task pane. The chosen colors also appear on the Fill Color, Line Color, and Font Color button menus.

Creating a Custom Color Scheme

The Holiday Trim brochure will use holiday accent colors of red and green, as well as a basic black main color for text. Publisher displays an option to create a custom color scheme on the Color Schemes task pane. Publisher then allows users to choose the various colors and name the scheme.

The following steps explain how to create a custom color scheme.

To Create a Custom Color Scheme

1

• **With the Font Schemes task pane still displayed, click Color Schemes.**

Publisher displays the Color Schemes task pane (Figure 3-6).

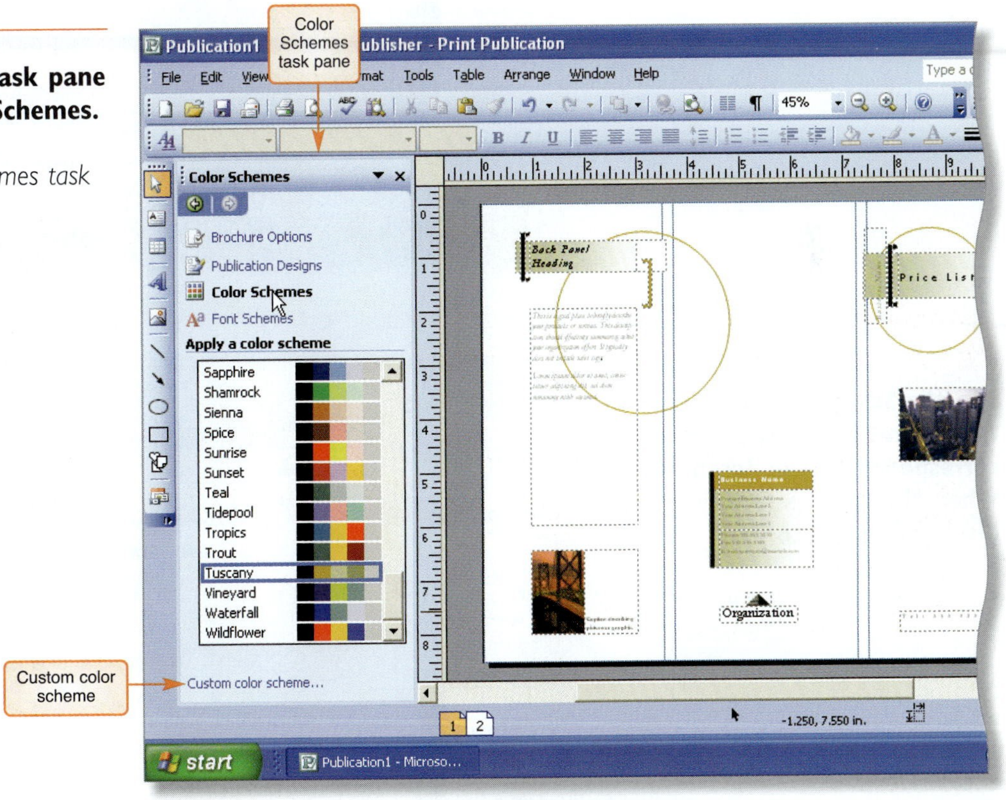

FIGURE 3-6

2

• **Click Custom color scheme in the lower portion of the Color Schemes task pane.**

• **When Publisher displays the Color Schemes dialog box, if necessary, click the Custom tab.**

The Color Schemes dialog box displays the Custom sheet (Figure 3-7).

FIGURE 3-7

3

• **In the Scheme colors area, click the second New box arrow that corresponds to the Accent 1 color. When the color palette is displayed, point to Red.**

The color palette is displayed (Figure 3-8).

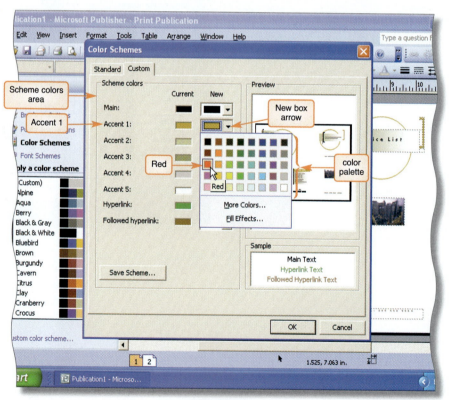

FIGURE 3-8

4

• **Click Red.**

• **Click the Accent 2, New box arrow. When the color palette is displayed, point to Lime.**

Publisher displays the color palette for Accent 2 (Figure 3-9).

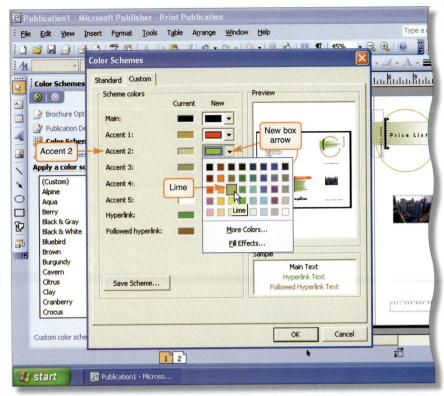

FIGURE 3-9

5

• **Click Lime.**

• **Click the Accent 3, New box arrow. When the color palette is displayed, point to Green.**

Publisher displays the color palette for Accent 3 (Figure 3-10).

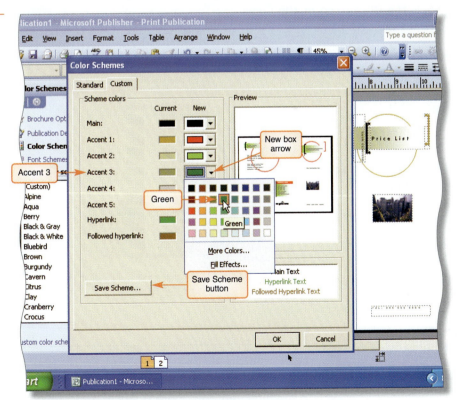

FIGURE 3-10

6

• **Click Green.**

• **Click the Save Scheme button.**

• **When Publisher displays the Save Scheme dialog box, type** Holiday **in the text box.**

The Save Scheme dialog box allows users to type a name for their custom color scheme (Figure 3-11).

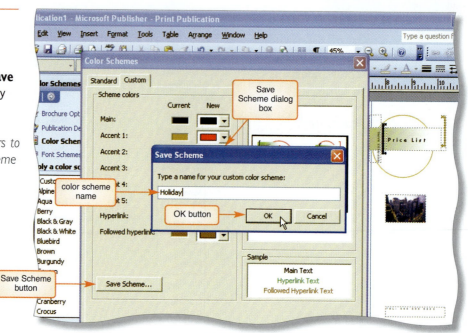

FIGURE 3-11

7

• **Click the OK button in the Save Scheme dialog box.**

• **Click the OK button in the Color Schemes dialog box.**

Publisher now displays the Holiday color scheme in the Apply a color scheme list (Figure 3-12). The selected color scheme is applied to the publication.

8

• **Click the Color Schemes task pane Close button.**

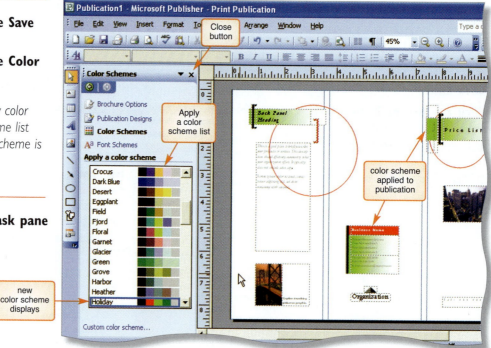

FIGURE 3-12

Other Ways

1. On Format menu click
   Color Schemes, click
   Color custom scheme

The scheme colors automatically apply to the standard publication objects in the brochure. Any objects, such as the default logo, that are filled with non-scheme colors, remain the same when you change the color scheme.

Now that several important options have been chosen, it is a good practice to save the publication. The following steps describe how to save the publication with the file name, Holiday Trim Brochure.

To Save the Publication

1 Click the Save button on the Standard toolbar.

2 Type Holiday Trim Brochure in the File name text box. If necessary, click 3½ Floppy (A:) in the Save in list.

3 Click the Save button in the Save As dialog box. If Publisher asks if you want to save the new logo to a personal information set, click the No button.

Publisher saves the publication on a floppy disk in drive A using the file name, Holiday Trim Brochure.

Replacing Text

Recall that editing text in the brochure involves selecting the current text and replacing it with new, appropriate text in one of two ways: edit text directly in Publisher or use Word to facilitate editing. If you need to edit only a few words, it is faster to use a Publisher text box with the accompanying Publisher tools. If you need to edit a long story, however, perhaps one that appears on different pages in a publication, it might be easier to edit the story in Word.

Publisher inserts placeholder text on page 1 of its supplied templates, which may be selected by a single click. Alternately, personal information components, designed to be changed or personalized for a company, are best edited by dragging through the text. When you change a personal information component, all matching components in the publication change due to synchronization.

Table 3-3 displays the text that needs to be replaced on page 1 of the brochure.

Table 3-3	Page 1 Text	
LOCATION	PUBLISHER-SUPPLIED TEXT AND TEXT BOXES	NEW TEXT
Right Panel	Pice List	Holiday Trim
Middle Panel	Address Text Box	Oak Park College Student Union 1306 127 S. Jordan Avenue Baring, NJ 08625
	Phone/Fax/E-mail Text Box	Phone: 609-555-9078 Fax: 609-555-9075 E-mail: opc.ccc@opc.edu
Left Panel	Back Panel Heading	About the College Computer Club
	Back Panel Story	The Oak Park College Computer Club is almost as old as personal computers themselves. It was formed in the early 80s, and now boasts the largest club membership on campus with 90 members from all departments. The College Computer Club is an educational and service organization whose objectives include providing an opportunity for its members and the OPC community to learn more about the use of computers and the Web; providing service to the community; and enhancing the image of the Oak Park College.
	Caption	The College Computer Club is open to all students on campus.

The following steps edit both placeholder and personal information text on page 1 of the brochure.

To Edit Text in the Brochure

1

• **Click the Price List heading in the right panel on page 1. Press the F9 key to zoom the placeholder text box.**

The placeholder text is selected with a single click (Figure 3-13). This text is the title of the brochure.

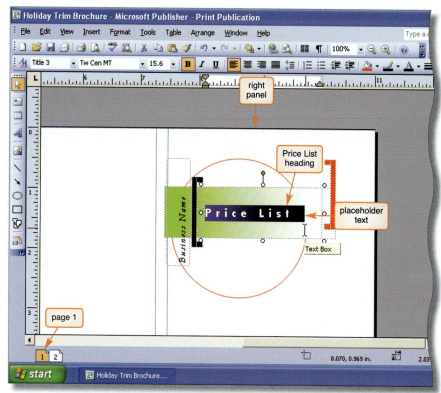

FIGURE 3-13

2

• **Type** Holiday Trim **to replace the title text. Select the text in the Organization Name Text Box to the left of the title by dragging through it.**

The new title text displays (Figure 3-14). The personal information component text is selected by dragging. Your text may differ.

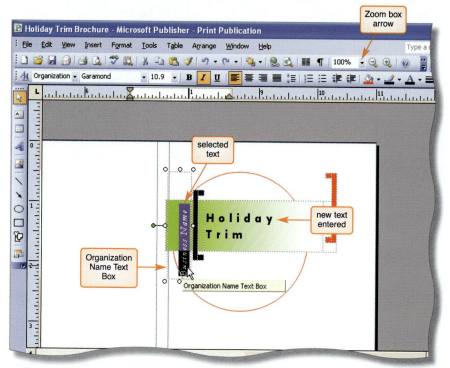

FIGURE 3-14

3

• **Type** College Computer Club **to replace the text.**

Publisher displays the new text (Figure 3-15).

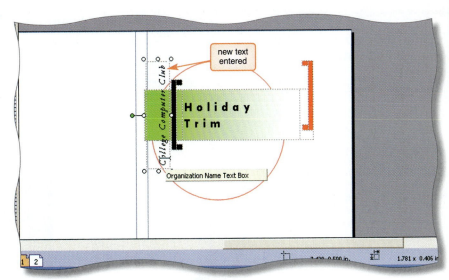

FIGURE 3-15

4

• **Click the Zoom box arrow (Figure 3-14) and then click Whole Page in the Zoom list.**

• **Click the Address Text Box in the middle panel.**

Publisher displays all of page 1 (Figure 3-16). The Address Text Box is selected.

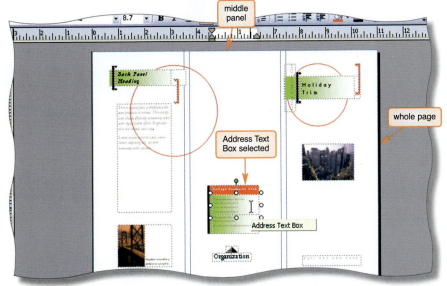

FIGURE 3-16

5

• **Press the F9 key to zoom the text box.**

• **Press CTRL+A to select the text.**

Publisher displays the selected text at 100% magnification (Figure 3-17).

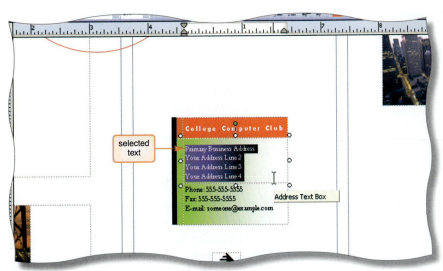

FIGURE 3-17

6

• **Enter the address from Table 3-3 on page PUB 141.**

The new text is displayed (Figure 3-18).

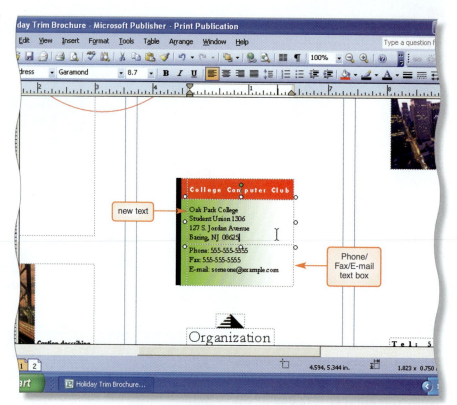

FIGURE 3-18

The following steps describe how to use similar zooming and editing techniques to edit the other text boxes on page 1 of the brochure as listed in Table 3-3 on page PUB 141.

To Edit Other Text Boxes on Page 1

1 Below the Address text box, click the text in the Phone/Fax/E-mail text box, press CTRL+A, and then type the new text from Table 3-3.

2 Scroll to the left panel of page 1 and click the Back Panel Heading located at the top of the panel. Type the new heading from Table 3-3.

3 Click the story below the heading and then type the new text from Table 3-3. Press the ENTER key at the end of each paragraph.

4 Click the caption of the picture in the lower portion of the left panel. Type the new text from Table 3-3.

The headings, placeholder text, personal information, and caption components have been edited.

Deleting Objects on Page 1

In a text box, simply selecting text and then cutting or deleting that text leaves an empty text box on the page. To delete unnecessary text boxes, you select the entire object rather than just the text. One text box in the front panel needs to be deleted, as well as the generic logo in the middle panel of page 1. The following steps describe how to delete each object.

To Delete Objects on Page 1

1 Click the Zoom box arrow and then click Whole Page in the Zoom list.

2 Right-click the telephone text box in the lower portion of the right panel. When the shortcut menu is displayed, click Delete Object.

3 Right-click the logo in the middle panel and then click Delete Object on the shortcut menu.

The two objects are deleted (Figure 3-19). Publisher displays the previously edited text boxes in Whole Page view.

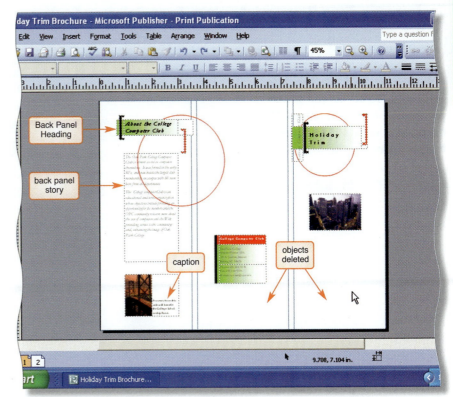

FIGURE 3-19

Font Scheme Styles

Recall that a style is a combination of formatting characteristics, such as font, font size, and formatting that are named and stored as a set. When you selected the Modern font scheme from the Font Schemes task pane, Publisher created styles for title text, headings, accent text, body text, and personal information components using the font scheme. The major font in the Modern font scheme is Tw Cen TM Bold. The minor font is Garamond. Publisher automatically creates more than 25 styles when you select a font scheme, using appropriate fonts, font sizes, font effects, and formatting. The styles include those for Headings, List Bullets, and Normal text, among others.

Applying a Font Scheme Style

When you apply a style, all of the formatting instructions in that style are applied at one time. To apply a style to new text, select the style from the Style list on the Formatting toolbar and then type the text. Alternately, you can select the text first and then select the style.

The steps on the next page create a new text box for the right panel of page 1, apply a Style, and then insert the text itself.

To Insert a Text Box and Apply a Font Scheme Style

1

• **With page 1 of the brochure still displayed, scroll to the lower portion of the right panel. If necessary, type** 100% **in the Zoom box to increase the magnification.**

Publisher displays the right panel at 100% (Figure 3-20).

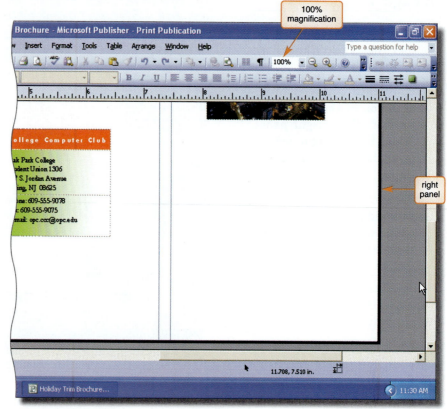

FIGURE 3-20

2

• **Click the Text Box button on the Objects toolbar and then drag a text box approximately 3 inches by 1 inch as shown in Figure 3-21.**

The Object Size box displays the size of the selected object.

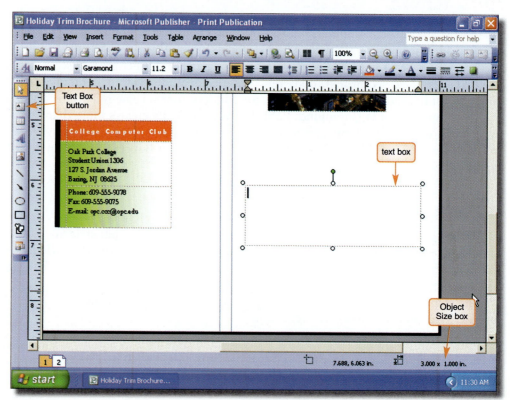

FIGURE 3-21

3

• **Click the Style box arrow on the Formatting toolbar. Scroll to display Heading 4.**

Publisher displays the various Styles created by the choice of the Modern Font Scheme (Figure 3-22).

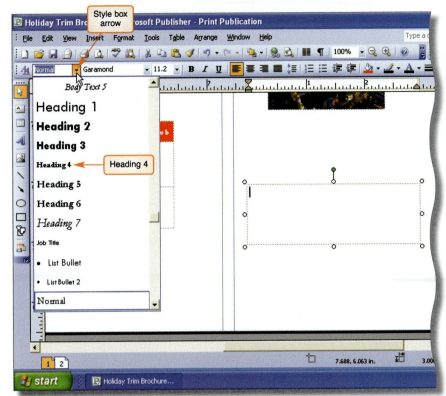

FIGURE 3-22

4

• **Click Heading 4.**

• **Click the Center button on the Formatting toolbar.**

• **Type** A College Computer Club fund-raising event for the Scholarship Fund **in the text box.**

• **Right-click the text. Point to Change Text on the shortcut menu. When the Change Text submenu is displayed, point to AutoFit Text. Click Best Fit on the AutoFit Text submenu.**

Publisher displays the new text centered in the text box (Figure 3-23).

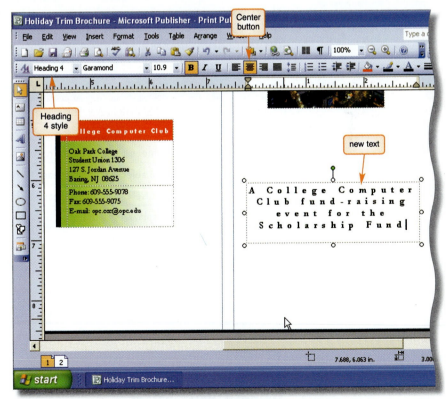

FIGURE 3-23

The text on page 1 is complete. After switching to page 2 of the brochure, the next steps are to format the text, edit the price list, and the order form, as shown in the following steps.

To Switch to Page 2

1 Click the Page 2 icon in the Page Navigation control on the Publisher status bar.

2 Click the Zoom box arrow on the Formatting toolbar and then click Whole Page in the Zoom list.

Formatting Fonts and Paragraphs

Publisher provides many ways to format fonts and paragraphs. Font schemes assist with major and minor fonts. Styles further specify sizes and formatting. Publisher also provides several font effects and line spacing options using menu options and toolbar buttons.

Font Effects

You have learned about font schemes, fonts, font sizes, formatting, and styles. Another way to format fonts is to use an effect. An **effect** is a special font option to add distinction to your text, including such things as outlining, embossing, and shadows.

Table 3-4 lists the font effects available in Publisher. The specific appearance of the font effects are printer- and screen-dependent.

More About

Fonts

You can download free fonts from the Web. For a list of Web addresses, visit the Publisher 2003 More About Web page (scsite.com/pub2003/more) and then click Downloading Fonts.

Table 3-4 Font Effects	
FONT EFFECT	**DESCRIPTION**
All caps	Formats lowercase letters as capitals. All caps formatting does not affect numbers, punctuation, nonalphabetic characters, or uppercase letters.
Emboss	The selected text appears to be raised off the page in relief.
Engrave	The selected text appears to be imprinted or pressed into the page.
Outline	Displays the inner and outer borders of each character.
Shadow	Adds a shadow beneath and to the right of the selected text.
Small caps	Formats selected lowercase text as capital letters and reduces their size. Small caps formatting does not affect numbers, punctuation, nonalphabetic characters, or uppercase letters.
Subscript	Lowers the selected text below the baseline.
Superscript	Raises the selected text above the baseline.

Using a Font Effect

The following steps apply an Outline font effect as new text is entered for the Main Inside Heading of the brochure.

To Apply a Font Effect

1

• **With page 2 displayed, right-click the text, Main Inside Heading.**

• **On the shortcut menu, point to Change Text.**

Publisher displays the shortcut menu and the Change Text submenu (Figure 3-24).

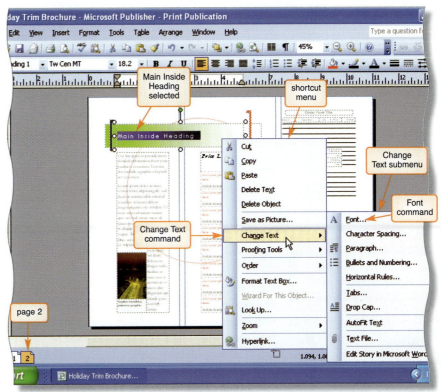

FIGURE 3-24

2

• **Click Font on the Change Text submenu. When the Font dialog box is displayed, click Outline in the Effects area.**

The Font dialog box displays font choices and a Sample preview area (Figure 3-25).

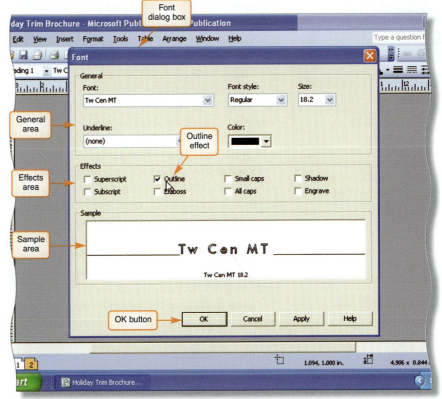

FIGURE 3-25

3

• **Click the OK button.**

• **Type** Our Products **to replace the selected main inside heading text.**

Publisher displays the new text with the Outline font effect (Figure 3-26).

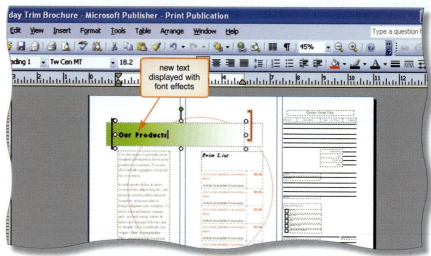

FIGURE 3-26

Two special font effects are superscript and subscript. A **superscript** is a character that appears slightly higher than other text on a line, such as that used in footnotes (reference[1]). A **subscript** describes text that is slightly lower than other text on a line, such as that used in scientific formulas (H_2O).

Formatting Paragraphs

A **paragraph,** in Publisher as well as in most word processing programs, consists of the text you type until you press the ENTER key. Pressing the ENTER key creates a **hard return**, or paragraph, in a text box. Recall that certain kinds of formatting are paragraph-dependent, such as bullets and numbering.

Publisher allows users to change the indentation, alignment, line spacing, baseline guides, and paragraph spacing of paragraphs. **Indentation** determines the distance of the paragraph from either the left or right margins. Within margins, you can increase or decrease the indentation of a paragraph or group of paragraphs. You also can create a negative indent (also known as an exdent), which pulls the paragraph out toward the left margin. You also can create a hanging indent, in which the first line of the paragraph is not indented, but subsequent lines are.

Alignment refers to horizontal appearance and orientation of the edges of the paragraph: left-aligned, right-aligned, centered, or justified. For example, in a left-aligned paragraph (the most common alignment), the left edge of the paragraph is flush with the left margin. **Justified** adjusts the horizontal spacing of text within text boxes, so that all lines, except the last line of the paragraph align evenly along both the left and right margins. Justifying text creates a smooth edge on both sides. Publisher also allows users to create a rarely used **Distribute** alignment, which justifies even the last line of the paragraph.

Line spacing is the amount of space from the bottom of one line of text to the bottom of the next line. Publisher adjusts the line spacing to accommodate the largest font or the tallest graphic in that line. You can use **baseline guides** to align text lines precisely across multiple columns. Publisher also allows you to set when and how lines and paragraphs break across text boxes. For example, you may want to specify that if one line of a paragraph moves to a new column, text box, or page, the entire paragraph should move.

Paragraph spacing determines the amount of space above or below a paragraph.

Formatting Paragraphs in the Main Inside Story

In the brochure, the main inside story details the specifics about the holiday wrapping paper, as displayed in Table 3-5.

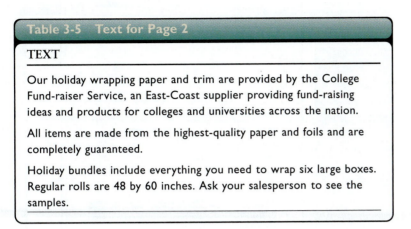

Table 3-5   Text for Page 2
TEXT
Our holiday wrapping paper and trim are provided by the College Fund-raiser Service, an East-Coast supplier providing fund-raising ideas and products for colleges and universities across the nation.
All items are made from the highest-quality paper and foils and are completely guaranteed.
Holiday bundles include everything you need to wrap six large boxes. Regular rolls are 48 by 60 inches. Ask your salesperson to see the samples.

The following steps illustrate how to adjust the alignment of the text to justified, change the line spacing of the paragraphs to 1.5 inches, and then type the text.

To Change the Alignment and Line Spacing

1

• **Right-click the story located below the Our Products heading. On the shortcut menu, point to Change Text and then click Paragraph on the Change Text submenu.**

• **When the Paragraph dialog box is displayed, if necessary, click the Indents and Spacing tab.**

Publisher displays the Paragraph dialog box (Figure 3-27).

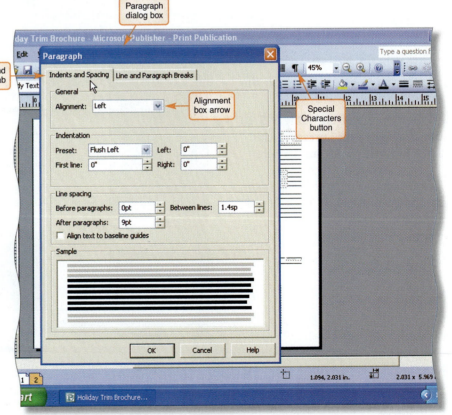

FIGURE 3-27

2

• **Click the Alignment box arrow and then click Justified in the list.**

• **In the Line spacing area, select the text in the Between lines box, and then type 1.5 to enter the new value.**

Justified alignment and the new value for line spacing between lines are entered (Figure 3-28).

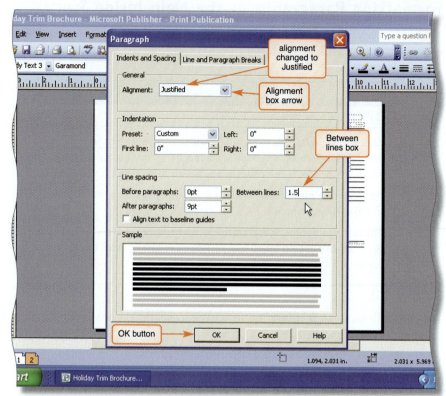

FIGURE 3-28

3

• **Click the OK button.**

• **Press the F9 key to increase the magnification.**

• **Type the text from Table 3-5 on the previous page, pressing the ENTER key after each paragraph.**

Publisher displays the text justified with line spacing of 1.5 (Figure 3-29). Notice the text automatically wraps around the graphic.

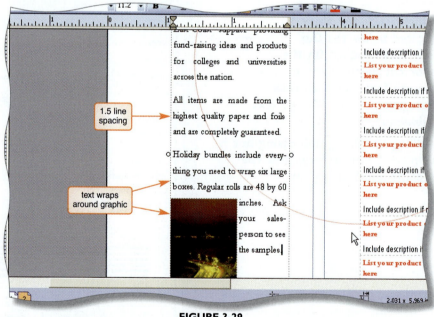

FIGURE 3-29

Other Ways

1. On Format menu click Paragraph

The Paragraph dialog box contains a Line and Paragraph Breaks tab where you can set widow and orphan control. A **widow** is the last line of a paragraph printed by itself at the top of a connected text box. An **orphan** is the first line of a paragraph printed by itself at the bottom of a connected text box. Choices include keeping the lines together and starting the paragraph in a new text box.

You can view the paragraph marks by clicking the Special Characters button on the Formatting toolbar. (See Figure 3-27 on page PUB 151.)

Editing the Caption, Price List, and Order Form Heading

To complete the text editing on page 2, the following steps describe how to edit the caption, price list, and order form heading. Table 3-6 displays the text for the price list. As you click and type parts of the price list, the formatting, complete with color and font, will be applied automatically.

Table 3-6 Text for Price List	
ITEM DESCRIPTION	PRICE
Holiday Bundle 2 large rolls, 8 bows, and ribbon	$14.00
Birthday Delight 1 roll, bow, and ribbon	$8.00
Evergreen/Winter Scene 1 roll, bow, and ribbon	$8.00
Bright Red or Bright Green Large, 8' roll	$6.00
Bows Galore 24 assorted colors and sizes	$6.00
Candle Holiday 2 rolls, 2 bows, and ribbon	$12.00
Angels on High Large, 8' roll	$6.00
That Jolly Ol' Man 1 roll, bow, and ribbon	$8.00

To Edit the Caption, Price List, and Order Form Heading

1

• **Scroll to display the caption below the graphic in the left panel of page 2. Click the caption to select it.**

• **Type** Holiday Bundles **to replace the selected caption text.**

Publisher replaces the placeholder text with the new caption (Figure 3-30).

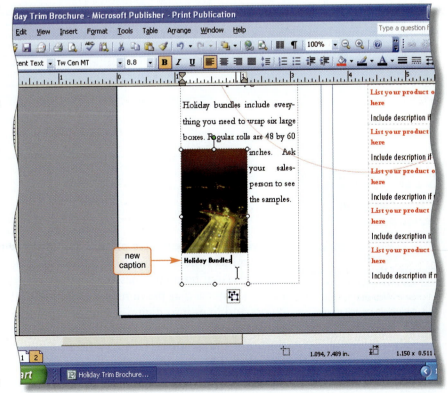

FIGURE 3-30

2

• **Scroll and zoom as necessary to display the price list in the middle panel. One at a time, click each part of the price list and then enter the new text from Table 3-6 on the previous page.**

The edited price list is entered (Figure 3-31).

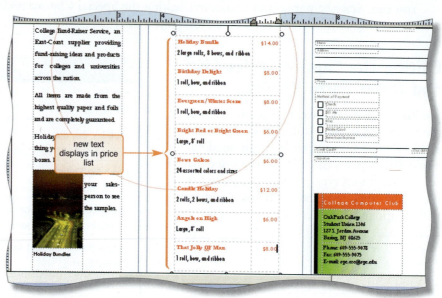

FIGURE 3-31

3

• **Scroll to the top of the right panel. Click the text in the Order form heading and then type** My Holiday Trim Order **to replace the heading.**

Publisher replaces the heading (Figure 3-32).

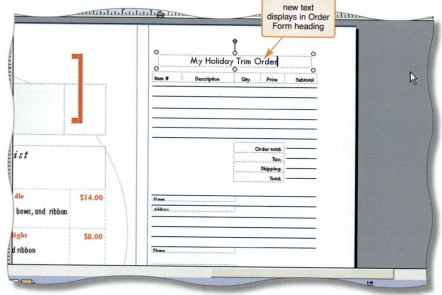

FIGURE 3-32

Using Photographs and Images in a Brochure

The advent of inexpensive photo CDs, along with Web access, has increased exponentially the possibilities for photographic reproduction in publications. Regular cameras using popular types of film now can take pictures that are ultimately digitized, a process that previously required digital cameras. **Digitizing** means converting colors and lines into digital impulses capable of being read by a computer. Digitized photos and downloaded graphics from the Web, combined with high-resolution production from scanners, create endless possibilities. Small businesses now can afford to include photographs in their brochures and other types of publications.

Publisher can accept photographs and images from a variety of input sources. Each graphic you import has a file name, followed by a dot or period, followed by a three-letter extension. Publisher uses **extensions** to recognize individual file formats. Table 3-7 displays some of the graphic formats and their extensions that Publisher can import.

Inserting a Photograph from a File

Publisher can insert a photograph into a publication by accessing the Clip Art task pane, by externally importing from a file, by directly importing an image from a scanner or camera, or by creating a new drawing.

When a Publisher template has grouped a picture with its caption, clicking either will select both. To further select only the picture or only the caption text box, a second click is required.

The next sequence of steps illustrates how to insert a previously scanned photograph from a file into the brochure. The photograph for the brochure is provided on the Data Disk. See the inside back cover of this book for instructions for downloading the Data Disk or see your instructor for information on accessing the files required for this book.

Table 3-7 Supported Graphic Formats
GRAPHIC FORMATS
Compressed Macintosh PICT (.pcz)
Compressed Windows Enhanced Metafile (.emz)
Compressed Windows Metafile (.wmz)
Computer Graphics Metafile (.cgm)
CorelDraw (.cdr)
Encapsulated PostScript (.eps)
Graphics Interchange Format, CompuServe format (.gif or .gfa)
JPEG File Interchange Format (.jpeg, .jpg, .jfif, or .jpe)
Macintosh PICT (.pct or .pict)
Microsoft Windows Bitmap (.bmp)
Portable Network Graphics (.png)
TIFF, Tagged Image File Format (.tif or .tiff)
Windows Enhanced Metafile (.emf)
Windows Metafile (.wmf)
WordPerfect Graphics (.wpg)

To Insert a Photograph from a File

1

• **Insert the Data Disk in drive A. If necessary, click the Page 2 icon in the Page Navigation Control and then click the graphic in the lower portion of the left panel.**

• **Click the picture again to select only the picture from the group.**

• **Right-click the picture and then point to Change Picture on the shortcut menu.**

The Change Picture submenu is displayed (Figure 3-33). Clicking one object in a group a second time selects only that object. The selected object displays a filled handle with an x in it.

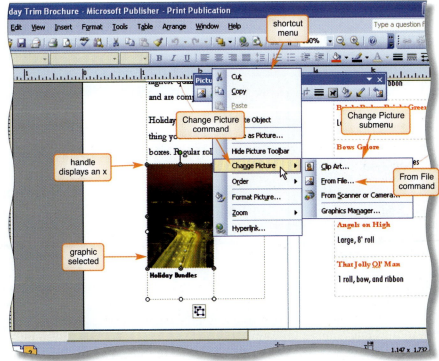

FIGURE 3-33

Microsoft Office
Publisher 2003

2

• Click **From File**.

• When the **Insert Picture** dialog box is displayed, click the **Look in** box arrow and then click **3½ Floppy (A:)** in the list.

• When the folders are displayed, double-click the **Project 3** folder and then double-click the file name, **paper**.

The wrapping paper picture replaces the original picture (Figure 3-34).

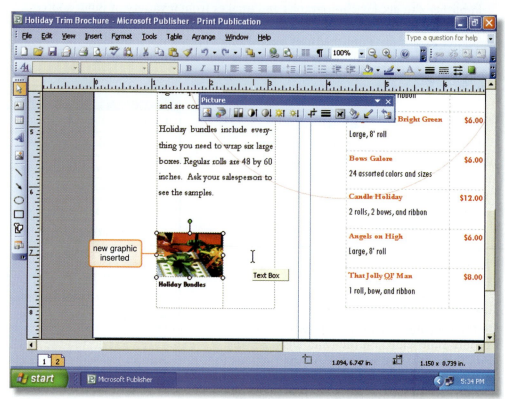

FIGURE 3-34

Other Ways

1. On Insert menu point to Picture, click From File
2. In Voice Command mode, say "Insert, Picture, From File"

Another common method of creating new image files, other than scanning, is to use **illustration software.** Designed for artists, illustration software packages such as CorelDRAW! and Adobe Illustrator create graphics to import into desktop publishing software.

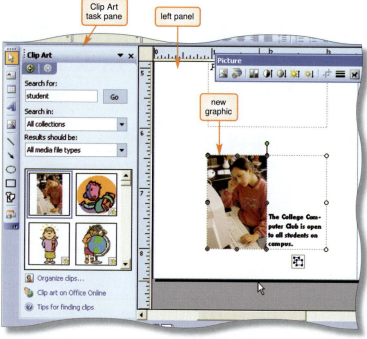

FIGURE 3-35

Replacing Graphics on Page 1

The graphics on page 1 come from the clip art included with a full installation of Publisher. The following steps describe how to use the Clip Art task pane to replace the graphics on page 1.

To Replace the Graphics in the Left Panel of Page 1

1 Click the Page 1 icon in the Page Navigation control on the status bar.

2 Zoom as necessary to display the lower portion of the left panel.

3 Click the graphic/caption grouped object in the lower portion of the left panel.

4 Double-click the graphic only. When the Clip Art task pane is displayed, select any text in the Search for text box, type student in the Search for text box, and then click the Go button.

5 When the clip art previews are displayed, click a picture similar to the one shown in Figure 3-35.

Publisher displays a graphic of a student sitting at a computer (Figure 3-35).

If the Clip Art task pane does not display as many graphics as you expect, it is possible that the search results may not include all media types. To verify that all media types are being searched, click the Results should be box arrow and confirm that the All media types check box displays a check mark (Figure 3-35).

To Replace the Graphics in the Right Panel of Page 1

1 Zoom as necessary to display the middle portion of the right panel.

2 Double-click the graphic. In the Clip Art task pane, select any text in the Search for text box, type bows in the Search for text box, and then click the Go button.

3 When the clip art previews are displayed, click a picture similar to the one shown in Figure 3-36.

4 Click the Close button in the Clip Art task pane.

new graphic

FIGURE 3-36

Publisher displays a holiday graphic (Figure 3-36).

In addition to the clip art images included in the previews, other sources for clip art include retailers specializing in computer software, the Internet, bulletin board systems, and online information systems. Some popular online information systems are The Microsoft Network, America Online, CompuServe, and Prodigy. A **bulletin board system** is a computer system that allows users to communicate with each other and share files. Microsoft has created a special page on its Web site where you can add new clips to the Clip Organizer.

Creating a Logo from Scratch

Many types of publications use logos to identify and distinguish the page. A **logo** is a recognizable symbol that identifies a person, business, or organization. A logo may be composed of a name, a picture, or a combination of symbols and graphics. In a later project, you will learn how to add a permanent logo to an information set for a company.

Creating a Shape for the Logo

The logo in the Holiday Trim brochure is a combination of a shape and three text boxes with symbols. Created individually in the workspace and then grouped together, the logo easily is positioned and sized to the proper places in the brochure. The logo appears both on the front of the brochure (right panel of page 1) and on the back of the brochure (middle panel of page 1).

More About

AutoShapes

You can set the fill color, line weight, and line color for new AutoShapes or drawing objects, such as curves, lines and WordArt in the current publication. Right-click an AutoShape or drawing object that has the attributes such as line fill or text color that you want to use as the default. Then, on the shortcut menu, click the Format option. In the dialog box, click the Colors and Lines tab. Finally, select the Apply settings to new AutoShapes check box.

The background of the logo is from the AutoShapes menu. Accessed through the Objects toolbar, the **AutoShapes** menu displays seven categories of shapes you may use as graphics in a publication. These shapes include lines, connectors, basic shapes, block arrows, stars, and banners, among others. AutoShapes differ from WordArt in that they do not contain text; rather, they are graphic designs with a variety of formatting options, such as color, border, size, and shadow.

The workspace, also called the **scratch area**, can serve as a kind of drawing board to create new objects. Without disturbing any object already on the publications page, you can manipulate and edit objects in the workspace and then move them to the desired location. The rulers and status bar display the exact size of the new object. Moving objects off the page and into the workspace is sometimes advantageous as well. Small objects that are difficult to revise on the publication can be moved into the workspace, magnified and edited, and then moved back. As you place new objects in the workspace, more workspace room is allocated.

The following steps illustrate creating the logo in Publisher's workspace to the right of the brochure.

To Create a Shape for the Logo

1

• **If necessary, click the Page 1 icon in the Page Navigation control on the status bar and then increase the magnification to view the whole page. Drag the scroll box to the right, to view more of the workspace.**

The brochure moves left as you scroll right, providing more workspace area (Figure 3-37).

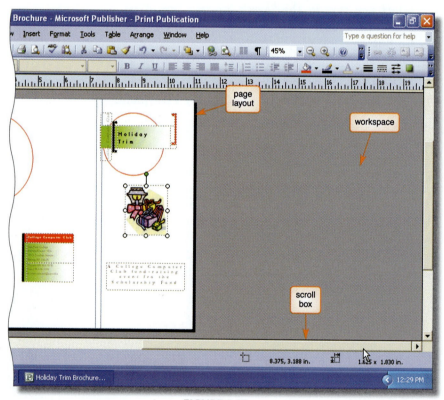

FIGURE 3-37

2

• **Click the AutoShapes button on the Objects toolbar.**

• **Point to Stars and Banners on the AutoShapes menu and then point to Horizontal Scroll.**

The AutoShapes menu is displayed (Figure 3-38).

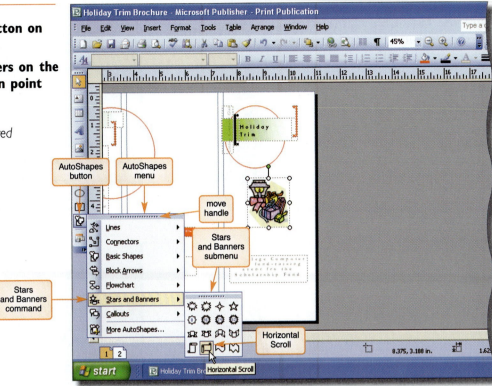

FIGURE 3-38

3

• **Click Horizontal Scroll and then move the mouse pointer to the workspace to the right of the brochure.**

• **Drag down and to the right until the shape is approximately 1.75 × 1.25 inches as displayed in the Object Size box on the status bar. Release the mouse button.**

• **Press the F9 key.**

The workspace displays the horizontal scroll shape for the logo (Figure 3-39). The Object Size box displays the size of the object. The AutoShape displays at 100% magnification.

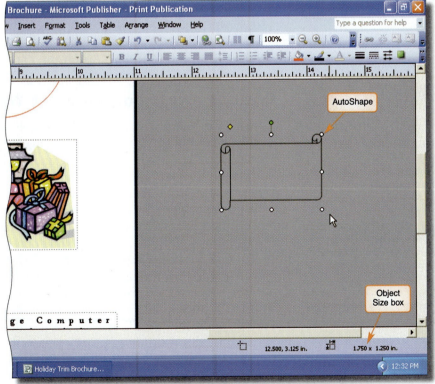

FIGURE 3-39

4

• **With the AutoShape still selected, click the Fill Color button arrow on the Formatting toolbar.**

The Fill Color palette is displayed (Figure 3-40).

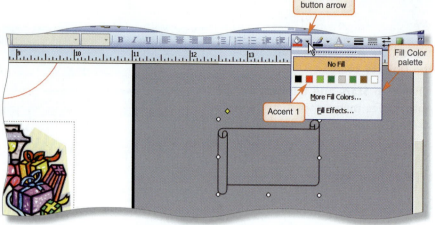

FIGURE 3-40

5

• **Click Accent 1 (Red).**

The shape's fill color changes to red to match the brochure's Holiday color scheme (Figure 3-41).

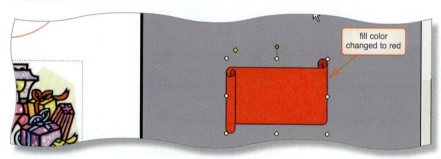

FIGURE 3-41

The AutoShape menu can be changed to a floating toolbar by dragging the move handle at the top of the menu (shown in Figure 3-38 on the previous page).

More About

Text Wrapping

Publisher text boxes automatically wrap around other objects on the page. If you want to change how text wraps around objects such as a picture, you can click the Text Wrapping button on the Picture toolbar. The Format dialog box associated with most objects also contains text wrapping options on the Layout sheet. If text wrapping appears to be unavailable, one of the objects may be transparent. In that case, press CTRL+T.

Creating a Text Box with Text Wrapping

The way that text wraps, or adjusts itself around objects, is not limited to wrapping around graphics. **Text wrapping** in Publisher implies how text wraps whenever it is close to or overlapping another Publisher object. You can choose how you want the text to wrap around an object using one of the following **wrapping styles**. **Square** wraps text around all sides of the selected object. **Tight** wraps text as closely as possible to the object. **Through** wraps text around the perimeter and inside any open portions of the object. **Top and bottom** wraps text above and below the object, but not on either side. The **None** option removes all text-wrapping formatting so that text does not wrap around the object. If the object is transparent, the text behind it will show through. Otherwise, the text will be hidden behind the object.

The Holiday Trim brochure needs a text box to hold a symbol used in the College Computer Club logo. The symbol should fill the text box. Recall that Publisher uses the Best Fit option to adjust the size of text to fill a text box.

Because this text box eventually will be displayed on top of the AutoShape, a transparent text box will allow the color of the AutoShape to show through. Black text on a dark background does not print as well as it displays on the screen. On a color desktop printer, the darker black is applied over the top of the background color, which lends itself to streaking. Therefore, a white symbol will be placed on top of the red AutoShape.

The text box should be formatted with a white font, centered text, with the Best Fit option, and no text wrapping, as described in the following steps.

To Create a Text Box with Text Wrapping

1

• **Click the Text Box button on the Objects toolbar. In a blank area of the workspace, near the horizontal scroll AutoShape, drag to create a text box approximately .75 × .75 inches.**

The text box is displayed in the workspace (Figure 3-42).

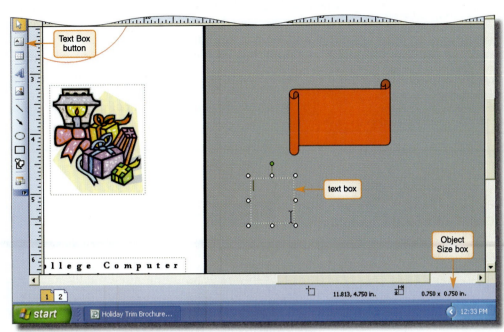

FIGURE 3-42

2

• **Press CTRL+E to center the text inside the text box.**

• **Click the Font Color button arrow on the Formatting toolbar and then click white on the color palette.**

• **With the insertion point still located in the text box, right-click the text box, point to Change Text, point to AutoFit Text on the Change Text Submenu, and then click Best Fit on the AutoFit Text submenu.**

• **Click Arrange on the menu bar. Point to Text Wrapping.**

Publisher displays the Arrange menu and the Text Wrapping submenu (Figure 3-43).

3

• **Click None on the Text Wrapping submenu.**

The text box will use no text wrapping as it is layered or moved closer to other objects.

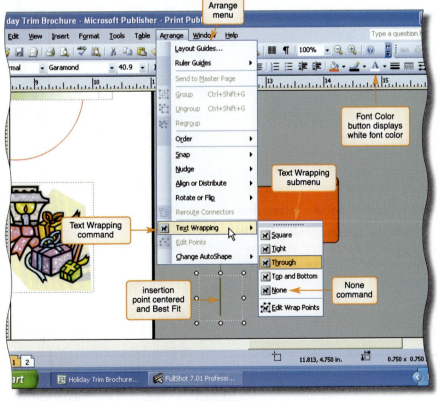

FIGURE 3-43

More About

Symbols

If you need a character that is not on your keyboard, such as a trademark symbol or a foreign language character, click Insert on the menu bar and then click Symbol. The Symbol dialog box contains a huge selection of characters in a variety of fonts and subsets. Click the character you want, and then click the Insert button.

Inserting a Symbol

The next step is to insert the symbol used for the College Computer Club logo, who is selling the holiday trim paper and bows. A **symbol** is a special character, not typically represented on the keyboard. Foreign language letters, mathematical symbols, and music notation symbols are examples of characters that you may want to use and print, but are not available on most keyboards. Publisher's Symbol command on the Insert menu displays a dialog box containing hundreds of symbols from which you may choose.

The following steps insert a symbol into the previously formatted text box.

To Insert a Symbol

1

• **Click Insert on the menu bar.**

Publisher displays the Insert menu (Figure 3-44).

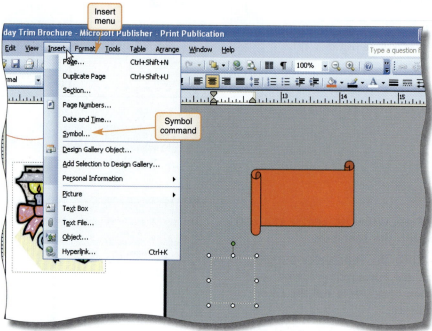

FIGURE 3-44

2

• **Click Symbol on the Insert menu.**

• **When the Symbol dialog box is displayed, if necessary, click the Symbols tab. Scroll to display the symbol, ©.**

The Symbol dialog box is displayed (Figure 3-45).

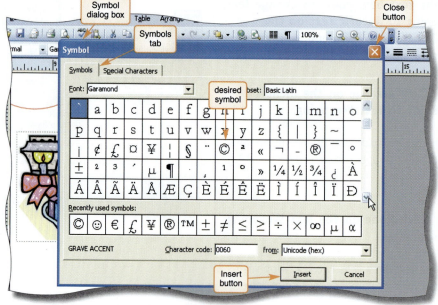

FIGURE 3-45

3

• **Click the symbol, ©, click the Insert button, and then click the Close button in the Symbol dialog box.**

The symbol is inserted in the text box (Figure 3-46).

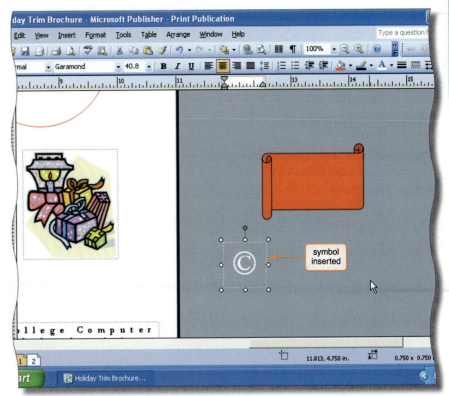

FIGURE 3-46

Mixed colors of layered objects create challenges for commercial printing. Professional printers use a technique known as knocking out. **Knocking out** removes the background colors underneath foreground objects or text so the foreground colors print directly on the paper instead of on top of other colors. When colors print on top of each other on a commercial printer, they can mix to create an undesired color. For example, if a blue circle prints on top of a red rectangle, the overlapping colors can mix to create purple.

A cost-saving alternative is to change the color as you did in the previous set of steps. Copy shops, printing services, and media design professionals all recommend white text on darker backgrounds. The white letters stand out and offer an appearance of distinction to the publication.

Copying Text Boxes

Because the Computer College Club logo combines three occurrences of the © symbol, the next task is to create two more identical text boxes, as shown in the step on the next page.

To Copy Text Boxes

1

• **With the symbol text box selected, right-click the text box and then click Copy on the shortcut menu.**

• **Right-click the workspace, away from the text box. Click Paste on the shortcut menu.**

• **Right-click the workspace again, away from the previous text boxes. Click Paste on the shortcut menu.**

The three text boxes are displayed in the workspace (Figure 3-47).

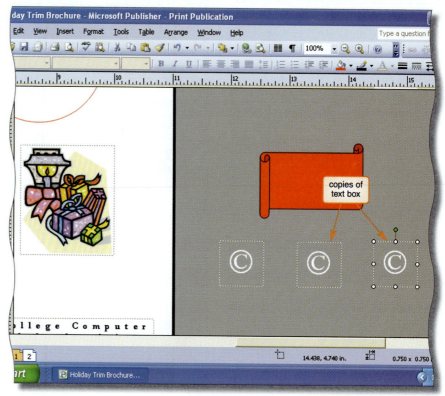

copies of text box

FIGURE 3-47

Aligning and Nudging the Logo Text Boxes

The logo, when complete, is a composite object: three text boxes and a background shape. Repositioning, aligning, and resizing objects independently can be tedious and prone to error. Placing objects on top of other objects, known as **layering**, can cause design errors if you are not careful. Moving the front objects first can cause an **order** error with parts of objects obscured behind others.

Publisher's Arrange menu contains choices for nudging, arranging, aligning, and rotating objects, among others. When you **align** objects, it means to line up or arrange them in relation to one another. For example, you might want to align tall and short graphics along their bottom edges to present a straight line appearance. Table 3-8 lists Publisher's align or distribute commands, available through the Arrange menu.

Table 3-8	Align or Distribute Commands
COMMAND	**RESULT**
Align Left	Lines up the left borders of the objects
Align Center	Lines up the centers of the objects vertically
Align Right	Lines up the right borders of the objects
Align Top	Lines up the top borders of the objects
Align Middle	Lines up the middles of the objects horizontally
Align Bottom	Lines up the bottom borders of the objects
Distribute Horizontally	Evenly arranges the objects horizontally
Distribute Vertically	Evenly arranges the objects vertically

When you **nudge** an object, it means to move it a set distance each time you press an arrow key (or ALT+ARROW key for text boxes). The default nudge distance is 0.13" (or its equivalent if you are using another measurement unit). You can change the nudge distance, however.

The following steps reposition the symbol text boxes, middle-aligning two of them and nudging the third into place, to create the College Computer Club logo.

To Align and Nudge the Logo Objects

1

• **Point to one of the symbol text boxes. When the mouse pointer changes to a double two-headed arrow, drag the text box to the left center of the AutoShape as shown in Figure 3-48.**

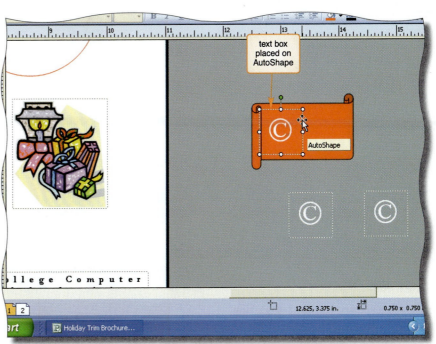

FIGURE 3-48

2

• **Drag another of the symbol text boxes to the right center of the AutoShape.**

The text box displays in front of the shape (Figure 3-49).

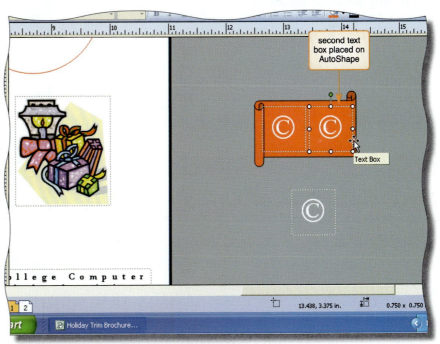

FIGURE 3-49

3

• **With the symbol text box still selected, SHIFT-click the first symbol text box so that both are selected.**

• **Click Arrange on the menu bar and then point to Align or Distribute on the Arrange menu.**

Pressing SHIFT-click selects multiple objects (Figure 3-50). Publisher displays the Align or Distribute submenu.

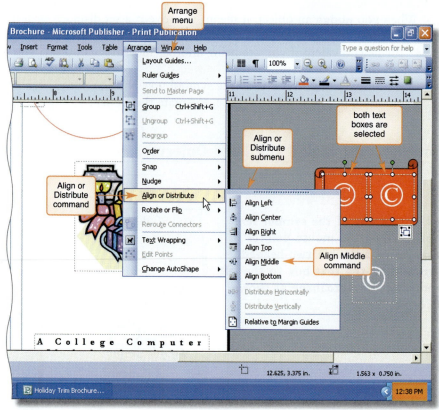

FIGURE 3-50

4

• **Click Align Middle.**

• **Drag the third symbol text box to the center of the AutoShape, so that it displays between the two other symbol text boxes and slightly lower, as shown in Figure 3-51.**

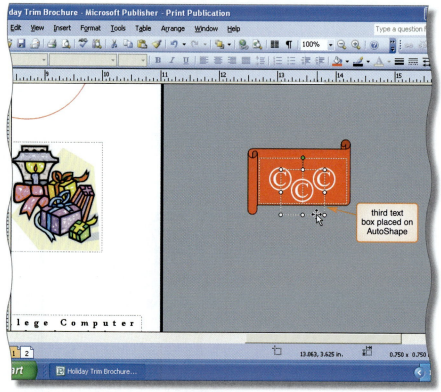

FIGURE 3-51

5

• **To place the text box precisely so that the © symbols overlap, with the center text box selected, press and hold the ALT key. Press the UP or DOWN ARROW key as necessary to nudge the text box in the direction that you want it to move.**

• **As necessary, select and nudge the other two text boxes left or right using the ALT key and the appropriate LEFT or RIGHT ARROW key. Be careful to select the text boxes individually and not the AutoShape.**

The three © symbols overlap so that their outside circles touch the inner c of each other (Figure 3-52).

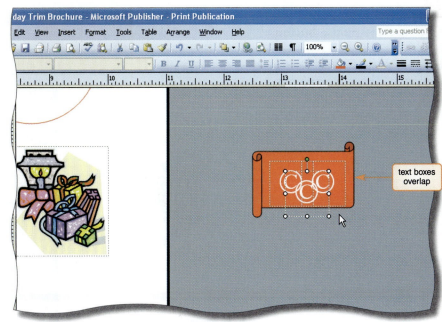

text boxes overlap

FIGURE 3-52

Grouping Objects

When you **group** objects, you combine them so you can work with them as though they were a single object. You can flip, rotate, resize, or scale all objects in a group as a single unit. You also can change the attributes of all objects in a group at one time — for example, you might change the fill color or add a shadow to all objects in the group.

Objects can be moved, resized, formatted, and copied easily, provided they are grouped and aligned carefully. It is important to adhere to the scheme colors, and pay close attention to layering.

The following steps describe how to group the logo.

To Group Objects

1

• **Above and to the left of the AutoShape and text boxes, click and drag the mouse pointer down and to the right to encompass the objects. Do not release the mouse button.**

The mouse pointer creates a visual rectangle as it drags through the area (Figure 3-53).

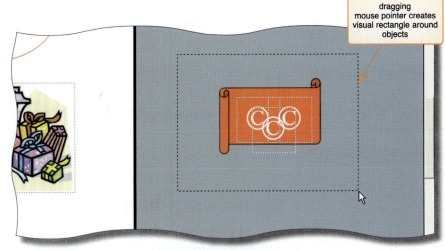

dragging mouse pointer creates visual rectangle around objects

FIGURE 3-53

2

• **Release the mouse button.**

Publisher selects all of the objects and displays the Group Objects button (Figure 3-54). The Group Objects button always is displayed when multiple objects are selected.

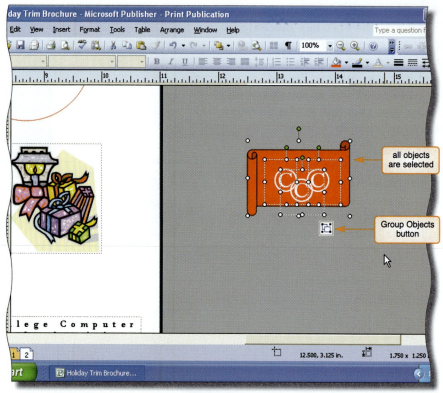

FIGURE 3-54

3

• **Click the Group Objects button.**

The objects display as a grouped object with a single set of handles (Figure 3-55). The Group Objects button becomes the Ungroup Objects button as indicated by the button's changed icon.

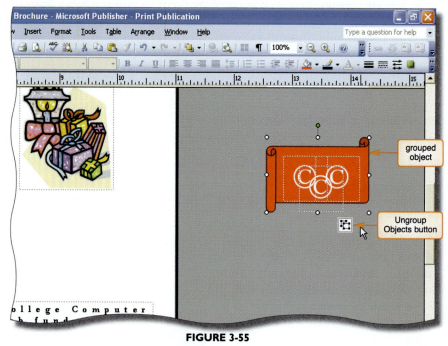

FIGURE 3-55

Repositioning Objects

The next series of steps repositions the logo in the page layout and then copies and pastes it to a second location in the brochure.

To Reposition the Logo

1

• **Click the Zoom Out button on the Standard toolbar several times until the entire page layout and workspace area is visible.**

Publisher displays the page layout and the logo in the workspace (Figure 3-56).

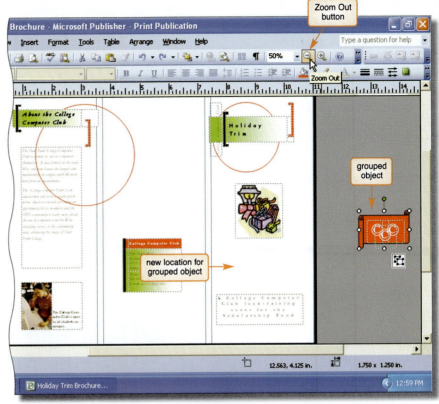

FIGURE 3-56

2

• **Point to the logo. When the mouse pointer changes to a double two-headed arrow, drag the logo to a position below the bows graphic in the right panel of page 1.**

The logo is displayed in the front panel of the brochure (Figure 3-57).

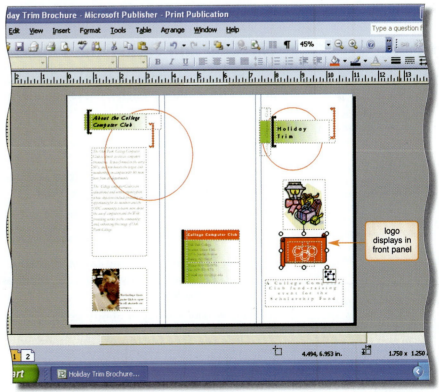

FIGURE 3-57

3

• **Right-click the logo and then click Copy on the shortcut menu.**

• **Right-click the middle panel below the address text box and then click Paste on the shortcut menu.**

The copy of the logo is inserted in the middle panel of the brochure (Figure 3-58). Drag the logo to the location shown, if necessary.

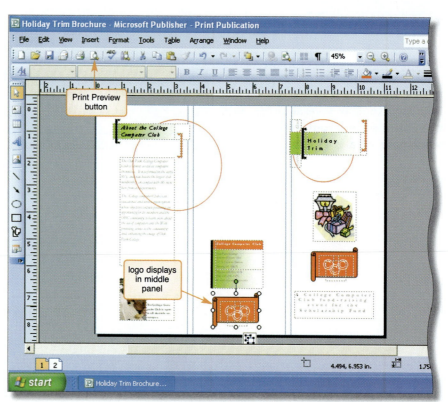

FIGURE 3-58

If the logos are not perfectly aligned horizontally or vertically with other objects in the panel, you can nudge or align them as necessary.

Checking and Saving the Publication

The publication now is complete. You should check for spelling errors in the publication, run the Design Checker, and then save the publication again.

To Check the Publication and Save Again

1 Click the Spelling button on the Standard toolbar. If Publisher flags any words that are misspelled, fix them.

2 When Publisher asks to check the entire document, click the Yes button.

3 Choose to ignore the abbreviated word, OI'. Fix any other errors.

4 Click Tools on the menu bar and then click Design Checker. If the Design Checker identifies any errors, fix them as necessary and then close the Design Checker task pane.

5 Ignore any messages about extra space below the top margin or RGB mode.

6 Click the Save button on the Standard toolbar.

The checked document saves in the same location with the same file name.

Outside Printing

When they need mass quantities of publications, businesses generally **outsource**, or submit their publications to an outside printer, for duplicating. You must make special considerations when preparing a document for outside printing.

Previewing the Brochure Before Printing

The first step in getting the publication ready for outside printing is to examine what the printed copy will look like from your desktop. The following steps preview the brochure before printing.

To Preview the Brochure Before Printing

1 **Click the Print Preview button on the Standard toolbar (Figure 3-58).**

Page 2 displays without the special characters and guides (Figure 3-59). You also may preview page 1 by clicking the Page 1 icon in the Page Navigation Control on the status bar.

2 **Click the Close button on the Print Preview toolbar.**

3 **Click the Page 2 icon in the Page Navigation Control on the status bar and then again click the Print Preview button on the Standard toolbar to view page 2.**

4 **Click the Close button on the Print Preview toolbar.**

You also can view two pages of the brochure at once by clicking the Multiple Pages button on the Print Preview toolbar. While viewing two full pages with intensive graphics and text may give

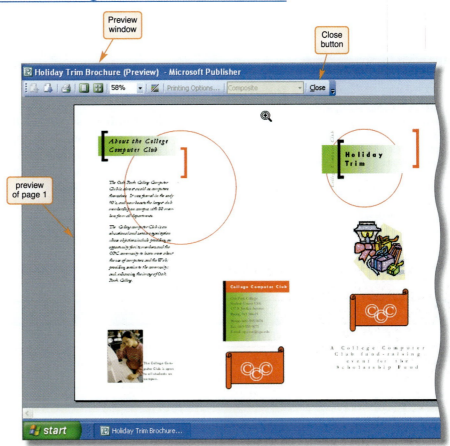

FIGURE 3-59

you a good overview of the publication, it provides few checking capabilities.

The next sequence of steps recommends publishing this brochure on a high grade of paper to obtain a professional look. A heavier stock paper helps the brochure to stand up better in display racks, although any paper will suffice. If you do use a special paper, be sure to click the Properties or Advanced Settings button in the Print dialog box for your printer and then specify the paper you are using. Following your printer's specifications, print one side of the paper, turn it over, and then print the reverse side. The completed brochure prints as shown in Figure 3-1 on page PUB 131. You then can fold the brochure to display the title panel on the front.

More About

Laser Printers

For details on laser printers, visit the Publisher 2003 More About Web page (scsite.com/pub2003/more) and then click Discovering Laser Printers.

The following steps print a copy of the brochure.

To Print the Brochure

1 Ready the printer according to the printer instructions, and insert paper.

2 With page 1 displaying in the workspace, click File on the menu bar and then click Print. When the Print dialog box is displayed, click Current page. If necessary, click the Properties button to choose a special paper. Click the OK button.

3 When page 1 finishes printing, turn the page over and reinsert it top first (or as your printer requires) into the paper feed mechanism on your printer.

4 Click the Page 2 icon in the Page Navigation Control on the status bar. Click File on the menu bar and then click Print. When the Print dialog box is displayed, again click Current page and then click the OK button.

The brochure prints as shown in Figure 3-1 on page PUB 131.

Printing Considerations

If you start a publication from scratch, it is best to **set up** the publication for the type of printing you want before you place objects on the page. Otherwise, you may be forced to make design changes at the last minute. You also may set up an existing publication for a printing service. In order to provide you with experience in setting up a publication for outside printing, this project takes you through the preparation steps — even if you are submitting this publication only to your instructor.

Printing options, such as whether to use a copy shop or commercial printer, have advantages and limitations. You may have to make some trade-offs before deciding on the best printing option. Table 3-9 shows some of the questions you can ask yourself about printing.

More About

Printing in Color

Some printers do not have enough memory to print a wide variety of images and color. In these cases, the printer prints up to a certain point on a page and then chokes — resulting in only the top portion of the publication printing. Check with your instructor to see if your printer has enough memory to work with colors.

Table 3-9 Picking a Printing Option

CONSIDERATION	QUESTIONS TO ASK	DESKTOP OPTION	PROFESSIONAL OPTIONS
Color	Is the quality of photographs and color a high priority?	Low- to medium-quality	High quality
Convenience	Do I want the easy way?	Very convenient and familiar	Time needed to explore different methods, unfamiliarity
Cost	How much do I want to pay?	Printer supplies and personal time	High-resolution color/high quality is expensive; the more you print, the less expensive the per copy price
Quality	How formal is the purpose of my publication?	Local event; narrow, personal audience	Business, marketing, professional services
Quantity	How many copies do I need?	1 to 10 copies	10 to 500 copies: copy shop 500+ copies: commercial printer
Turnaround	How soon do I need it?	Immediate	Rush outside printing, probably an extra cost

Paper Considerations

Professional brochures are printed on a high grade of paper to enhance the graphics and provide a longer lasting document. Grades of paper are based on weight. Desktop printers commonly use **20 lb. bond paper**, which means they use a lightweight paper intended for writing and printing. A commercial printer might use 60 lb. glossy or linen paper. The finishing options and their costs are important considerations that may take additional time to explore. **Glossy paper** is a coated paper, produced using a heat process with clay and titanium. **Linen paper**, with its mild texture or grain, can support high-quality graphics without the shine and slick feel of glossy paper. Users sometimes pick a special stock of paper such as cover stock, card stock, or text stock. This textbook is printed on 45 lb., blade-coated paper. **Blade-coated paper** is coated and then skimmed and smoothed to create the pages you see here.

These paper and finishing options may sound burdensome, but they are becoming conveniently available to desktop publishers. Local office supply stores have shelf after shelf of special computer paper specifically designed for laser and ink-jet printers. Some of the paper you can purchase has been prescored for special folding.

Color Considerations

When printing colors, desktop printers commonly use a color scheme called **Composite RGB**. RGB stands for the three colors — red, green, and blue — that are used to print the combined colors of your publication. Professional printers, on the other hand, can print your publication using color scheme processes, or **libraries.** These processes include black-and-white, spot-color, and process-color.

In **black-and-white printing**, the printer uses only one color of ink (usually black, but you can choose a different color if you want). You can add accent colors to your publication by using different shades of gray or by printing on colored paper. Your publication can have the same range of subtleties as a black-and-white photograph.

A **spot color** is used to accent a black and white publication. Newspapers, for example, may print their masthead in a bright, eye-catching color on page 1 but print the rest of the publication in black and white. In Publisher, you may apply up to two spot colors with a color matching system called **Pantone**. **Spot-color printing** uses semitransparent, premixed inks typically chosen from standard color-matching guides, such as Pantone. Choosing colors from a **color-matching library** helps ensure high-quality results, because printing professionals who license the libraries agree to maintain the specifications, control, and quality.

In a spot-color publication, each spot color is **separated** to its own plate and printed on an offset printing press. The use of spot colors has become more creative in the last few years. Printing services use spot colors of metallic or florescent inks, as well as screen tints to get color variations without increasing the number of color separations and cost. If your publication includes a logo with one or two colors, or if you want to use color to emphasize line art or text, then consider using spot-color printing.

Process-color printing means your publication can include color photographs and any color or combination of colors. One of the process-color libraries, called **CMYK**, or **four-color printing**, is named for the four semitransparent process inks — cyan, magenta, yellow, and black. CMYK process-color printing can reproduce a full range of colors on a printed page. The CMYK color model defines color as it is absorbed and reflected on a printed page rather than in its liquid state.

Process-color printing is the most expensive proposition; black-and-white printing is the cheapest. Using color increases the cost and time it takes to process the publication. When using either the spot-color or process-color method, the printer

---

More About

Spot Color Printing

If you choose black plus one spot color in a publication, Publisher converts all colors except for black to tints of the selected spot color. If you choose black plus two spot colors, Publisher changes only exact matches of the second spot color to 100 percent of the second spot color. All other colors in the publication, other than black, are changed to tints of the first spot color. You then can apply tints of the second spot color to objects in the publication manually.

More About

CMYK Process Colors

When CMYK Process is selected, Publisher converts all colors in text, graphics, and other objects to CMYK values and then creates four plates, regardless of the color scheme originally used to create the publication. Some RGB colors, including some of Publisher's standard colors, cannot be matched exactly to a CMYK color. After setting up for process-color printing, be sure to evaluate the publication for color changes. If a color does not match the color you want, you will have to include the new color library when you pack the publication.

More About

Printing Service Colors

Your printing service may use the initials SWOP, which stand for Standard for Web Offset Printing — a widely accepted set of color standards used in web offset printing. Web offset printing has nothing to do with the World Wide Web. It is merely the name for an offset printing designed to print thousands of pieces in a single run from a giant roll of paper.

More About

Flipping Objects to Print on T-Shirts

You can use Publisher to create T-shirt designs with pictures, logos, words, or any of the Publisher objects. You need thermal T-shirt transfer paper that is widely available for most printers. Then create your design in Publisher. On the File menu, click Page Setup. On the Printer & Paper sheet, select Letter. If your design is a picture, clip art, or WordArt, flip it horizontally. If your design includes text, cut it from the text box, and insert it into a WordArt object; then flip it horizontally.

first must output the publication to film on an **image setter**, which recreates the publication on film or photographic paper. The film then is used to create color **printing plates**. Each printing plate transfers one of the colors in the publication onto paper in an offset process. Publisher can print a preview of these individual sheets showing how the colors will separate before you take your publication to the printer.

A new printing technology called **digital printing** uses toner instead of ink to reproduce a full range of colors. Digital printing does not require separate printing plates. Although not yet widely available, digital printing promises to become cheaper than offset printing without sacrificing any quality.

Publisher supports all three kinds of printing and provides the tools commercial printing services need to print the publication. You should ask your printing service which color-matching system it uses.

Choosing a Commercial Printing Tool

After making the decisions about printing services, paper, and color, you must prepare the brochure for outside printing. The first task is to assign a color library from the commercial printing tools, as illustrated in the following steps.

To Choose a Commercial Printing Tool

1

• **Click Tools on the menu bar. Point to Commercial Printing Tools.**

The Commercial Printing Tools submenu displays (Figure 3-60).

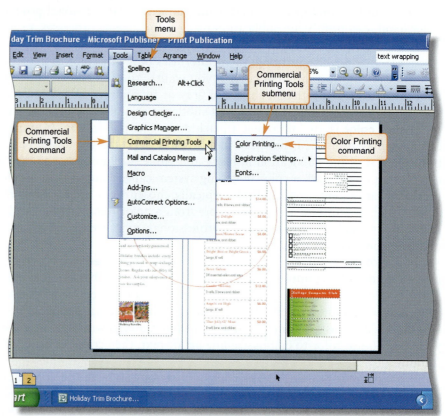

FIGURE 3-60

2

• **Click Color Printing on the Commercial Printing Tools submenu. When the Color Printing dialog box is displayed, click Process colors (CMYK). If a dialog box is displayed, click its OK button.**

Publisher will convert all colors in text, graphics, and other objects to CMYK values and then internally create four plates, regardless of the color model originally used to create the colors (Figure 3-61).

3

• **Click the OK button.**

Depending on your screen colors and resolution, you may or may not see a noticeable difference.

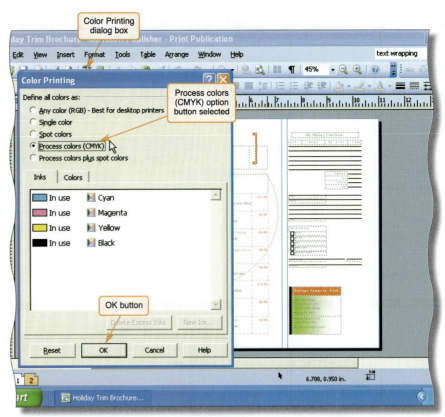

FIGURE 3-61

Other Ways

1. In Voice Command mode, say "Tools, Commercial Printing Tools"

Packaging the Publication for the Printing Service

The publication file can be packaged for the printing service in two ways. The first way is to give the printing service the Publisher file in Publisher format using the Pack and Go Wizard. The second way is to save the file in a format called Encapsulated PostScript. Both of these methods are discussed in the following sections.

Using the Pack and Go Wizard

The **Pack and Go Wizard** guides you through the steps to collect and pack all the files the printing service needs and then compress the files to fit on one or more disks. Publisher checks for and embeds the TrueType fonts used in the publication. **Embedding** ensures that the printing service can display and print the publication with the correct fonts. The Pack and Go Wizard adds a program called **Unpack.exe** to the disk that the printing service can use to unpack the files. At the end of Publisher's packing sequence, you are given the option of printing a composite color printout or color separation printouts on your desktop printer.

You need either sufficient space on a floppy disk or another formatted disk readily available when using the Pack and Go Wizard. Graphic files and fonts require a great deal of disk space. The Pack and Go Wizard also creates on disk a **Readme file** intended for the printing service. In the steps on the next page, if you use a disk other than the one on which you previously saved the brochure, save it again on the new disk before beginning the process.

More About

The Pack and Go Readme File

To look at a sample Pack and Go Readme file, visit the Publisher 2003 More About Web page (scsite.com/pub2003/more) and then click Pack and Go.

The following steps illustrate using the Pack and Go Wizard to ready the publication for submission to a commercial printing service.

To Use the Pack and Go Wizard

1

• **With a floppy disk in drive A, click File on the menu bar. Point to Pack and Go.**

The File menu and Pack and Go submenu are displayed (Figure 3-62). Publisher also uses a Pack and Go Wizard to transport publications to other computers for printing and viewing purposes only.

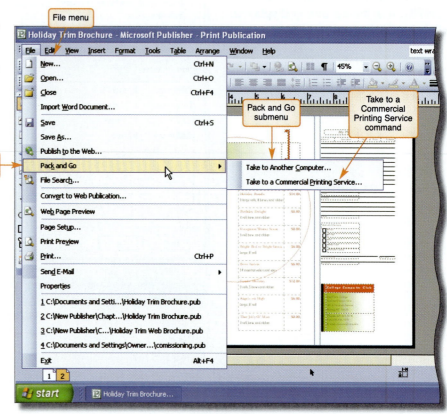

FIGURE 3-62

2

• **Click Take to a Commercial Printing Service on the Pack and Go submenu.**

The first Pack and Go Wizard dialog box is displayed (Figure 3-63). This wizard guides you through each step of the packing process. Read each individual screen as you progress through the steps.

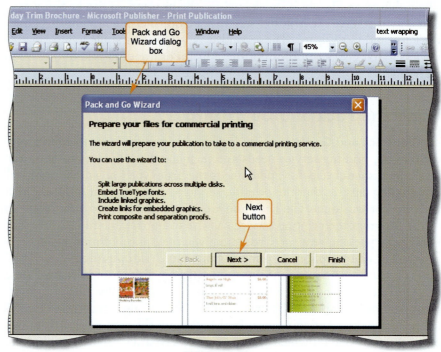

FIGURE 3-63

3

• **Click the Next button for each of the wizard steps, accepting the preset options.**

The last dialog box of the Pack and Go Wizard is displayed (Figure 3-64).

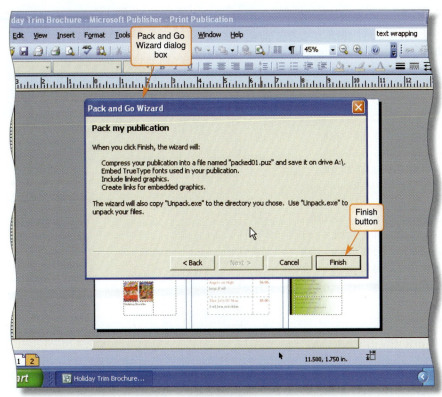

FIGURE 3-64

4

• **Click the Finish button. If you used graphics from an external source, Publisher will ask you to insert the disk. If you used system fonts that cannot be embedded, Publisher will display a dialog box in which you may click the OK button for the purposes of this project.**

After Publisher finishes packing your publication, a confirming dialog box is displayed (Figure 3-65). Both print check boxes are selected.

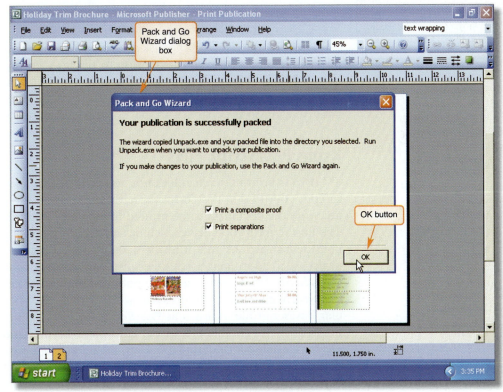

FIGURE 3-65

5

• **If necessary, click both print check boxes so neither one is selected.**

The check marks are removed from the check boxes (Figure 3-66). You already have printed the brochure and unless you are actually submitting this publication to a printing service, a separation print is unnecessary. If you want to see what the separations look like, you may print them.

6

• **Click the OK button.**

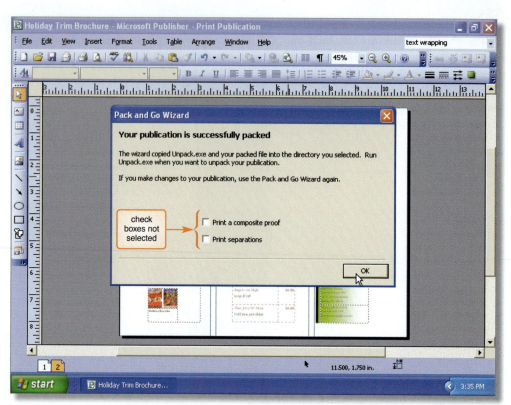

FIGURE 3-66

The files are saved on the disk in drive A. Publisher names and numbers the packed files and adds a .puz extension to the files. For example, the first file will be named Packed01.puz, the second file will be Packed02.puz, and so on. If you make changes to the publication after packing the files, be sure to run the Pack and Go Wizard again so the changes are part of the packed publication.

Using PostScript Files

If your printing service does not accept Publisher files, you can hand off, or submit, your files in PostScript format. **PostScript** is a page definition language that describes the document to be printed in language that the printer can understand. The PostScript printer driver includes a page definition language translator to interpret the instructions and print the document on a printer or a PostScript output device, such as an image setter. Because you cannot open or make changes directly to a PostScript file, everything in the publication must be complete before saving it.

Nearly all printing services can work with some type of PostScript file, either regular PostScript files, known as **PostScript dumps**, or **Encapsulated PostScript** (**EPS**) files, which are graphic pictures of each page. If you hand off a PostScript file, you are responsible for updating graphics, including the necessary fonts, and ensuring that you have all the files your printing service needs. Publisher includes several **PostScript printer drivers** (**PPD**s) and their description files to facilitate printing at the publisher. You must install a PPD before saving in PostScript form. Because the most common installation of Publisher is for a single user in a desktop environment, this project will not take you through the steps involved to install a PostScript printer driver. That process would necessitate using original operating system disks and a more thorough knowledge of PostScript printers. Ask your printing service representative for the correct printer driver, and see your Windows documentation for installing it. Then use the Save As command on the File menu to save the publication in PostScript format.

Another question to ask your printing service is whether it performs the **prepress tasks** or a **preflight check**. You may be responsible for making color corrections, separations, setting the printing options, and other printing tasks.

More About

Submitting PostScript Files

If you decide to hand off a PostScript "dump," or file, to an outside printer or service bureau, include a copy of the original document as well — for backup purposes. Many shops slowly are changing over from Macintosh-based to cross-platform based operations. If something happens, the printer technician can correct the error from the original without another trip by you to the print shop.

Quitting Publisher

The following steps quit Publisher.

To Quit Publisher

1 **Click the Close button on the Publisher title bar.**

2 **If a dialog box displays reminding you to save the document, click its No button.**

The Publisher window closes.

Project Summary

Project 3 introduced you to the brochure medium. You learned how to create custom color schemes, apply font effects, and change paragraph formatting. You learned about the use of photographs versus images, and how to insert a photograph from a file. After entering new text and deleting unwanted objects, you created a logo from scratch using a custom shape and symbols grouped in the workspace. You also learned about design and printing considerations such as overlapping, separations, color libraries, paper types, and costs. In anticipation of taking the brochure to a professional publisher, you previewed and printed your publication and then used the Pack and Go Wizard to create the necessary files.

What You Should Know

Having completed this project, you should be able to perform the tasks below. The tasks are listed in the same order they were presented in this project. For a list of the buttons, menus, toolbars, and commands introduced in this project, see the Quick Reference Summary at the back of this book and refer to the Page Number column.

1. Start Publisher   (PUB 133)
2. Choose Brochure Options   (PUB 134)
3. Create a Custom Color Scheme   (PUB 137)
4. Save the Publication   (PUB 141)
5. Edit Text in the Brochure   (PUB 142)
6. Edit Other Text Boxes on Page 1   (PUB 144)
7. Delete Objects on Page 1   (PUB 145)
8. Insert a Text Box and Apply a Font Scheme Style (PUB 146)
9. Switch to Page 2   (PUB 148)
10. Apply a Font Effect   (PUB 149)
11. Change the Alignment and Line Spacing (PUB 151)
12. Edit the Caption, Price List, and Order Form Heading   (PUB 153)
13. Insert a Photograph from a File   (PUB 155)
14. Replace the Graphics in the Left Panel of Page 1 (PUB 156)

What You Should Know *(continued)*

15. Replace the Graphics in the Right Panel of Page 1 (PUB 157)
16. Create a Shape for the Logo   (PUB 158)
17. Create a Text Box with Text Wrapping (PUB 161)
18. Insert a Symbol   (PUB 162)
19. Copy Text Boxes   (PUB 164)
20. Align and Nudge the Logo Objects   (PUB 165)
21. Group Objects   (PUB 167)

22. Reposition the Logo   (PUB 169)
23. Check the Publication and Save Again (PUB 170)
24. Preview the Brochure Before Printing   (PUB 171)
25. Print the Brochure   (PUB 172)
26. Choose a Commercial Printing Tool   (PUB 174)
27. Use the Pack and Go Wizard   (PUB 176)
28. Quit Publisher   (PUB 179)

More About

The Publisher Help System

The best way to become familiar with the Publisher Help system is to use it. Appendix A includes detailed information on the Publisher Help system and exercises that will help you gain confidence using it.

More About

Quick Reference

For a table that lists how to complete tasks covered in this book using the mouse, menu, shortcut menu, and keyboard, see the Quick Reference summary at the back of this book or visit the Shelly Cashman Series Office XP Web page (scsite.com/offxp/qr), and then click Microsoft Publisher 2003.

Learn It Online

Instructions: To complete the Learn It Online exercises, start your browser, click the Address bar, and then enter the Web address scsite.com/pub2003/learn. When the Publisher 2003 Learn It Online page is displayed, follow the instructions in the exercises below. Each exercise has instructions for printing your results, either for your own records or for submission to your instructor.

1 Project Reinforcement TF, MC, and SA

Below Publisher Project 3, click the Project Reinforcement link. Print the quiz by clicking Print on the File menu for each page. Answer each question.

2 Flash Cards

Below Publisher Project 3, click the Flash Cards link and read the instructions. Type 20 (or a number specified by your instructor) in the Number of playing cards text box, type your name in the Enter your Name text box, and then click the Flip Card button. When the flash card is displayed, read the question and then click the ANSWER box arrow to select an answer. Flip through Flash Cards. If your score is 15 (75%) correct or greater, click Print on the File menu to print your results. If your score is less than 15 (75%) correct, then redo this exercise by clicking the Replay button.

3 Practice Test

Below Publisher Project 3, click the Practice Test link. Answer each question, enter your first and last name at the bottom of the page, and then click the Grade Test button. When the graded practice test is displayed on your screen, click Print on the File menu to print a hard copy. Continue to take practice tests until you score 80% or better.

4 Who Wants To Be a Computer Genius?

Below Publisher Project 3, click the Computer Genius link. Read the instructions, enter your first and last name at the bottom of the page, and then click the PLAY button. When your score is displayed, click the PRINT RESULTS link to print a hard copy.

5 Wheel of Terms

Below Publisher Project 3, click the Wheel of Terms link. Read the instructions, and then enter your first and last name and your school name. Click the PLAY button. When your score is displayed, right-click the score and then click Print on the shortcut menu to print a hard copy.

6 Crossword Puzzle Challenge

Below Publisher Project 3, click the Crossword Puzzle Challenge link. Read the instructions, and then enter your first and last name. Click the SUBMIT button. Work the crossword puzzle. When you are finished, click the Submit button. When the crossword puzzle is redisplayed, click the Print Puzzle button to print a hard copy.

7 Tips and Tricks

Below Publisher Project 3, click the Tips and Tricks link. Click a topic that pertains to Project 3. Right-click the information and then click Print on the shortcut menu. Construct a brief example of what the information relates to in Publisher to confirm you understand how to use the tip or trick.

8 Newsgroups

Below Publisher Project 3, click the Newsgroups link. Click a topic that pertains to Project 3. Print three comments.

9 Expanding Your Horizons

Below Publisher Project 3, click the Expanding Your Horizons link. Click a topic that pertains to Project 3. Print the information. Construct a brief example of what the information relates to in Publisher to confirm you understand the contents of the article.

10 Search Sleuth

Below Publisher Project 3, click the Search Sleuth link. To search for a term that pertains to this project, select a term below the Project 3 title and then use the Google search engine at google.com (or any major search engine) to display and print two Web pages that present information on the term.

11 Publisher Online Training

Below Publisher Project 3, click the Publisher Online Training link. When your browser displays the Microsoft Office Online Web page, click the Publisher link. Click one of the Publisher courses that covers one or more of the objectives listed at the beginning of the project on page PUB 130. Print the first page of the course before stepping through it.

12 Office Marketplace

Below Publisher Project 3, click the Office Marketplace link. When your browser displays the Microsoft Office Online Web page, click the Office Marketplace link. Click a topic that relates to Publisher. Print the first page.

1 Editing a Publication

Instructions: Start Publisher. Open the publication named, Apply-3-1, from the Data Disk. See the inside back cover of this book for instructions for downloading the Data Disk or see your instructor for information on accessing the files required for this book. The edited publication is shown in Figures 3-67a and 3-67b.

Perform the following tasks:

1. With page 1 displayed, click View on the menu bar and then click Task Pane on the View menu. Click the Other Task Panes buttons, and then click Brochure Options. Click Include in the Customer address area and click Response form in the Form area.
2. On page 1, make the following text changes, zooming as necessary:
   a. Click the text, Seminar or Event Title. Type Music among the Maples to replace the text.
   b. Drag through the text, Business Name. Type The Performing Arts Center to replace the text.
   c. In the lower portion of the right panel of page 1, insert a text box below Performing Arts Center. Click the Font Color button arrow on the Formatting toolbar and then click white on the color palette. Press CTRL+E to center the text. Press F9 to increase the magnification. Type In conjunction with the Dayton Symphonic Orchestra and then press the ENTER key. Type 2005 Fall Concert Series to complete the entry.
   d. Delete the organization logo if it displays.
3. In the left panel, double-click each of the three graphics, one at a time. Use the keywords, violin, conductor, and entertainment, respectively, to search for pictures similar to Figure 3-67a.
4. Click the Page 2 icon in the Page Navigation control on the status bar. Delete the text box in the center panel by right-clicking the text box and then clicking Delete Object on the shortcut menu. Delete the picture of the graduate and its caption. Drag the instruments picture upward to the center of the panel.
5. SHIFT-drag the red rectangle from the center panel to the left panel and place it to the left of the text.
6. Select all of the story on page 2. Change the line spacing to 1.5 and the alignment to justified.
7. Create a 5-point Star AutoShape button in the workspace. Use the Accent 1 scheme color to fill the star. Create a centered text box using the Best Fit option and a white font color. Insert a musical notation symbol. (*Hint*: the musical notes in Figure 3-67b are found using the Times New Roman Font in the Symbol dialog box.) Drag the text box on top of the star and group. Drag the grouped object to the center panel.
8. Check spelling and run the Design Checker. Correct errors if necessary.
9. Click File on the menu bar and then click Save As. Use the file name, Apply 3-1 Concert Series Brochure.
10. Click Tools on the menu bar, point to Commercial Printing Tools, and then click Color Printing on the Commercial Printing Tools submenu. When the Color Printing dialog box is displayed, click Process colors (CMYK) and then click the OK button.
11. With a floppy disk in drive A, click File on the menu bar. Point to Pack and Go and then click Take to a Commercial Printing Service on the Pack and Go submenu. Click the Next button in each progressive dialog box. When the final dialog box is displayed, click the Finish button.
12. When the wizard completes the packing process, if necessary click the Print a composite check box to select it. The brochure will print on two pages.

Apply Your Knowledge

(a)

2005 Fall Concert Series

This year's Fall Concert Series promises to be the best yet. The Performing Arts Center has brought in some of the more gifted and talented conductors from across the United States. Whether you want to hear the latest Broadway medley or Straus's "Also Sprach Zarathustra" used in 2001: A Space Odyssey, the 2005 Fall Concert Series will entertain and delight you.

Robert Stewart
Director of the Dayton Symphonic Orchestra for the last five years

Amy Hayes
The first woman conductor of the Ohio Pops Orchestra

Our Own Jazz
The newest member of the series

The Performing Arts Center
2003 Fall Concert Series
1728 Nottingham Drive
Dayton, OH 45402

Music Among the Maples

The Performing Arts Center

In conjunction with the
Dayton Symphonic Orchestra
2005 Fall Concert Series

(b)

The Concerts

The Classical Series: Performed by the Dayton Symphonic Orchestra, the Classical Series has been the mainstay of the summer repertoire since the series' inception in 1987. This 80-piece orchestra, made up of professional and semiprofessional musicians, has performed all over the northeast. This year's theme is music of the late nineteenth and twentieth centuries

The Broadway Series: The Ohio Pops Orchestra is back by popular demand playing, show tunes by famous duos. Performances of music by Rogers & Hammerstein and Lerner & Lowe highlight this family-oriented series.

The Jazz Series: The group, Our Own Jazz brings its unique interpretation of jazz greats, Duke Ellington and Count Basie to the Fall Concert Series. Don't miss this newest addition.

Friday and Saturday evening concerts begin at 8:00 p.m.; Sunday Matinees at 2:00 p.m.

For more information, visit our web site at www.arts.dayton.oh.org.

Order Fall Concert Series Tickets

Enter the number of tickets you wish to purchase in the boxes. All orders are filled using best seating available.

Classical Series
- [ ] September 19
- [ ] September 28
- [ ] October 4

Broadway Series
- [ ] September 20
- [ ] September 26
- [ ] October 5

Jazz Series
- [ ] September 21
- [ ] September 27
- [ ] October 3

Season Tickets
- [ ] Friday Series
- [ ] Saturday Series
- [ ] Sunday Matinee Series

Name _____
Address _____
_____
_____

Telephone _____

Method of Payment
- [ ] Check
- [ ] Bill Me
- [ ] Visa
- [ ] MasterCard
- [ ] American Express

Credit Card # _____ Exp. date _____
Signature _____

The Performing Arts Center
Ticket Hotline: 802-555-8484
2005 Fall Concert Series
1728 Nottingham Drive
Dayton, OH 45402

FIGURE 3-67

In the Lab

1 Creating a Brochure Layout with One Spot Color

Problem: A large marketing firm is planning a seminar for salesmen in the oil industry. They would like you to create a sample publication, advertising the event. Their theme is "Reach Your Goal." They would like a tri-fold brochure with a graphic related to the oil industry and a large blue arrow with white diagonal lettering, spelling the word, GOAL. On the inside of the brochure, the marketing firm would like a response form to gain some knowledge of the participants' backgrounds. If they like the sample, the firm then will submit text for the other text boxes.

Instructions: Start Publisher and perform the following tasks to create the one spot color brochure shown in Figures 3-68a and 3-68b.

1. From the New Publication task pane, choose the Accent Box Informational Brochure. Choose to display the customer address and a response form.
2. Edit the text frames in the right panel as shown in Figure 3-68a. Delete the logo in the middle panel.
3. Double-click the graphic in the front panel. Insert a clip using the keyword, oil.
4. Click the AutoShapes button on the Objects toolbar. Point to Block Arrows and then click the arrow shape that points right. In the workspace, SHIFT-drag to create an arrow approximately two inches square. Use the Fill Color button to choose Accent 1 (Medium Blue).
5. Drag to create a text frame in the workspace approximately .35 inch square. Use the Fill Color button to choose Accent 1 (Medium Blue). Use the Font Color button to choose Accent 5 (White). Type G in the text frame. On the Format menu, point to AutoFit Text and then click Best Fit. Choose no text wrapping.
6. Copy the text frame three times. Drag each copy away from the original. Replace the text in each copy with the letters O, A, and L, respectively.
7. Drag the text frames on top of the large arrow so they display diagonally across the arrow as shown in Figure 3-68a. Click the G text frame and then SHIFT-click each of the other letters. SHIFT-click the large arrow itself, away from the letters. Group the objects to create a composite logo. Drag the logo to the empty space above the picture.
8. Click the Response form (page 2). Make the text changes as indicated in Figure 3-68b.
9. Click Tools on the menu bar and then point to Commercial Printing Tools. Click Color Printing. When the Color Printing dialog box is displayed, click Spot colors. Click the OK button.
10. Save the publication using the file name, Lab 3-1 GOAL Brochure. Print a copy.

In the Lab

(a)

(b)

FIGURE 3-68

In the Lab

2 Creating a CD Liner

Problem: Your friend has recorded a new CD of his original guitar music. Knowing of your interest in desktop publishing, he has asked you to create the CD liner. You decide to create a publication with four pages, using Publisher's CD liner template.

Instructions: Perform the following tasks to create the two-panel, two-sided CD liner as shown in Figures 3-69a and 3-69b.

1. Start Publisher.
2. In the New Publication task pane, click Publications for Print, click Labels, and then click CD/DVD Labels. When Publisher displays the previews, click CD/DVD Case Insert Booklet.
3. Choose the Glacier color scheme and the Modern font scheme.
4. Edit the text in both panels as shown in Figure 3-69a.
5. Select the large rectangle border in the right panel. Press CTRL+T to make the rectangle transparent, in preparation for the watermark.
6. Replace the picture in the right panel using the Clip Art task pane. Search using the keyword, guitar.
7. Copy the graphic using the Copy button on the Standard toolbar.
8. On the Insert menu, click Page to insert a new blank page to follow page 1. Click the Page 2 icon in the Page Navigation control, if necessary.
9. Paste the picture from page 1. Drag it to the left panel and SHIFT-drag a corner handle, resizing so it fills the entire panel.
10. Use the Clip Art task pane to search for an appropriate line drawing graphic, similar to the one in Figure 3-69b, for a watermark effect using the keyword, music.
11. Drag the music graphic to the right panel and SHIFT-drag a corner handle, resizing so it fills the entire panel.
12. Create a large text frame in the left panel. Make it transparent so the picture shows through. Use a white font color. Type the text as shown in Figure 3-69b.
13. Using the Design Gallery Object button, insert a Voyage style table of contents. Use the Size and Position dialog box to place it exactly as follows: Width: 3.4; Height: 4.5; Horizontal: 5.4; and Vertical .1 in the right panel. Make it transparent. Edit the table of contents as shown in Figure 3-69b.
14. Save the publication on a floppy disk using the file name, Lab 3-2 Guitar CD Liner.
15. Print a copy of the CD liner, using duplex printing. The default settings will print the liner in the middle of an 8½-by-11-inch piece of paper, with crop marks. Trim the printout.

In the Lab

(a)

Manufactured in the United States by Starks Recording Corporation.
Printed in the United States. All Rights Reserved.

<u>Warning:</u> unauthorized reproduction of this recording is prohibited by
federal law and subject to criminal prosecution.

© Starks Recording Corporation

137 East 25th Street
New York, New York 10001

Visit the artist's home page at
www.starks.net\gobert

Jonathan Gobert

MUSIC OF MY LIFE

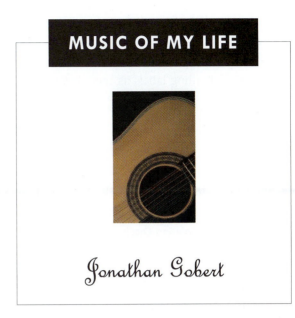

Jonathan Gobert

(b)

Jon Gobert's style of guitar crosses the boundaries among classical, rock, and blues. His unique style of fingering and his use of percussive wood sounds mark him as one of the up and coming artists of the twenty-first century.

Jon studied at the New England Conservatory of Music and has performed with the Greater New York Chamber Guitar Society.

He tours regularly on college campuses and performs at night clubs and coffee houses. Hon also plays studio guitar and has performed with artists such as singer David J. Taylor and blues great Billie Davis.

Music of My Life

All I Have	1
Your Love	2
The City	3
Street Musician	4
Classical, But Not a Gas	5
Forever Bach	6
Winter Blues	7

FIGURE 3-69

In the Lab

3 Creating a Travel Brochure

Problem: Alpha Zeta Mu fraternity is planning a ski trip to Sunset Mountain, Colorado during spring break. They have asked you to design a brochure that advertises the trip. They would like a full-color tri-fold brochure on glossy paper that includes pictures of Sunset Mountain, a sign-up form, and the Alpha Omega logo. The fraternity plans to use mailing labels as they distribute the brochures.

Instructions: Perform the following tasks to create the two-panel, two-sided CD liner as shown in Figures 3-70a and 3-70b.

1. From the New Publication task pane, choose the Straight Edge Informational Brochure. Choose a 3-panel display, choose to include the customer address, and select the Sign-up form.
2. Choose the Clay color scheme and the Modern Font Scheme.
3. On Page 1, in the right panel, edit the brochure title as shown in Figure 3-70a. Delete the tag line and telephone number text boxes in the lower portion of the right panel. Delete the address text box in the center of the middle panel.
4. Table 3-10 displays the text for the left panel. Enter the text. Press CTRL+A to select all of the text. On the Format menu, click Paragraph. Choose justified alignment and type 2 in the line spacing text box. Close the Paragraph dialog box. With the text still selected, click the Font Color button and select white in the color palette.

Table 3-10	Text for Page 1
LOCATION	**TEXT**
Left Panel Heading	Sunset Mountain
Left Panel	Located in the beautiful Colorado Rockies, Sunset Mountain's extreme elevation allows it to boast the latest ski season in Colorado and one of the longest ski runs at more than a mile! Sunset Mountain is off the beaten path, so lifts are not crowded. Four double chair lifts accommodate 1,000 people per hour, so you never have a long wait to begin your skiing adventure. Whether you are into "bunny" slopes or telemark skiing, you will love Sunset Mountain.
Left Panel Caption	Sunset Mountaintop
Middle Panel	University Spring Break Alpha Zeta Mu 1050 Greek Row P.O. Box 1050-3211 Kansas City, MO 64118
Right Panel	University Spring Break March 7-10, 2005

5. Click the Page 2 icon in the Page Navigation Control.
6. Table 3-11 on page PUB 190 displays the text for the three stories on Page 2. Enter the text and headings as shown in Figure 3-70b.
7. Using the Clip Art task pane, search for graphics, similar to the ones shown in Figure 3-70, that are related to lodge, mountain, fireplace, and skiing. Replace the placeholder graphics in the brochure.

In the Lab

University Spring Break
March 7-10, 2005

Alpha Zeta Mu
1050 Greek Row
P.O. Box 1050-3211
Kansas City, MO 64118

University Spring Break

Spring Break
Ski Trip

Sunset Mountain

Located in the beautiful Colorado Rockies, Sunset Mountain's extreme elevation allows it to boast the latest ski season in Colorado and one of the longest ski runs at more than a mile!

Sunset Mountain is off the beaten path, so lifts are not crowded. Four double chair lifts accommodate 1,000 people per hour, so you never have a long wait to begin your skiing adventure. Whether you are into "bunny" slopes or telemark skiing, you will love Sunset Mountain.

Sunset Mountaintop

(a)

Winter Sports: Skiing and Beyond

Ski rental available

Sunset Mountain offers a wide variety of winter sports, including downhill and cross-country skiing, as well as snowboarding, tubing, and bobsledding runs. Downhill slopes for beginner, intermediate, and advanced skiers are groomed daily. Experienced ski instructors conduct small group lessons.

If skiing isn't your "thing," think variety! Sunset Mountain is offering an advanced tubing course this season, with banked turns and jumps to make your trip down the mountain more exciting.

Alpha Zeta Mu Ski Trip

Alpha Zeta Mu Sorority is sponsoring a 4-day, 3-night ski trip to Colorado. Sorority members and their guests will fly from Kansas City International to Denver on JLM Airlines and then board a free shuttle to Sunset Mountain. All package option prices are based on Alpha Zeta Mu's ability to book at least 20 people, two to a room, with a maximum of 40. You may mix and match any of the options. You will receive a confirmation postcard in the mail.

Lodging

Sunset Mountain Lodge is the only bed and breakfast among the seven lodging experiences on Sunset Mountain. Nestled among the tall lodge pole pines, the lodge offers modern rooms with full baths. An optional dinner package is available at a modest cost. Other amenities include a game room, hot tub, meeting room, and of course the grand hearth — where the fireplace always is lit and the hot cinnamon cocoa always is ready!

Visit the lodge at:
www.skicolorado.com

Alpha Zeta Mu Ski Trip March 7-10

Sign up for:	Price
☐ Round-trip KCI/Denver/KCI	$300.00
☐ 4 days, 3 nights w/breakfast	$325.00
☐ 3 days ski rental and lift tickets	$125.00
☐ 2-hour ski lesson	$ 50.00
☐ 3 dinner option	$ 50.00
☐ Single-day lift ticket	$ 40.00
	Subtotal: _____
	Tax: _____
	Total: _____

Name _____
Address _____
_____
_____
Phone _____

Method of Payment
☐ Check
☐ Bill Me
☐ Visa
☐ MasterCard
☐ American Express

Credit Card # _____ Exp. date _____
Signature _____

University Spring Break
March 7-10, 2005

Alpha Zeta Mu
1050 Greek Row
P.O. Box 1050-3211
Kansas City, MO 64118
Phone: 816-555-1217
Fax: 816-555-1218
Email: greekao@midland.edu

(a)

FIGURE 3-70

(continued)

In the Lab

Creating a Travel Brochure *(continued)*

Table 3-11	Text for Page 2
HEADING	**TEXT**
Winter Sports: Skiing and Beyond	Sunset Mountain offers a wide variety of winter sports, including downhill and cross-country skiing, as well as snowboarding, tubing, and bobsledding runs. Downhill slopes for beginner, intermediate, and advanced skiers are groomed daily. Experienced ski instructors conduct small group lessons. If skiing isn't your "thing," think variety! Sunset Mountain is offering an advanced tubing course this season, with banked turns and jumps to make your trip down the mountain more exciting.
Left Panel caption	Ski rental available
Alpha Zeta Mu Ski Trip	Alpha Zeta Mu Fraternity is sponsoring a 4-day, 3-night ski trip to Colorado. Fraternity members and their guests will fly from Kansas City International to Denver on JLM Airlines and then board a free shuttle to Sunset Mountain. All package option prices are based on Alpha Zeta Mu's ability to book at least 20 people, two to a room, with a maximum of 40. You may mix and match any of the options. You will receive a confirmation postcard in the mail.
Lodging	Sunset Mountain Lodge is the only bed and breakfast among the seven lodging experiences on Sunset Mountain. Nestled among the tall lodge pole pines, the lodge offers modern rooms with full baths. An optional dinner package is available at a modest cost. Other amenities include a game room, hot tub, meeting room, and of course the grand hearth — where the fireplace always is lit and the hot cinnamon cocoa always is ready!
Middle Panel Caption	Visit the lodge at: www.skicolorado.com
Order Form Detail	Add 6 lines from upper right of Figure 3-70a on the previous page.

8. Click the AutoShapes button on the Objects toolbar, point to Stars and Banners, and then click the Wave shape. Drag a wave shape in the scratch area, approximately 1.6 by 1.2 inches in size. Use the Fill Color button to fill the shape with Accent 1 (Dark Red).

9. Create a text box in the scratch area, approximately .5 by 5. inches. Change the text box to Best Fit with gray text. Copy the text box and paste it twice, creating three boxes. Using the Insert Symbol dialog box, enter the Greek letters Alpha, Zeta, and Mu as shown in Figure 3-70a. Drag each of the text boxes on top of the Wave shape and group them with the shape.

10. Click the Copy button. Drag the grouped shape to the right panel of page 2.

11. Click the Paste button. With the copy of the grouped shape selected, click Arrange on the menu bar and then click Rotate Right. Drag a corner handle to resize the shape to approximately 1 by .75 inches. Drag the shape to the middle panel as shown in Figure 3-70a.

12. Check the publication for Spelling. Run the Design Checker. Fix any errors.

13. Click Tools on the menu bar and then point to Commercial Printing Tools. Click Color Printing. When the Color Printing dialog box is displayed, click Process Colors (CMYK).

14. Save the publication using the file name, Lab 3-3 Ski Trip Brochure.

15. Print the publication two sided. Fold the brochure and submit it to your instructor.

Cases and Places

The difficulty of these case studies varies:
■ are the least difficult and ■■ are more difficult. The last exercise is a group exercise.

1 ■ You recently have joined Success America, Incorporated as the new in-house desktop publisher. You are to design a tri-fold event brochure for their October 2005 training event in Indianapolis. The theme will be "Every American Can Win." Featured speakers will include former U.S. Senator Charles Goolsby, television news anchor Holly Schulke, and prominent businessman Dennis Louks. Your employer wants to mail the brochures to potential attendees. The company logo is a blue triangle with a white Sigma S (Greek S) symbol in the center. Create a rough draft using an Event brochure that includes a sign-up form with a placeholder for the customer address. The technical writer will send you content for the stories at a later date.

2 ■ Use the Blends Information brochure to create a brochure announcing the Youth Baseball League. Pick an appropriate color and font scheme. Type Spring Sign-Up as the brochure title. Type The Youth Baseball League as the Organization name. Type your address and telephone number in the appropriate text boxes. Delete the logo. Replace all graphics with sports-related clip art. Edit the captions to match. The league commissioner will send you content for the stories at a later date. Include a sign-up form on page 2. Edit the sign-up form event check boxes as displayed in Table 3-12.

Table 3-12 Sign-Up Form Check Box Content		
EVENT NAME	TIME	PRICE
Preschool T-Ball: ages 4 and 5	10:00	$25.00
Pee-Wee T-Ball: ages 6 and 7	11:00	$25.00
Coach Pitched: ages 8 and 9	1:00	$40.00
Intermediate: ages 10 and 11	2:30	$40.00
Advanced: ages 12 and 13	4:00	$40.00
City Team, audition only	6:00	TBA

On a separate piece of paper, make a table similar to Table 3-1 on page PUB 132, listing the type of exposure, kinds of information, audience and purpose of communication. Turn in the table with your printout.

3 ■ Create a new color scheme named, My Favorite Colors. Use the Color Scheme task pane to access the Color Schemes dialog box. Choose colors that complement one another. Using the New Publication task pane, create a blank publication. Insert six different AutoShapes and fill each with a color from your color scheme. Create text box captions for each of the AutoShapes, identifying the name of the shape and the color. Print the publication.

Cases and Places

4 ■■ Using the Blank Print Publications link on the New Publication task pane, recreate as closely as possible your school or company logo on a full-page publication. Use the AutoShapes button, fill and font colors, text boxes, and symbols to match the elements in your logo. You also may use WordArt. Ask your instructor or employer for clip art files, if necessary. Use the workspace scratch area to design portions of the logo and then layer and group them before dragging them onto the publication.

5 ■■ Bob Bert of Bert's Beanery has hired you to "spice up" and modernize the look of the restaurant's menu. You decide to use a menu template to create a full color menu for publication at a local copy shop. Bob wants special attention paid to his famous "Atomic Chili®," which is free if a customer can eat five spoonfuls without reaching for water. You will find the registered trademark symbol in the Symbol dialog box. Bob serves salads, soups, and sandwiches a la carte. He has several family specials, as well as combo meals and a variety of drinks and side dishes.

6 ■■ **Working Together** Individually, visit or call several local copy shops or commercial printers in your area. Ask them the following questions: What kind of paper stock do your customers choose for brochures? What is the most commonly used finish? Do you support all three color processes? Will you accept files saved with Microsoft Publisher Pack and Go, or EPS files? What prepress tasks do you perform? Come back together as a group and create a blank Publisher publication to record your answers. Create a table with the Insert Table button on the Objects toolbar. Insert the questions down the left side. Insert the names of the print shops across the top. Fill in the grid with the answers they provide.

MICROSOFT
Office Publisher 2003

Creating an E-Mail Letter Using Publisher

CASE PERSPECTIVE

Your friend, Burt Carlo, is the president of the Community Action Group that looks at public policy related to the town of Marshall, Missouri. The steering committee members of his group recently have created a listserv of e-mail addresses so they may communicate with members of the community more quickly. Many residents have subscribed to the committee's listserv.

Burt knows of your interest in Microsoft Publisher and wonders if you can create a publication that he can send out via e-mail. Together you look through the available templates in the New Publication task pane and discover an e-mail letter template that will serve Burt's purpose. The Community Action Group wants to invite people to a special zoning meeting where a contractor will present a proposal to build new homes in the area.

Burt wants the e-mail message to catch the recipient's eye with strong colors and fonts so they will not delete it right away. He wants to display his group's motto, Building a better community, at the top of the e-mail. Burt also wants the Marshall County logo, as well as an interesting graphic, to appear in the body of the e-mail message. The text of the e-mail letter should remind people of the purpose, date, and time of the meeting.

In the lower portion of the e-mail message, Burt wants a return e-mail address and telephone number to be displayed. You remind him that listserv e-mails always should provide a way for the recipient to unsubscribe.

Objectives

You will have mastered the material in this project when you can:

- Select and format an e-mail letter template
- Edit text boxes in an e-mail letter
- Choose a logo design
- Insert an e-mail hyperlink
- Preview an e-mail letter
- Send an e-mail message using Publisher

Introduction

E-mail, short for electronic mail, is a popular form of communication to transmit messages and files via a computer network. People use e-mail in ways similar to traditional mail, sending correspondence, business communication, greeting cards, letters, brochures, newsletters, and other type of publications.

You can send any Publisher publication as an attachment to an e-mail message; however, if you use Microsoft Outlook 2003 or Microsoft Outlook Express version 5.0 or later as your e-mail program, you can use Publisher 2003 to create and send just a page of the publication as an e-mail letter or message.

This Special Feature illustrates how to send an e-mail letter using Publisher to create the publication. An **e-mail letter** displays both traditional correspondence-related text and graphics, as well as hyperlinks similar to a Web page. All of the objects in an e-mail letter are displayed in the body of the e-mail message rather than as a separate publication attached to the e-mail message.

Q&A

Q: Do most people prefer to receive a publication as an e-mail attachment?

A: It is not necessarily better to use attachments. For immediate viewing, such as an announcement, letter, or card, it is better to send a single page in the body of an e-mail. If you do send an attachment, the person receiving your e-mail will have to have Publisher installed on his or her system in order to open and view the publication. Additionally, with a large attachment, you may run the risk of the e-mail being blocked by firewalls and filters at the receiving end.

More About

E-Mail Letter Templates

Microsoft has additional e-mail letter templates that you may download. For a link to the Microsoft Office Publisher download site, visit the Publisher 2003 More About Web page (scsite.com/pub2003/more) and then click Download Templates.

Publisher provides several ways to create an e-mail letter. You can use a template, create an e-mail letter from scratch, or convert a single page of another publication into an e-mail letter, expanding the use of your existing content. Publisher's e-mail letter templates are preformatted to the correct page size. The templates use placeholder text and graphics that download quickly and are suitable for the body of an e-mail message. When sending a page of another publication type as an e-mail message, some adjustments may need to be made to the width of your publication in order for it to fit in an e-mail message.

When you send a single page of a publication as an e-mail message, recipients can read the message using an HTML-enabled e-mail program such as Hotmail, AOL, and Yahoo!, as well as the current versions of Outlook and Outlook Express. Recipients do not need to have Publisher installed to view the message, because the page you send will be displayed as the body of the e-mail message. Sending a one-page publication by e-mail to a group of customers or friends is an efficient and inexpensive way to deliver a message. When you send an entire publication as an e-mail attachment, the recipient must have Microsoft Publisher 2002 or Microsoft Office Publisher 2003 installed to view it. When the recipient opens the attached file, Publisher automatically opens and displays the publication. An attachment is the only way to send a multipage publication in e-mail.

Figure 1 displays an e-mail letter sent to a list of residents interested in community housing and zoning matters. The e-mail letter includes a colorful heading, a logo, a graphic, and directions for obtaining more information.

This E-Mail Feature is for instructional purposes only. You do not have to be connected to the Internet or have an e-mail program on your system in order to create the e-mail letter. You can create and save the e-mail letter on a floppy disk rather than send it via e-mail.

Starting Publisher

To start Publisher, Windows must be running. The following steps explain how to start Publisher.

To Start Publisher

1 Click the Start button on the Windows taskbar, point to All Programs on the Start menu, point to Microsoft Office on the All Programs submenu, and then click Microsoft Office Publisher 2003 on the Microsoft Office submenu.

2 If the Publisher window is not maximized, double-click its title bar to maximize it.

3 If Publisher does not display the New Publication task pane, click View on the menu bar and then click Task Pane. If the Publication Designs task pane is displayed, click the Other Task Panes button on the task pane title bar, and then click New Publication.

4 If the Language bar is displayed, click its Minimize button.

You now are ready to use Publisher's New Publication task pane to create a tri-fold brochure.

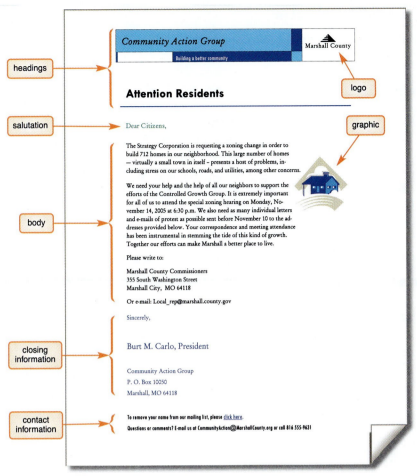

headings

salutation

body

closing information

contact information

logo

graphic

FIGURE 1

E-Mail Templates

E-mail can be an efficient and cost-effective way to keep in touch with friends, customers, co-workers, or other interested parties. It is easy to design and send professional-looking e-mail using Publisher. Each of Publisher's design sets features several e-mail publication types, so you can create and send e-mail that is consistent in design with the rest of the business communication and marketing materials that you create using Publisher. Table 1 lists the types of e-mail publications and their purpose.

Table 1 E-mail Template Publications	
E-MAIL TEMPLATE	**PURPOSE**
Newsletter	Informs interested clientele about an organization or business with stories, dates, contact information, and upcoming events
Letter	A more personalized document to correspond with one or more people, including specific information on a single topic
Event/Speaker	A notice of a specific upcoming event that includes a speaker and usually contains pictures, dates, times, and a map
Event/Activity	A notice of a specific upcoming activity or event containing a combination of pictures, dates, times, maps, agenda, and the ability to sign up
Product List	A sales-oriented publication to display products, prices, and special promotions including Web page links for more information
Featured Product	A publication that provides information about a company and a specific product or service, including graphics and Web page links for more information

Creating an E-mail Letter

The following steps describe how to open an e-mail letter template.

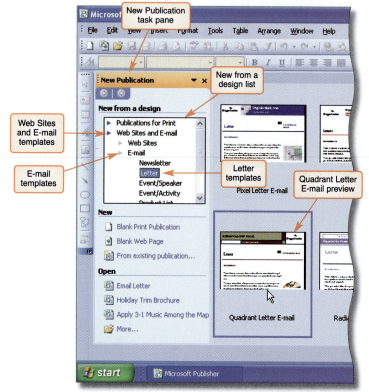

FIGURE 2

To Open an E-Mail Letter Template

1 In the New Publication task pane, click Web Sites and E-mail in the New from a design list.

2 When the Web Sites and E-mail list is displayed, click E-mail.

3 When the E-mail list is displayed, click Letter.

4 When the previews are displayed, scroll to the Quadrant Letter E-mail preview.

Publisher displays the New Publication task pane and the Quadrant Letter E-mail preview (Figure 2).

The following steps describe how to select the design set, color scheme, and font scheme for the e-mail letter.

To Select Publication Options

1 Click the Quadrant Letter E-mail preview. If Publisher displays the Personal Information dialog box, click its Cancel button.

2 When the Publication Design task pane is displayed, click Color Schemes and then click Marine in the Apply a color scheme list.

3 Click Font Schemes and then click Modern in the Apply a font scheme list.

4 Click the Close button on the Font Schemes task pane title bar.

5 On the Standard toolbar, click the Zoom box arrow and then click 100% in the Zoom list.

6 Scroll to display the upper portion of the page layout.

Publisher displays the upper portion of the e-mail letter template in the workspace (Figure 3).

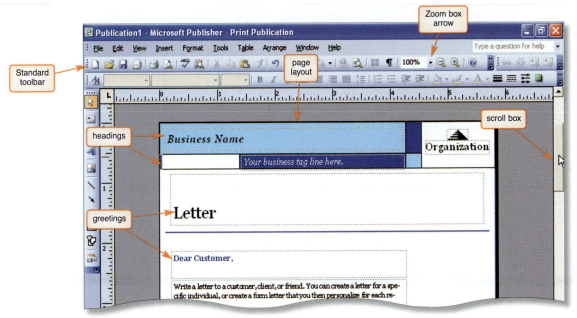

FIGURE 3

E-mail letter templates contain text boxes, logos, hyperlinks, and graphics. To customize the e-mail letter, you replace the placeholder text and graphics with your own content, just as you would in any other template publication.

Editing Text

The text boxes in an e-mail letter template include headings, the greeting, the salutation, the body of the letter, the closing, the signature block, and the informational text box at the bottom of the e-mail letter.

Editing the Headings and Greeting

The following steps show how to edit the placeholder text in the various heading and personal information text boxes. Your placeholder text may differ from that shown in the figures.

To Edit the Headings and Greeting

1 **Drag through the text in the Organization Name Text Box to select it. Type** `Community Action Group` **to replace the text.**

2 **Drag through the text in the Tag Line Text Box to select it. Type** `Building a better community` **to replace the text.**

3 **Click the text, Letter, in the text box below the Tag Line Text Box to select it. Type** `Attention Residents` **to replace the text.**

4 **Click the text, Dear Customer, in the salutation text box to select it. Type** `Dear Citizens,` **to replace the text.**

The edited text boxes are displayed in the publication (Figure 4 on the next page).

More About

Business Letters

For more information about the proper formatting and style of business letters, visit the Publisher 2003 More About Web page (scsite.com/pub2003/more) and then click Business Letters.

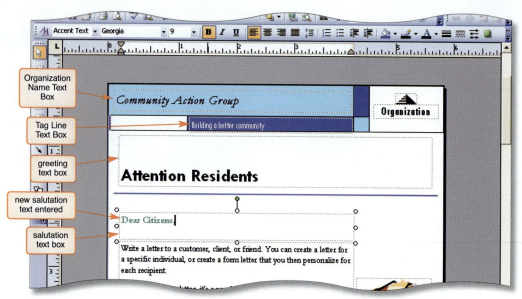

FIGURE 4

Editing the Body of the E-mail Letter

Table 2 displays the text for the body of the e-mail letter.

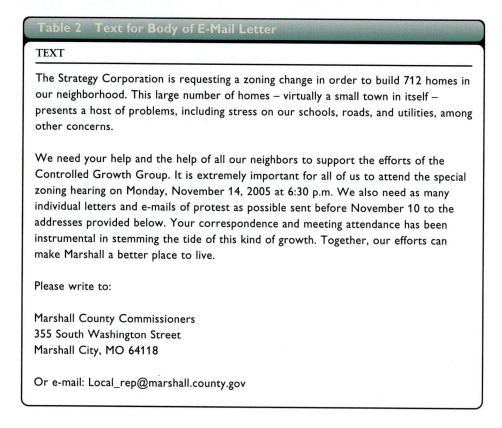

Table 2   Text for Body of E-Mail Letter
TEXT
The Strategy Corporation is requesting a zoning change in order to build 712 homes in our neighborhood. This large number of homes – virtually a small town in itself – presents a host of problems, including stress on our schools, roads, and utilities, among other concerns.
We need your help and the help of all our neighbors to support the efforts of the Controlled Growth Group. It is extremely important for all of us to attend the special zoning hearing on Monday, November 14, 2005 at 6:30 p.m. We also need as many individual letters and e-mails of protest as possible sent before November 10 to the addresses provided below. Your correspondence and meeting attendance has been instrumental in stemming the tide of this kind of growth. Together, our efforts can make Marshall a better place to live.
Please write to:
Marshall County Commissioners 355 South Washington Street Marshall City, MO 64118
Or e-mail: Local_rep@marshall.county.gov

The placeholder text in the e-mail template formats single-spaced lines within paragraphs, and a double-space, or blank line, between paragraphs. While this is normal for the regular text, you commonly do not double-space each line in an address. Because Publisher creates a new paragraph each time you press the ENTER key, the address would be double-spaced. You can override this spacing between paragraphs by pressing SHIFT+ENTER after the first two lines of the address. Sometimes called a soft return or new line, pressing SHIFT+ENTER creates a new line of text using single spacing.

To facilitate editing with paragraphs, you can click the Special Characters button on the Standard toolbar to display paragraph marks and special characters, such as the space between words.

The following steps show how to enter the text in the body of the e-mail letter.

To Edit the Body of the E-Mail Letter

1 If necessary, click the Special Characters button on the Standard toolbar to display paragraph marks.

2 Click the text in the body of the e-mail letter to select it.

3 Enter the text from Table 2, pressing the ENTER key after each paragraph. Press SHIFT+ENTER after each of the first two lines in the address.

The body of the letter is entered (Figure 5).

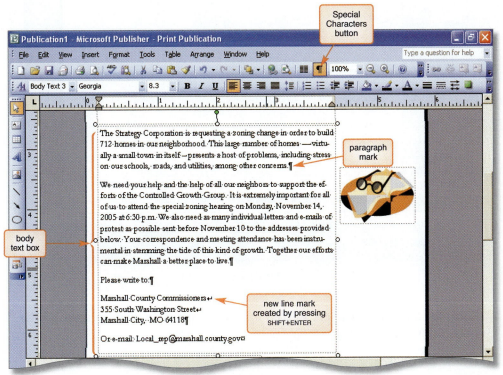

FIGURE 5

Other uses for the SHIFT+ENTER key combination include multiple lines of text within bullets and numbering, as well as short lines in addresses, lists, and titles.

Editing the Closing Text Boxes

To complete the text box editing in the e-mail letter, the steps on the next page describe editing the closing, signature block, and contact information.

More About

Pressing SHIFT+ENTER

When you press SHIFT+ENTER, you create a manual line break. A manual line break ends the current line and continues the text on the next line. For example, suppose your paragraph style includes an extra blank line before each paragraph. To omit this extra space between short lines of text, such as those in an address block or a poem, insert a manual line break after each line instead of pressing the ENTER key. Using a manual line break in a bulleted list will keep the next bullet from displaying as you create a new line. Pressing the ENTER key then will add a new bullet.

To Edit the Closing Text Boxes

1 **Click the text in the signature text box and then type** `Burt M. Carlo, President` **to replace the text.**

2 **Click the text in the address text box and then type** `Community Action Group` **to replace the text. Press SHIFT+ENTER and then type** `P. O. Box 10050` **as the second line of the address. Press SHIFT+ENTER and then type** `Marshall, MO 64118` **to complete the address.**

3 **In the contact text box at the bottom of the page, click the text, someone@example.com. Type** `CommunityAction@MarshallCounty.org` **to replace the text.**

4 **Click the text, or call 555-555-5555. Type** `or call 816 555-9631` **to replace the text.**

The new text is entered (Figure 6).

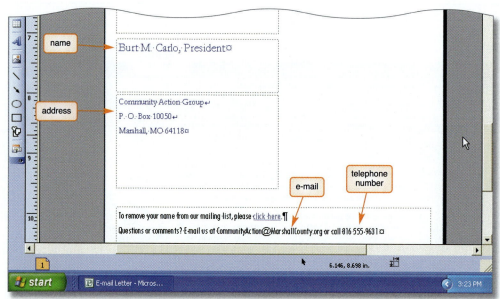

FIGURE 6

5 **Click the Special Characters button on the Standard toolbar to turn off the paragraph mark display.**

More About

Editing Hyperlinks

To change the destination of a hyperlink, select the hyperlink you want to change and then click the Insert Hyperlink button. When the Edit Hyperlink dialog box is displayed, edit the Address text box. To remove a hyperlink, click the Remove Link button in the Edit Hyperlink dialog box.

Creating a Hyperlink

E-mail letters can contain hyperlinks just as Web pages do. Recall that a hyperlink is a colored and underlined text or a graphic that you click to go to a file, a location in a file, a Web page, or an e-mail address. When you insert a hyperlink, you select the text or object and then click the Insert Hyperlink button on the Standard toolbar. When clicked, hyperlinks can take the viewer to an existing file or Web page, another place in the publication, a new document, or open an e-mail program and create a new message.

Editing the Hyperlink

In the e-mail letter template, the words, click here, display as a hyperlink. The following steps illustrate how to create a clickable link that opens the user's e-mail program and creates a new message.

To Edit the Hyperlink

1 Select the text, click here, in the contact information text box at the bottom of the page.

2 Click the Insert Hyperlink button on the Standard toolbar.

3 When the Insert Hyperlink dialog box is displayed, click E-mail Address in the Link to bar on the left.

4 In the E-mail address text box, type unsubscribe@MarshallCounty.org **as the entry.**

Publisher automatically adds the mailto: prefix as you type in the E-mail address text box (Figure 7).

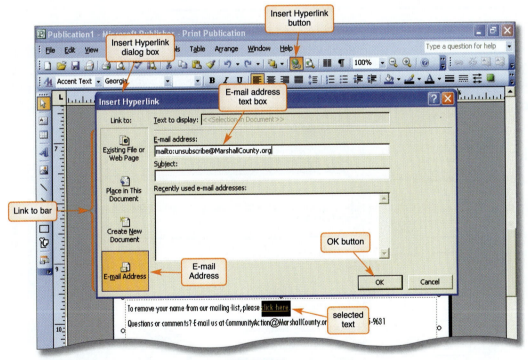

FIGURE 7

5 Click the OK button.

The **mailto:** prefix is added to the e-mail address automatically by Publisher. The prefix is necessary to direct the user's system to start an e-mail program rather than a browser or other application.

E-Mail Logos and Graphics

Most of the e-mail templates contain both logos and graphics that you can edit to suit your publication. In the upper-right corner of the e-mail letter template, Publisher displays one of the predesigned logos from the Design Gallery. Recall that

More About

Logos

For more information about logos and graphics in e-mail letters, visit the Publisher 2003 More About Web page (scsite.com/pub2003/more) and then click E-mail Logos and Graphics.

a logo is a recognizable symbol that identifies a person, business, or organization. A logo may be composed of text, a picture, or a combination of symbols.

Further down in the e-mail letter, Publisher displays a graphic that you can change to reflect the purpose of your publication. You edit e-mail graphics in the same way as you edit graphics in other publications. You can select a clip art clip, insert a graphic from a file, or import a graphic from a scanner or digital camera.

Editing the Logo

A Publisher-provided logo may be formatted in several ways. When selected, a logo displays a small wizard button with a picture of a wand. Clicking this button causes Publisher to display the Logo Designs task pane (Figure 8). In that task pane, you may select an alternate design or click Logo Options to choose a different combination of graphics and text, or even insert your own graphic as a logo.

The following steps show how to select an alternate design and edit the text in the logo.

To Edit the Logo

1

• **Scroll to the upper-right portion of the publication.**

• **Click the logo to select it. When Publisher displays the wizard button, click the button.**

Publisher displays the Logo Designs task pane (Figure 8).

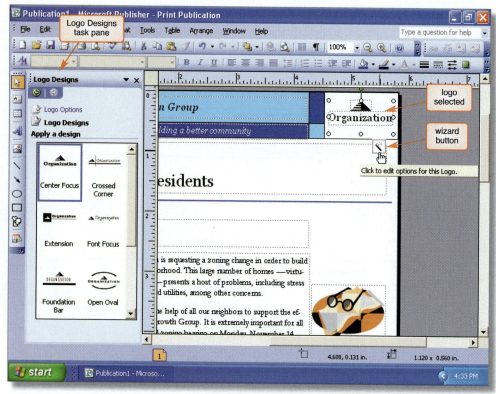

FIGURE 8

2

• In the Apply a design list, click the Open Oval preview.

Publisher changes the logo design in the publication (Figure 9).

3

• Within the logo, double-click the text, Organization, to select it. Type `Marshall County` to replace the text, as shown in Figure 10.

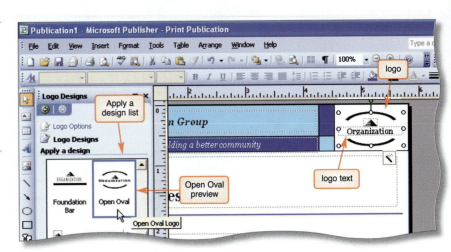

FIGURE 9

Editing the Graphic

Because the purpose of the letter is to inform residents about a housing and zoning meeting of the town council, a graphic representing a home is appropriate. The following steps describe how to edit the graphic.

To Edit the Graphic

1 Double-click the graphic in the e-mail letter.

2 When the Clip Art task pane is displayed, type homes in the Search for text box. If necessary, click the Search in box arrow and then click Everywhere in the list. If necessary, click the Results should be box arrow and then click All media types in the list.

3 Click the Go button (Figure 10).

4 Click a graphic similar to the one shown in the task pane in Figure 10.

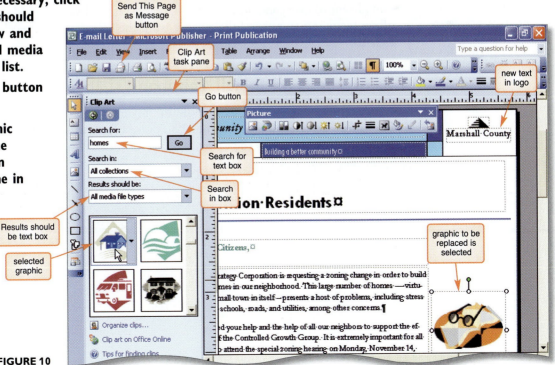

FIGURE 10

The publication is now complete. The following steps describe how to check the publication for spelling and design errors.

To Check for Spelling and Design Errors

1 Click the Spelling button on the Standard toolbar. Correct any errors. Click the Yes button when Publisher asks you to check the rest of the document.

2 On the Tools menu, click Design Checker. Correct any problems and then close the Design Checker task pane.

The following steps illustrate how to save the e-mail letter.

To Save the E-Mail Letter

1 Click the Save button on the Standard toolbar.

2 When the Save As dialog box is displayed, click the Save in box arrow and then click 3½ Floppy (A:) in the Save in list. Type E-mail Letter in the File name text box.

3 Click the Save button in the Save As dialog box.

The publication saves on the floppy disk.

Sending an E-Mail Letter

E-mail letters can be sent to one or more people. Many organizations create a **listserv**, which is a list of interested people with e-mail addresses who want to receive news and information e-mails about the organization. A listserv e-mail is one e-mail sent to everyone on the list. Listserv e-mails always should contain a link to allow recipients to remove their name from the list to prevent receiving future e-mails.

Using the Send E-Mail Command

The following steps describe how to preview and then send an e-mail using Publisher's Send E-Mail command. You do not have to send the e-mail, nor do you have to be connected to the Internet to perform the steps.

To Preview and Send a Publication Via E-Mail

1

• **With the publication displayed, click File on the menu bar and then point to Send E-Mail.**

Publisher displays the Send E-Mail submenu (Figure 11).

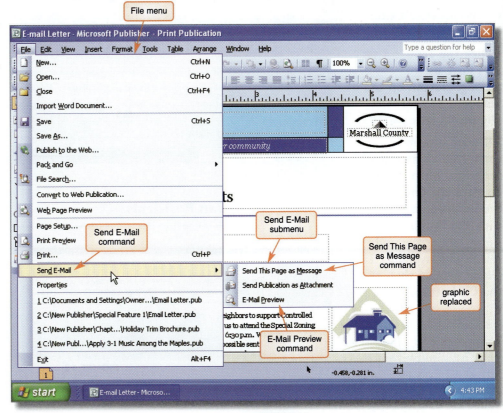

FIGURE 11

2

• **Click the E-Mail Preview command on the Send E-Mail submenu.**

The browser window displays a preview of the E-mail letter (Figure 12).

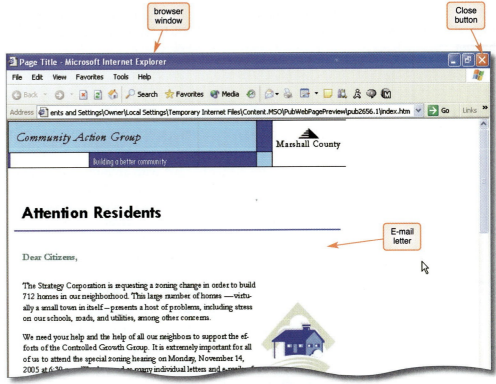

FIGURE 12

3

• **Click the Close button on the browser's title bar.**

• **Click the Send This Page as Message button on the Standard toolbar (Figure 10 on page 203).**

• **If your system is connected to an e-mail program, when Publisher displays the Choose Profile dialog box, click the Profile Name box arrow and select your system's e-mail profile; then click the OK button.**

Publisher displays the E-mail toolbar (Figure 13). If your system is not connected to the Internet, Publisher may not display the Send button.

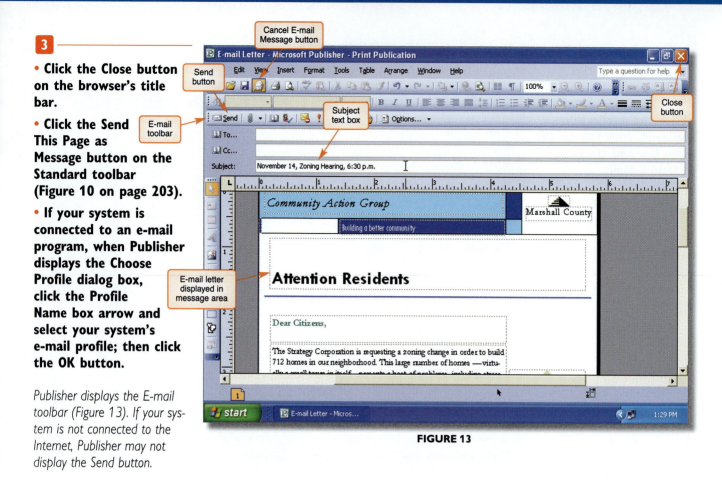

FIGURE 13

4

• **If you want to send the e-mail, type your e-mail address in the To box and then click the Send button. To cancel the request, click the Cancel E-Mail Message button.**

Sending Print Publications as E-Mail Messages

In general, it is better to start with an e-mail publication template such as the e-mail letter or e-mail newsletter. If, however, you want to send a page of another publication as an e-mail message, you may need to modify the width and margins to ensure that the message will display attractively for e-mail recipients. The typical page size of an e-mail message is 5.8 by 11 inches so that the recipients will not need to scroll horizontally to view the entire width of message.

TO MODIFY THE PAPER SIZE AND MARGINS

1. Click File on the menu bar and then click Page Setup.
2. When the Page Setup dialog box is displayed, if necessary click the Layout tab.
3. Enter the new width and height entries in the Width and Height boxes.
4. Click the OK button.

It is a good idea to send the publication to yourself first to see how it will look before sending it to other recipients.

Occasionally, you may encounter unexpected formatting results when sending a page of a publication as an e-mail message. Some of these problems have easy solutions, while others involve the unavoidable loss of formatting. You can take measures to prevent formatting problems as you add and manipulate text and graphics in your publication.

The final task is to quit Publisher, as described in the following step.

To Quit Publisher

1 **Click the Close button on the Publisher title bar. If Publisher displays a dialog box, click its No button.**

The Publisher window closes.

> ### More About
>
> ### Sending Publications Via E-Mail
>
> You can avoid formatting problems in publications sent via e-mail by using one of the many e-mail templates. For a list of possible problems and solutions when sending other types of publications via e-mail, type `troubleshoot e-mail` in the Type a question for help box on the menu bar.

E-Mail Feature Summary

This E-Mail Feature introduced you to creating an e-mail letter by illustrating how to select and format an e-mail letter template. The feature then showed how to edit both the text boxes and graphics. Next, you learned how to choose a logo design and create an e-mail hyperlink. Finally, the project showed how to preview and send a publication as an e-mail message.

What You Should Know

Having completed this project, you should be able to perform the tasks below. The tasks are listed in the same order they were presented in this project. For a list of the buttons, menus, toolbars, and commands introduced in this project, see the Quick Reference Summary at the back of this book and refer to the Page Number column.

1. Start Publisher   (PUB 194)
2. Open an E-Mail Letter Template   (PUB 196)
3. Select Publication Options   (PUB 196)
4. Edit the Headings and Greeting   (PUB 197)
5. Edit the Body of the E-Mail Letter   (PUB 199)
6. Edit the Closing Text Boxes   (PUB 200)
7. Edit the Hyperlink   (PUB 201)
8. Edit the Logo   (PUB 202)
9. Edit the Graphic   (PUB 203)
10. Check for Spelling and Design Errors (PUB 204)
11. Save the E-Mail Letter   (PUB 204)
12. Preview and Send a Publication Via E-Mail (PUB 205)
13. Modify the Paper Size and Margins   (PUB 206)
14. Quit Publisher   (PUB 207)

In the Lab

1 Creating an E-mail Featured Product List

Problem: Your work for a telecommunications company in the marketing department. Your boss wants you to send an e-mail out to all previous customers advertising the latest cell phone that your company sells. You decide to use a Publisher E-mail Featured Product template to design the e-mail message.

Instructions:

1. Start Publisher and choose the Watermark Featured Product E-mail. Select the Sapphire color scheme and the Foundry font scheme.
2. Think of a name for your telecommunications company and replace it in the heading. Use the phrase, Everything Cellular, as the tag line text.
3. Use the Clip Art task pane to replace the graphic with one picturing a cell phone.
4. Use the Logo Designs task pane to replace the logo.
5. Describe your cell phone or a friend's cell phone and its features in the lower text boxes.
6. Edit the hyperlink at the bottom to reflect your e-mail address.
7. Check the publication for spelling and design errors.
8. Save the publication with the file name, Lab E-1 Cell Phone E-mail. Preview the e-mail.
9. If you have permission, send the publication to your instructor as an e-mail message. Include an appropriate subject line in the Subject text box.

2 Sending a Newsletter as an E-mail Message

Problem: You created the newsletter shown in Figure 2-1 on page PUB 195. You decide to send the first page of the newsletter as an e-mail publication.

Instructions:

1. Open the file you created in Project 2. (If you did not create the publication in Project 2, see your instructor for a copy.)
2. Right-click page 2 in the Page Navigation Control on the status bar, and then click Delete Page on the shortcut menu.
3. Delete the Special Points of Interest sidebar toward the upper-left of the page and then delete the pull quote in the lower portion of the page.
4. Insert a text box toward the bottom of the page that lists your contact information and a link to your e-mail.
5. On the File menu, click Page Setup. In the Page Setup dialog box, if necessary, click the Layout tab. Click Custom in the Publication type list. Type 5.8 in the Width box. Click the OK button. If Publisher asks to adjust your publication for the margins, click the Yes button.
6. Check the publication for spelling and design errors.
7. Save the publication as Lab E-2 Extreme E-mail. Preview the e-mail.
8. If you have permission, send the publication to your instructor as an e-mail message. Include an appropriate subject line in the Subject text box.

MICROSOFT

Office Publisher 2003

Personalizing and Customizing Publications with Information Sets

PROJECT

4

Cakes For All Occasions

Only Cakes

CASE PERSPECTIVE

Your friend, Teresa Chen, recently has turned her passion for baking into a small business named Only Cakes. Teresa has contacted you about preparing various publications to publicize her new business, including letterhead, business cards, envelopes, and an introductory Web page. She also would like to be able to store her customers' names and addresses so she can send them thank you cards and keep them up-to-date about specials and events. Eventually, Teresa will offer cake decorating classes and Web sales — after her business is the huge initial success that you both know it will be!

Teresa wants to use Microsoft Publisher because of its wide variety of business publications as well as its capability of maintaining her company information and customer database. Teresa already has names and addresses of several customers, as she has been selling baked goods out of her home for the past several years.

The stationery must be eye-catching, yet tasteful, and include her tag line, Cakes for all occasions.

As e-commerce eventually is going to be an important part of her business, Teresa would like a prototype of the Web page to send to a usability tester at the local college.

As you read through this project, you will learn how to use Publisher to create, save, and print letterhead, business cards, and envelopes, and create a simple Web page. Additionally, you will learn how to complete the personal information set for a company and enter customer names and addresses.

Office Publisher 2003

Personalizing and Customizing Publications with Information Sets

Objectives

You will have mastered the material in this project when you can:

- Start Publisher with a blank publication
- Edit layout and ruler guides
- Create a personal information set
- Use letterhead production techniques to create a letterhead
- Format an object with a gradient fill, differentiating among tints, shades, patterns, and textures
- Crop a photograph
- Use the Measurement toolbar to position objects
- Explain character spacing techniques
- Format using the Format Painter
- Create a business card
- Create an envelope
- Create an address list and labels
- Use field codes to merge an address list with a main document
- Use the Easy Web Site Builder to create a simple Web page

Introduction

Customizing desktop publications with personal information unique to the business, organization, or individual user expands the possibilities for using Publisher as a complete application product for small businesses. People create large text boxes and use Publisher like a word processor. Others create a table and perform mathematical and statistical operations or embed charts as they would with a spreadsheet. Still others create a database and use Publisher for mass mailings, billings, and customer accounts. Publisher's capability of merging these features and transferring objects between publications makes it an efficient tool in small business offices — without the cost and learning curve of some of the high-end dedicated application software.

Project Four — Personalizing and Customizing Publications with Information Sets

To illustrate some of the business features of Microsoft Publisher, this project presents a series of steps to create a letterhead, business card, envelope, and Web page using a personal information set for a bakery named Only Cakes, as shown in Figure 4-1. Additionally, it demonstrates the creation and use of a simple database, the sort a small business would use to keep track of its customers.

letterhead

envelope

business card

Web page

FIGURE 4-1

Creating Letterhead from Scratch

When you first start Publisher, the New Publication task pane displays a list of templates and links. Most users select a publication template and then begin editing. It is not always the case, however, that a template will fit every situation. Sometimes you want to think through a publication while manipulating objects on a blank page, trying different shapes, colors, pictures, and effects. Other times you may have specific goals for a publication that do not match any of the templates. In these cases, Publisher makes available a **blank publication** with no preset objects or design, allowing you to start from scratch.

Starting Publisher with a Blank Publication

The New Publication task pane displays two ways to start a blank publication: you can choose a type of blank publication in the New from a design area, or you can click the link for a standard blank print publication. The preset page options for a standard blank page include an 8½-by-11-inch publication with one-inch margins, although you can change the size of the paper by clicking Page Setup on the File menu. For the Only Cakes letterhead, you will use the standard blank page.

The following steps describe how to start Publisher and choose a blank print publication from the task pane.

To Start Publisher with a Blank Publication

1 Click the Start button on the Windows taskbar, point to All Programs on the Start menu, point to Microsoft Office on the All Programs submenu, and then click Microsoft Office Publisher 2003 on the Microsoft Office submenu.

2 If the Publisher window is not maximized, double-click its title bar to maximize it.

3 If Publisher does not display the New Publication task pane, click View on the menu bar and then click Task Pane. If the Publication Designs task pane is displayed, click the Other Task Panes button on the task pane title bar, and then click New Publication.

4 If the Language bar is displayed, click its Minimize button.

The New Publication task pane is displayed as shown in Figure 4-2.

FIGURE 4-2

5 **Click Blank Print Publication in the New area.**

The next steps show how to set the color and font schemes for the blank publication.

To Set the Color and Font Schemes

1 **Click Color Schemes in the Publication Designs task pane. If necessary, scroll to and then click Parrot in the Apply a color scheme list.**

2 **Click Font Schemes in the Color Schemes task pane. If necessary, scroll to and then click Casual in the Apply a font scheme list.**

3 **Click the Close button on the Font Schemes task pane title bar.**

Using Layout and Ruler Guides

Publisher displays each publication with layout guides around the edge of the page to use as a **margin**. This is not to say that you cannot position objects closer to the edge of the paper if your printer is capable of printing close to the edge. The guides are there to help you edit object placement and alignment. The size of the **printing area**, or printable region, varies among printers and depends on paper size. Most printers have a small area around the edge of the paper that they cannot use. On a desktop printer, the printable area can include the space up to three-tenths of an inch from the edge; others can require five-tenths to seven-tenths of an inch. If you know your printer's nonprintable area, you can ensure that the printing area is large enough to include everything on each page. If your publication is destined for a commercial printer, you should consult the print professional about printable areas.

The size of the paper also makes a difference. Labels, envelopes, and business cards display a variety of different margins in Publisher depending on the number of copies per sheet and the size of the publication. Web pages, designed for electronic publication rather than print, display layout guides at the edge of the publication page.

Publisher's object boundaries and layout guides help you align and position objects on the page. Recall that layout guides are the nonprinting blue, dotted lines that display on the pages of a publication. These guides reside on the background and repeat on each page of a publication, serving as a template for uniformity in multipage publications. Additionally, when more than one person works on a publication, the final product has a consistent look. The layout guides help organize text, pictures, and other objects into straight columns and rows. Object boundaries display as nonprinting gray, dotted lines around each object.

Editing the Layout Guides

The steps on the next page change the margins to three-quarter inch by editing the layout guides.

More About

Guides

If the nonprinting lines such as object boundaries and layout and ruler guides are not displayed in the page layout, click View on the menu bar and then click Boundaries and Guides.

To Edit the Layout Guides

1

• **If the layout guides are not displayed, click View on the menu bar and then click Boundaries and Guides.**

• **Click Arrange on the menu bar.**

The Arrange menu is displayed (Figure 4-3). The layout guides display as blue, dotted lines.

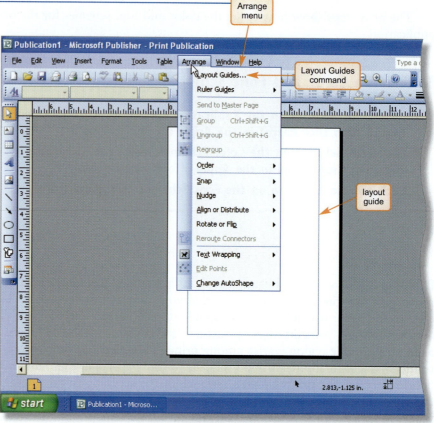

FIGURE 4-3

2

• **Click Layout Guides.**

• **When Publisher displays the Layout Guides dialog box, click the Margin Guides tab, if necessary. Select the text in the Left box and then type** .75 **to replace it. Press the TAB key. Repeat the process typing** .75 **in each of the other three boxes in the Margin Guides area.**

The boxes display .75, which equates to a three-quarter inch margin (Figure 4-4). The result of the new margin settings is reflected in the Preview area.

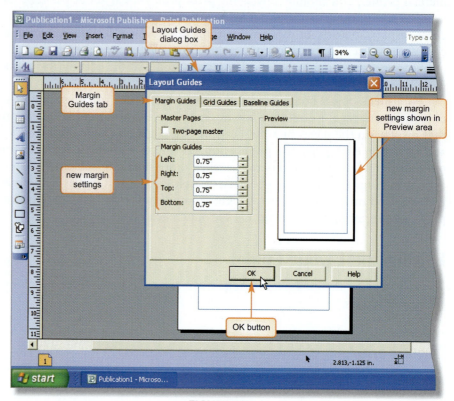

FIGURE 4-4

3

• **Click the OK button.**

The publication is displayed with a .75-inch margin (Figure 4-5).

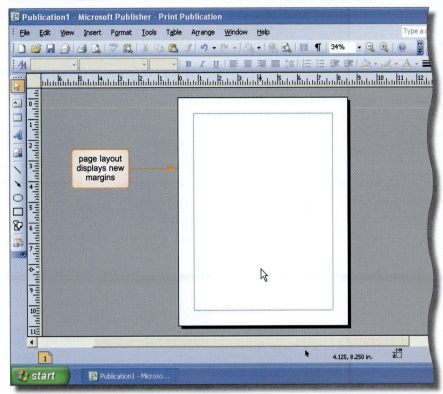

page layout displays new margins

FIGURE 4-5

In addition to the page margins, each object on the page has its own individual boundary margins. For instance, text boxes are preset with a 0.04-inch margin, which means that text on all four sides begins 0.04 inches from the edge of the frame, and thus away from any other object snapped to the text box.

Using Rulers and Ruler Guides

To further measure and place objects on the page layout, you can use Publisher's rulers. Recall that vertical and horizontal rulers are displayed at the left and top of the workspace. These rulers can be moved to any place in the workspace. You also can drag a ruler guide from the ruler, which results in a green dotted line that is displayed across the page. Added to individual pages on an as-needed basis, ruler guides help align objects.

The steps on the next page show how to move a ruler and then drag from the ruler to create two ruler guides.

To Move a Ruler and Create Ruler Guides

1

• **If the rulers are not displayed, click View on the menu bar and then click Rulers. SHIFT-DRAG the vertical ruler to the left margin of the page layout.**

The mouse pointer changes to a two-headed arrow as you SHIFT-DRAG the ruler (Figure 4-6).

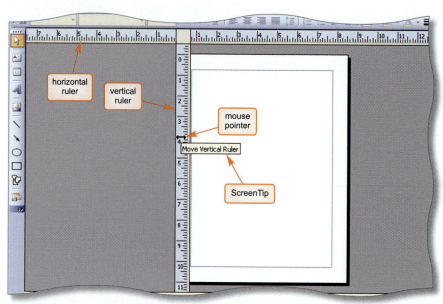

FIGURE 4-6

2

• **Point to the horizontal ruler at the top of the workspace. When the mouse pointer changes to a two-headed horizontal arrow, drag the ruler guide down to the 2-inch mark on the vertical ruler.**

The green dotted ruler guide is displayed horizontally two inches from the top of the page (Figure 4-7).

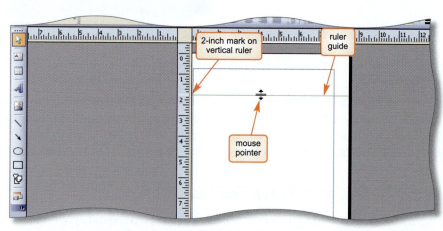

FIGURE 4-7

3

• **Release the mouse button. Drag another ruler guide from the horizontal ruler to 2.5 inches in the page layout.**

• **SHIFT-DRAG the vertical ruler back to the left edge of the workspace.**

The two ruler guides are displayed (Figure 4-8).

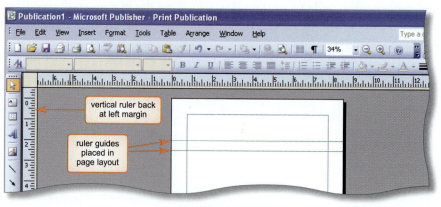

FIGURE 4-8

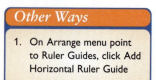

Other Ways

1. On Arrange menu point to Ruler Guides, click Add Horizontal Ruler Guide

Publisher allows users to move both rulers at once by SHIFT-dragging the gray box at the intersection of the two rulers. Double-clicking the gray box resets the ruler origin.

The next section describes how to insert company data about Only Cakes into a personal information set in Publisher.

Personal Information Sets

A **personal information set** is a set of fields, or components, containing information about a person, a business, or an organization — components that Publisher maintains for use across publications. Many of the templates create personal information text box components that incorporate the data from the personal information set. Publications created from scratch also can integrate a personal information set by including one or more of the components in the publication. For example, you can save your name, address, and telephone number in the personal information set. It then automatically is displayed when inserted by you or by a template.

Publisher provides four different, independent personal information sets for use in business and home: Primary Business, Secondary Business, Other Organization, and Home/Family. Although every new publication has the Primary Business personal information set selected by default, it is easy to apply a different personal information set to the publication.

> **More About**
>
> **Personal Information Sets**
>
> If you want Publisher to update the personal information set automatically from your publication, click Tools on the menu bar, and then click Options. Click the User Assistance tab and then click Update personal information when saving.

Editing the Personal Information Set

Each personal information set contains eight components: name, job title, organization name, address, phone/fax/e-mail, tag line, logo, and color scheme. When you first install Publisher, the personal information components contain preset, generic information for each of the four sets. If you edit a text box within a publication that contains personal information, you change that publication only. To affect changes for all future publications, you edit the components through the Edit menu. You can edit the personal information set at any time — before, during, or after performing other publication tasks.

Table 4-1 displays the data for each of the personal information components. The steps on the next page show how to edit the Secondary Business personal information set. You will edit each component and select a color scheme.

Table 4-1 Data for Personal Information Components	
FIELDS	DATA
Select a personal information set	Secondary Business
My name	Teresa Chen
Job or position title	Owner & Baker
Organization name	Only Cakes
Address	1422 Airport Road Suite 1217 Charleston, SC 29424
Phone, fax, and e-mail	Phone: 843-555-BAKE Fax: 843-555-2254 E-mail: teresa@onlycakes.com
Tag line or motto	Cakes for all occasions
Select a color scheme	Parrot

To Edit a Personal Information Set

1

• **Click Edit on the menu bar.**

The Edit menu is displayed (Figure 4-9).

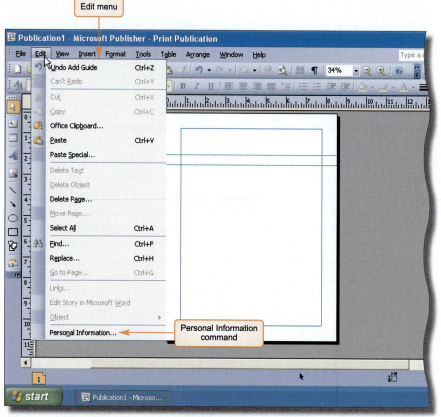

FIGURE 4-9

2

• **Click Personal Information.**

Publisher displays the Personal Information dialog box (Figure 4-10).

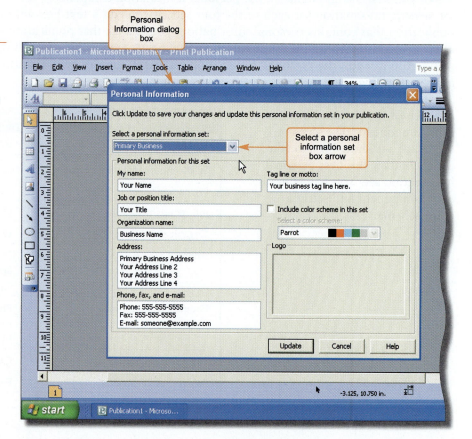

FIGURE 4-10

3

• **Click the Select a personal information set box arrow. Click Secondary Business.**

• **Press the TAB key and type Teresa Chen as the entry.**

• **Repeat the process to enter the data from Table 4-1 on page PUB 217. Press the TAB key to progress from one text box to the next.**

The personal information set for the Secondary Business is entered (Figure 4-11).

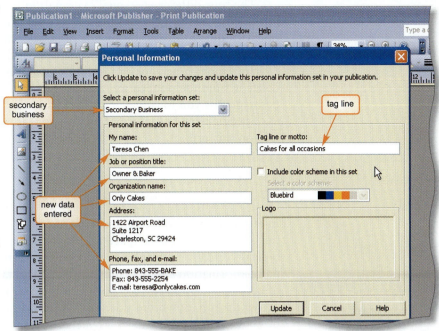

FIGURE 4-11

4

• **Click Include color scheme in this set to select it.**

• **Click the Select a color scheme box arrow and scroll as necessary to point to Parrot.**

The Parrot color scheme will be included in the secondary personal information set (Figure 4-12).

5

• **Click Parrot in the Select a color scheme list.**

• **Click the Update button.**

The publication again is displayed.

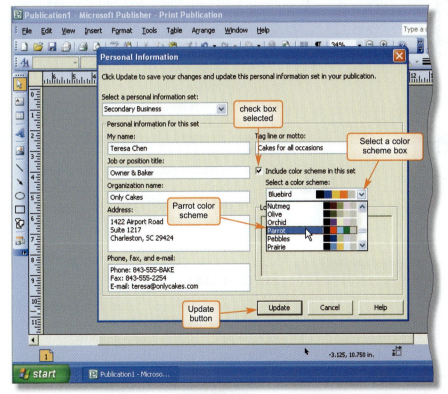

FIGURE 4-12

You can edit any of Publisher's four personal information sets in the Personal Information dialog box. It is not necessary to save the publication in order to save the changes to the set. When you click the Update button, Publisher uses the displayed set in the current publication.

Other Ways

1. In publication, edit personal information component text box, save publication
2. In Voice Command mode, say "Edit, Personal Information"

The four different personal information sets allow you to maintain alternate information about your business; a second or related business, such as a major supplier or home business; an outside organization for which you maintain information, such as scouting or sports; and your personal home/family information.

To remove a personal information component in a single publication, you can delete it from the publication itself. To remove a personal information component permanently, you must delete its text from the Personal Information dialog box.

Specific personal information components will be inserted into the publication later in this project.

Creating a Company Letterhead

In many businesses, **letterhead** is preprinted stationery with important facts about the company and blank space to display the text of the correspondence. Letterhead, typically used for official business communication, is an easy way to convey company information to the reader and quickly establish a formal and legitimate mode of correspondence. The company information is displayed in a variety of places — across the top, down the side, or split between the top and bottom. Although most business letterhead is 8½-by-11-inches, other sizes are becoming more popular, especially with small agencies and not-for-profit organizations.

Generally, it is cost effective for companies to outsource their letterhead. Designing the letterhead in-house and then sending the file to a commercial printer saves design consultation time, customization, and money. Large firms order thousands of copies at a time, as the data seldom changes. Black-and-white or spot-color letterhead is more common and less expensive than composite or process color.

Sometimes preprinted letterhead may not be purchased because of its expense, color, or limited quantity. In these cases, companies can design their own letterhead and save it in a file. Employees open the letterhead file, create the rest of their document, and then save the finished product with a new name — thus preserving the original letterhead file. Alternately, businesses can print multiple copies of their letterhead only, and then, using other application software, prepare documents to print on the letterhead paper. All of these types of letterhead production can be used in any combination to produce professional publications.

For the Only Cakes company, the letterhead will consist of personal information components, a picture, and decorative rectangles, as shown in Figure 4-1 on page PUB 211.

Fill Effects

The next step is to create a rectangle and fill the inside. In Publisher, you can **fill**, or paint, the inside of a drawing object with a color or with an effect. **Fill effects** include gradient (two-toned) colors, textures, patterns, pictures, and tints/shades. Fill effects can be applied to text boxes, shapes, and even WordArt objects in Publisher. Fill effects add subtle contrast and create an illusion of texture and depth.

Publisher suggests using gradient fills to draw attention and heighten interest. A **gradient** is a gradual progression of colors and shades, usually from one color to another color, or from one shade to another shade of the same color. Gradient fills create a sense of movement and add dimension to a publication. Publisher also displays more than 40 available gradients with patterns ranging from stars and swirls to arrows to three-dimensional abstractions.

The following steps show how to draw a rectangle and fill it with a gradient fill effect.

More About

Letterhead

To look at some samples of letterhead and for more information on content, visit the Publisher 2003 More About Web page (scsite.com/pub2003/more) and then click Letterhead.

More About

Fills

When you use a picture, pattern, or texture as a background fill, the graphic is tiled, or repeated, to fill the page or object frame. When you save a document as a Web page, the textures and gradients are saved as JPEG files and the patterns are saved as GIF files.

To Create a Gradient Fill Effect

1

• **Zoom to Whole Page if necessary. Click the AutoShapes button on the Objects toolbar and then point to Basic Shapes.**

The Basic Shapes submenu is displayed (Figure 4-13).

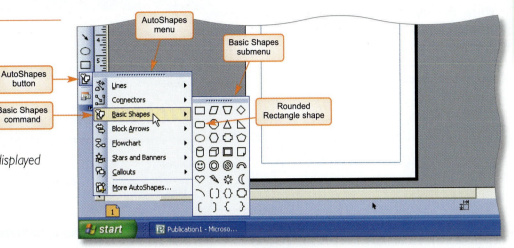

FIGURE 4-13

2

• **Click the Rounded Rectangle shape in the second row.**

• **In the publication, drag from the upper-left corner of the layout guide down to the 2" ruler guide, and then right to the right edge of the layout guide.**

The rounded rectangle fills the area between the left and right layout guides down to the first green ruler guide (Figure 4-14).

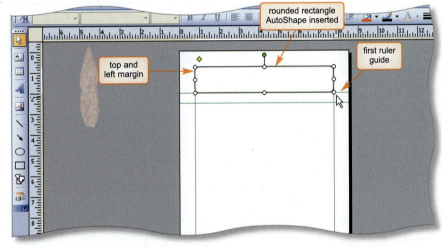

FIGURE 4-14

3

• **Press the F9 key to zoom to 100% and then, with the rounded rectangle still selected, click the Fill Color button arrow on the Formatting toolbar.**

The color palette is displayed (Figure 4-15).

FIGURE 4-15

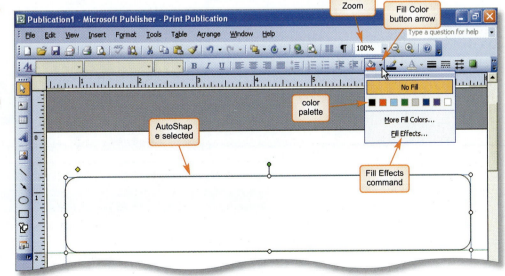

Microsoft Office Publisher 2003

4

• **Click Fill Effects.**

• **When the Fill Effects dialog box is displayed, if necessary click the Gradient tab. In the Colors area, click Two colors. Click the Color 1 box arrow.**

The available colors and options are displayed (Figure 4-16).

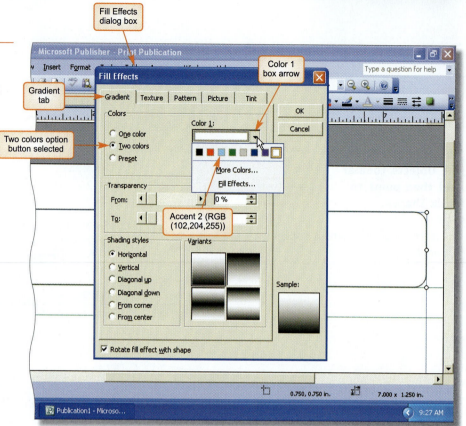

FIGURE 4-16

5

• **Click Accent 2 (RGB (102,204,255)).**

• **Click the Color 2 box arrow.**

The selected color is displayed in the Color 1 box as well as in the Variants and Sample areas (Figure 4-17). The Color 2 color palette is displayed.

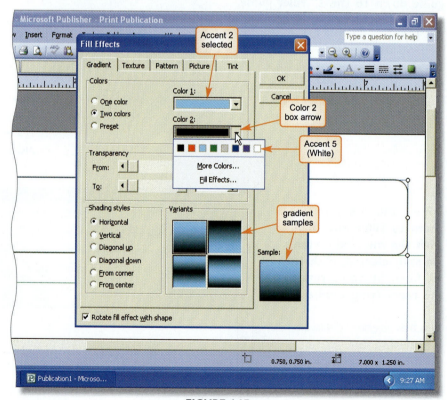

FIGURE 4-17

6

- **Click Accent 5 (White).**

Publisher displays a sample of the gradient background for the rectangle (Figure 4-18). The rounded rectangle will be displayed with the first variant of the Horizontal shading styles.

7

- **Click the OK button.**

The rectangle is displayed with the gradient fill effect (shown in Figure 4-19 on the next page).

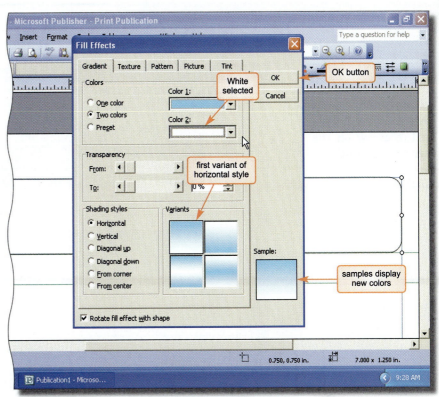

FIGURE 4-18

Four other tabs in the Fill Effects dialog box contain choices for filling shapes. A **texture fill** is a combination of color and patterns without gradual shading. Publisher provides 24 different textures from which you may choose.

Patterns include variations of repeating designs such as lines, stripes, checks, and bricks. Publisher uses the base color and a second color to create the pattern. Patterns destined for commercial printing usually are more expensive than tints and shades, because they increase the time it takes to image the file to film.

You can use a **picture fill** to insert clip art or your own graphic to create a unique and personal texture in a Publisher object.

A **tint** is a gradation of a color with reference to its mixture with white. A **shade**, on the other hand, is a mixture of a base color and black. You use tints and shades to create a more sophisticated color scheme. Tints and shades are incremented in ten-percent intervals. For example, the first tint of red is nine parts red and one part white. Therefore, Publisher displays 10 tints and 10 shades of each basic color on the Tints sheet in the Fill Effects dialog box.

Line Color

The rounded rectangle still displays a black border. Publisher adds **line colors** to the edge of each shape. Black is the default color. The color can be changed or removed entirely, as shown in the steps on the next page that remove the line color.

More About

Color Palettes

If your color palette contains fewer colors than shown in this book, then your system may be using a different color palette setting. The figures in this book were created using High Color (16 bit). To check your color palette setting, return to the desktop, right-click the desktop, click Properties on the shortcut menu, click the Settings tab, and locate the Color quality list box.

To Change the Line Color

1

• **With the rounded rectangle still selected, click the Line Color button arrow on the Formatting toolbar.**

The Line Color palette is displayed (Figure 4-19).

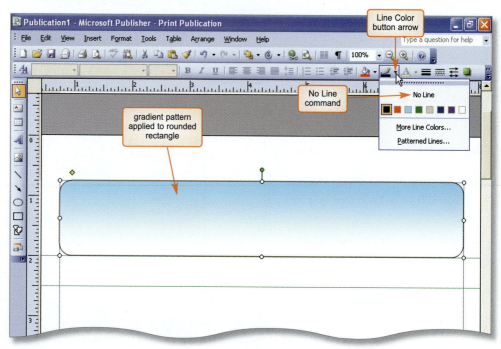

FIGURE 4-19

2

• **Click No Line.**

The rounded rectangle's border disappears (Figure 4-20).

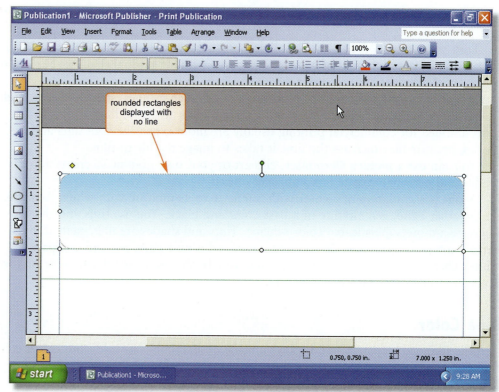

FIGURE 4-20

Inserting and Formatting Personal Information Components

The upper portion of the letterhead will contain three text box components from the Secondary Business personal information set: the Organization Name, the Address, and the Phone/Fax/E-mail. When you insert a component, Publisher places it in the center of the screen with a preset font and font size. You then may move it and format the text as necessary. Applied formatting affects the current publication only.

The following steps insert and format personal information components in the letterhead.

To Insert and Format Personal Information Components

1

• **Click Insert on the menu bar and then point to Personal Information.**

The Insert menu and the Personal Information submenu appear (Figure 4-21).

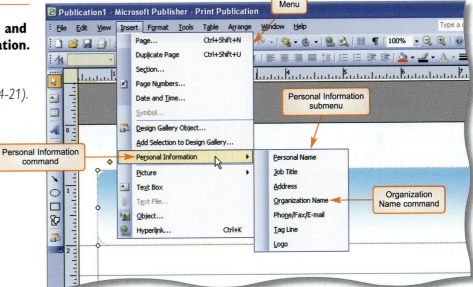

FIGURE 4-21

2

• **Click Organization Name.**

• **When the text box is displayed, if necessary, select the text by pressing CTRL+A. Click the Font Color button arrow on the Formatting toolbar.**

Publisher displays the Organization Name Text Box with the data from the personal information set (Figure 4-22). The color palette also is displayed.

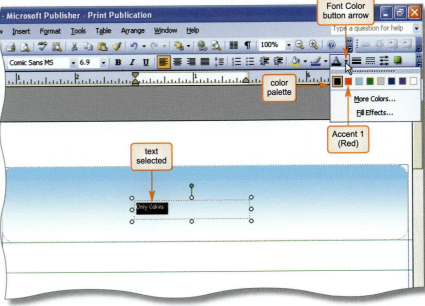

FIGURE 4-22

3

• **With the text still selected, click Accent 1 (Red).**

• **To further format the text for best fit within the text box, right-click the text box. When the shortcut menu is displayed, point to Change Text, point to AutoFit Text, and then click Best Fit.**

• **Click the Bold button on the Formatting toolbar.**

• **Drag the text box to the upper-left corner of the page layout so it touches the layout guides. Drag the lower-right handle down and to the right so the text box is sized and positioned approximately as shown in Figure 4-23.**

The text displays its new formatting (Figure 4-23). The Object Size box on the status bar shows that the text box is 2.5 × 1.25 inches.

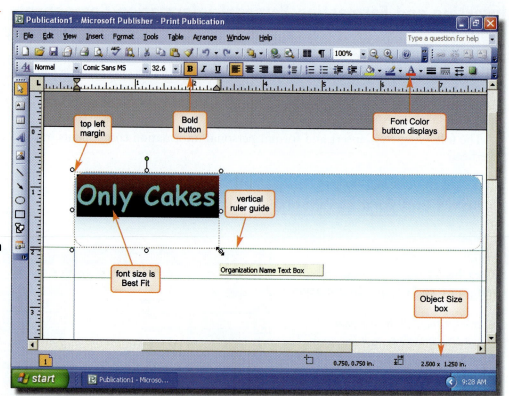

FIGURE 4-23

4

- Click Insert on the menu bar, point to Personal Information, and then click Address.

- When Publisher displays the Address text box, if necessary, drag it to the right so it snaps next to the Organization Name just above the green ruler guide.

- Press CTRL+A to select all the text and then click the Font Color button on the Formatting toolbar.

- Click Insert on the menu bar, point to Personal Information, and then click Phone/Fax/E-mail.

- When Publisher displays the Phone/Fax/E-mail text box, drag it to the right of the Address Text Box.

- Press CTRL+A to select all the text and then click the Font Color button on the Formatting toolbar.

The personal information data for Address and Phone/Fax/E-mail is displayed in red (Figure 4-24). When you click the Font Color button instead of the button arrow, the selected text is formatted with the color last used, in this case red.

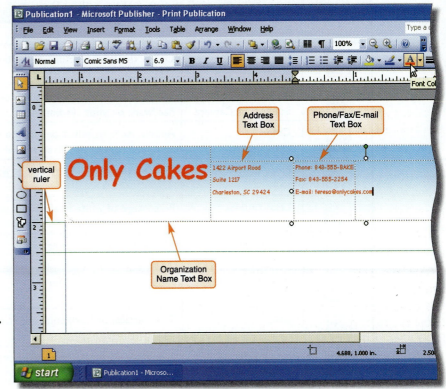

FIGURE 4-24

Searching for and Editing Photographs

Recall that using photographs rather than drawings brings a sense of reality to a publication. Sales brochures typically use real pictures to advertise their products. A newsletter story about an employee would be more interesting to read with a photograph rather than a clip art image; however, searching through a large number of previews, looking for just the right picture can be tedious. In those cases, Publisher allows users to narrow the search to clip art, photographs, sounds, movies (animated graphics), or any combination thereof. Limiting the search is more efficient; users do not have to scroll through extra clip art previews to find the one they want.

Once located, a graphic can be manipulated using the Picture toolbar. Table 4-2 on the next page lists the buttons on the Picture toolbar and their function.

Table 4-2   Picture Toolbar Buttons

BUTTON	NAME	FUNCTION
	Insert Picture	Opens the Insert Picture dialog box to browse for pictures on your system
	Insert Picture from Scanner or Camera	Automatically retrieves picture scanned or digitized from the installed hardware on your system
	Color	Allows users to select one of the color effects for the picture, including automatic, grayscale, black and white, and washout
	More contrast	Percentage of black in all colors will be increased
	Less contrast	Percentage of white in all colors will be increased
	More brightness	All colors become lighter
	Less brightness	All colors become darker
	Crop	Trim vertical or horizontal edges of an object
	Line/Border Style	Presents a variety of lines and borders to display at the edges of the picture
	Text Wrapping	Changes the way text will be displayed around the edges of the picture — choices include square, tight, through, top and bottom, none, and edit wrap points
	Format Picture	Opens the Format Picture dialog box to make more changes to the picture, such as exact size, position, or Web text
	Set Transparent Color	Allows you to click a picture color which then changes to transparent
	Reset Picture	Resets all changes to the picture so it is displayed in its original size, format, and color

The picture in this project will be cropped. A line border then will be added.

Searching for Photographs

In the Only Cakes letterhead, the owner would like to use a real picture of a cake rather than a drawing or graphic representation. The following steps demonstrate how to limit the search using the Clip Art task pane.

To Search for a Photograph

1

• **Scroll to the workspace, left of the page layout.**

• **Click the Picture Frame button on the Objects toolbar.**

The Picture Frame menu is displayed (Figure 4-25). Scroll to the workspace, left of the page layout.

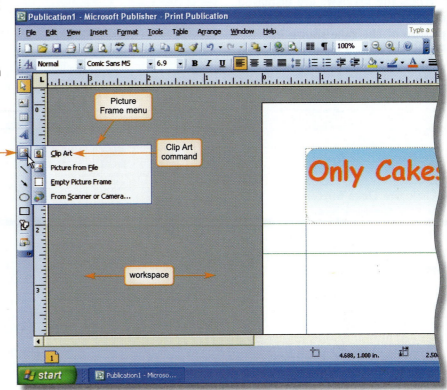

FIGURE 4-25

2

• **Click Clip Art.**

• **When Publisher displays the Clip Art task pane, select any text in the Search for text box and then type** cake **to replace the text.**

• **Click the Results should be box arrow. Click each check box so only Photographs is selected.**

The selected media file types will include only photographs (Figure 4-26).

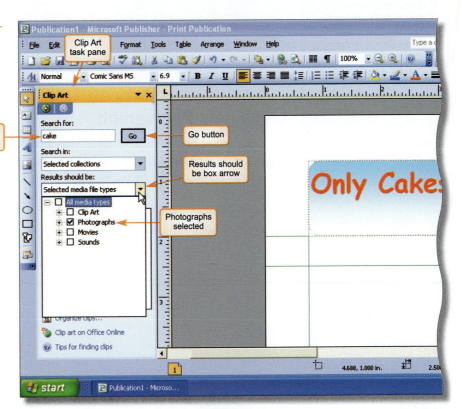

FIGURE 4-26

3

• **Click the Go button.**

• **When the previews are displayed in the Clip Art task pane, click the picture of the cake shown in Figure 4-27, or a similar picture in your previews.**

Publisher displays the graphic in the workspace (Figure 4-27). The Picture toolbar also is displayed.

4

• **Click the Close button in the Clip Art task pane.**

• **Drag the picture into the workspace to the left of the page layout.**

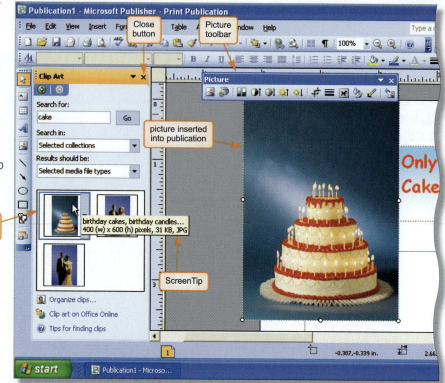

FIGURE 4-27

The cake picture is a jpeg file, which is a standard compressed picture format used for full-color or grayscale images of natural, real-world scenes. The file format, as well as the pixel width and height, is shown in the ScreenTip when you point to a preview in the Clip Art task pane.

Cropping a Photograph

If a picture is too large to fit in the space you designated for it, or if you want to display only a portion of a picture, Publisher allows you to **crop**, or trim, vertical or horizontal edges of an object. Pictures often are cropped to focus attention on a particular area.

In the Only Cakes letterhead, the picture needs to be trimmed to eliminate the extra space around the sides of the cake. The following steps show how to crop a picture.

To Crop a Picture

1

• **If the Picture toolbar is not displayed, right-click the picture and then click Show Picture Toolbar on the shortcut menu. Click the Crop button on the Picture toolbar.**

The picture displays cropping handles on all corners and sides (Figure 4-28).

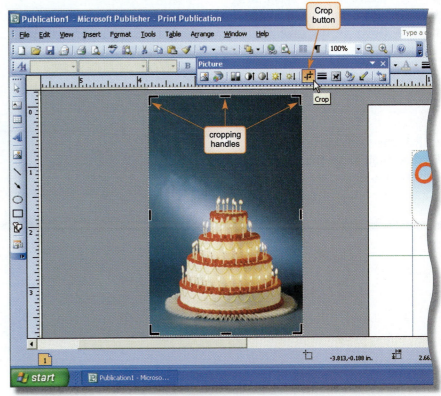

FIGURE 4-28

2

• **Drag the top center cropping handle down until it is close to the candles on the cake.**

The mouse pointer changes to a pushpin when positioned over a cropping handle (Figure 4-29).

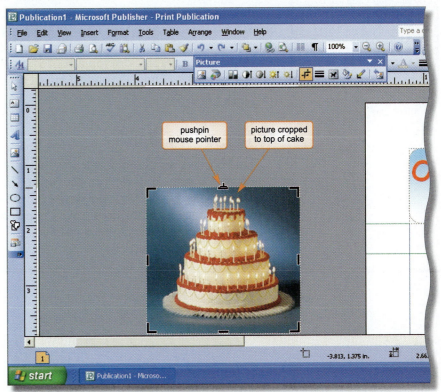

FIGURE 4-29

3

• **If necessary, click the Crop button on the Picture toolbar again. Drag the left, right, and top cropping handles closer to the cake.**

The picture is cropped to include just the cake (Figure 4-30).

4

• **Click the Crop button on the Picture toolbar so the cropping handles no longer are displayed.**

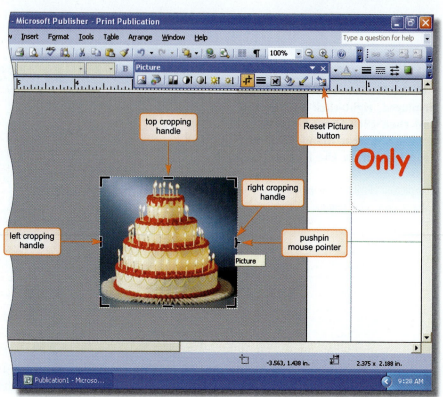

FIGURE 4-30

Cropping is different from resizing. Both techniques reduce the overall size of the graphic display; however, with cropping you eliminate part of the graphic from the display while maintaining the size of the objects in the picture. With resizing, the entire graphic is displayed smaller. For additional editing possibilities, you can both resize a cropped graphic or crop a resized graphic.

If you want to undo a cropping effect, you can click the Reset Picture button on the Picture toolbar.

Adding a Line Border

Line borders for graphics, such as the cake picture, are measured in ¼- and ½-inch increments. You also can choose no line and variety lines such as dashed, double-lines, and BorderArt. **BorderArt** is the use of a graphical border, such as hearts, Christmas trees, or decorative squares and triangles. The following steps add a line border around the cropped graphic.

To Add a Line Border

1

• **With the picture of the cake still selected, click the Line/Border Style button on the Picture toolbar.**

The Line/Border Style menu is displayed (Figure 4-31).

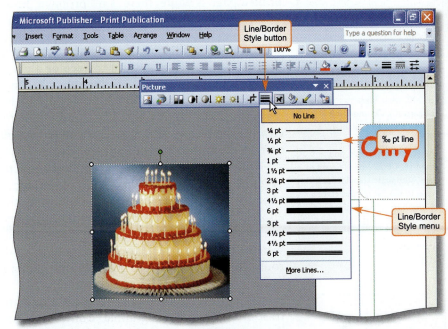

FIGURE 4-31

2

• **Click ½ pt on the Line/Border Style menu.**

The picture is displayed with a thin (½ pt) black border (Figure 4-32).

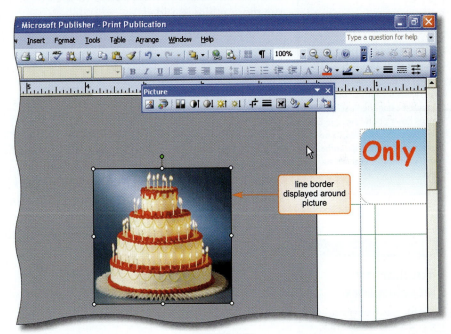

FIGURE 4-32

Other Ways

1. Click Line/Border Style button on Formatting toolbar

More About

Trapping

Publisher uses luminance values to calculate trapping for spot-color objects throughout your publication. A higher luminance value is a lighter color. For example, white has a luminance value of 100, while black has a value of zero (0). On the Tools menu, point to Commercial Printing Tools, point to Registration Settings, and then click Publication. Select the Automatic trapping check box. In the list of spot colors under Spot color options, select a spot color, and then select a value in the Luminance box.

Q&A

Q: Can I recolor any type of picture?

A: Most pictures imported into Publisher can be recolored. This procedure does not apply to pictures that are in Encapsulated PostScript (EPS) format, however. EPS is a graphic file format that is created using the PostScript page description language. EPS graphics are designed to be printed to PostScript compatible printers and cannot be recolored.

More About

Toolbar Accelerators

Toolbar accelerators include shortcut keys, designated by an underlined character; button menus, designated by an arrow attached to a box or button; combination key-strokes, listed to the right of many menu commands; and several floatable toolbar palettes, such as the Font and Fill Color button menus and the Bring to Front button menu.

When printed by a professional printer using spot colors or process colors, Publisher creates a **trap** or small overlap where the colors of the AutoShape meet the color of the printed page. The amount of overlap varies between printers. If the printed page is white, there is no problem; however, if there is a background object or color on the page around the AutoShape, the colors will trap depending on the kind of separations you print. The borders around an AutoShape filled with color will trap to the fill color, if necessary.

Sometimes you may want to **recolor** a graphic, which means making a large-scale color change to the entire graphic. When chosen, the color applies to all parts of the graphic, with the option of leaving the black parts black. It is an easy way to convert a color graphic to a black and white line drawing in order to print more clearly. The reverse also is true; if you have a black and white graphic, you can convert it to a tint or shade of any one color.

Other graphic effects you can apply to pictures include scaling, contrast, and brightness. **Scaling**, when it applies to graphics, means changing the vertical or horizontal size of the graphic by a percentage. Scaling can create interesting graphic effects. For example, a square graphic could become a long thin graphic suitable for use as a single border, if the scale height were increased to 200% and the scale width were reduced to 50%. Caricature drawings and intentionally distorted photographs routinely use scaling. Used for resizing, scaling is appropriate for subtle changes to make a graphic fit in tight places.

Using the Picture toolbar (Table 4-2 on page PUB 228), you can increase the contrast or brightness of a graphic. **Contrast** is the saturation or intensity of the color; the higher the contrast percentage, the more intense the color. **Brightness** is the amount of black or white added to the color. The higher the brightness percentage, the more white is added.

Using the Measurement Toolbar

To place objects precisely, rather than estimate by dragging and resizing, you use the Measurement toolbar to enter the exact values for width, height, left, and top of the object. The **Measurement toolbar** not only sets the location and size of an object, but sets the angle of rotation, as well. If the object is text, the Measurement toolbar offers additional character spacing or typesetting options. Accessed either by clicking Toolbars on the View menu or by double-clicking one of the Object boxes on the status bar, the Measurement toolbar is a floating toolbar with nine text boxes. Entries can be typed in each box or chosen by clicking the appropriate arrows. Table 4-3 lists the boxes available on the Measurement toolbar, their purpose, and their preset unit of measurement.

Table 4-3	Measurement Toolbar Boxes		
TOOLBAR SYMBOL	**BOX NAME**	**SPECIFIES**	**PRESET UNIT OF MEASUREMENT**
x	Horizontal Position	Horizontal distance from the upper-left corner of the page to the upper-left corner of the object	Inches
y	Vertical Position	Vertical distance from the upper-left corner of the page to the upper-left corner of the object	Inches
	Width	Width of object	Inches
	Height	Height of object	Inches
	Rotation	Rotate the object counterclockwise from the original orientation	Degrees
aaa	Text Scaling	Width of the text	Percent
A	Tracking	General space between characters	Percent
AV	Kerning	Subtle space between paired characters	Point size
A	Line Spacing	Vertical spacing between lines of selected text	Space (1 for single)

The lower four boxes on the Measurement toolbar edit text only, however, they are useful because they provide many possible combinations for spacing characters. Early typesetters were limited to just a few typefaces and sizes of type. The only way to change the spacing between characters was to insert or remove metal on each side of a piece of type. To stretch a title across the top of a page, they inserted several equally sized pieces of metal between each character. To position characters closer together, some typesetters actually used a knife to shave bits of lead from the sides of wide characters. The resulting overhang was called a **kern**.

In modern desktop publishing, the word, font, essentially has eliminated the word, typeface; in many instances, font size has replaced pitch and point; tracking and scaling have taken the place of proportional spacing; and kern has become a verb referring to both the subtraction and addition of subtle spacing.

Scaling, the process of shrinking or stretching text, changes the width of individual characters in text boxes. Recall that the WordArt toolbar has a button for scaling; however, scaling also is available for any text box using the Measurement toolbar or, alternately, using Character Spacing on the Format menu. **Tracking**, on the other hand, refers to the adjustment of the general spacing between characters. Tracking text compensates for the spacing irregularities caused when you make text much bigger or much smaller. For example, smaller type is easier to read when it has been tracked loosely. Tracking both maintains the original height of the font and overrides adjustments made by justification of the margins.

Kerning, or **track kerning**, is a special form of tracking related to pairs of characters that can appear too close together, even with standard tracking. For instance, certain letters such as T, V, W, and Y often are kerned when they are preceded or followed by a, e, o, or u. Automatic kerning is applied to 14-point text and larger.

Text in a smaller point size usually does not need to be kerned. With manual kerning Publisher lets you choose from normal, expanded, and condensed kerning for special effects. Kerning fine-tunes the amount of space between specific character pairs that otherwise would appear to be too close together or too far apart.

The following step demonstrates how to position the rectangle precisely using the Measurement toolbar. Then, you will kern text using the Measurement toolbar.

To Position Objects Using the Measurement Toolbar

1

• **With the picture selected, double-click the Object Size box on the status bar. When the Measurement toolbar is displayed, type** 6.875 **in the x box and then press the TAB key. Type** 1.613 **in the y box. Type** .875 **in the Width box. Type** .887 **in the Height box. Press the TAB key to move from box to box.**

The Measurement toolbar displays the new measurements (Figure 4-33). The picture of the cake has been moved and resized. The placement of your graphic may differ slightly depending on how closely you cropped.

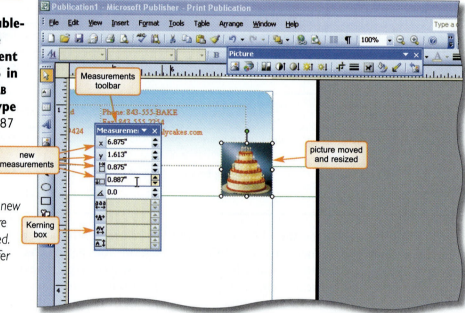

FIGURE 4-33

The letters n and the l in the name of the organization, Only Cakes, are close together due to the Comic Sans proportional font. You can use kerning to adjust the distance between the two letters, as shown in the following steps.

To Kern Letters

1 **In the Organization Name Text Box, select the letters n and l.**

2 **On the Measurement toolbar, in the Kerning box, type** 2 **to widen the space between the letters.**

Publisher displays the letters further apart, as shown in Figure 4-34.

3 **Click the Close button on the Measurement toolbar.**

Now that the upper portion of the letterhead is complete, you will copy and paste the fill effect rectangle and insert the Tag Line component from the personal information set to create the lower portion of the letterhead.

Creating the Lower Portion of the Letterhead

The lower portion of the letterhead consists of a rounded rectangle similar to the one at the top of the page. The tag line of the Only Cakes company also is displayed. The following sections describe how to copy, paste, and rotate the rounded rectangle; insert the tag line; use the Format Painter button on the Standard toolbar to apply the format, and then group the object and move it to the lower portion of the page.

To Copy and Paste an Object

1

• **Click the upper-right corner of the rounded rectangle at the top of the page layout.**

• **Click the Zoom box arrow and then click Page Width in the Zoom list.**

• **Press CTRL+C to copy the object to the Clipboard.**

The selected object is copied to the Clipboard (Figure 4-34).

2

• **Press CTRL+V to paste the object. If necessary, drag the new AutoShape down so it displays below the other objects as shown in Figure 4-35 on the next page.**

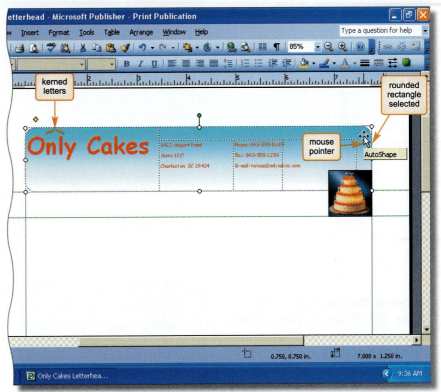

FIGURE 4-34

Other Ways

1. Click Copy button or Paste button on Standard toolbar
2. On Edit menu click Copy or Paste
3. Right click object, click Copy or Paste on shortcut menu

Rotating an Object

When you **rotate** an object in Publisher, you turn it so it faces a different direction. For example, a picture of a person facing left could be rotated 180° or flipped horizontally so it would appear that the person would be facing right.

Each selected object in Publisher displays a green rotation handle that can be used to freely rotate the object. To rotate in 15-degree increments, hold down the SHIFT key while dragging the rotation handle. To rotate an object on its base, hold down the CTRL key and drag the green rotation handle — the object will rotate in a circle by pivoting around the handle.

Publisher provides four options to **flip** an object. You can flip horizontally, flip vertically, flip right 90°, or flip left 90°. The following steps rotate the copied and pasted rectangle.

To Rotate an Object

1

• **Point to the rotation handle of the pasted rectangle.**

The mouse pointer changes to the rotation symbol (Figure 4-35).

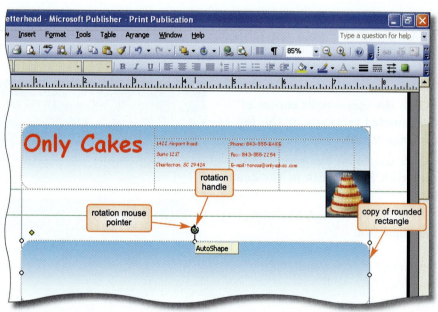

FIGURE 4-35

2

• **SHIFT-drag the rotation handle 180° so the object is upside down.**

Publisher rotates the object (Figure 4-36).

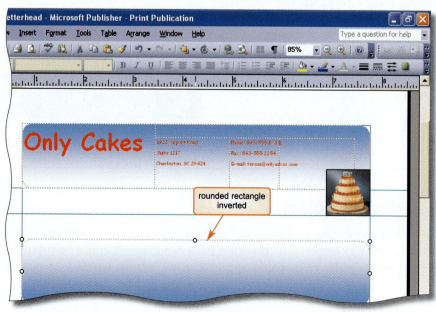

FIGURE 4-36

Other Ways

1. Click Rotation text box on Measurement toolbar, type 180
2. On Arrange menu point to Rotate or Flip, click Flip Vertical
3. Right-click selected object, click Format AutoShape on shortcut menu, click Size tab, click Rotation text box, type 180

Formatting with the Format Painter

If you have a text box containing a font, size, and color that you would like to use in another text box, you can use the **Format Painter** button on the Standard toolbar to copy the format and apply it to the second text box. In the Only Cakes letterhead, you will copy the formatting from the letterhead title to the text box that contains the company's tag line in the lower portion of the page layout.

The following steps insert and format the personal information tag line using the Format Painter.

To Format the Tag Line with the Format Painter

1

• **Click Insert on the menu bar, point to Personal Information, and then click Tag Line.**

• **When the Tag Line Text Box is displayed, double-click the Object Size box on the status bar to display the Measurement toolbar.**

• **Type** 1.5 **in the x box,** 3.125 **in the y box,** 5.5 **in the Width box, and** .625 **in the Height box. Use the TAB key to progress to each box.**

Publisher displays the object at its new location and resized (Figure 4-37).

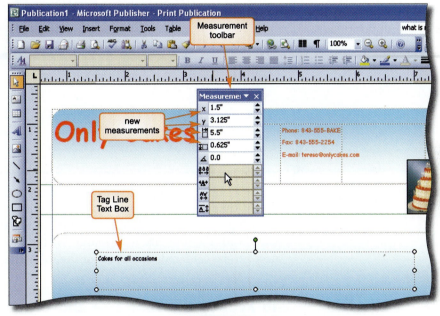

FIGURE 4-37

2

• **Click the Close button on the Measurement toolbar.**

• **Click the text, Only Cakes, in the Organization Name Text Box and then click the Format Painter button on the Standard toolbar.**

The Format Painter button will copy the formatting of the letterhead title (Figure 4-38).

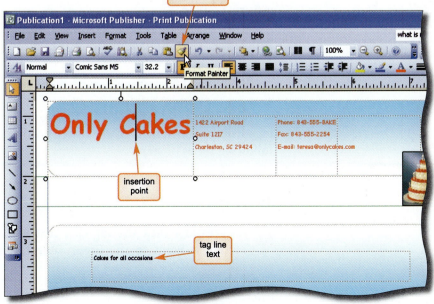

FIGURE 4-38

3

• **Drag through the text in the tag line.**

Publisher changes the formatting of the tag line so it matches the letterhead title (Figure 4-39). The mouse pointer has a paintbrush attached to it when the Format Painter button is selected.

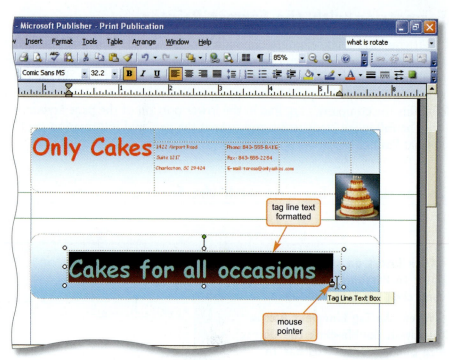

FIGURE 4-39

At times, you may decide to make a minor change to the formatting, even though you like the font, color, and effect (bold). In the case of the Only Cakes letterhead, the font size is too large for the lower portion of the page and the text needs to be centered, as shown in the following steps.

To Reduce the Font Size and Center

1 **With the text still selected, press CTRL+SHIFT+< four times to reduce the font size.**

2 **Click the Center button on the Formatting toolbar.**

Publisher displays the tag line in a smaller font size and centered, as shown in Figure 4-40.

Editing and formatting any personal information component except the logo changes the current publication only.

The final steps in formatting the tag line and AutoShape is to group them together and move them to the lower portion of the letterhead, as shown in the following series of steps.

To Group Objects

1 **If necessary, click the Tag Line Text Box to select it. SHIFT+CLICK the rounded rectangle. Point to the Group Objects button.**

Publisher always displays the Group Objects button whenever more than one object is selected (Figure 4-40).

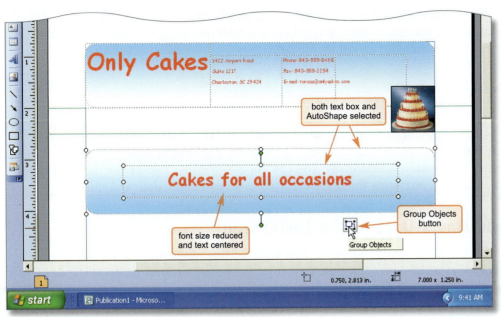

FIGURE 4-40

2 **Click the Group Objects button.**

To Move an Object

1 **Click the Zoom box arrow on the Standard toolbar and then click Whole Page in the Zoom list.**

2 **Drag the grouped object to the lower portion of the page so it snaps to the bottom margin.**

The object is displayed in the lower portion of the letterhead (Figure 4-41).

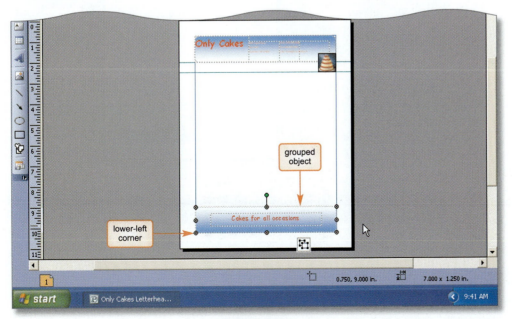

FIGURE 4-41

More About

Rotating

The Rotation text box on the Measurements toolbar allows you to enter any degree of rotation from -360 to +360. Positive numbers rotate counterclockwise. Negative numbers rotate clockwise and then are converted on the toolbar to their complemented angles. For example, an entry of -90 is converted to 270 (360 minus 90) and then the object is rotated 90 degrees clockwise. You can rotate any object or grouped objects, including text boxes, for special effects.

Now that the static components of the letterhead are complete, the next section describes the process to enter a text box in which users can type the body of their letters, which includes an automatic date.

Using an Automatic Date

Publisher and other Microsoft Office applications can access your system's stored date and time. You then can retrieve the current date and/or time and display it in a variety of formats. Additionally, you can choose to either update the date and time automatically each time the file is accessed or keep a static date and time.

Inserting a Date in the Letterhead

To make the letterhead more functional for the company, you will insert a large text box in which users can type their text. At the top of most letters is the date. Using the Date and Time dialog box, the following steps show how to insert a date that will be current whenever the user opens the letterhead to prepare a new letter.

To Insert an Automatic Date

1

• **Click the Text Box button on the Objects toolbar and then drag a rectangle that begins at the left margin of the second ruler line and continues to the right margin, just above the grouped object.**

Publisher inserts the text box (Figure 4-42).

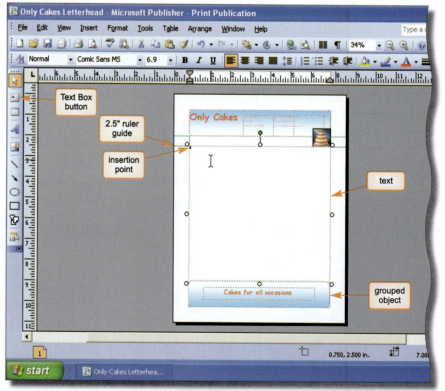

FIGURE 4-42

2

• **Press the F9 key to zoom in on the text box.**

• **Click the Font box arrow and click Times New Roman in the Font list.**

• **Click the Font Size box arrow and click 10 in the Font Size list.**

• **Click Insert on the menu bar.**

Publisher displays the Insert menu (Figure 4-43).

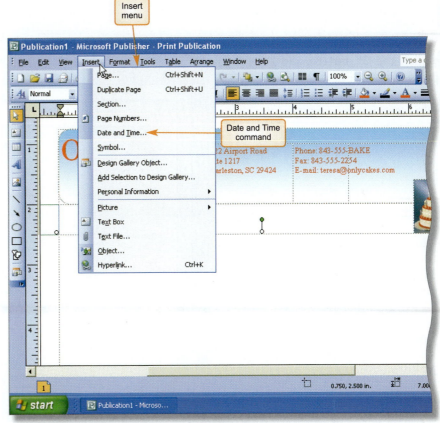

FIGURE 4-43

3

• **Click Date and Time.**

• **When the Date and Time dialog box is displayed, click the third format in the list and then select the Update automatically check box.**

Publisher displays the Date and Time dialog box (Figure 4-44). The date will be current every time the letterhead is accessed.

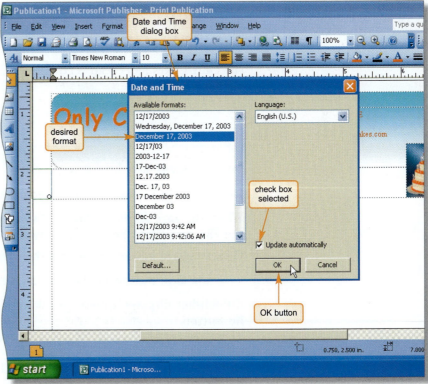

FIGURE 4-44

4

• **Click the OK button and then press the ENTER key twice.**

The date is displayed (Figure 4-45).

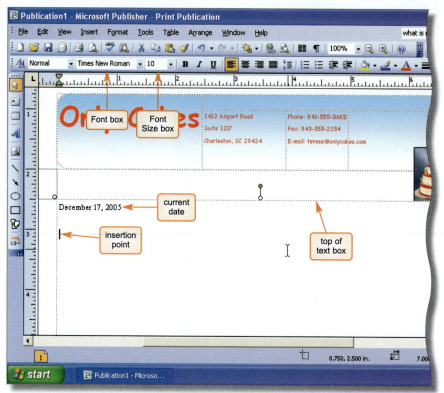

FIGURE 4-45

Saving the Letterhead

The Only Cakes letterhead is complete. The following steps demonstrate how to save the letterhead.

To Save the Letterhead

1 **Insert a floppy disk into drive A.**

2 **Click the Save button on the Standard toolbar.**

3 **When the Save As dialog box is displayed, type** Only Cakes Letterhead **in the File name text box. Do not press the ENTER key.**

4 **Click the Save in box arrow and then click 3½ Floppy (A:).**

5 **Click the Save button in the Save As dialog box.**

6 **If Publisher displays a message asking if you want to save the logo, click the No button.**

Publisher saves the publication on a floppy disk in drive A with the file name, Only Cakes Letterhead. The letterhead is shown in Figure 4-1 on page PUB 211.

Finally, before you start the business card publication, close the letterhead file without quitting Publisher, as shown in the following step.

To Close a Publication without Quitting Publisher

1 **Click File on the menu bar and then click Close.**

The letterhead file is closed, but Publisher remains open. The New Publication task pane is displayed.

If the users routinely plan to open the letterhead file and type in it, it is a good idea to change the file's attribute to read-only. That way, users will be forced to save the publication with a new file name, keeping the original letterhead intact for the next user. If you wanted to assign the read-only attribute to a file, you would perform the following steps.

To Set a File to Read-Only

1 **In any Windows Explorer window, right-click the file icon. On the shortcut menu, click Properties.**

2 **If necessary, click the General tab. Place a check mark in the Read-only check box.**

3 **Click the OK button.**

Business Cards

Another way companies are saving money on publishing costs is by designing their own business cards. A **business card** is a small publication, 3½ by 2 inches, printed on heavy stock paper. It usually contains the name, title, business, and address information for an employee, as well as a logo, distinguishing graphic, or color to draw attention to the card. Many employees want their telephone, pager, and fax numbers on their business cards in addition to their e-mail and Web page addresses, so colleagues and customers can reach them quickly.

Business cards can be saved as files to send to commercial printers or printed by desktop color printers on special perforated paper.

The Business Card Template

Because the personal information set contains information about the Only Cakes company, using a business card template is the quickest way to create a business card. Not only does the template set the size and shape of a typical business card, it also presets page and printing options for the easiest production.

The next sequence of steps uses the New Publication task pane to produce a business card for the owner at the Only Cakes company. The created template automatically uses information from the personal information set edited earlier in this project.

To Create a Business Card

1 **With the New Publication task pane displayed, click Publications for Print in the New from a design area.**

2 **Click Business Cards. If necessary, click Plain Paper.**

3 **Scroll down in the Plain Paper Business Cards preview pane and then click the Retro Business Card preview.**

4 | **Close the task pane.**

Publisher displays the business card in the workspace.

The **Business Card Options task pane** displays choices for logo, orientation, and copies.

Editing the Business Card

The template created from the New Publication task pane uses information from the Primary Business personal information set, placing typical business card fields in appropriate places in the publication. Choosing a different personal information set and editing the layout customizes the business card even further. The term **layout** refers to both the process and the result of planning and arranging objects in a publication. Sending objects behind other objects, layering, and aligning objects are part of editing the layout.

The following step shows how to select the Secondary Business personal information set created earlier in the project.

To Edit the Business Card

1

• **Click Edit on the menu bar and then click Personal Information.**

• **When the Personal Information dialog box is displayed, click the Select a personal information set box arrow, and then click Secondary Business in the list.**

• **Click the Update button. If the logo is displayed, right-click it and click Delete Object on the shortcut menu. If Publisher displays a dialog box asking if you want to change to a design without a logo, click the No button.**

The change is made in the business card (Figure 4-46).

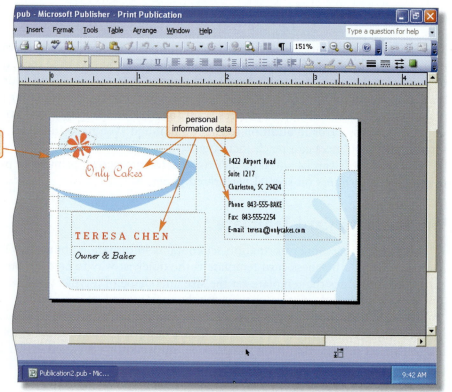

FIGURE 4-46

The color scheme is saved with the personal information set, so the colors change when you select Secondary Business.

Saving, Printing, and Closing the Business Card

The business card is complete, and you are ready to save and print it. If you have perforated paper available, the Print dialog box contains buttons to customize the number of cards per sheet.

Follow these steps to save, print, and then close the business card publication.

To Save, Print, and Close the Business Card

1 Insert a floppy disk in drive A.

2 Click the Save button on the Standard toolbar.

3 When the Save As dialog box is displayed, type Only Cakes Business Card in the File name text box. Do not press the ENTER key.

4 If necessary, click the Save in box arrow and then click 3½ Floppy (A:).

5 Click the Save button in the Save As dialog box.

6 Click the Print button on the Standard toolbar.

7 Click File on the menu bar and then click Close.

Publisher saves the publication on a floppy disk in drive A with the file name, Only Cakes Business Card, and then prints a copy on the printer. The business card is shown in Figure 4-1 on page PUB 211.

Envelopes

Envelopes are manufactured in a variety of sizes and shapes. The most common sizes are #6 personal envelopes that measure 3⅝ by 6½ inches, and #10 business envelopes that measure 4⅛ by 9½ inches. You also can customize the page layout to instruct Publisher to print envelopes for invitations, cards, and mailers.

Although the majority of businesses outsource their preprinted envelopes, most desktop printers have an envelope feeding mechanism that works especially well for business envelopes. Check your printer documentation for any limitations on the size and shape of envelopes. You can print the envelope for this project on 8½-by-11-inch paper, if necessary.

Creating an Envelope

The following steps create an envelope for Only Cakes. You will create mailing labels later in this project. Therefore, you will delete the Mailing Address text box on the envelope.

To Create an Envelope

1 If the New Publication task pane is not displayed, click File on the menu bar and then click New. In the New Publication task pane, click Publications for Print and then click Envelopes.

2 Scroll as necessary and click the Retro Envelope preview.

3 When Publisher displays the Envelope Options task pane, click None in the Logo area and click #10 in the Size area.

4 Click Edit on the menu bar and then click Personal Information. When the Personal Information dialog box is displayed, click the Select a personal information set box arrow, and then click Secondary Business in the list. Click the Update button.

5 Right-click the Mailing Address text box. Click Delete Object on the shortcut menu.

The envelope is displayed in the workspace (Figure 4-47).

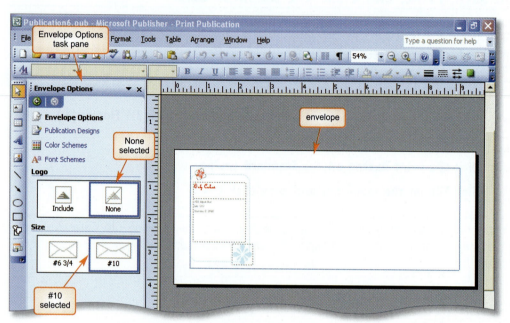

FIGURE 4-47

The following steps save, print, and then close the envelope publication.

To Save, Print, and Close the Envelope

1 Insert a floppy disk in drive A.

2 Click the Save button on the Standard toolbar.

3 In the Save As dialog box, type `Only Cakes Envelope` in the File name text box. Do not press the ENTER key.

4 If necessary, click the save in box arrow and then click 3½ Floppy (A:).

5 Click the Save button in the Save As dialog box.

6 Click the Print button on the Standard toolbar.

7 Click File on the menu bar and then click Close.

Publisher saves the envelope on the floppy disk in drive A and then prints it on the printer. If you are using standard size paper in your printer, the envelope will print in landscape orientation on a single sheet of paper. The envelope is shown in Figure 4-1 on page PUB 211.

If you have an unusual sized envelope, you can adjust the print settings by performing the following steps.

To Create a Custom Size Envelope

1. On the File menu, click Page Setup, and then click the Layout tab.
2. In the Publication type area, click Envelope.
3. In the Page size area, click Custom Size.
4. Enter the width and height of your envelope.

Using the Mail Merge Feature

Whether you want individual letters sent to everyone on a **mailing list**, personalized envelopes, an invoice sent to all customers, or a printed set of mailing labels to apply to your brochures, you can use Publisher to maintain your names and addresses and make the task of mass mailing easier.

Readers expect documents such as these to be timely and professional looking, yet at the same time, individualized and personal. Take, for example, a form letter. Used regularly in both business and personal correspondence, a **form letter** has the same basic content no matter to whom it is sent; however, items such as name, address, city, state, and zip code change from one form letter to the next. Thus, form letters are personalized to the addressee. An individual is more likely to open and read a personalized letter than a standard Dear Sir or Dear Madam letter. With word processing and database techniques, it is easy to generate individual, personalized documents even for a large group. Publisher extends that capability to any type of publication.

The process of generating an individualized publication for mass mailing involves creating a main publication and a data source. The two then are merged, or blended, into a series of publications ready for printing or saving. **Merging** is the process of combining the contents of a data source with a main publication. The **main publication** contains the constant or unchanging text, punctuation, space, and graphics. Conversely, the data source contains the variable or changing values in each publication. A **data source** or database is a file where you store all addresses or other information for customers, friends and family, or merchants with whom you do business. The term **database** generically describes a collection of data, organized in a manner that allows access, retrieval, and use of that data.

Microsoft Publisher allows users to create data sources internally, which means using Publisher as both the creation and editing tool. Publisher creates a special database that can be edited independently by using Microsoft Access; however, you do not need to have Microsoft Access, or any database program, installed on your computer to create and use a database in Publisher.

If you plan to **import**, or bring in data from another application, Publisher can accept data from a variety of other formats, as shown in Table 4-4.

More About

Printing a Custom Size Publication

If you are working on a network printer, choosing a custom size publication may cause the printer to pause, waiting for custom size paper. Many labs have a hands-off policy on loading printer paper yourself. Check with your instructor on the best way to print custom sizes.

Table 4-4   Data Formats

DATA-CREATION PROGRAM	VERSION	FILE EXTENSION
ASCII text files	Text delimited	.txt
dBase	III, IV, and V	.dbf
Microsoft Access	All versions	.mdb
Microsoft Excel	3.0, 4.0, 5.0, 7.0, and 8.0	.xls
Microsoft FoxPro	2.0, 2.5, and 2.6	.fxd
Microsoft Outlook	All versions	.pst
Microsoft Word tables or merge data documents	All versions	.doc
Microsoft Works (no formulas)	All Windows versions and MS-DOS 3.0	.wdb

Creating a Publisher Address List

The internally created data sources are called **Publisher address lists**. Each customer or client is an entry in Publisher's address lists. Similar to a record in other database applications, an **entry** represents all the information about one person or one business. In Table 4-5, an entry is equivalent to a row of information. Entries are broken down into pieces of information called **fields**. The preset fields in a typical Publisher address list include Title, First Name, Last Name, Company Name, Address Line 1, Address Line 2, City, State, ZIP Code, Country, Home Phone, Work Phone, and E-mail Address. In Table 4-5, a field is equivalent to a column. Each field contains a piece of data about a customer. In Table 4-5, the data is located in the intersection of the row and column where one piece of information is displayed.

Table 4-5	Customer Address List Data						
TITLE	FIRST NAME	LAST NAME	ADDRESS LINE 1	ADDRESS LINE 2	CITY	STATE	ZIP CODE
Dr.	Elias	Wooster	1400 Mall Drive	Suite B	Charleston	SC	29424
Mr.	Javier	Nunez	8006 Howard		Charleston	SC	29424
Mr.	Ali	Nasser	150 Grant Building	Office 24 East	Charleston	SC	29424
Rev.	Solomon	Walter	Eastwood Church	247 Antioch Ave.	Nearby	SC	29420
Ms.	Rose	Li	942 Main		Charleston	SC	29424
Mr.	Fredrick	Montgomery	1400 Mall Drive	Suite K	Charleston	SC	29424
Ms.	Katie	Marie	1135 Calumet		Nearby	SC	29420

The following steps describe how to create a Publisher address list containing information about the customers at Only Cakes and then save it on a floppy disk. Notice in Table 4-5 that some customers have no Address Line 2. You will leave that field blank. You can create or edit address lists at any time, from any publication, just as you did with personal information sets.

To Create the Address List

1

• **If necessary, close the New Publication task pane. Click Tools on the menu bar and then point to Mail and Catalog Merge.**

The Mail and Catalog Merge submenu is displayed (Figure 4-48).

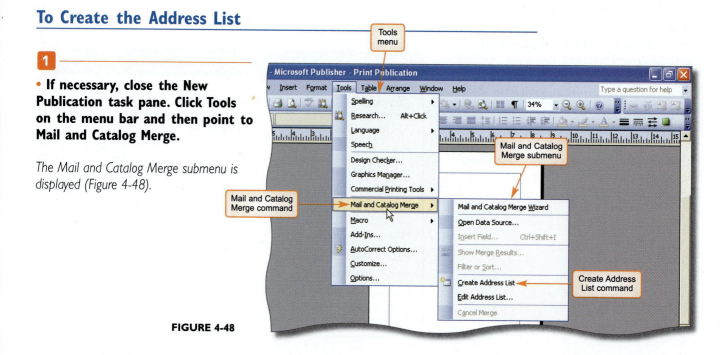

FIGURE 4-48

2

- **Click Create Address List.**
- **When the New Address List dialog box is displayed, type** Dr. **in the Title text box and then press the TAB key. Type** Elias **in the First Name text box and then press the TAB key. Type** Wooster **in the Last Name text box and then press the TAB key twice to skip the Company Name.**

The title, first name, and last name are displayed in their respective text boxes, and the insertion point is positioned in the Address Line 1 text box (Figure 4-49).

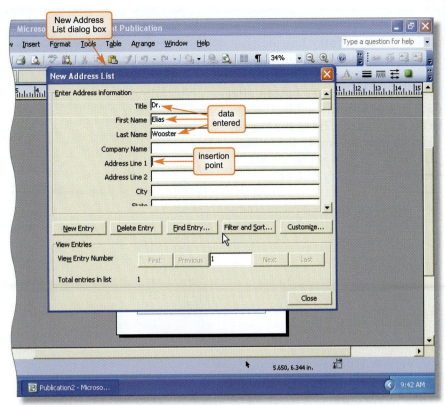

FIGURE 4-49

3

- **Continue to enter data from the first row in Table 4-5. Press the TAB key to advance to each new text box.**

The first record is complete (Figure 4-50). The data entry fields automatically scroll as you enter each field. This entry number is 1.

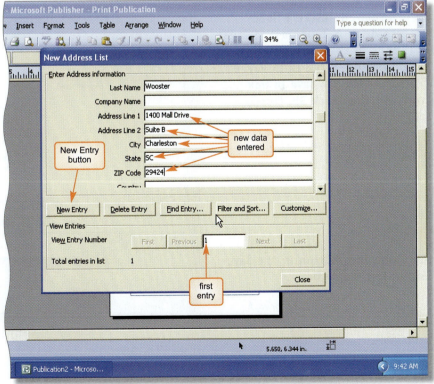

FIGURE 4-50

4

• **Click the New Entry button. Continue to add all the entries from Table 4-5 on page PUB 250, clicking the New Entry button after each row of information in the table is complete. Press the TAB key twice to skip an empty field. When you finish the last entry, do not click the New Entry button.**

The last fields are entered for entry number 7 (Figure 4-51).

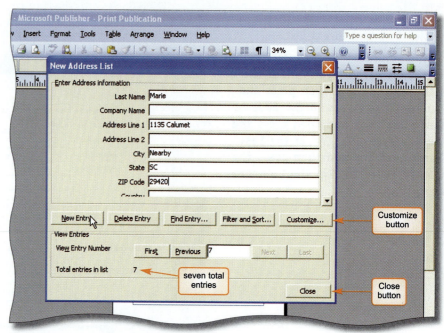

FIGURE 4-51

5

• **Click the Close button in the New Address List dialog box.**

• **When the Save Address List dialog box is displayed, insert a floppy disk into drive A. Type** Only Cakes Customers **in the File name text box. Do not press the ENTER key. If necessary, click the Save in box arrow and then click 3½ Floppy (A:).**

The file name, Only Cakes Customers, is displayed in the File name text box (Figure 4-52). The database file will be saved on drive A.

6

• **Click the Save button in the Save Address List dialog box.**

The address list file is saved on drive A.

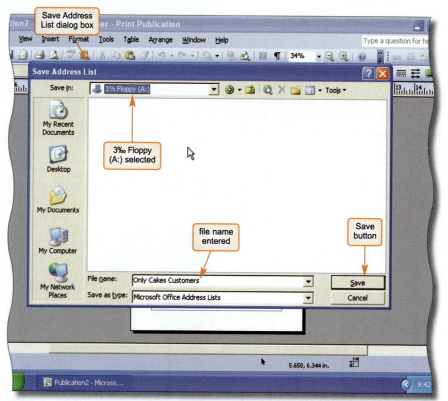

FIGURE 4-52

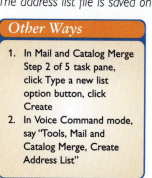

Other Ways

1. In Mail and Catalog Merge Step 2 of 5 task pane, click Type a new list option button, click Create
2. In Voice Command mode, say "Tools, Mail and Catalog Merge, Create Address List"

You can use Publisher address lists for additional, non-address information, because Publisher does not restrict the data entered into the address list in any way. If you want to keep track of other information, such as charges, rates, prices, or time, you still can use Publisher to maintain the data. The Customize button in the New Address List dialog box (Figure 4-51) allows you to add, delete, and rename fields in your data source.

You also can maintain multiple address lists for data sources such as customers, employees, or vendors, if you create and name the lists with different names. The Edit Address List command on the Mail and Catalog Merge submenu (Figure 4-48 on page PUB 250) permits you to specify to which data source you want to connect.

When you create an address list in Publisher, you can edit its entries without closing the current publication. If you are using a data source from another program, such as Microsoft Excel or Microsoft Word, you cannot edit the data source without closing the Publisher publication.

More About

Filter and Sort

The Filter and Sort button (shown in Figure 4-51) allows you either to merge a subset of records from your total data source or to merge your data in a particular order. The filter and sort orders do not permanently change your data source or mail merge.

Creating a Main Publication Using a Label Wizard

Another application for merging involves the use of mailing labels. For documents that are not available electronically and for large quantities that have been mass-produced, a mailing label sometimes is the most economical method of addressing correspondences. Several paper supply companies produce labels for desktop printers in a variety of sizes and configurations.

The following steps illustrate how to create a main publication using the Label Wizard to merge with the address list.

More About

Main Publications

When you open a main publication, Publisher attempts to open the associated data source file, too. If the data source is not in exactly the same location (i.e., drive and folder) as when it originally was merged and saved, Publisher displays a dialog box indicating that it cannot find the data source. When this occurs, click the Find Data Source button to display the Open Data Source dialog box, where you can locate the data source file.

To Use the Label Wizard

1. **With a blank publication still displaying, press CTRL+F1 to display the New Publication task pane.**
2. **In the New Publication task pane, click Publications for Print and then click Labels. Click the Medium Mailing Address Label (Avery 5161) preview.**

The label is displayed in the workspace (Figure 4-53).

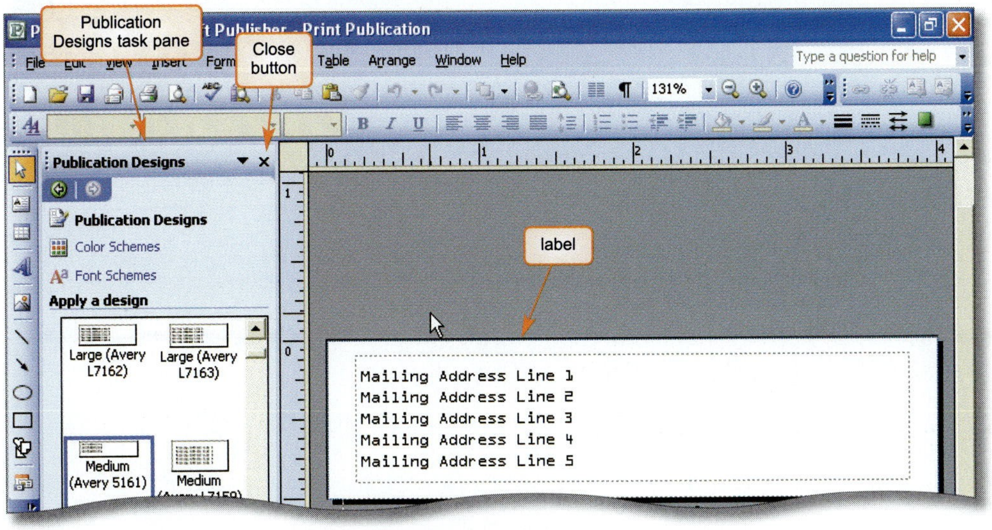

FIGURE 4-53

3. **Close the Publication Designs task pane.**

Inserting Field Codes

A publication designed for merging not only must be connected to its data source, it also must contain field codes. A **field code** is placeholder text in the publication that shows Publisher where to insert the information from the data source. You can format, copy, move, or delete a field code just as you would regular text. Field codes need to be spaced and punctuated appropriately.

Publisher supplies some grouped field codes. A **grouped field code** is a set of standard fields, such as typical address fields or salutation fields, preformatted and spaced with appropriate words and punctuation. For example, instead of entering the field codes for Title, First Name, Last Name, Company Name, Address Line 1, etc., you can choose an Address Block that includes all the fields displayed correctly.

With the floppy disk containing the customer database in drive A, the next series of steps show how to insert the field codes from the address list using the Mail and Catalog Merge Wizard. The **Mail and Catalog Merge Wizard** displays task panes to guide you step-by-step through the merging process.

To Insert Field Codes and Merge

1

• **If necessary, insert the floppy disk containing the data source file Only Cakes Customers. With the label still displayed in the workspace, click Tools on the menu bar, and then point to Mail and Catalog Merge.**

The Mail and Catalog Merge submenu is displayed (Figure 4-54).

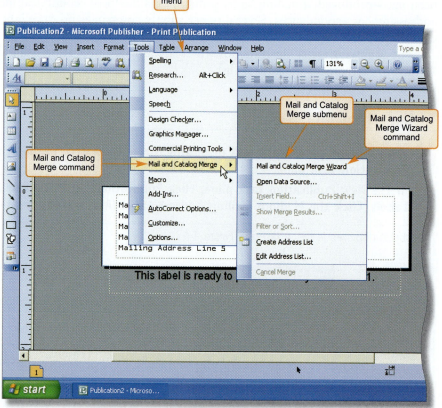

FIGURE 4-54

2

• **Click Mail and Catalog Merge Wizard.**

• **When the Mail and Catalog Merge task pane is displayed, if necessary, click the Mail Merge option button to select it.**

Step 1 of 5 is displayed in the Mail and Catalog Merge task pane (Figure 4-55).

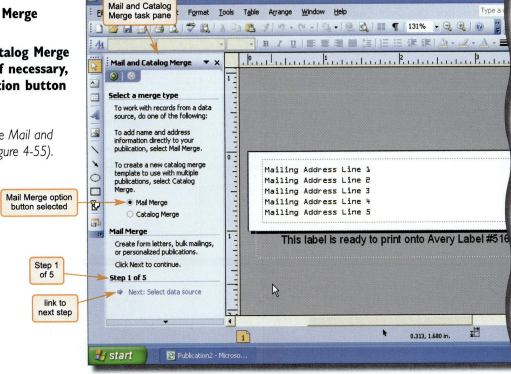

FIGURE 4-55

3

• **In the lower portion of the task pane, click Next: Select data source.**

• **When Step 2 of 5 is displayed, click Browse.**

• **When the Select Data Source dialog box is displayed, click the Look in box arrow and then click 3½ Floppy (A:) in the list.**

Publisher displays the list of files on the disk in drive A (Figure 4-56). Step 2 of 5 is displayed in the Mail and Catalog Merge task pane.

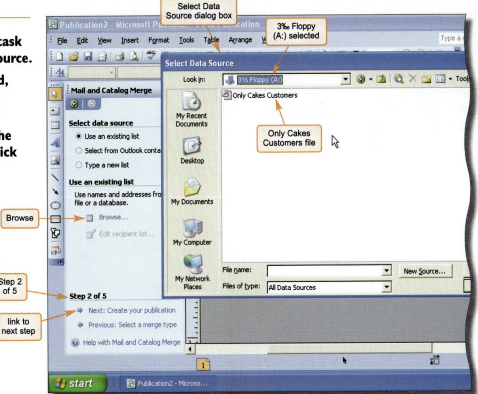

FIGURE 4-56

4

• **Double-click the Only Cakes Customers file in the list.**

The *Mail Merge Recipients dialog box* provides ways to sort, select, and edit the fields in the address list (Figure 4-57).

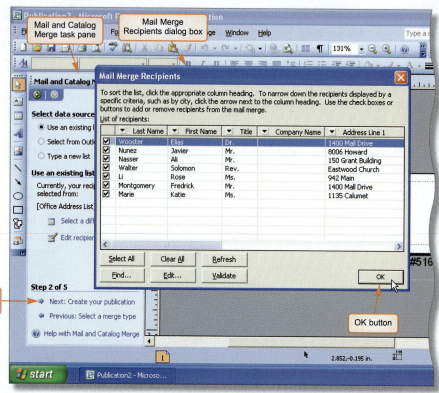

FIGURE 4-57

5

• **Click the OK button.**

• **In the Mail and Catalog Merge task pane, click Next: Create your publication.**

• **When Step 3 of 5 is displayed in the task pane, click the placeholder text in the mailing label to select it.**

Step 3 of 5 allows you to choose blocks of data or specific individual fields (Figure 4-58).

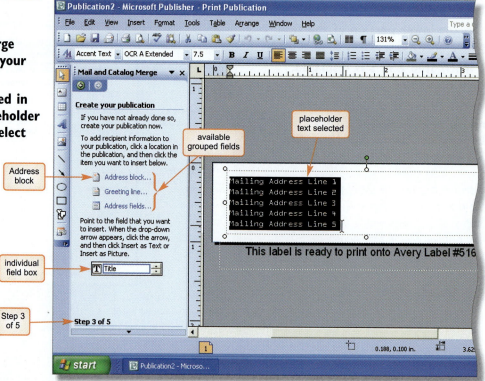

FIGURE 4-58

6

• **Click Address block.**

The *Insert Address Block dialog box* specifies address elements you can include in the publication (Figure 4-59).

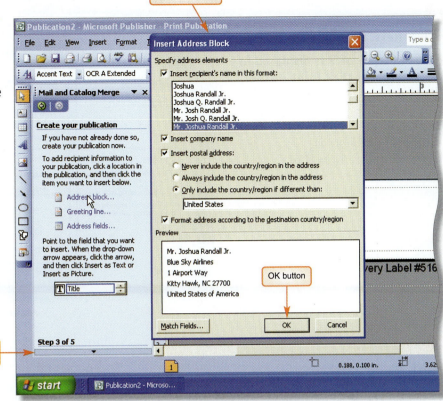

FIGURE 4-59

7

• **Click the OK button.**

• **If necessary, click the down arrow at the bottom of the task pane and then click Next: Preview your publication.**

The mailing address text box displays the first entry's address data (Figure 4-60). Step 4 of 5 allows you to make changes or view each recipient. You can click the previous and next buttons to traverse and display the records in the address list file.

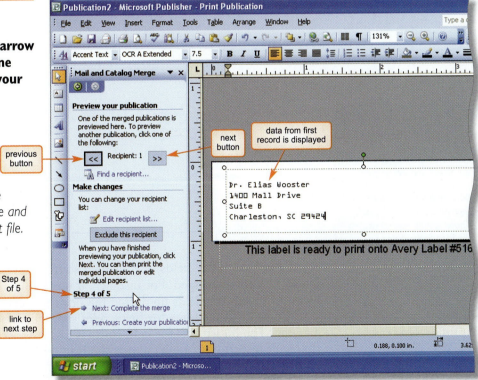

FIGURE 4-60

8

• **Click Next: Complete the merge.**

• **When Step 5 of 5 is displayed in the task pane, click Print in the Merge area.**

The Print Merge dialog box contains options for printing merged documents (Figure 4-61).

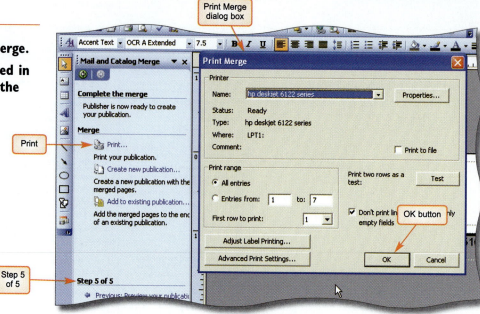

FIGURE 4-61

9

• **Click the OK button.**

The mailing labels print as shown in Figure 4-62. The preset label layout is two per row and 10 per column for a total of 20 labels per sheet.

Dr. Elias Wooster
1400 Mall Drive
Suite B
Charleston, SC 29424

Mr. Ali Nasser
150 Grant Building
Office 24 East
Charleston, SC 29424

Ms. Rose Li
942 Main
Charleston, SC 29424

Ms. Katie Marie
1135 Calumet
Nearby, SC 29420

labels display
in two columns

Mr. Javier Nunez
8006 Howard
Charleston, SC 29424

Rev. Solomon Walter
Eastwood Church
247 Antioch Ave.
Nearby, SC 29420

Mr. Fredrick Montgomery
1400 Mall Drive
Suite K
Charleston, SC 29424

FIGURE 4-62

More About

Printing Multiples

If the publication page size is one-half the size of your paper or smaller, you can print multiple copies of the page on each printed sheet. These special sizes, chosen in the Page Setup dialog box, will create a Page Options button that displays in the Print dialog box. You can choose how many copies of the publication to print per page and specify custom margin and gap measurements. The book fold option or book fold imposition will place two pages on opposite facing pages. If your printer supports paper as large as 11-by-17 inches, you can print two standard publication pages, side by side.

If you have blank fields in your data source, Publisher will omit the field when the publication is merged. For instance, if no second address line exists, Publisher will move the other fields up during the print process, in order to fill the gap.

You can edit the fonts for field codes that will affect the way they print after merging. The preset font for field codes is OCR A Extended. **OCR** stands for optical character recognition, which means that the post office can scan the address easily with electronic equipment, thereby speeding up the processing.

Publisher can save the merged files as one large file on the disk, and if you are planning to print labels many times, it might be beneficial to do so. It requires a large amount of disk space, and the data is **static**, which means that updates to the data source are not reflected. It is easy to merge the label and address list again if you need to print at a future time, and you can include any updates to the address list.

The next step is to close the envelope publication without saving the merged file.

To Close the Envelope

1 **Click File on the menu bar and then click Close. When Publisher asks if you want to save the changes, click the No button.**

The New Publication task pane again is displayed.

Web Sites

The final publication that Only Cakes has asked for is a prototype of a Web site. A **prototype** is a functional working model of a proposed system, created to make sure it meets the users' needs. Recall that a Web page is a combination of text, graphics, and links that are displayed via the Internet. The Web page prototype may contain only one Web page, some links that are not yet active, and placeholder graphics and text. A Web page prototype gives the user an idea of how the page will look over the Web, allowing the user to make suggestions and edits to the content. Web page prototypes sometimes are sent to professional usability testers who look at design issues and functionality.

Creating a Web Site

The Only Cakes Web site prototype will be created with Publisher's Easy Web Site Builder as described in the following steps.

To Use the Easy Web Site Builder

1

• **In the New Publication task pane, click Web Sites and E-mail.**

• **Click Web Sites and then click Easy Web Site Builder.**

• **Scroll as necessary to view the Marker Easy Web Site preview.**

The previews are displayed (Figure 4-63).

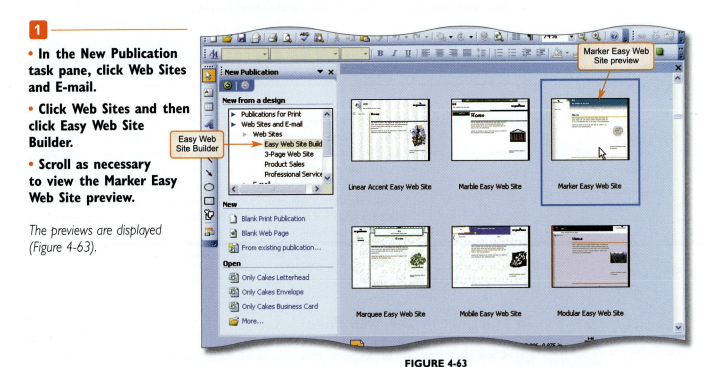

FIGURE 4-63

2

• **Click the Marker Easy Web Site preview.**

• **When the Easy Web Site Builder dialog box is displayed, click its Cancel button.**

• **Close the Web Site Options task pane.**

• **Click Edit on the menu bar and then click Personal Information. When the Personal Information dialog box is displayed, click the Select a personal information set box arrow, and then click Secondary Business.**

• **Click the Update button.**

• **If Publisher displays an Organization Logo, right-click it, and then click Delete Object on the shortcut menu.**

The Web site displays the personal information and its color scheme (Figure 4-64).

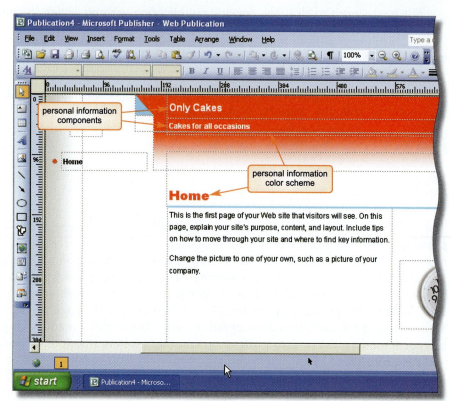

FIGURE 4-64

Editing Web Page Text

The next step is to edit text in the various text boxes as shown in Table 4-6.

Table 4-6	Text for Web Page
TEXT BOX	**NEW TEXT**
Home	Welcome to our Web site!
main text box	Only Cakes is a bakery specializing in cakes for all occasions. Teresa Chen recently has turned her passion for baking into a small business located on Airport Road. As owner and chief baker, Teresa is on site daily to help you with your cake decisions. Teresa has a degree in Culinary Art and Business from the University of Charleston and has been baking for five years. Eventually, Teresa will offer cake decorating classes and Web sales. Check back soon for more ways to order cakes. Our address and phone number are listed below.
caption	We specialize in big cakes and quick turnarounds!

To Edit Text in the Web Page

1 Click the text, Home. Replace the placeholder text with the new text from Table 4-6.

2. **Click the main text below the heading. Replace the placeholder text with the next text from Table 4-6.**

3. **Click the caption below the graphic on the right of the Web page. Replace the placeholder text with the new text from Table 4-6.**

The new text is entered (Figure 4-65).

FIGURE 4-65

Replacing the Web Page Graphic

Only Cakes wants to use the same picture on its Web Page that it uses on its letterhead. See pages PUB 228 through PUB 234 for the steps to retrieve the graphic of the cake, crop it, and add a border. Alternately, you can open the Only Cakes Letterhead and copy the graphic as described in the following steps.

To Copy a Graphic from Another Publication

1. **Click the Open button on the Standard toolbar. When the Open Publication dialog box is displayed, click the Look in box arrow and then click 3½ Floppy (A:) in the Look in list. Double-click Only Cakes Letterhead.**

2. **Right-click the cake graphic and then click Copy on the shortcut menu.**

3. **Click the Close button on the Publisher title bar to exit the publication. If Publisher asks if you want to save the contents of the clipboard, click the Yes button.**

4. **When the Web page again is displayed, right-click the placeholder graphic and then click Delete Object on the shortcut menu.**

5. **Right-click the page layout where the graphic was, and then click Paste on the shortcut menu.**

6. **Resize the picture of the cake to fill the space.**

The cake graphic is pasted in the Web page (Figure 4-66 on the next page).

More About

Graphics on the Web

You can use Vector Markup Language (VML) to speed up the downloading time for graphics on your Web site. VML is a system of marking up, or tagging, two-dimensional vector graphics for publishing on the Web. VML graphics are scalable and editable; they usually take less time to download and require less disk space. To enable VML, click Options on the Tools menu. Then, on the Web tab, click the Rely on VML for faster graphics downloading check box in the Saving area.

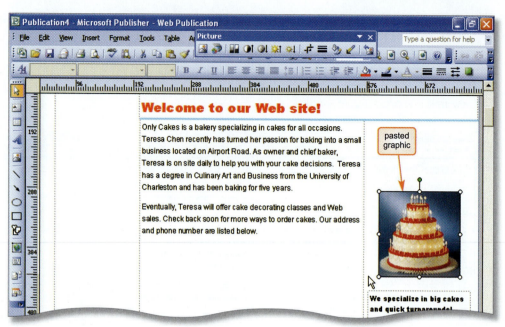

FIGURE 4-66

More About

Search Engines

For more information about using keywords with Web pages, visit the Publisher 2003 More About Web page (scsite.com/pub2003/more) and then click Search Engine Keywords.

Setting Web Page Options

While Publisher provides many options to tailor Web pages and Web sites, this prototype will edit only four: the title, the description, the keywords, and a background sound. The **Web page title** is the text that is displayed on the browser title bar when viewing the Web page. The **Web page description** is the short description that is displayed in most search engine references. **Keywords** are the words used by search engines to generate search results. The **background sound** is a short audio clip that plays when the user first visits a Web page.

The following steps show how to set the Web page options for the Only Cakes Web page.

To Set Web Page Options

1

• **Click Tools on the menu bar and then click Web Page Options.**

• **When Publisher displays the Web Page Options dialog box, type** Only Cakes **in the Page title text box.**

• **Type** This is the Web site of Only Cakes bakery. **in the Description text box.**

• **Type** cake bakery online orders custom cakes **in the Keywords text box.**

The title, description, and keywords are entered (Figure 4-67).

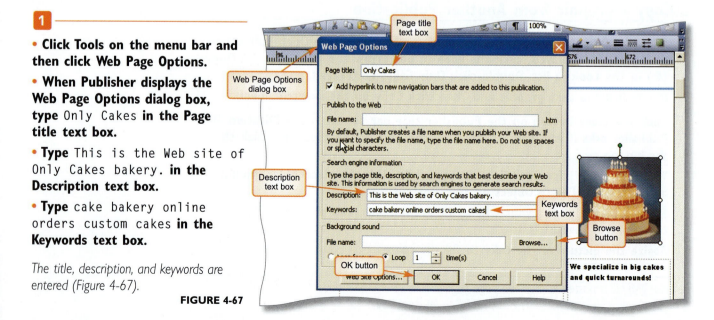

FIGURE 4-67

2

• **Click the Browse button.**

• **When Publisher displays the Background Sound dialog box, click SPRNG_01 in the list.**

Publisher displays the Background Sound dialog box (Figure 4-68).

3

• **Click the Open button in the Background Sound dialog box.**

• **Click the OK button in the Web Page Options dialog box.**

Publisher again displays the Web page.

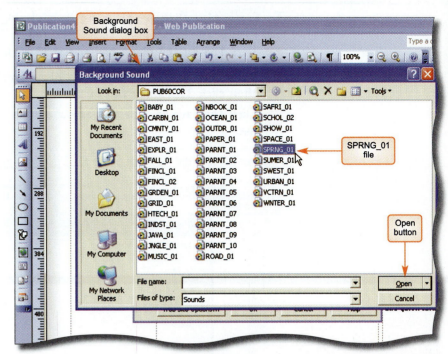

FIGURE 4-68

Other Ways

1. In Web Site Options task pane, click Page Content, click Rename Page

The following steps preview the Web page to see the effects of the selected Web page options.

To Preview the Web Page

1 **Click the Web Page Preview button on the Standard toolbar.**

The Web page is displayed in the browser. If your system is connected to speakers, the background sound will begin to play after a few moments.

2 **Click the Close button on the browser's title bar.**

The final task is to save the Web page for future editing, which requires you to save it as a Publisher file with a .pub extension, and then to save it as a filtered Web page file with the .mht extension. The following steps save the publication, first as a Publisher file, then as a Web page.

To Save the Publication as a Publisher File

1 **Insert a floppy disk in drive A.**

2 **Click the Save button on the Standard toolbar.**

3 **In the Save As dialog box, type** Only Cakes Web Publication **in the File name text box. Do not press the ENTER key.**

4 **If necessary, click the Save in box arrow and then click 3½ Floppy (A:).**

5 **Click the Save button in the Save As dialog box.**

To Save the Publication as a Web Page

1 Click File on the menu bar and then click Save As.

2 When the Save As dialog box is displayed, click the Save in box arrow and then click 3½ Floppy (A:) in the list.

3 Click the Save as type box arrow and then click Single File Web Page in the list.

Publisher will save the file in the Single File Web Page format (Figure 4-69).

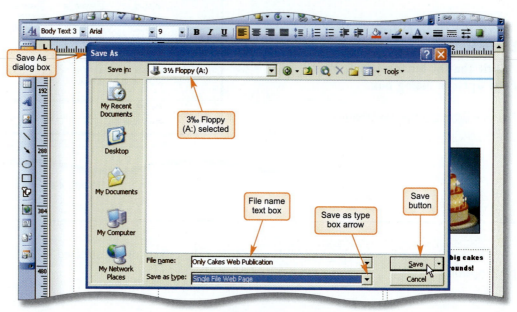

FIGURE 4-69

4 Click the Save button in the Save As dialog box.

Recall that a filtered HTML format is smaller than regular HTML files and can be published to and downloaded from the Internet quickly. Publisher encodes its filtered HTML with **Vector Markup Language** (**VML**), which is a system of marking up, or tagging, two-dimensional vector graphics for publishing on the World Wide Web. VML graphics are scalable and editable. Filtered Web pages usually require less disk space. VML information speeds up the downloading time for graphics on your Web site.

Quitting Publisher

The following steps quit Publisher.

To Quit Publisher

1 Click the Close button on the Publisher title bar.

2 If a dialog box is displayed reminding you to save the document, click its No button.

The Publisher window closes.

Project Summary

Project 4 introduced you to personalizing and customizing publications. First, you created the personal information set with its many components; then you used the information, along with a fill effect, to create a letterhead complete with a picture to which you added a border and cropped. Next, you applied the same components to a business card using a template to help you get started. You created an envelope for mass mailing along with a database of customers and then merged it with a mailing label file. Finally, you used the Easy Web Site Builder to create a prototype of a Web page for Only Cakes.

What You Should Know

Having completed this project, you should be able to perform the tasks below. The tasks are listed in the same order they were presented in this project. For a list of the buttons, menus, toolbars, and commands introduced in this project, see the Quick Reference Summary at the back of this book and refer to the Page Number column.

1. Start Publisher with a Blank Publication (PUB 212)
2. Set the Color and Font Schemes (PUB 213)
3. Edit the Layout Guides (PUB 214)
4. Move a Ruler and Create Ruler Guides (PUB 216)
5. Edit a Personal Information Set (PUB 218)
6. Create a Gradient Fill Effect (PUB 221)
7. Change the Line Color (PUB 224)
8. Insert and Format Personal Information Components (PUB 225)
9. Search for a Photograph (PUB 229)
10. Crop a Picture (PUB 231)
11. Add a Line Border (PUB 233)
12. Position Objects Using the Measurement Toolbar (PUB 236)
13. Kern Letters (PUB 236)
14. Copy and Paste an Object (PUB 237)
15. Rotate an Object (PUB 238)
16. Format the Tag Line with the Format Painter (PUB 239)
17. Reduce the Font Size and Center (PUB 240)
18. Group Objects (PUB 240)
19. Move an Object (PUB 241)
20. Insert an Automatic Date (PUB 242)
21. Save the Letterhead (PUB 244)
22. Close a Publication without Quitting Publisher (PUB 245)
23. Set a File to Read-Only (PUB 245)
24. Create a Business Card (PUB 245)
25. Edit the Business Card (PUB 246)
26. Save, Print, and Close the Business Card (PUB 247)
27. Create an Envelope (PUB 247)
28. Save, Print, and Close the Envelope (PUB 248)
29. Create the Address List (PUB 250)
30. Use the Label Wizard (PUB 253)
31. Insert Field Codes and Merge (PUB 254)
32. Close the Envelope (PUB 259)
33. Use the Easy Web Site Builder (PUB 259)
34. Edit Text in the Web Page (PUB 260)
35. Copy a Graphic from Another Publication (PUB 261)
36. Set Web Page Options (PUB 262)
37. Preview the Web Page (PUB 263)
38. Save the Publication as a Publisher File (PUB 263)
39. Save the Publication as a Web Page (PUB 264)
40. Quit Publisher (PUB 264)

Learn It Online

Instructions: To complete the Learn It Online exercises, start your browser, click the Address bar, and then enter the Web address scsite.com/pub2003/learn. When the Publisher 2003 Learn It Online page is displayed, follow the instructions in the exercises below. Each exercise has instructions for printing your results, either for your own records or for submission to your instructor.

1 Project Reinforcement TF, MC, and SA

Below Publisher Project 4, click the Project Reinforcement link. Print the quiz by clicking Print on the File menu for each page. Answer each question.

2 Flash Cards

Below Publisher Project 4, click the Flash Cards link and read the instructions. Type 20 (or a number specified by your instructor) in the Number of playing cards text box, type your name in the Enter your Name text box, and then click the Flip Card button. When the flash card is displayed, read the question and then click the ANSWER box arrow to select an answer. Flip through Flash Cards. If your score is 15 (75%) correct or greater, click Print on the File menu to print your results. If your score is less than 15 (75%) correct, then redo this exercise by clicking the Replay button.

3 Practice Test

Below Publisher Project 4, click the Practice Test link. Answer each question, enter your first and last name at the bottom of the page, and then click the Grade Test button. When the graded practice test is displayed on your screen, click Print on the File menu to print a hard copy. Continue to take practice tests until you score 80% or better.

4 Who Wants To Be a Computer Genius?

Below Publisher Project 4, click the Computer Genius link. Read the instructions, enter your first and last name at the bottom of the page, and then click the PLAY button. When your score is displayed, click the PRINT RESULTS link to print a hard copy.

5 Wheel of Terms

Below Publisher Project 4, click the Wheel of Terms link. Read the instructions, and then enter your first and last name and your school name. Click the PLAY button. When your score is displayed, right-click the score and then click Print on the shortcut menu to print a hard copy.

6 Crossword Puzzle Challenge

Below Publisher Project 4, click the Crossword Puzzle Challenge link. Read the instructions, and then enter your first and last name. Click the SUBMIT button. Work the crossword puzzle. When you are finished, click the Submit button. When the crossword puzzle is redisplayed, click the Print Puzzle button to print a hard copy.

7 Tips and Tricks

Below Publisher Project 4, click the Tips and Tricks link. Click a topic that pertains to Project 4. Right-click the information and then click Print on the shortcut menu. Construct a brief example of what the information relates to in Publisher to confirm you understand how to use the tip or trick.

8 Newsgroups

Below Publisher Project 4, click the Newsgroups link. Click a topic that pertains to Project 4. Print three comments.

9 Expanding Your Horizons

Below Publisher Project 4, click the Articles for Microsoft Publisher link. Click a topic that pertains to Project 4. Print the information. Construct a brief example of what the information relates to in Publisher to confirm you understand the contents of the article.

10 Search Sleuth

Below Publisher Project 4, click the Search Sleuth link. To search for a term that pertains to this project, select a term below the Project 4 title and then use the Google search engine at google.com (or any major search engine) to display and print two Web pages that present information on the term.

11 Publisher Online Training

Below Publisher Project 4, click the Publisher Online Training link. When your browser displays the Microsoft Office Online Web page, click the Publisher link. Click one of the Publisher courses that covers one or more of the objectives listed at the beginning of the project on page PUB 210. Print the first page of the course before stepping through it.

12 Office Marketplace

Below Publisher Project 4, click the Office Marketplace link. When your browser displays the Microsoft Office Online Web page, click the Office Marketplace link. Click a topic that relates to Publisher. Print the first page.

Apply Your Knowledge

1 Working with a Form Letter

Instructions: Start Publisher. Open the publication, Apply 4-1a from the Data Disk. See the inside back cover for instructions for downloading the Data Disk or see your instructor for information about accessing the files required in this book. The publication is a main document for Prairie University (Figure 4-70). The Data Disk also contains an address list for prospective graduate students in a file named, Apply 4-1b. You will edit the address list to insert your own personal information into the database, insert the date and field codes, and then merge the main publication with the data source.

FIGURE 4-70

(continued)

Apply Your Knowledge

Working with a Form Letter *(continued)*

Perform the following tasks:

1. Start Publisher. Open the existing file Apply 4-1a from the Data Disk. When the publication is displayed, click Tools on the menu bar, point to Mail and Catalog Merge, and then click Mail and Catalog Merge Wizard.
2. When the Mail and Catalog Merge task pane is displayed, click Next: Select data source. Click Browse. When the Select Data Source dialog box is displayed, click the Look in box arrow and click 3½ Floppy (A:) in the list. When the files are displayed, double-click the file name, Apply 4-1b.
3. When the Mail Merge Recipients dialog box is displayed, click the Edit button. When the Apply 4-1b dialog box is displayed, click the New Entry button. Enter your name and address into the appropriate fields and then click the Close button. Click the OK button.
4. In the publication, click the Enter date here text box and then press the F9 key. Press CTRL+A to select the text and then on the Insert menu, click Date and Time. In the Date and Time dialog box, choose an appropriate style from the Available formats list. Click the Update Automatically check box to display its check mark. Click the OK button.
5. In the publication, click the Enter address block here text box. Press CTRL+A to select the text. At the bottom of the Mail and Catalog Merge task pane, click Next: Create your publication. Click Address block. When the Insert Address Block dialog box is displayed, click the OK button.
6. In the publication, click the Enter greeting line here text box. Press CTRL+A to select the text. In the Mail and Catalog Merge task pane, click Greeting line. When the Greeting Line dialog box is displayed, click the OK button.
7. On the File menu, click Save As. Save the publication using the file name, Apply 4-1 Prairie Form Letter.
8. At the bottom of the Mail and Catalog Merge task pane, click Next: Preview your publication. When the step is displayed in the task pane, click the arrows until the letter with your name is displayed.
9. At the bottom of the Mail and Catalog Merge task pane, click Next: Complete the merge. When the step is displayed in the task pane, click Print. Click the OK button in the Print Merge dialog box to print the letters. Close the file. Turn in the printouts to your instructor.

In the Lab

1 Creating Stationery

Problem: Your uncle is the volunteer commissioner for the local children's baseball league. Because he is responsible for organizing the teams, ordering equipment, and scheduling games, fields, and umpires, he has asked you to create some stationery for his correspondences (Figure 4-71).

In the Lab

Instructions: Perform the following tasks with a computer:

1. Start Publisher with a blank publication. On the Arrange menu, click Layout Guides and then set the margins to .5 inches.

2. At the bottom of the page, insert a graphic relating to baseball. Resize and crop it as necessary. Insert a text box next to the graphic. Change the font size to 20 and then type the name and address as shown in Figure 4-71.

3. Click the AutoShapes button on the Objects toolbar. Point to Basic Shapes and then click Bevel. Draw a bevel shape at the top of the page. Use the Measurement toolbar to adjust the size of the bevel as follows: 7.5 inches wide, 1.5 inches tall, and .5 inch margins.

4. Click the Fill Color button arrow on the Formatting toolbar and then click Fill Effects. Click the Gradient tab. Click the One Color option button. Choose a color that complements the graphic. Drag the Dark to Light scroll box all the way to the right.

5. Click the Line Color button on the Formatting toolbar. On the color palette, choose a red color.

6. In front of the bevel, insert a text box for the heading. Use a script font that resembles handwriting and a font size of at least 24. Type From the desk of the commissioner ... in the text box. Click the Line Color button to make the text box line color red.

7. Select all the text in the heading and then use the Measurement toolbar to change the text scaling to 150%. If necessary, adjust the size and position of the text box as shown in Figure 4-71. Choose Best Fit.

8. Save the publication with the file name, Lab 4-1 Baseball Stationery, and then print a copy.

9. Click the graphic at the bottom of the page and then SHIFT-click the address text box. Click the Copy button on the Standard toolbar to copy both objects to the Clipboard.

10. Click the New button on the Standard toolbar. When the blank publication is displayed, click File on the menu bar and then click Page Setup. When the Page Setup dialog box is displayed, click Envelope in the Publication type list. Click Size 10 in the Page Size list. Click the OK button. When the envelope is displayed in the workspace, click the Paste button to paste from the Clipboard to the envelope. Use the Measurement toolbar and the Best Fit option to reposition as necessary for an appropriate return address.

11. Save the publication with the file name, Lab 4-1 Baseball Envelope, and then print a copy.

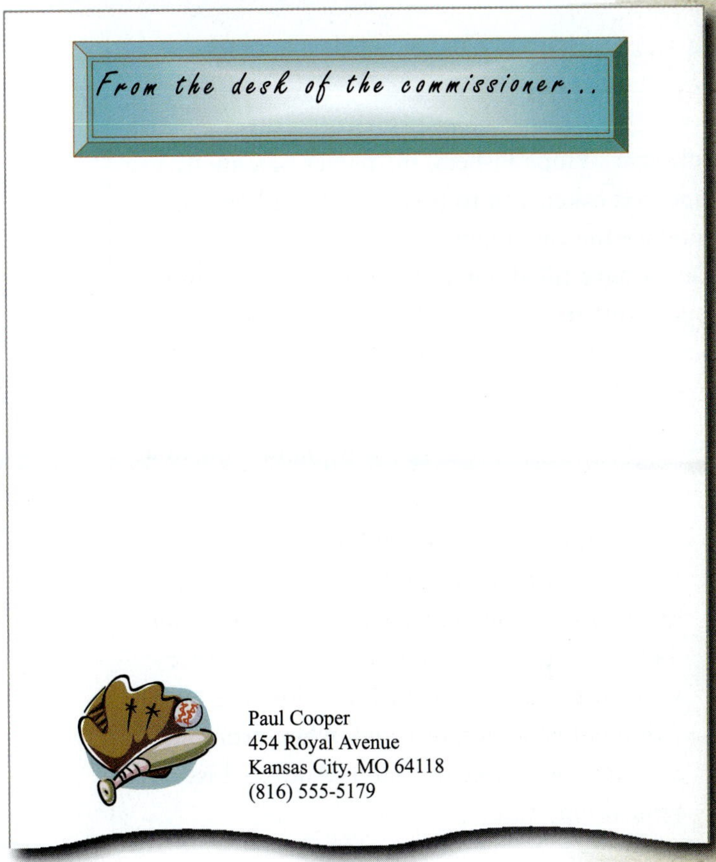

From the desk of the commissioner...

Paul Cooper
454 Royal Avenue
Kansas City, MO 64118
(816) 555-5179

FIGURE 4-71

2 Creating a Data Source and Form Letter

Problem: Hope Fishers, the owner of Café of Hope, has asked you to prepare a form letter to announce the cafe's new hours. Customers recently have filled out a satisfaction survey, and Hope wants to start a Publisher Address list. You decide to create the form letter shown in Figure 4-72.

Instructions: Perform the following tasks with a computer:

1. Start Publisher with a blank publication.
2. Using the Mail and Catalog Merge feature, create a Publisher address list using data from Table 4-7. Click the New Entry button after each customer except the last. Close the New Address List dialog box and, when prompted, save the file as Lab 4-2 Hope Address List on your floppy disk.

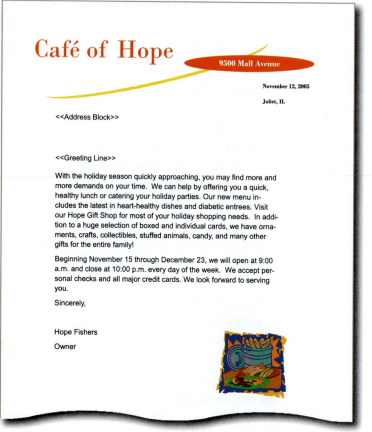

FIGURE 4-72

	FIRST NAME	LAST NAME	ORGANIZATION	ADDRESS LINE 1	ADDRESS LINE 2	CITY	STATE	ZIP CODE
TITLE								
Mr.	Ian	Peters	Carr & Associates, CPAs	P. O. Box 19		Orland Park	IL	60462
Mrs.	Karen	Bissell		105 Lake Street	Apt. 3D	New Lenox	IL	60451
Dr.	John	Groves	Medical Associates	P. O. Box 67		Mokena	IL	60448
Mr.	Samuel	Easton		123 Michigan	Apt. 5A	Joliet	IL	60435

Table 4-7   Hope Address List Data

3. Using the Design Gallery Object button on the Objects toolbar, choose the Arcs Masthead. Choose the Sunrise color scheme and the Breve font scheme.
4. Drag the masthead to the top of the page. Edit the text boxes in the masthead as shown in Figure 4-72. Use the Symbol command on the Insert menu to insert an e with an accent. Use the Measurement toolbar to position the name of the shop and adjust the tracking, scaling, and/or kerning.
5. Insert empty text boxes below the masthead for the address and greeting line blocks.
6. Create a large text box and enter the remainder of the letter text shown in Figure 4-72.
7. Click the Address block text box. SHIFT-click the greeting line text box. SHIFT-click the text box containing the body of the letter. Use the Arrange menu to align the three text boxes on the left.
8. Save the publication on a floppy disk with the file name, Lab 4-2 Hope Form Letter.

In the Lab

9. Using the Mail and Catalog Merge wizard, merge the letter with the address list, using the Hope Address list. In Step 3, click the address text box you created and then click Address block in the task pane. Click the greeting text box you created and then click Greeting line in the task pane.

10. Preview the publication and then print all the pages of the merged file.

3 Creating a Web Page

Problem: Your friend runs Miracle Maids house cleaning service and has asked you to produce a Web page he can use to advertise his services. He wants the name, address, and telephone number in the header. You decide to use the Axis Easy Web Site, the Mountain color scheme, and the Online font scheme (Figure 4-73).

Instructions: Perform the following tasks with a computer:

1. Start Publisher. In the New Publication task pane, select Web Sites and E-mail. Select the Easy Web Site Builder. Click the Axis Easy Web Site preview. If Publisher displays an Easy Web Site Builder dialog box, click its Cancel button.

2. Click Color Schemes in the task pane. Select Mountain in the Apply a color scheme list. Click Font Schemes in the task pane. Select Online in the Apply a font scheme list.

3. Replace the Organization Name Text Box with the text, Miracle Maids. Replace the Home text box text and the Tag Line Text Box text with the phrase, We clean it all!

4. Find a suitable clip art graphic using the Clip Art task pane. Crop the graphic to focus on the most important part. Add a line border in a color that complements the graphic.

5. Click Tools on the menu bar and then click Web Page Options. When the Web Page Options dialog box is displayed, change the title to Miracle Maids and the description to: This is the home page of Miracle Maids, a house cleaning service in the greater Chicago area. Edit the keywords to include: maids house cleaning Chicago clean maid service. Edit the other text boxes to describe a typical maid and house cleaning service or copy the text from Figure 4-73.

FIGURE 4-73

6. Check the publication for spelling errors and then run the publication through the Design Checker.

7. Save the publication as Publisher file on a floppy disk using the file name, Lab 4-3 Miracle Maids Publication.

8. Save the publication as a filtered Web page on a floppy disk using the file name, Lab 4-3 Miracle Maids Web Publication. Print the publication and turn in a copy to your instructor.

Cases and Places

The difficulty of these case studies varies:
■ are the least difficult and ■■ are more difficult. The last exercise is a group exercise.

1 ■ Copy Cat Creations has asked you to create a new letterhead. They would like an arrow shape with a gradient fill to serve as a background for the words, Copy Cat Creations. Use a blank page publication and insert an arrow from the AutoShapes button on the Objects toolbar. Position the arrow in the upper-left corner of the page. Use a text box for the company name. Insert a text box at the bottom of the page and type the address and telephone number: 1350 Ridgeway Avenue, Mesa, AZ 85211, (480) 555-3770. Insert a graphic of a cat or tiger. Crop the graphic to show just the animal's face.

2 ■ Start Publisher and choose a Business Card template from the list. Edit the personal information set for the Secondary Business. Use your own name and the title, Student Extraordinaire. Enter the name and address of your school or workplace as the organization. Choose a color scheme. In the Personal Information dialog box, click Update. Print the business card with the personal information components.

3 ■ Using a blank publication, create your own personal stationery. Insert a graphic or a background shape with a fill effect. Include your name, address, and telephone number in text boxes. If your first or last name begins with the letter, A, T, V, W, Y, M, or Z, kern that letter and the following letter. Save the file on a floppy disk using the file name, My Letterhead. Create a matching #6 envelope using the concepts and techniques presented in this project. Print a copy of the stationery and the envelope to use in your own correspondence.

4 ■■ You currently are seeking employment in your field of study. You already have prepared a resume and would like to send it to a group of potential employers. You decide to design a cover letter to send with the resume. Obtain a recent newspaper and cut out five classified advertisements pertaining to your field of study. Create the cover letter for your resume as a main publication to merge with a data source. Be sure the cover letter has an attractive letterhead containing your name, address, and telephone number. Use the information in the classified ads for the address list. Insert the personal information components as the inside mailing address underneath the letterhead. Create a large text box for the body of your letter. Merge the letter with the address list and print all five copies. Turn in the classified ads with your printouts.

5 ■■ **Working Together** Individually, create a large mailing label using the New Publication task pane. Choose an appropriate font scheme. Use the Mail and Catalog Merge Wizard to create an address list of the students in your class. Insert data into the fields for first name and e-mail address. Create a new field called Year in School, in which you will enter freshman, sophomore, junior, or senior. If your instructor permits you to do so, go from one computer station to the next, inserting your personal data. On your computer, in the label's address text box, delete the text. Use the More Items link in the task pane to insert the three fields. Print multiple labels on the page.

Creating Business Forms and Tables

PROJECT

5

CASE PERSPECTIVE

Teresa Chen, owner and chief baker of Only Cakes, was very happy with the stationery and Web page created earlier in Project 4. She liked the eye-catching fonts and colors and appreciated the consistency across publications that Publisher's design set provides. With your help, she has entered each customer into her Publisher address list, printed labels, and has used Publisher to create simple thank-you cards for customer orders. Now that her business is up and running in its new location, Teresa would like to automate some of the paper and pencil tasks that she has been performing on a daily basis.

Teresa has asked you to create an invoice that is easy to fill out on the screen (Figure 5-1a on page 275). She then plans to print the invoice and attach it to the box of each cake she sells. She would like to have a coupon at the bottom of the invoice that advertises 10% off the customer's next order. She reminds you to put her new Web site address on the invoice.

The workers who have been taking orders in the store have been using plain paper to fill out the customer requests. Teresa mentions that she has had to call several customers when the order clerk forgets to ask all the right questions about size, shape, filling, icing, etc. Teresa wonders if you could create a short form, approximately 5 inches by 7 inches that would include boxes and fields for the clerks to fill out (Figure 5-1b).

Finally, Teresa wants to proceed with her Web site construction, as well. She would like to add a page to her site that displays a calendar of events. Teresa is planning several cake decorating workshops including Kids in the Kitchen, Just for Men, and Cake Decorating 101 (Figure 5-1c).

Creating Business Forms and Tables

Objectives

You will have mastered the material in this project when you can:

- List common business forms
- Create an invoice template
- Use styles and drop caps
- Set a tab stop
- Create a border using BorderArt

- Add a shadow effect
- Create and format tables
- Navigate through table cells to enter data
- Insert Design Gallery calendars
- Format a navigation bar

Introduction

Computers commonly are used to produce modern business forms, such as invoices, statements, purchase orders, expense reports, fax covers, time records, and inventory lists. Not only do computers make it easy to maintain a consistent look and style for business forms, but they also update and manipulate the forms more quickly and inexpensively than manual processing. Some of Publisher's forms typical to business applications are defined below.

An **invoice** is an itemized list of goods or services, stating quantities, prices, fees, and other charges with a request for payment (Figure 5-1a). Invoices usually accompany delivered orders; occasionally they are mailed to customers. A **statement** is a form sent to customers at regular intervals, displaying a compilation of invoices, charges, and payments. A formal request to buy a product from a vendor and bill it to a business account is called a **purchase order**. When employees travel or entertain for business purposes they prepare an **expense report** as a means of itemizing incurred business expenses for reimbursement. A **fax cover** is a cover sheet for a facsimile transmission to send images over telephone lines. For payroll purposes, companies use **time cards**, or time records, to keep track of the exact time employees begin and end their workdays. An **inventory list** may take any of several different forms, but usually includes fields for quantities, serial numbers, descriptions, warranties, and values.

Other types of business publications are specific to individual industries. For example, a college might need a student registration form, manufacturing companies might need production schedules, the travel industry might use a reservation form, and the bakery in this project needs a customer order form with specific information about cake sizes, flavors, and decorations.

Project Five — Creating Business Forms and Tables

Project 5 illustrates the generation of three business forms for a small bakery: an invoice with a coupon (Figure 5-1a), an order form (Figure 5-1b), and a Web page calendar (Figure 5-1c).

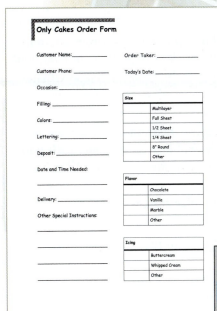

(a) Invoice

(b) Order form

(c) Web page calendar

FIGURE 5-1

The invoice for Only Cakes will become a reusable template with fields for individualizing customer data and charges. The coupon that is displayed in the lower right portion of the invoice is a Design Gallery object with text boxes and a specialized border. The order form includes a formatted table that clerks will complete when ordering cakes. The Web page includes a calendar of Only Cakes events.

Starting Publisher

To start Publisher, Windows must be running. The following steps show how to start Publisher.

To Start Publisher

1 Click the Start button on the Windows taskbar, point to All Programs on the Start menu, point to Microsoft Office on the All Programs submenu, and then click Microsoft Office Publisher 2003 on the Microsoft Office submenu.

2 If the Publisher window is not maximized, double-click its title bar to maximize it.

3 If Publisher does not display the New Publication task pane, click View on the menu bar and then click Task Pane. If the Publication Designs task pane is displayed, click the Other Task Panes button on the task pane title bar, and then click New Publication.

4 If the Language bar is displayed, click its Minimize button.

You now are ready to use Publisher's New Publication task pane to create an invoice template.

Creating Invoices

Invoices come in a variety of styles and sizes. Some invoices are handwritten on generic invoice pads, while others may be multipart carbonless forms sold commercially. Most invoices have several elements in common. First, they display the name of the company, its location, and contact information. Invoices generally include the creation date, an invoice number, and the name of the customer to whom the invoice is presented. Invoices may contain different addresses for billing and shipping. Finally, invoices display quantities, descriptions, prices, taxes, and totals.

While larger businesses may use accounting programs, point-of-sale terminals, or transaction processing systems to create invoices automatically from inventory databases or work records, smaller businesses that use a computer to keep track of billing and customers usually generate invoices on an as-issued basis. That means that when a customer orders an item, an employee accesses an **invoice template** on the computer and then fills in the parts of the invoice that change. Once saved, this data-enriched template becomes an **instance** of the invoice.

Creating an Invoice Template

Using one of the invoice templates provided by Publisher, you will create an invoice template for Only Cakes employees to complete on the screen (Figure 5-1a on the previous page). The following steps show how to choose an appropriate invoice preview and create a template.

Q: How can I make sure no one overwrites my template?

A: Right-click the template file in any Explorer window. Click Properties on the shortcut menu. Then, on the General sheet, click the Read-only check box so it displays a checkmark. Setting the read-only attribute will force users to save with a different file name.

To Create an Invoice Template

1

• **Click Publications for Print in the New Publication task pane.**

• **Click Business Forms in the New from a design list.**

• **When the list of available business forms is displayed, click Invoice.**

• **In the previews pane, click the down scroll arrow until the Punctuation Invoice is visible.**

Publisher displays previews of the invoice business forms (Figure 5-2). Your previews may vary.

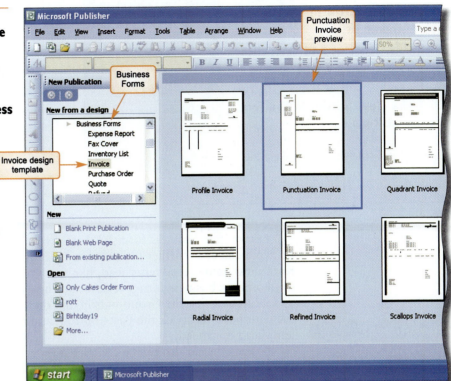

FIGURE 5-2

2

• **Click Punctuation Invoice.**

• **When the Business Form Options task pane is displayed, click None in the Logo area.**

The invoice will not include a logo from the personal information set (Figure 5-3).

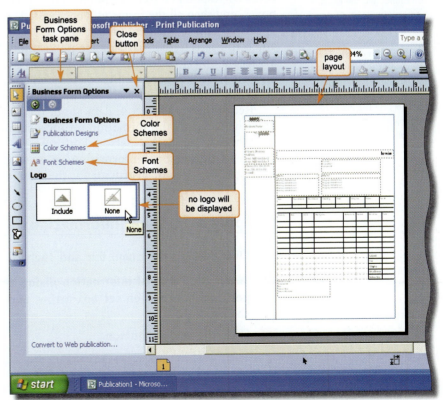

FIGURE 5-3

3

• **Click Color Schemes in the Business Form Options task pane and then click Parrot in the Apply a color scheme list.**

• **Click Font Schemes and then click Casual in the Apply a font scheme list.**

• **Click the Close button in the Font Schemes task pane.**

The Casual font scheme is displayed in the invoice (Figure 5-4).

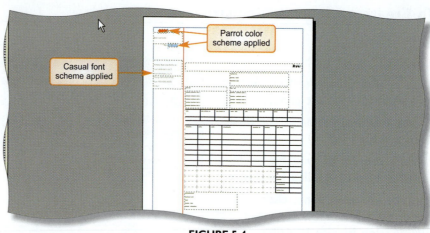

Parrot color scheme applied

Casual font scheme applied

FIGURE 5-4

Automating business forms such as invoices, statements, and purchase orders can be expedited even further in Publisher by cutting and pasting the input portion of the form onto predesigned letterhead, like that you created in Project 4. To use letterhead, open a business form preview and then select all of the objects below the name and address. Click the Group button and then click the Copy button. Finally, open the letterhead file, click the Paste button, and then drag the pasted objects below the letterhead masthead.

Business forms also can be completed using merged data sources. As you learned in Project 4, Publisher's capability of using an external data source can facilitate the processing of standard forms and letters. If a company uses a database such as Microsoft Access to store charges, they can merge the business form with the data source. Field codes corresponding to those in the database can be inserted into the appropriate text boxes, and then all the forms will be updated, automating the process even more.

Many times, when editing, it is necessary to zoom to different magnifications and scroll to different parts of the publication. Recall that the F9 key is used to zoom a selected object to 100%. The Zoom In and Zoom Out buttons and the Zoom box arrow on the Standard toolbar display other magnifications including Whole Page and Page Width. The steps in this project use these zooming techniques.

Recall that in Project 4, data about the Only Cakes business was entered in Publisher's personal information set for a secondary business. The following steps show how to apply that personal information set to the invoice template. If you did not create the personal information set, see pages PUB 217 through PUB 219 in this textbook, or see your instructor for the data.

To Apply a Personal Information Set

1 Click Edit on the menu bar and then click Personal Information.

2 When the Personal Information dialog box is displayed, click the Select a personal information set box arrow, and then click Secondary Business in the list.

3 Click the Update button.

The personal information components now are displayed in the publication.

The Invoice template does not include the company's tag line. The following steps illustrate how to insert that personal information component.

To Insert a Personal Information Component

1 Press the F9 key to zoom to 100%.

2 Click Insert on the menu bar, point to Personal Information, and then click Tag Line.

3 When the Tag Line text box is displayed, select the text and then click the Font Size box on the Formatting toolbar.

4 Type 12 in the Font Size box and then press the ENTER key.

5 Drag the Tag Line text box to the upper-right portion of the publication as shown in Figure 5-5.

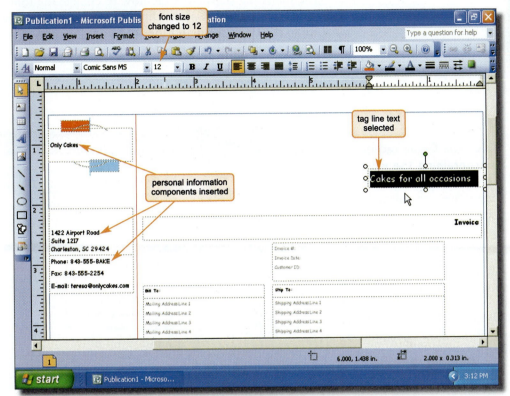

FIGURE 5-5

The Tag Line component is inserted in the invoice.

Creating Styles

Formatting the invoice template involves creating a style for the company name and applying the style to make the word, Invoice, more prominent. Second, you will create a large dropped initial capital letter called a drop cap. Finally, you will insert a coupon from the Design Gallery with BorderArt.

The owner of Only Cakes has used a special font and color scheme for her business. She would like this style of formatting to be used across all of the publications she creates. If you want to save formatting for use in future publications, Publisher uses a concept called styles, as do many word processing applications. A **style** is a set of formatting characteristics that you apply to text to change its appearance quickly. A style contains all text formatting information: font, font size, font color, indents, character and line spacing, tabs, and special formatting, such as numbered lists. When you apply a style, you apply a whole group of formats in one step. For example, you may want to format the Web page address of a company to make it stand out. Instead of taking four separate steps to format the address as underlined, blue, 16-point, and center-aligned, you can achieve the same result in one step by applying a saved style. The formatting changes affect the entire paragraph.

Publisher contains a predefined Normal style that uses a left-aligned, 10-point Times New Roman font. Other text styles can come from a variety of sources. You can define your own styles in Publisher, import text styles from other publications, or use text styles you have saved. For example, styles from Microsoft Word documents can be imported into Publisher.

Creating a New Style

The following steps illustrate how to change the font settings to create a new style and name it Only Cakes. Once created, you can import the style from the invoice to the order form and the Web page.

To Create a New Text Style

1

• **Click the Organization Name text box containing the words, Only Cakes, at the top of the invoice. Press CTRL+A to select all of the text.**

• **Click Format on the menu bar.**

The text is selected, and Publisher displays the Format menu (Figure 5-6). Depending on which personal information set is selected and previous changes to personal information data, your organization name may differ.

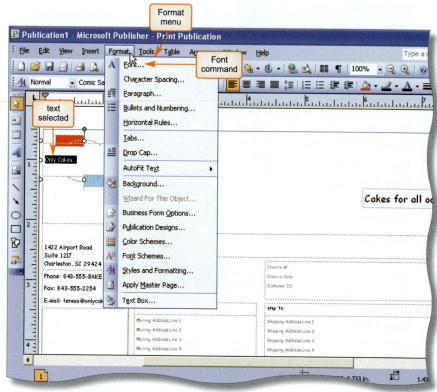

FIGURE 5-6

2

• **Click Font.**

• **When the Font dialog box is displayed, if necessary, click the Font box arrow, and then click Comic Sans MS or a similar font. Click the Font style box arrow and then click Bold. Click the Size box arrow, scroll as necessary, and then click 16 in the Size list. Click the Color box arrow and then click Accent 1 (Red).**

The new font settings are displayed in the preview (Figure 5-7). Your preview may differ.

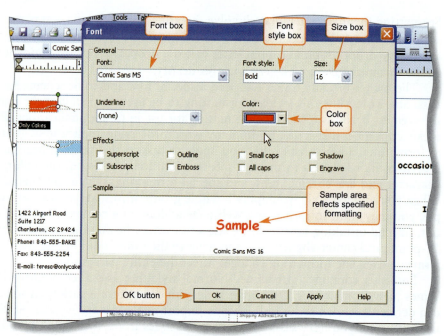

FIGURE 5-7

3

- Click the OK button.
- Click the Styles and Formatting button on the Formatting toolbar.

The new formatting is applied to the selected company name (Figure 5-8). Publisher also displays the Styles and Formatting task pane that contains a list of standard styles from which you may choose, as well as buttons to import and create new styles (Figure 5-8).

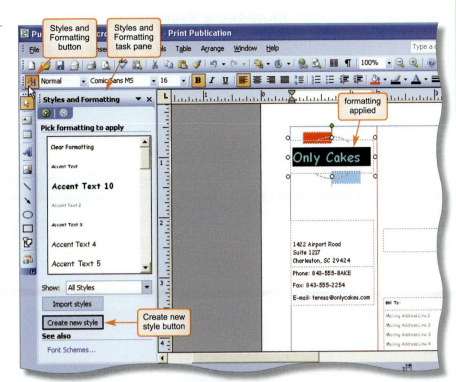

FIGURE 5-8

4

- Click the Create new style button in the Styles and Formatting task pane.
- When the New Style dialog box is displayed, type Only Cakes in the Enter new style name text box.

The New Style dialog box displays a description of the new style and a sample (Figure 5-9). Your preview may differ. The buttons in the Click to change area allow you to customize the new style even further.

5

- Click the OK button.
- Close the Styles and Formatting task pane by clicking its Close button.

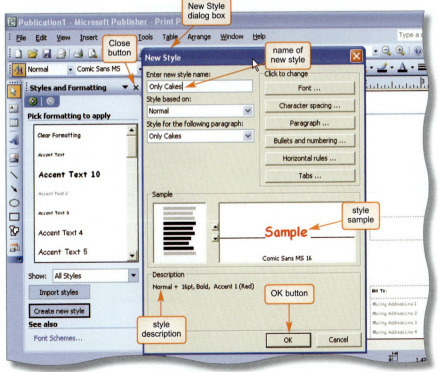

FIGURE 5-9

The Normal style (Figure 5-9) on which Only Cakes is based is left-justified and single-spaced. The color, size, and bold effect are added to the Normal Style.

Styles are saved when the publication is saved. The next step is to apply the new style to more text.

Other Ways

1. Click formatted text, type new style name in Style box
2. In Voice Command mode, say "Styles and Formatting, Create new style"

Applying a Style

When you want to use a previously created style or a style from Publisher's standard list, you select the text, click the Style box arrow, and then click the Style you wish to use as shown in the following steps.

To Apply a Style

1

• **Zoom to Page Width. Click the word, Invoice, on the right side of the page layout to select it, as shown in Figure 5-10.**

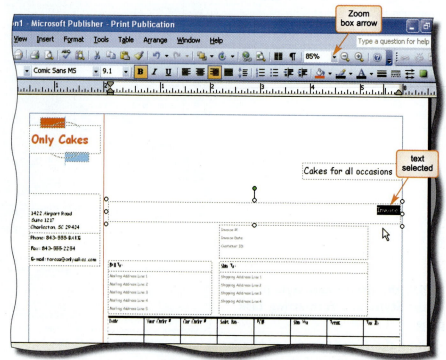

FIGURE 5-10

2

• **Click the Style box arrow on the Formatting toolbar.**

Publisher displays the styles associated with this publication (Figure 5-11).

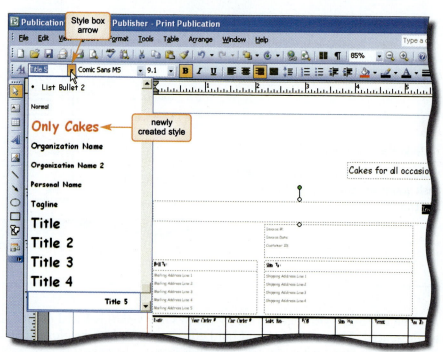

FIGURE 5-11

3

• **Click Only Cakes in the Style list.**

The word, Invoice, is formatted using the new Only Cakes style (Figure 5-12).

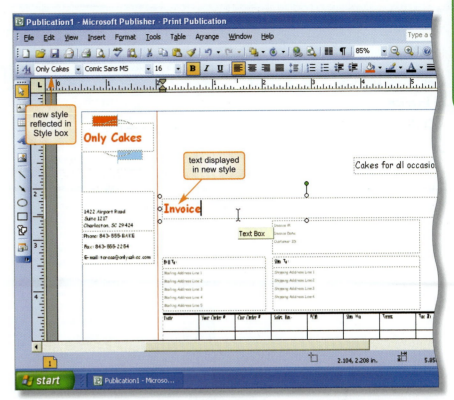

FIGURE 5-12

Using a style is easier than using the Format Painter button when you have multiple pages or multiple documents. You do not have to search for the text with the formatting you like. Rather, you can choose the preferred style from the Formatting toolbar.

The next step is to create a drop cap on the first letter of the word, Invoice.

Using a Drop Cap

A dropped capital letter, or **drop cap,** is a decorative large initial capital letter extending down below the other letters in the line. A drop cap is displayed larger than the rest of the characters in the line or paragraph and commonly is used to mark the beginning of an article or text box. If the text wraps to more than one line, the paragraph typically wraps around the dropped capital letter. You can format up to 15 contiguous letters and spaces as drop caps at the beginning of each paragraph.

Formatting a Drop Cap

The steps on the next page show how to create a dropped capital letter I to be placed in the Invoice text box.

To Format a Drop Cap

1

- **Click to the left of the letter I in Invoice.**

- **Click Format on the menu bar.**

The page layout in Figure 5-13 has been scrolled slightly in order to view both the word, Invoice, and the Format menu. Your screen may differ.

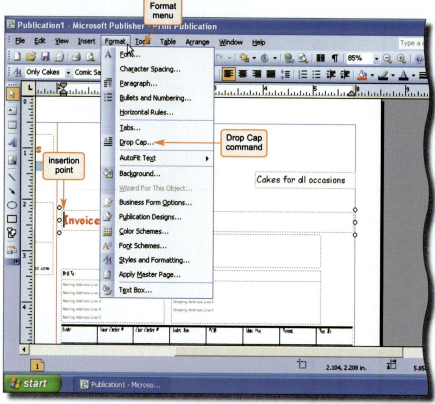

FIGURE 5-13

2

- **Click Drop Cap.**

- **When the Drop Cap dialog box is displayed, if necessary, click the Drop Cap tab. In the Available drop caps area, click a preview that is similar to the one shown in Figure 5-14.**

The Available drop caps list is displayed using colors from the color scheme of the publication (Figure 5-14). Your list may vary.

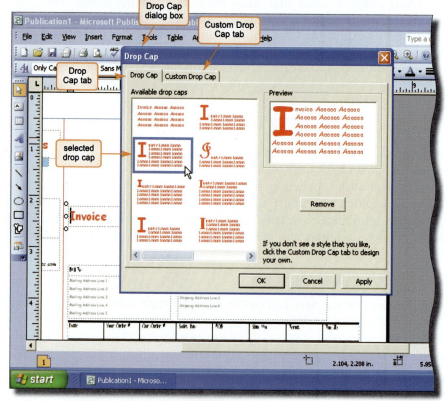

FIGURE 5-14

3

- **Click the Custom Drop Cap tab. In the Select letter position and size area, if necessary, click Dropped.**
- **Drag through any number in the Size of letters box and then type** 2 **to enter the new size.**

The Custom Drop Cap sheet allows you to customize the drop cap further (Figure 5-15).

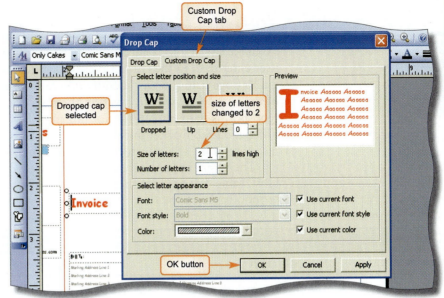

FIGURE 5-15

4

- **Click the OK button.**

The drop cap letter is displayed in the text box (Figure 5-16).

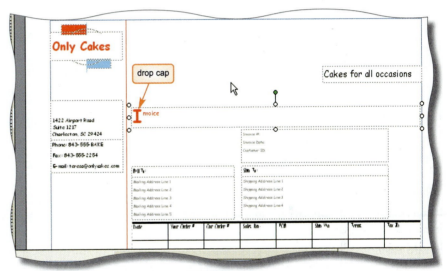

FIGURE 5-16

Other Ways

1. In Voice Command mode, say "Format, Drop Cap"

More About

Embedding Fonts

To embed the fonts for a commercial printing service, click Tools on the menu bar, point to Commercial Printing Tools, and then click Fonts. In the Fonts dialog box, you will see options for embedding the entire font set, or a subset.

When you create a custom drop cap, the custom style is added to the Available drop caps list in the Drop Cap sheet. You can use this style to create other drop caps in the current publication. Another option is to use an **Up cap**, which extends above the paragraph, rather than sinking into the first few lines of the text.

Drop caps deserve special consideration if you are sending the file to a commercial printer. A file prepared for commercial submission includes all fonts from the publication. If you use only a small number of characters from a font, as in drop caps or for headlines, you can have Publisher embed only the characters you used from the font. Embedding only part of a font is called **subsetting**. The advantage of font subsetting is that it decreases the overall size of the file. The disadvantage is that it limits the ability to make corrections at the printing service. If the printing service does not have the full font installed on its computer, corrections can be made using only the characters included in the subset. Using the Fonts command on the Format menu, you are able to turn on font subsetting so that all the fonts you use in the publication will be subsetted when you embed them.

Working with Tabs and Markers

To make the invoice template as user-friendly as possible, it is important to help the user enter data in the correct places as much as you can. Text boxes with exact margin settings help the user identify where to place the text as well as the typical length of the entry. One way to position the insertion point inside the text box, at the correct spot, is with tabs. A **tab**, or tab stop, is a horizontal location on the page as noted by a tab marker in the Publisher ruler. Once the tab is set, you position the insertion point at a tab stop by pressing the TAB key.

The ruler contains several tools to help you set text box margins, indents, and tabs. Table 5-1 explains the functions of the tools displayed in Figure 5-18, and how to modify them.

Table 5-1   Ruler Tools

TOOL NAME	DESCRIPTION	HOW TO CHANGE	OTHER WAYS
First-Line Indent marker	The position at which paragraphs begin	Drag to desired location	On Format menu click Tabs
Left Indent marker	A small rectangle used to move both markers at once	Drag to desired location	On Format menu click Tabs
Hanging Indent marker	The left position at which text will align	Drag to desired location	On Format menu click Tabs
object margins	Gray indicates the area outside the object margin; white indicates the area inside the object margin	Resize object	On Format menu click Text Box, click Size tab
Right Indent marker	The right position at which text wraps to the next line	Drag to desired location	On Format menu click Tabs
Markers button (tab alignment button)	Displays the current alignment setting: left, right, center, or leader	Click to toggle choice	Double-click tab stop marker
tab stop marker	Displays the location of a tab stop	Click to create; drag to move	On Format menu click Tabs
zero point	A ruler setting commonly used to measure distances from the upper-left corner of a page or object	SHIFT+right-click ruler at desired location	Double-click to move both horizontal and vertical zero points

The triangles and rectangles on the ruler are called **markers**. You drag markers to any place on the ruler within the object margin. You can click a marker to display a dotted line through the publication to see in advance where the marker is set. Markers are paragraph-specific, which means that the tabs and indents apply to the whole paragraph. If you are typing a long passage of text, pressing the ENTER key carries forward the paragraph formatting.

Recall that the Special Characters button shown in Figure 5-17 on the Standard toolbar makes visible special nonprinting characters to help you format text passages, including tab characters, paragraph marks, and end-of-frame marks.

Inserting a Tab Stop

The following steps show how to add a tab stop at .75 inches to the Invoice # text box by clicking the horizontal ruler. A tab stop will ensure that the data is properly aligned when entered by the user.

More About

Hanging Indents

A first-line indent placed to the left of the left margin sometimes is called a hanging indent or exdent. Exdents typically are found in bibliographies and alphabetized listings. Creating an exdent saves keystrokes and formatting time.

To Insert a Tab Stop

1

- **Click the placeholder text in the Invoice # text box and then zoom to 150%.**

- **Click the Special Characters button on the Standard toolbar.**

The paragraph marks are displayed in the text box (Figure 5-17). Each line of this text box is a paragraph. The end-of-frame marker is displayed as an embellished circle.

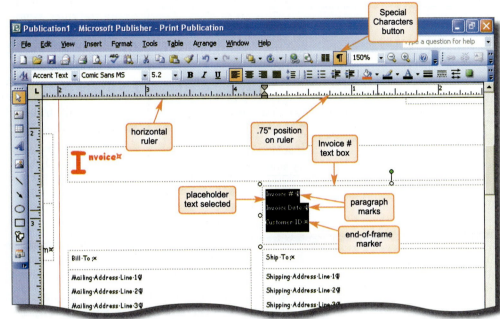

FIGURE 5-17

2

- **Click the horizontal ruler at the .75" position. Type** Invoice # **and then press the TAB key.**

- **Press the ENTER key. Type** Invoice Date **and then press the TAB key. Press the ENTER key. Type** Customer Name **and then press the TAB key.**

The tab stop marker is displayed on the horizontal ruler, and the nonprinting tab characters display in each line to indicate that the TAB key was pressed (Figure 5-18). The measurement of the tab stop location is relative to the left edge of the text box.

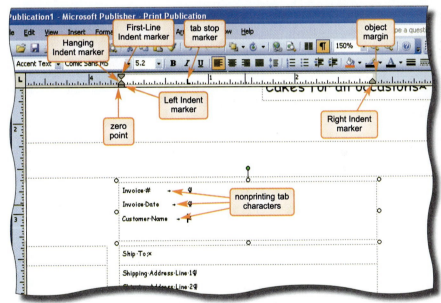

FIGURE 5-18

Sometimes it is difficult to determine whether to use tab stops or indents. Use tab stops when you want to indent paragraphs as you go or when you want a simple column. Using the TAB key to indent the first line of each paragraph in a long passage of text is inefficient, however, because you must press it each time you begin a new paragraph. In those cases, it is better to use an **indent** because it automatically carries forward when you press the ENTER key. Use indents when you want the lines in a paragraph to be automatically adjusted for you, or when you want to indent all the lines in a paragraph without inserting tab stops at the beginning of each line.

Table 5-2	Types of Tab Alignments	
SYMBOL	NAME	ACTION AND USE
L	Left Tab	Creates a left-justified tab, used for most tabbing
⌐	Right Tab	Creates a right-justified tab, used for indexes, programs, and lists
⊥	Center Tab	Creates a center-justified tab used to center a list within a column
⊥.	Decimal Tab	Creates a tab stop aligned at the decimal point, used for aligning currency amounts

The **tab stop alignment** can be changed by SHIFT-clicking the intersection of the horizontal and vertical rulers (Figure 5-19) and then clicking the ruler. SHIFT-clicking the button toggles among the types of tabs displayed in Table 5-2.

The Tabs dialog box, accessed through the Tools menu, allows you to customize the tab stop further with leaders. A **leader** is a character that repeats from the previous text or tab stop to fill in the tabbed gap. Available leaders include None, Dot, Dash, Line, and Bullet.

The next step is to add a date that updates automatically each time you open the template, as shown in the following steps.

To Insert a System Date

1 Click just to the left of the paragraph mark on the Invoice Date line. Click Insert on the menu bar and then click Date and Time.

2 When the Date and Time dialog box is displayed, click the format, January 24, 2005 (or the current date on your screen). Click Update automatically to select the check box.

3 Click the OK button. Click the Special Characters button so it is not selected.

Publisher displays the current system date (Figure 5-19). Your date will differ.

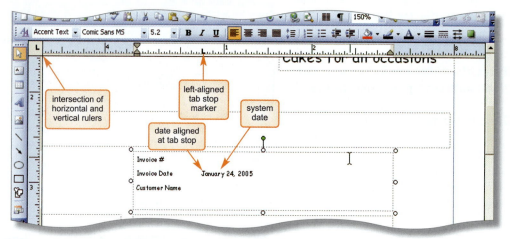

FIGURE 5-19

You may insert a system date, a system time, or both in a text box or table cell. In addition, you can determine the language and format you want. When you open or print the publication, Publisher will update the date or time you inserted to reflect the current date or time.

Editing Invoice Tables

The next step in creating the invoice is to edit the tables to reflect more accurately the items sold by Only Cakes. The following steps first delete the table with shipping and sales rep information and then edit the column headings in the second table.

To Edit the Tables

1

• **Zoom to 150%.**

• **Right-click the first table located just below the mailing address text box.**

The table's shortcut menu is displayed (Figure 5-20).

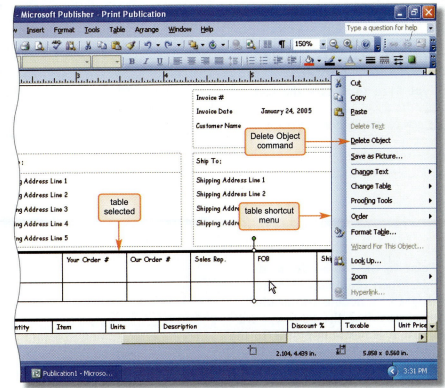

FIGURE 5-20

2

• **Click Delete Object.**

• **In the next table directly below, click the word, Quantity, in the first column.**

The placeholder text is selected (Figure 5-21).

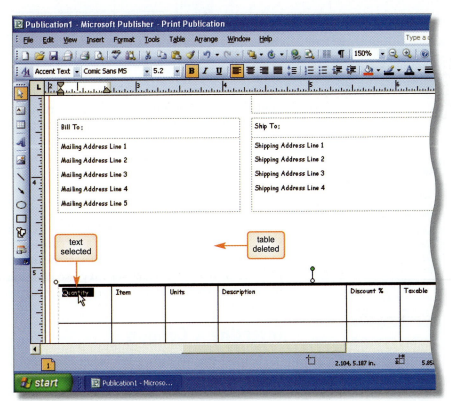

FIGURE 5-21

3

- **Type** Date **and then press the TAB key.**
- **Type** Quantity **and then press the TAB key.**
- **Type** Type of Cake **and then press the TAB key twice.**
- **Type** Size **to replace the text.**

The new column headings are entered (Figure 5-22). Pressing the TAB key moves the insertion point to the next column and automatically selects the text in the cell.

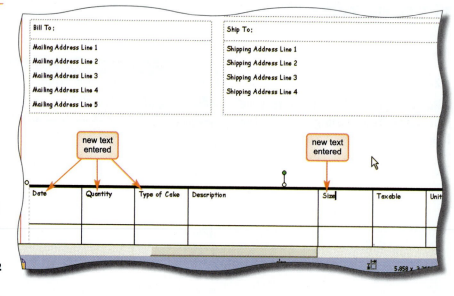

FIGURE 5-22

4

- **Point to the top border of the table. When the mouse pointer changes to a double two-headed arrow, SHIFT-drag the table upward so that it is positioned close to the address text boxes, as shown in Figure 5-23.**

The table is displayed in its new location.

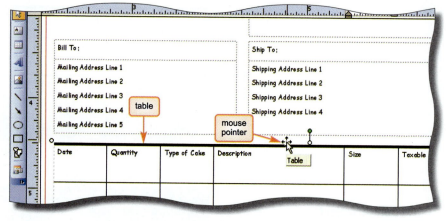

FIGURE 5-23

Recall that SHIFT-dragging moves an object in a straight line. That way, the alignment is maintained, and the table remains aligned with the text boxes above it.

The next step is to insert a coupon in the lower-right portion of the invoice, to entice customers to make more purchases.

Coupons

Coupons are a popular way for businesses to attract customers to a product or to a store. A coupon also is a valued advertising tool. Because many coupons never are used, they are an inexpensive investment in advertising, to remind the customer of a product or service. Businesses may use coupons as a promotion, to offer a special deal to move merchandise, or to gain advantage over a competitor.

Inserting a Coupon

The Microsoft Office Publisher Design Gallery, accessed via the Design Gallery Object button on the Objects toolbar, contains many kinds of desktop publishing objects that users may add to their publications. Design Gallery objects include coupons, advertisements, table of contents objects, sidebars, pull quotes, and attention getters, among others.

The following steps demonstrate how to insert a Design Gallery object.

To Insert a Design Gallery Object

1

- **Zoom to Whole Page.**

- **Click the Design Gallery Object button on the Objects toolbar.**

Publisher displays the Design Gallery dialog box that contains three sheets: Objects by Category, Objects by Design, and My Objects (Figure 5-24).

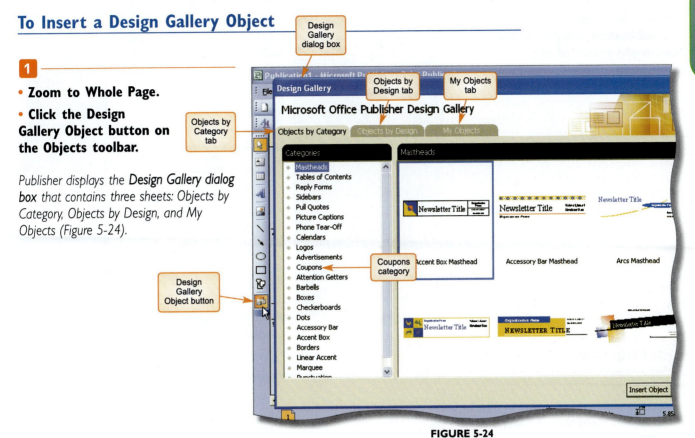

FIGURE 5-24

2

- **Click Coupons in the Categories list.**

- **Click the Tilted Box Coupon preview in the Coupons pane.**

Publisher displays three coupon previews (Figure 5-25).

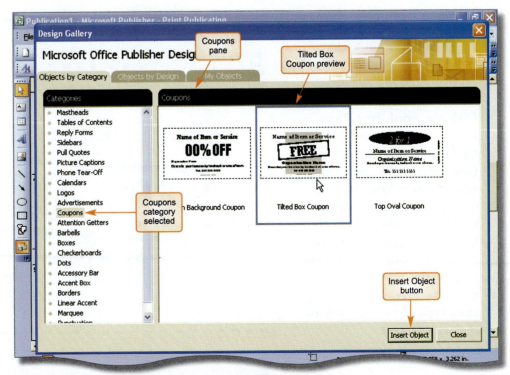

FIGURE 5-25

3

• **Click the Insert Object button.**

• **When the coupon is inserted in the publication, drag it to the lower-right corner of the publication.**

Publisher displays the inserted coupon and snaps it to the layout guides in the lower-right corner (Figure 5-26).

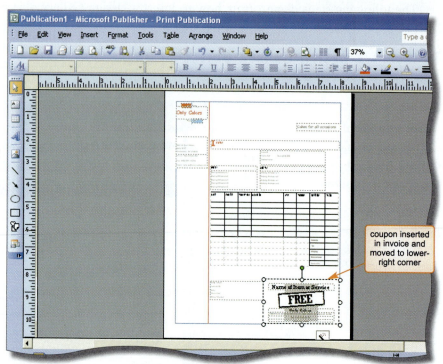

FIGURE 5-26

The next task is to edit the text boxes of the coupon, as shown in the following steps.

To Edit Coupon Text Boxes

1 **Zoom to 200%. Click the words, Name of Item or Service. Type** Any Cake or Class **to replace the text.**

2 **Click the word, Free. Type** 10% Off **to replace the text.**

3 **Click the words, Describe your location by landmark or area of town. Type** In the mall on Airport Road **to replace the text.**

4 **Click the telephone number. Type** Call 843-555-BAKE **to replace the text.**

5 **Click the text, 00/00/00, and then type** June 1, 2005 **to replace the text.**

The text boxes display their new text (Figure 5-27).

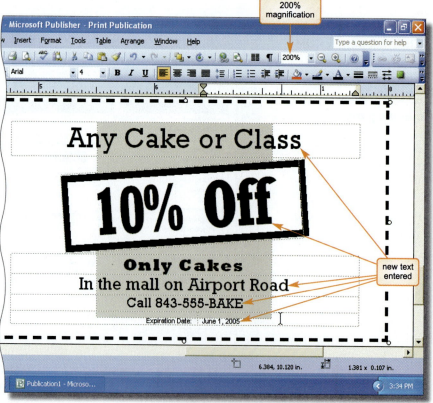

FIGURE 5-27

Coupons can be a publication by themselves as well as an added object to other publications. Later in this project, you will learn how to create a custom-size publication containing a single object used for publications such as coupons, order forms, bookmarks, or handouts.

BorderArt

The final tasks to complete the invoice involve adding a border to the coupon. A **border** is a visible line or design around the edge of an object. Borders may be as simple as a single black line or as complex as repeated pictures from a graphics file. Borders can add interest and emphasis to publications.

Using BorderArt

Project 3 used a line border around an object. The following steps show how to add a customized BorderArt around the coupon. Recall that BorderArt is a graphical, decorative border in place of a solid or dashed line to set off an object and add eye appeal.

To Add BorderArt

1

• **Click the dashed line border of the coupon. Click the Line/Border Style button on the Formatting toolbar.**

Publisher displays the Line/Border Style list (Figure 5-28).

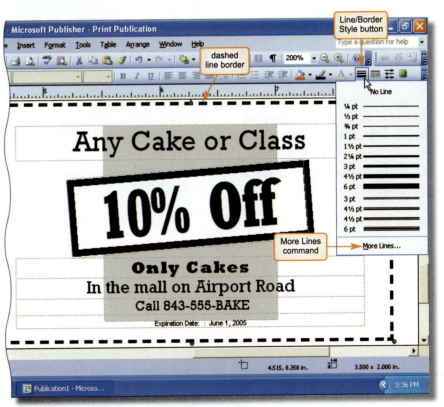

FIGURE 5-28

2

• **Click More Lines.**

• **When the Format AutoShape dialog box is displayed, if necessary, click the Colors and Lines tab.**

Publisher displays the Format AutoShape dialog box (Figure 5-29).

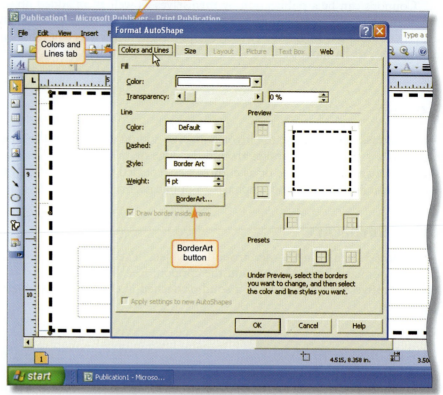

FIGURE 5-29

3

• **Click the BorderArt button.**

• **When the BorderArt dialog box is displayed, scroll as necessary to display Cake Slice in the Available Borders list. Click Cake Slice.**

• **Click Don't stretch pictures to select it.**

The BorderArt dialog box displays many available borders, as well as a button to create a customized border from a graphic on your system (Figure 5-30).

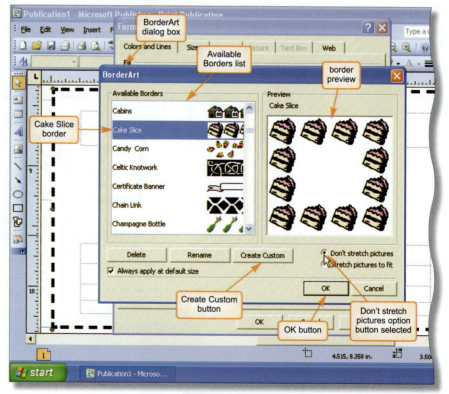

FIGURE 5-30

4

• **Click the OK button.**

• **When the Format AutoShape dialog box is visible again, select the text in the Weight box, and then type 10 as the new weight.**

In the case of BorderArt, weight refers to the size of the individual graphics around the edge (Figure 5-31).

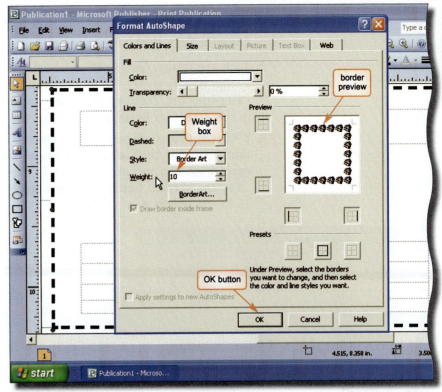

FIGURE 5-31

5

• **Click the OK button.**

The coupon with the new border around the edge of the text box is displayed (Figure 5-32).

FIGURE 5-32

The final step is to insert an attention getter from the design gallery to display the company's Web address, as shown in the steps on the next page.

Other Ways

1. Right-click coupon, click Format AutoShape, click BorderArt
2. In Voice Command mode, say "Format, AutoShape, BorderArt"

To Insert and Format an Attention Getter

1 Zoom to Page Width.

2 Click the Design Gallery Object button on the Objects toolbar. When the Design Gallery dialog box is displayed, click Attention Getters in the Categories list. Scroll as necessary and click Side Curves Attention Getter in the Attention Getters pane. Click the Insert Object button.

3 With the attention getter still selected, double-click the Object Size box on the status bar to display the Measurement toolbar. Using the TAB key to move from box to box, type 5.5 in the Horizontal Position (x) box, type .5 in the Vertical Position (y) box, type 2.5 in the Width box, and type .5 in the Height box.

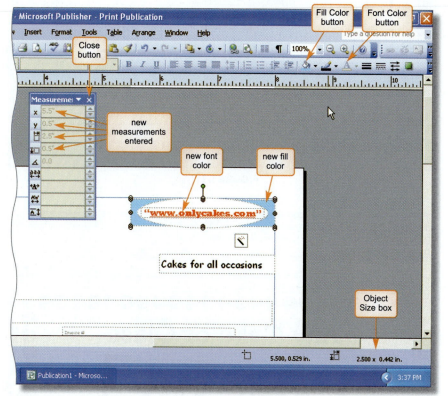

FIGURE 5-33

4 Click the text in the attention getter to select it. Click the Font Color button arrow on the Formatting toolbar and then click Accent 1 (Red) on the color palette. Type "www.onlycakes.com" to replace the selected attention getter text.

5 Click the black shading around the text. Click the Fill Color button arrow on the Formatting toolbar and then click Accent 2 (RGB (102, 204, 255)) on the color palette.

The attention getter is displayed with red lettering and light blue trim (Figure 5-33).

6 Close the Measurement toolbar by clicking its Close button.

Now that the invoice template is complete, the publication file can be used to generate instances on an as-needed basis. The following series of steps checks the publication for spelling and design errors, and then saves and prints the invoice template.

To Check the Invoice for Spelling and Design Errors

1 Click the Spelling button on the Standard toolbar. If Publisher detects any spelling errors, correct them. Click the Ignore button when Publisher flags the Web address. When Publisher asks if you want to check the rest of the publication, click the Yes button. When Publisher notifies you that the spelling check is complete, click the OK button.

2 Click **Tools** on the menu bar, and then click **Design Checker**. If Publisher displays errors in the Design Checker task pane, other than an RGB mode reminder, fix the errors as necessary. Close the Design Checker task pane.

To Save and Print the Invoice Template

1 Insert a floppy disk into drive A.

2 Click the **Save** button on the Standard toolbar.

3 When the Save As dialog box is displayed, type `Only Cakes Invoice Template` in the File name text box. Do not press the ENTER key.

4 If necessary, click the **Save in** box arrow and then click **3½ Floppy (A:)**.

5 Click the **Save** button in the Save As dialog box.

6 Click the **Print** button on the Standard toolbar.

Publisher saves the publication on a floppy disk in drive A with the file name, Only Cakes Invoice Template, and then prints a copy on the printer. The completed invoice template is shown in Figure 5-1a on page PUB 275.

You can protect this template file from accidental deletion by forcing users to save each instance with a different name, thereby preserving the original file. This is accomplished by changing the **read-only attribute**. The Windows operating system provides a Properties command on every file's shortcut menu. If you want to protect the file, click the Read-only check box in the General sheet.

The following step closes the file without quitting Publisher.

To Close the File without Quitting Publisher

1 Click **File** on the menu bar and then click **Close**. If a Microsoft Publisher dialog box is displayed asking if you want to save, click the **No** button.

A blank page is displayed to start the next business publication.

Custom-Size Publications

Not all publication pages measure 8½ by 11 inches. Some publications, such as envelopes, invitations, CD liners, or postcards are smaller. Others, such as banners, posters, and legal briefs are larger than a typical piece of copy paper. The Page Setup command can be used to create a custom size, or clicking Blank Publications on the New Publication task pane displays 11 different sizes and folds.

Creating a Custom-Size Publication

Only Cakes wants to provide clerks with an order form to help them obtain the required information from customers who order cakes. The order form (Figure 5-34 on the next page) should be 5 inches by 7 inches and include blanks for the customer's name, address, and cake information. A shadowed text box displays the organization name from the personal information set using a font from the Casual font scheme. The order form also should include three small tables for the clerk to enter information about size, flavor, and icing.

More About

Imposition

Imposition means inserting an entire printed page as an object in another publication. This book uses imposition to display output from the printer. Even though Publisher does not support full-page imposition, several ways exist to work around the problem. You can select all of the objects from a publication page, group and copy, and then in a new publication, create a white rectangle with a shadow. Paste the objects on top of the rectangle and then resize as necessary.

Q&A

Q: Can I create oversized publications?

A: If your system is connected to a printer or plotter than can support larger paper, you can set the width and height of your publication to match the paper size using the Page Setup dialog box.

The bakery plans to send the order form to an outside printing service to create pads of order forms for use in the store, so it has chosen a black and white color scheme in order to save money.

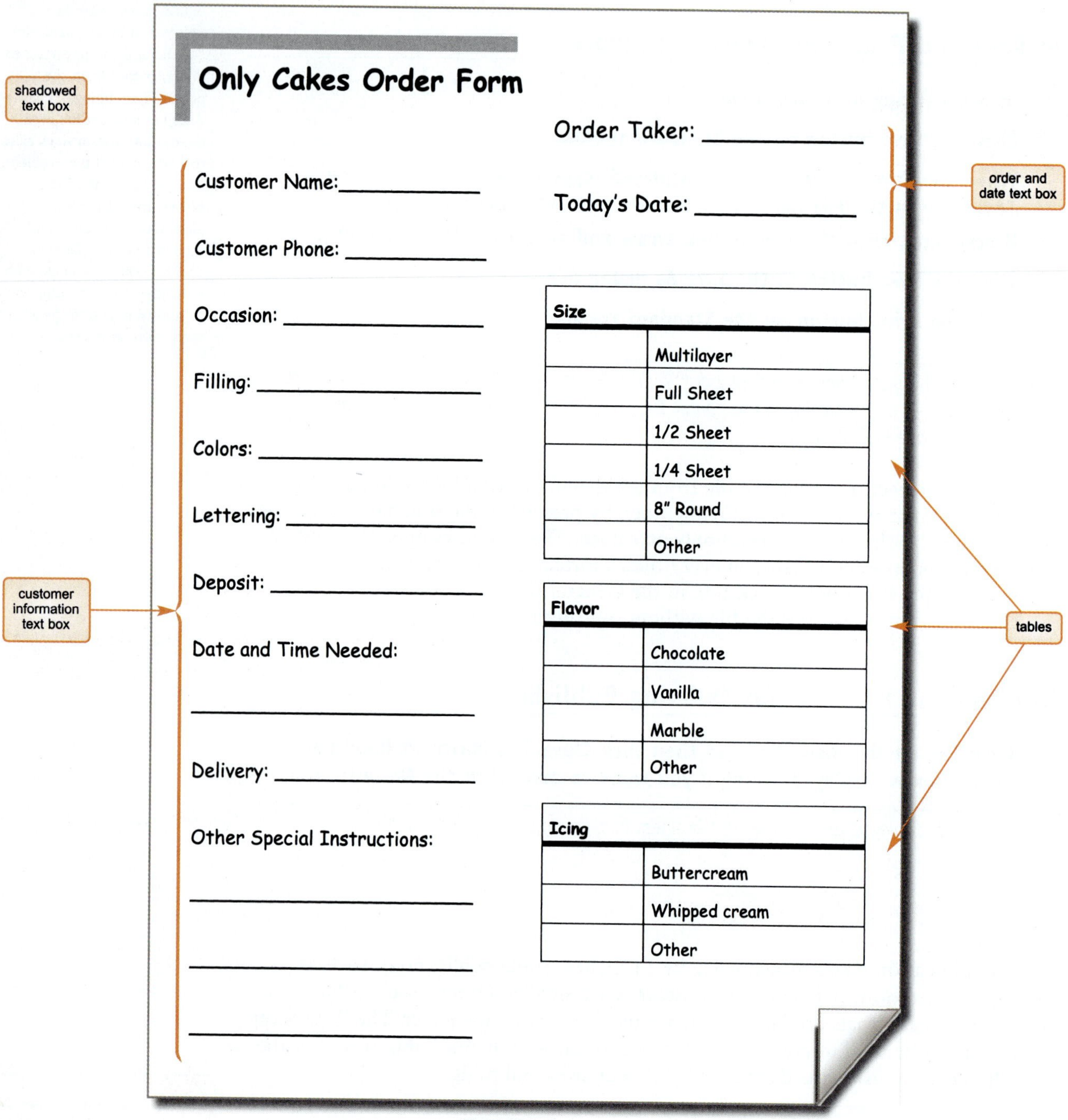

FIGURE 5-34

The following steps illustrate how to create a custom-size publication.

To Create a Custom-Size Publication

1

• **If a blank publication is not displayed, click the New button on the Standard toolbar. Click File on the menu bar.**

The File menu is displayed (Figure 5-35).

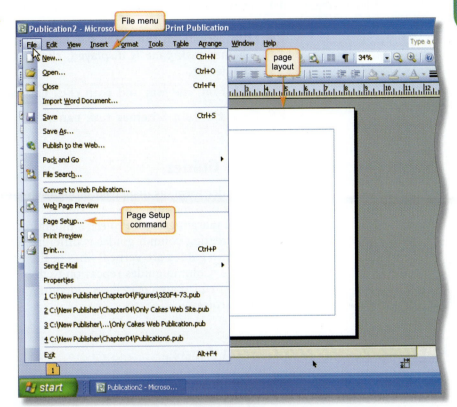

FIGURE 5-35

2

• **Click Page Setup.**

• **When the Page Setup dialog box is displayed, if necessary, click the Layout tab. In the Publication type list, click Custom and then press the TAB key. Type 5 in the Width text box and then press the TAB key. Type 7 in the Height text box and then press the TAB key.**

The order form will be 5 inches wide and 7 inches tall (Figure 5-36).

3

• **Click the OK button in the Page Setup dialog box.**

The page layout is displayed.

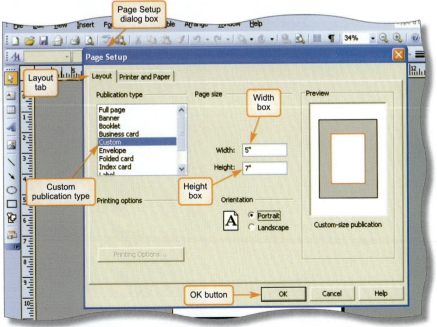

FIGURE 5-36

Other Ways

1. In Voice Command mode, say "File, Page Setup"

More About

Page Setup

In Publisher, page size refers to the size of your publication, not to the paper. Page orientation refers to the portrait (vertical) or landscape (horizontal) layout of the publication. The publication layout you choose includes the page size and orientation most often used for that particular type of publication. You can change page size, change orientation, and preview your changes using the Page Setup dialog box.

Only Cakes wants to apply the font schemes from the invoice to the order form. The following steps show how to choose the Black and Gray color scheme and the Casual font scheme.

To Select a Color and Font Scheme

1 **Click Format on the menu bar and then click Color Schemes. When the Color Schemes task pane is displayed, click Black & Gray in the Apply a color scheme list.**

2 **Click Font Schemes and then click Casual in the Apply a font scheme list.**

3 **Close the Font Schemes task pane.**

Column Guides

The order form, as displayed in Figure 5-34 on page PUB 298, contains two columns of information. The next step is to create column guides for the order form and set the margin guides. Project 2 illustrated creating columns within a text box; however, creating column guides is different from creating columns within a text box. **Column guides** are vertical lines in the background to help you align and separate objects. Column guides repeat on each page of a publication, as opposed to ruler guides which are created on individual pages by dragging from the horizontal or vertical ruler.

To Create Margin and Column Guides

1

• **Click Arrange on the menu bar.**

The Arrange menu is displayed (Figure 5-37).

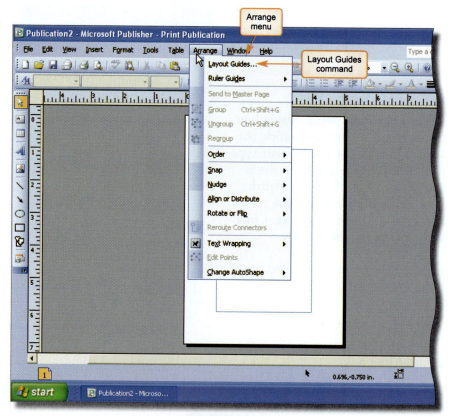

FIGURE 5-37

2

• **Click Layout Guides.**

• **When the Layout Guides dialog box is displayed, if necessary, click the Margin Guides tab.**

• **Type .5 in each of the four margin guide boxes as shown in Figure 5-38.**

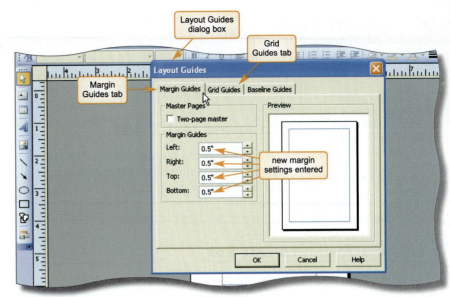

FIGURE 5-38

3

• **Click the Grid Guides tab.**

• **Type 2 in the Columns box.**

The Grid Guides sheet contains boxes to set row and column guides that will be displayed in the page layout (Figure 5-39).

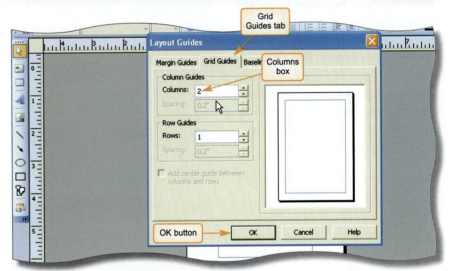

FIGURE 5-39

4

• **Click the OK button.**

Publisher displays the page layout with the .5-inch margins and column guides down the middle of the page (Figure 5-40).

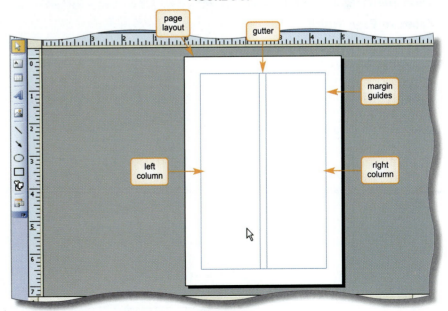

FIGURE 5-40

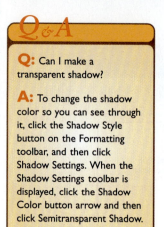

Q&A

Q: Can I make a transparent shadow?

A: To change the shadow color so you can see through it, click the Shadow Style button on the Formatting toolbar, and then click Shadow Settings. When the Shadow Settings toolbar is displayed, click the Shadow Color button arrow and then click Semitransparent Shadow.

Publisher automatically makes the two columns the same width and evenly spaces them on the page. Once the columns are created, if you want a wider **gutter**, or spacing between the two columns, you can enter a larger number in the Spacing box in the Grid Guides sheet shown in Figure 5-39 on the previous page.

Shadowed Text Boxes

The following steps show how to create a shadowed text box. A **shadow** is a light gray extension of an object's border, on one or more sides, to simulate a direction of light at various angles. The bakery wants a shadow on the left and top of the form's title.

To Create a Shadowed Text Box

1

• **Click the Text Box button on the Objects toolbar. Drag the mouse pointer to draw a text box in the upper-left portion of the order form.**

• **Double-click the Object Size box. When the Measurement toolbar is displayed, enter the amounts as shown in Figure 5-41.**

The new dimensions and location of the text box are displayed (Figure 5-41).

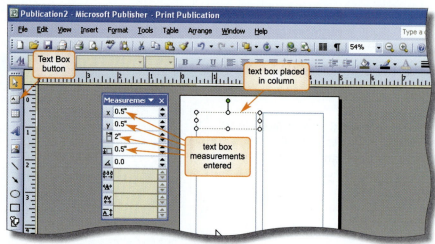

FIGURE 5-41

2

• **Close the Measurement toolbar.**

• **Zoom to Page Width.**

• **Click the Shadow Style button on the Formatting toolbar.**

The various styles and placement of shadows are listed in the Shadow Style list (Figure 5-42). Your toolbar buttons may differ.

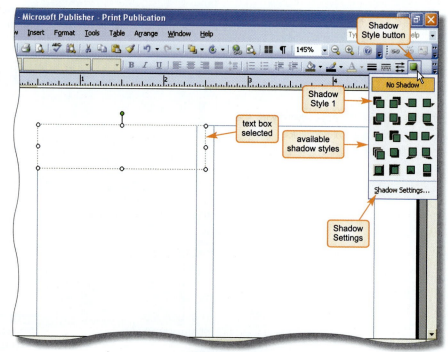

FIGURE 5-42

3

• **Click Shadow Style 1 in the list.**

The text box is displayed with a shadow on the left and top edges (Figure 5-43).

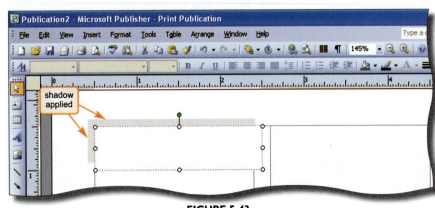

FIGURE 5-43

If your system does not display a shadow, the shadow color may be set to white. In that case, click the Shadow Style button, click Shadow Settings, click the Shadow Color button arrow and then click a gray color.

The next step is to select a style, choose a font size for the text box, and then enter text.

To Select a Style and Enter Text

1 **If necessary, click inside the shadowed text box. Click the Style box arrow on the Formatting toolbar and then click Heading 5 in the list.**

2 **Type** Only Cakes Order Form **to complete the text.**

The text is entered using the new style (Figure 5-44).

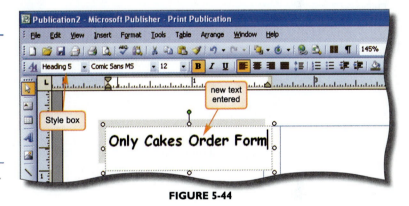

FIGURE 5-44

Creating Additional Text Boxes

The next step is to create a text box to display the text and lines that clerks will use to write customer information. Table 5-3 on the next page displays the text for the customer text box.

To Create a Customer Text Box

1 **Zoom to 75%. Scroll as necessary. Click the Text Box button on the Objects toolbar.**

2 **Drag the mouse pointer to draw a new text box below the shadowed text box, which approximately fills the left column as shown in Figure 5-45 on the next page.**

3 **Click inside the text box.**

4 **Click the Font Size box arrow on the Formatting toolbar and then click 8 in the list.**

5 **Press CTRL+2 to change to double spacing.**

6 Enter the text for each piece of customer information from Table 5-3, zooming as necessary. To create the lines shown in Figure 5-45, press the SPACEBAR after typing each text entry and then press underline (SHIFT+—) several times until the insertion point reaches the right edge of the text box. For the last item, create four additional lines. If necessary, drag the bottom of the text box so that all lines are displayed.

The fields for customer information are entered in the text box (Figure 5-45).

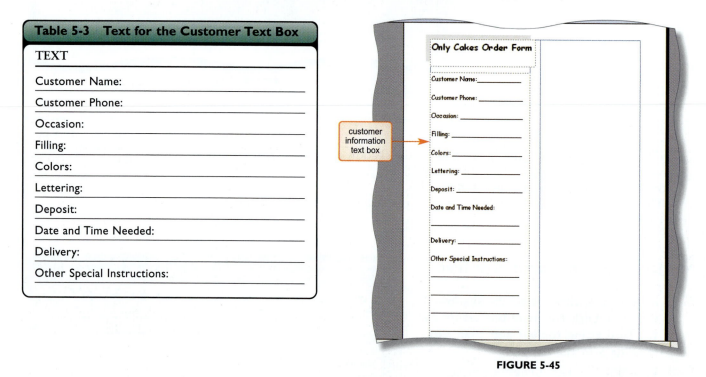

Table 5-3   Text for the Customer Text Box
TEXT
Customer Name:
Customer Phone:
Occasion:
Filling:
Colors:
Lettering:
Deposit:
Date and Time Needed:
Delivery:
Other Special Instructions:

FIGURE 5-45

The following steps create the text and lines that clerks will use to write order taker and date information.

To Create an Order and Date Text Box

1 Click the Text Box button on the Objects toolbar. Drag the mouse pointer to draw another text box in the upper portion of the right column, approximately .75 inches tall as shown in Figure 5-46. Zoom as necessary.

2 Click inside the text box.

3 Click the Font Size box arrow on the Formatting toolbar and then click 8 in the list.

4 Press CTRL+2 to change to double spacing.

5 Enter the text as shown in Figure 5-46. Press the SPACEBAR after each item and then press underline (SHIFT+—) several times until the insertion point reaches the right edge of the text box to create the blank lines.

The fields for order taker and date information are entered in the text box (Figure 5-46).

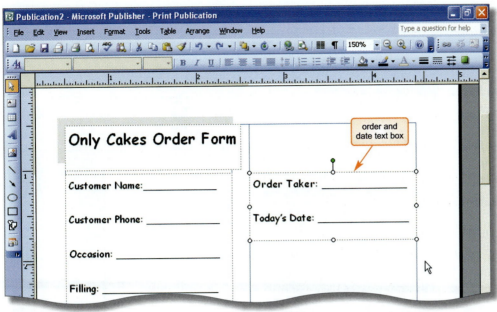

FIGURE 5-46

If you want to align text boxes with each other, the Align or Distribute command on the Arrange menu displays choices for left, center, right, top, middle, or bottom. Simply SHIFT-click the boxes to select them and then make a selection from the Arrange menu.

Using Tables

You may recall that a Publisher table is a collection of rows and columns, and that the intersection of a row and column is called a cell. Cells are filled with data. Within a table, you easily can rearrange rows and columns, change column widths and row heights, and insert diagonal lines, pictures, and text. You can format the cells to give the table a professional appearance. You also can add a border to the entire table. For these reasons, many Publisher users create tables rather than using large text boxes with tabs. Tables allow you to input data in columns as you would for a schedule, price list, a resume, or a table of contents.

Creating Tables

The steps on the next page show how to draw the tables for the order form for Only Cakes. You will format it using the Create Table dialog box. The first step is to draw an empty table in a blank publication with the **Insert Table button** on the Objects toolbar and then choose the number of rows and columns and a table style.

To Create a Table

1

• **If necessary, zoom to Whole Page.**

• **Click the Insert Table button on the Objects toolbar. In the right column, below the order and date text box, drag from the column guide downward and to the right.**

• **Do not release the mouse button.**

The outline of the table is displayed before you release the mouse button (Figure 5-47).

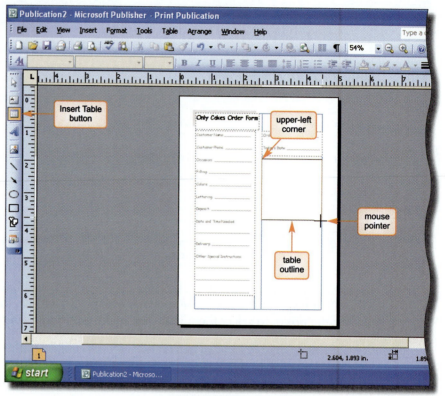

FIGURE 5-47

2

• **Release the mouse button. When the Create Table dialog box is displayed, type 7 in the Number of rows box. Press the TAB key. Type 2 in the Number of columns box. Click List 1 in the Table format list.**

The Create Table dialog box is displayed (Figure 5-48). The Table format list includes formats with and without titles.

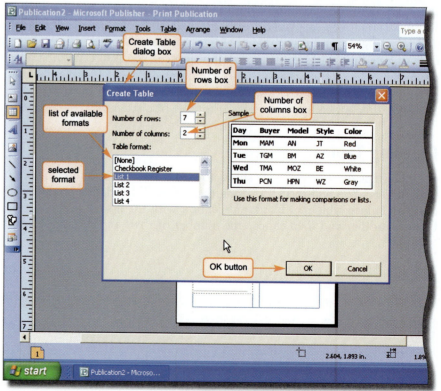

FIGURE 5-48

3

- **Click the OK button. If Publisher displays a dialog box asking if you want to resize the table, click the Yes button.**
- **When the table is displayed in the publication, double-click the Object Size box on the Publisher status bar.**
- **When Publisher displays the Measurement toolbar, enter the values as shown in Figure 5-49.**

The table is inserted in the workspace.

4

- **Click the Close button on the Measurement toolbar.**

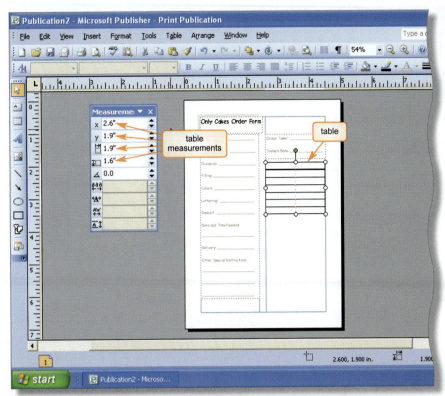

FIGURE 5-49

An unformatted table looks different from a text box. When selected, Publisher tables display vertical and horizontal gray gridlines. The non-printing gridlines are displayed in the frame so you can see the rows and columns. Cell heights automatically increase as inserted text wraps to the next line.

To customize a table, or data within a table, first you must select the cell(s) and then apply the appropriate formats. Table 5-4 describes techniques to select items in a table.

Entering Data into the Table

Efficiently navigating cells is an important skill when entering data into a table. To advance from one cell to the next, press the TAB key. To advance from one column to the next, also press the TAB key; do not press the ENTER key. The ENTER key is used to begin new paragraphs within a cell. To advance from one row to the next, press the DOWN ARROW key.

The steps on the next page show how to enter the data into the table.

Table 5-4 Selecting Items in a Table

ITEMS TO SELECT	ACTION
Cell	Triple-click the cell or drag through the text.
Column	Point to the top of the column. When the mouse pointer becomes a downward pointing arrow, click.
Contiguous cells, rows, or columns	Drag through the cells, rows, or columns.
Entire table	On the Table menu, click Select, and then click Table.
Row	Point to the left of the row. When the mouse pointer becomes a right block arrow, click.
Text in next cell	Press the TAB key.
Text in previous cell	Press the SHIFT+TAB keys.

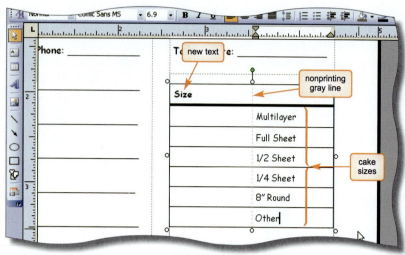

FIGURE 5-50

To Enter Data into a Table

1 Zoom to 150%. If necessary, click the first cell of the table. Type Size and then press the TAB key three times.

2 Type Multilayer and then press the DOWN ARROW key.

3 Continue to enter data as shown in Figure 5-50.

The data is entered in the table (Figure 5-50).

Formatting Tables

When you insert a table, Publisher creates evenly spaced columns in the table. The List 1 table format applies line borders that will print around each row. The final step to finish the table is to adjust the column width and create a vertical line that prints between the columns.

To Format the Table

1

• **SHIFT**-drag the nonprinting gray line between the two columns to 3.25 inches on the horizontal ruler.

The mouse pointer changes to a two-headed vertical arrow while dragging the column border (Figure 5-51). The right column now is wider than the left.

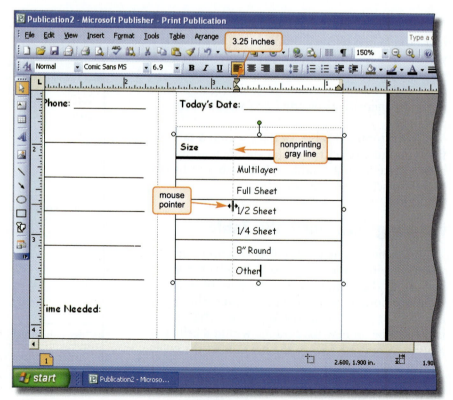

FIGURE 5-51

2

• **Drag through the cells containing the cake sizes. Right-click the selected area.**

Publisher displays the shortcut menu (Figure 5-52).

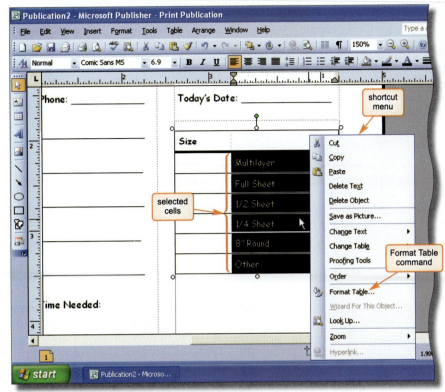

FIGURE 5-52

3

• **Click Format Table.**

• **When the Format Table dialog box is displayed, if necessary, click the Colors and Lines tab.**

• **In the Preview area, click any selected preview buttons so they no longer are selected. Click the left border preview button so it is the only one selected.**

• **In the Line area, click the Color box arrow and then click Main (Black) on the color palette.**

• **Type .5 in the Weight box.**

The new table settings are displayed (Figure 5-53). The Format Table dialog box also contains three Presets to create printable borders.

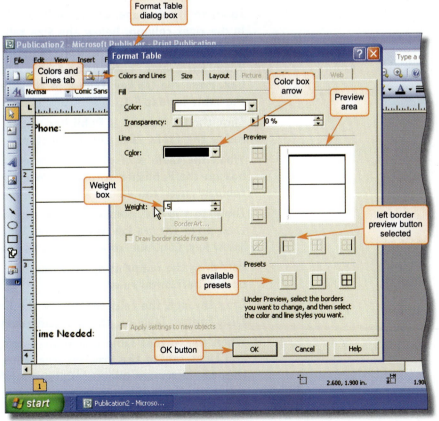

FIGURE 5-53

4

- **Click the OK button.**

- **When the table again is displayed, click outside the selected area to view the border.**

The border between the columns for the cake sizes now will print (Figure 5-54).

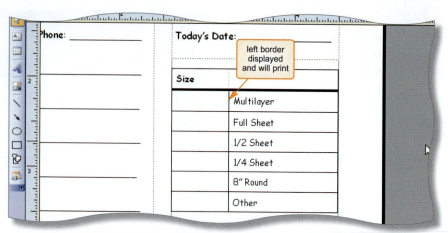

FIGURE 5-54

Dragging a cell border without using the SHIFT key moves all rows below the cell or all columns to the right of the cell. SHIFT-dragging adjusts only the border being dragged.

The next steps show how to insert and format two more tables in the order form.

To Create a Second Table

1 Zoom to Whole Page. Click the Insert Table button on the Objects toolbar. In the right column, below the Size table, drag from the column guide downward and to the right.

2 When the Create Table dialog box is displayed, type 5 in the Number of rows box. Press the TAB key. Type 2 in the Number of columns box. Click List 1 in the Table format list.

3 Click the OK button. If Publisher displays a dialog box asking if you want to resize the table, click the Yes button.

4 When the table is displayed in the publication, double-click the Object Size box on the Publisher status bar. When Publisher displays the Measurement toolbar, enter the values as shown in Figure 5-55.

5 Zoom to 150%. If necessary, click the first cell of the table. Type Flavor and then press the TAB key three times. Type Chocolate and then press the DOWN ARROW key. Continue to enter data as shown in Figure 5-55.

6 SHIFT-drag the nonprinting gray line between the two columns to 3.25 inches on the horizontal ruler.

7 Drag through the cells containing the flavors. Right-click the selected area. Click Format Table on the shortcut menu.

8 When the Format Table dialog box is displayed, if necessary, click the Colors and Lines tab. In the Preview area, click any selected preview buttons so they no longer are selected. Click the left border preview button so it is the only one selected. In the Line area, click the Color box arrow and then click Main (Black) on the color palette. Type .5 in the Weight box. Click the OK button.

The data is entered in the table (Figure 5-55).

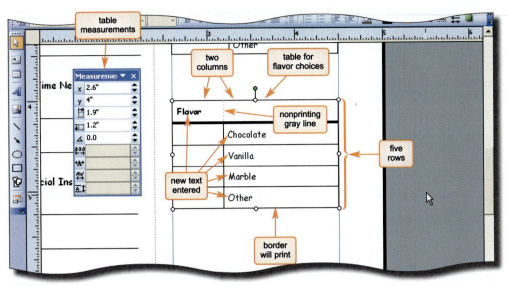

FIGURE 5-55

To Create a Third Table

1 Zoom to Whole Page. Click the Insert Table button on the Objects toolbar. In the right column, below the Size table, drag from the column guide downward and to the right.

2 When the Create Table dialog box is displayed, type 4 in the Number of rows box. Press the TAB key. Type 2 in the Number of columns box. Click List 1 in the Table format list.

3 Click the OK button. If Publisher displays a dialog box asking if you want to resize the table, click the Yes button.

4 When the table is displayed in the publication, double-click the Object Size box on the Publisher status bar. When Publisher displays the Measurement toolbar, enter the values as shown in Figure 5-56.

5 Zoom to 150%. If necessary, click the first cell of the table. Type Icing and then press the TAB key three times. Type Buttercream and then press the DOWN ARROW key. Continue to enter data as shown in Figure 5-56.

6 SHIFT-drag the nonprinting gray line between the two columns to 3.25 inches on the horizontal ruler.

7 Drag through the cells containing the icing flavors. Right-click the selected area. Click Format Table on the shortcut menu.

8 When the Format Table dialog box is displayed, if necessary, click the Colors and Lines tab. In the Preview area, click any selected preview buttons so they no longer are selected. Click the left border preview button so it is the only one selected. In the Line area, click the Color box arrow and then click Main (Black) on the color palette. Type .5 in the Weight box. Click the OK button.

The data is entered in the table (Figure 5-56).

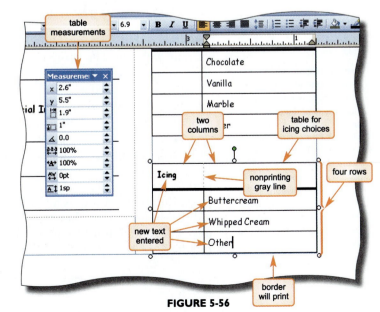

FIGURE 5-56

The Table menu contains options to insert, delete, select, format, and change other table settings. If you wish to combine two or more cells, you can select the cells and then choose the **Merge Cells command** to create one large cell instead of several smaller ones. If you wish to divide a cell, the **Cell Diagonals command** splits the cell in half diagonally.

The order form now is complete. The following steps show how to save and print the order form.

To Save and Print the Order Form

1 Insert a floppy disk into drive A. Click the Save button on the Standard toolbar.

2 When the Save As dialog box is displayed, type Only Cakes Order Form in the File name text box. Do not press the ENTER key.

3 Click the Save in box arrow and then click 3½ Floppy (A:).

4 Click the Save button in the Save As dialog box.

5 Click the Print button on the Standard toolbar.

Publisher saves the publication on a floppy disk in drive A with the file name, Only Cakes Order Form, and then prints a copy on the printer. The completed order form is shown in Figure 5-34 on page PUB 298.

The following step closes the Only Cakes Order Form before beginning the final publication.

To Close the Publication without Quitting Publisher

1 Click File on the menu bar and then click Close.

Publisher closes the publication.

Calendar Web Page

The final publication for Only Cakes is a Web page that can be added to their current Web site. The company wants a calendar of events to advertise cake-decorating classes and special events.

Project 4 created a one-page Web site with a home page. A **home page** is the first page of a Web site, usually named index, which visitors reach by entering the basic Web address or **URL** (universal resource locator) of a company.

The next series of steps will create a **calendar**, which is a specialized table that Publisher can format with any month and year. Calendar cells, like table cells, can be formatted with color, borders, text, and styles. The calendar Web page is the second Web page of the company, which will be accessed by clicking a link on the first page. Recall that a link is an underlined word or phrase that when clicked, moves to a different location within the page, or opens a new page. The calendar Web page also will contain links to other pages the company plans to create in the future (Figure 5-1c on page PUB 275).

Creating a Calendar Web Page

The following steps open the Web page created in Project 4. If you did not create a Web page in Project 4, see your instructor for a copy of the file.

To Open a Web Publication and Insert a New Page

1

• **With the floppy disk containing the Only Cakes Web Publication file in drive A, click the Open button on the Standard toolbar.**

• **When the Open Publication dialog box is displayed, if necessary, click the Look in box arrow and then click 3½ Floppy (A:) in the list.**

The Publisher publications on drive A are displayed (Figure 5-57). Your display may differ.

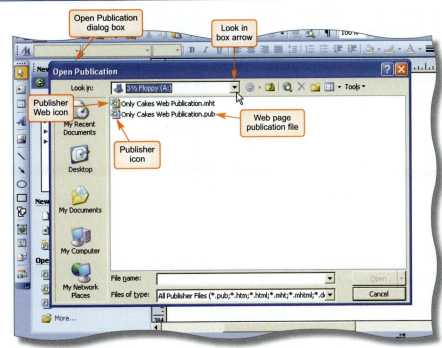

FIGURE 5-57

2

• **Double-click the Only Cakes Web Publication file. If you have two files, a .pub and an .mht, double-click the one with the .pub extension and the Publisher icon.**

• **When the publication is displayed in the Publisher window, right-click the page 1 icon in the page sorter.**

The Only Cakes Web Publication is displayed (Figure 5-58). Publisher displays a shortcut menu when you right-click a page icon.

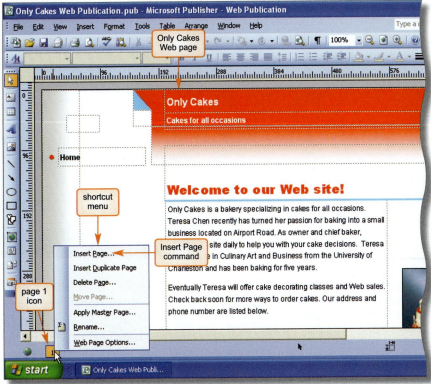

FIGURE 5-58

3

• **Click Insert Page on the shortcut menu.**

• **When the Insert Web Page dialog box is displayed, click Calendar in the Select a page type list. When the types of Calendar Web pages are displayed, click Calendar.**

Two types of Calendar Web pages are available (Figure 5-59).

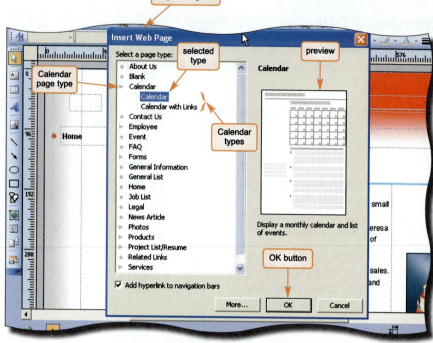

FIGURE 5-59

4

• **Click the OK button.**

• **Zoom to Page Width.**

A new page is added with a calendar that displays January 2005 (Figure 5-60). Your month and year will differ.

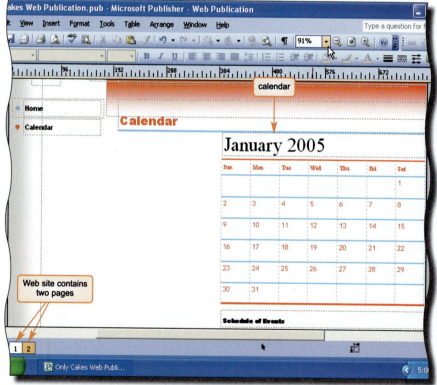

FIGURE 5-60

Other Ways

1. On menu bar click Insert, click Page
2. Press CTRL+SHIFT+N

Calendars are not restricted to Web publications. You can insert a calendar in any type of publication by clicking the Design Gallery Object button on the Objects toolbar and then select the type of calendar you want.

Changing the Calendar Date

Publisher calendars can be edited in several ways. The design style can be changed as well as the month and year. The following steps change the calendar date.

To Change the Calendar Date

1

• **Click the Calendar to select it. When the wizard button is displayed, click it. When Publisher displays the Calendar Designs task pane, click the Change date range button.**

The Calendar Designs task pane displays many design styles including the Layers style that is selected (Figure 5-61). Publisher displays the Change Calendar Dates dialog box.

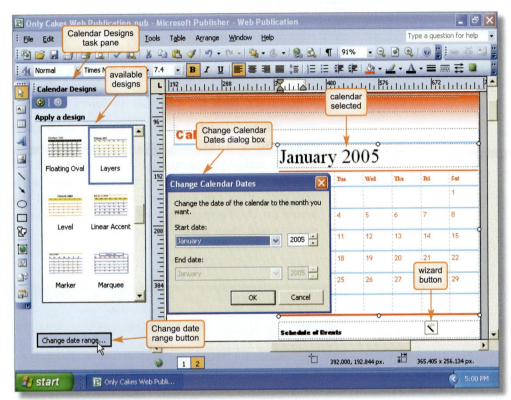

FIGURE 5-61

2

• **Click the Start date box arrow and then click February in the list.**

• **Click the up or down arrow next to the year box until it displays 2005.**

The Change Calendar Dates dialog box displays settings to change the month and year (Figure 5-62). Selecting multiple calendars would enable the ending date settings.

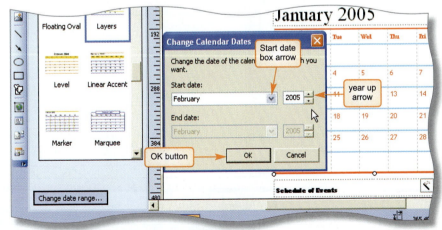

FIGURE 5-62

3

• **Click the OK button in the Change Calendar Dates dialog box.**

• **Click the Close button in the Calendar Designs task pane.**

> ### Other Ways
>
> 1. On View menu click Task Pane, click task pane title bar, click Calendar Designs

Table 5-5   Calendar Data

DATES	TEXT
February 1, 8, 15, and 22	Cake Decorating 101
February 2	Groundhog Cake Walk
February 4, 11, 18, and 25	Fun Fridays
February 7	Just for Men
February 12	Kids in the Kitchen

Resizing the Calendar and Entering Text

The next steps in formatting the calendar include resizing the calendar and then inserting text in various cells of the calendar table. Table 5-5 shows the dates and the text. Because the cells are small, you will select a font size of 8 as you enter the text.

To Resize the Calendar and Enter Text

1 If necessary, click the calendar to select it.

2 Drag the middle-left handle to the left until the border of the calendar aligns with the text box above the calendar.

3 Use the techniques discussed on pages PUB 307 through 310 to move through the table and enter the text shown in Table 5-5. In each appropriate cell, click after the numeric calendar date and then click the Font Size box arrow on the Formatting toolbar. Click 8 in the Font Size list. Press the SPACEBAR and then enter the appropriate text.

The new text is entered with a font size of 8 (Figure 5-63).

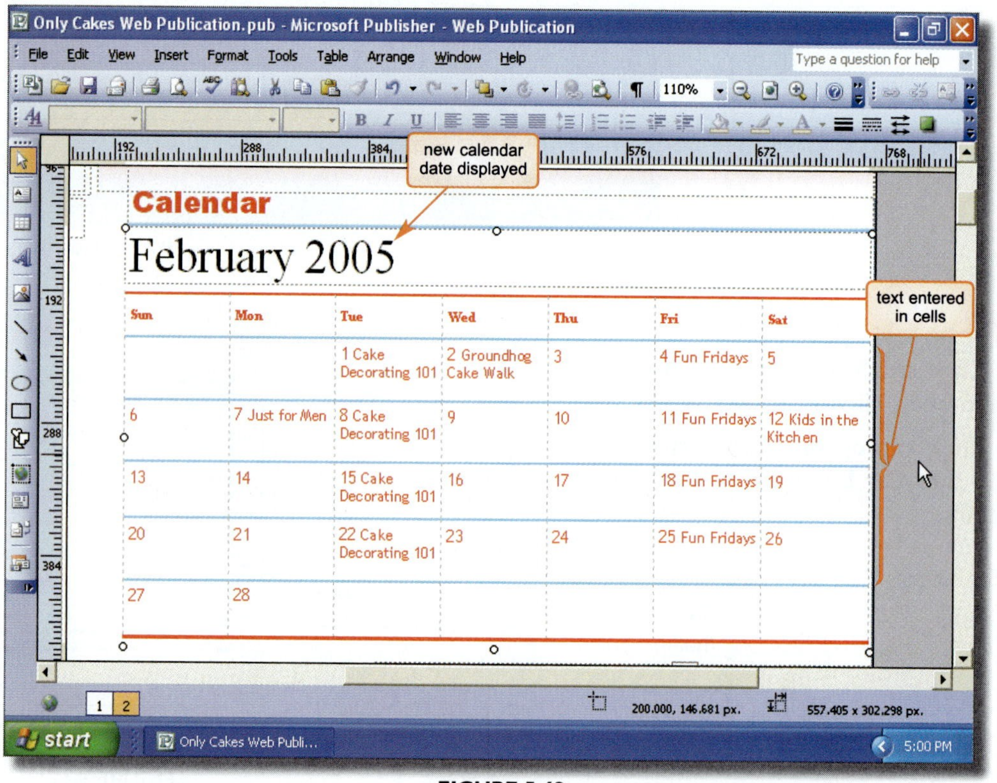

FIGURE 5-63

Editing the Schedule of Events

The events sponsored by Only Cakes are described in detail below the calendar and are shown in Table 5-6.

The following steps illustrate how to edit the Schedule of Events.

To Edit the Schedule of Events

1 Click the first text box below the heading, Schedule of Events.

2 Enter the text as shown in Table 5-6.

3 Edit the other three description text boxes in the same manner.

Descriptions of the four events are entered (Figure 5-64).

Table 5-6 Calendar Events
EVENT DESCRIPTION
Cake Decorating 101, Tuesday mornings at 9:00 a.m. The class is free, but you must purchase your supplies.
Groundhog Cake Walk, February 2 at 1:00 p.m. Join us for cake decorating tips that will make the sun come out.
Just for Men, February 7 at 7:00 p.m. Come on out guys, for an evening dedicated to making something special for that someone special.
Fun Fridays, Friday mornings from 10:00 a.m. until noon. We have free taste testing of all of our cake flavors, icings, and fillings. Every cake ordered during the taste testing is 10% off.

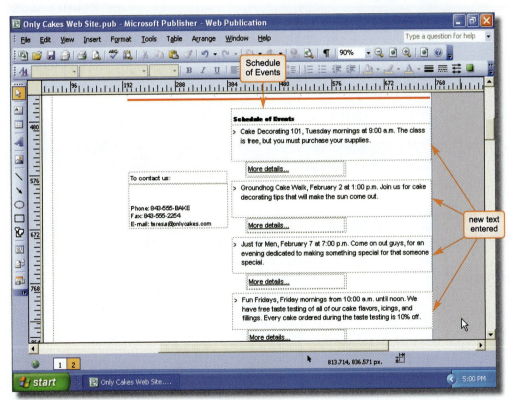

FIGURE 5-64

Navigating the Web Site

Publisher customizes the navigation bar with the Navigation Bar task pane. A **navigation bar** is a set of buttons, graphics, or text boxes that are linked individually to other pages in a Web site. The Web Page Preview button on the Standard toolbar allows you to test the navigation of your Web site before uploading it to the Web. The steps on the next page format the navigation bar and then preview the Web site using the navigation bar to test its ability to move from one page to the next.

To Format and Test the Navigation Bar

1

• **Scroll to the upper-left corner of page two.**

• **Click the word, Calendar.**

• **When Publisher displays the wizard button, click it.**

Publisher displays the Navigation Bar task pane (Figure 5-65).

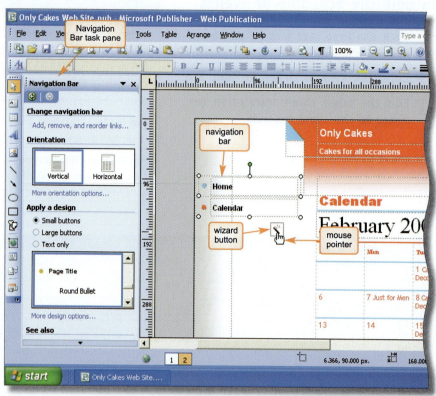

FIGURE 5-65

2

• **If necessary, click Vertical in the Orientation area.**

• **Click Large Buttons in the Apply a design area.**

• **Below the option buttons in the Apply a design area, scroll as necessary and then click Rectangle Navigation Bar in the list.**

The Web page changes to match the new settings (Figure 5-66).

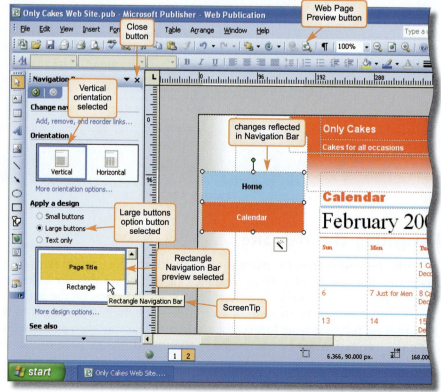

FIGURE 5-66

3

• **Close the Navigation Bar task pane.**

• **Click the Web Page Preview button on the Standard toolbar.**

The Web page is displayed (Figure 5-67).

4

• **Click the Home button to test the link to the home page.**

• **When the browser displays the home page, click Calendar to test the link.**

• **Close the browser by clicking the Close button in the browser's title bar.**

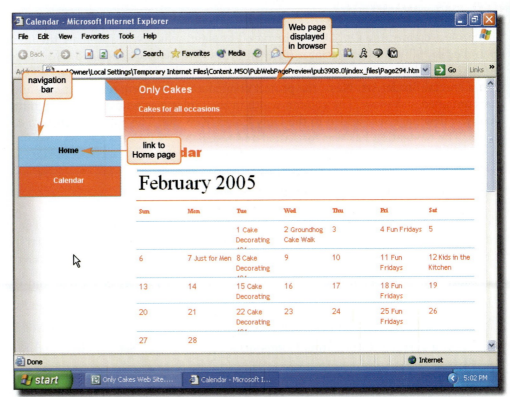

FIGURE 5-67

The second page of the Only Cakes Web site is complete. The following steps save the Web pages and quit Publisher.

To Save the Web Pages and Quit Publisher

1 Insert a floppy disk into drive A.

2 Click File on the menu bar and then click Save As.

3 When the Save As dialog box is displayed, type `Only Cakes Web Site` in the File name text box. Do not press the ENTER key.

4 If necessary, click the Save in box arrow and then click 3½ Floppy (A:).

5 Click the Save button in the Save As dialog box.

6 Click File on the menu bar again and then click Save As.

7 When the Save As dialog box is displayed, click the Save as type box arrow and then click Single File Web Page in the list.

8 Click the Save button in the Save As dialog box.

9 Click the Print button on the Standard toolbar.

Publisher saves the publication first with the extension .pub and then with the extension .mht on a floppy disk in drive A with the file name, Only Cakes Web Site. Finally, Publisher prints a copy on the printer. The completed invoice template is shown in Figure 5-1c on page PUB 275.

10 Click the Close button on the Publisher title bar.

Project Summary

This project created the Only Cakes Invoice Template, which will automate the invoice process. Workers will open the file, fill it out, and print it for each order. The invoice contained a formatted attention getter, special tab settings to help the users, a drop cap, and a new style. The coupon from the Design Gallery was formatted with a special BorderArt. Next, the project created an order form with columns and tables. The heading text box contained a shadow. The column width in the tables was adjusted and a printing border line was added. Finally, a new page was added to the Only Cakes Web site. The page contained a calendar and a schedule of events. The navigation bar was formatted and tested.

What You Should Know

Having completed this project, you should be able to perform the tasks below. The tasks are listed in the same order they were presented in this project. For a list of the buttons, menus, toolbars, and commands introduced in this project, see the Quick Reference Summary at the back of this book, and refer to the Page Number column.

1. Start Publisher   PUB 276
2. Create an Invoice Template   PUB 277
3. Apply a Personal Information Set   PUB 278
4. Insert a Personal Information Component   PUB 279
5. Create a New Text Style   PUB 280
6. Apply a Style   PUB 282
7. Format a Drop Cap   PUB 284
8. Insert a Tab Stop   PUB 287
9. Insert a System Date   PUB 288
10. Edit the Tables   PUB 289
11. Insert a Design Gallery Object   PUB 291
12. Edit Coupon Text Boxes   PUB 292
13. Add BorderArt   PUB 293
14. Insert and Format an Attention Getter   PUB 296
15. Check the invoice for Spelling and Design Errors   PUB 296
16. Save and Print the Invoice Template   PUB 297
17. Close the File without Quitting Publisher   PUB 297
18. Create a Custom-Size Publication   PUB 299
19. Select a Color and Font Scheme   PUB 300
20. Create Margin and Column Guides   PUB 300
21. Create a Shadowed Text Box   PUB 302
22. Select a Style and Enter Text   PUB 303
23. Create a Customer Text Box   PUB 303
24. Create an Order and Date Text Box   PUB 304
25. Create a Table   PUB 306
26. Enter Data into a Table   PUB 308
27. Format the Table   PUB 308
28. Create a Second Table   PUB 310
29. Create a Third Table   PUB 311
30. Save and Print the Order Form   PUB 312
31. Close the Publication without Quitting Publisher   PUB 312
32. Open a Web Publication and Insert a New Page   PUB 313
33. Change the Calendar Date   PUB 315
34. Resize the Calendar and Enter Text   PUB 316
35. Edit the Schedule of Events   PUB 317
36. Format and Test the Navigation Bar   PUB 318
37. Save the Web Pages and Quit Publisher   PUB 319

Learn It Online

Instructions: To complete the Learn It Online exercises, start your browser, click the Address bar, and then enter the Web address scsite.com/pub2003/learn. When the Publisher 2003 Learn It Online page is displayed, follow the instructions in the exercises below. Each exercise has instructions for printing your results, either for your own records or for submission to your instructor.

1 Project Reinforcement TF, MC, and SA

Below Publisher Project 5, click the Project Reinforcement link. Print the quiz by clicking Print on the File menu for each page. Answer each question.

2 Flash Cards

Below Publisher Project 5, click the Flash Cards link and read the instructions. Type 20 (or a number specified by your instructor) in the Number of playing cards text box, type your name in the Enter your Name text box, and then click the Flip Card button. When the flash card is displayed, read the question and then click the ANSWER box arrow to select an answer. Flip through Flash Cards. If your score is 15 (75%) correct or greater, click Print on the File menu to print your results. If your score is less than 15 (75%) correct, then redo this exercise by clicking the Replay button.

3 Practice Test

Below Publisher Project 5, click the Practice Test link. Answer each question, enter your first and last name at the bottom of the page, and then click the Grade Test button. When the graded practice test is displayed on your screen, click Print on the File menu to print a hard copy. Continue to take practice tests until you score 80% or better.

4 Who Wants To Be a Computer Genius?

Below Publisher Project 5, click the Computer Genius link. Read the instructions, enter your first and last name at the bottom of the page, and then click the PLAY button. When your score is displayed, click the PRINT RESULTS link to print a hard copy.

5 Wheel of Terms

Below Publisher Project 5, click the Wheel of Terms link. Read the instructions, and then enter your first and last name and your school name. Click the PLAY button. When your score is displayed, right-click the score and then click Print on the shortcut menu to print a hard copy.

6 Crossword Puzzle Challenge

Below Publisher Project 5, click the Crossword Puzzle Challenge link. Read the instructions, and then enter your first and last name. Click the SUBMIT button. Work the crossword puzzle. When you are finished, click the Submit button. When the crossword puzzle is redisplayed, click the Print Puzzle button to print a hard copy.

7 Tips and Tricks

Below Publisher Project 5, click the Tips and Tricks link. Click a topic that pertains to Project 5. Right-click the information and then click Print on the shortcut menu. Construct a brief example of what the information relates to in Publisher to confirm you understand how to use the tip or trick.

8 Newsgroups

Below Publisher Project 5, click the Newsgroups link. Click a topic that pertains to Project 5. Print three comments.

9 Expanding Your Horizons

Below Publisher Project 5, click the Articles for Microsoft Publisher link. Click a topic that pertains to Project 5. Print the information. Construct a brief example of what the information relates to in Publisher to confirm you understand the contents of the article.

10 Search Sleuth

Below Publisher Project 5, click the Search Sleuth link. To search for a term that pertains to this project, select a term below the Project 5 title and then use the Google search engine at google.com (or any major search engine) to display and print two Web pages that present information on the term.

11 Publisher Online Training

Below Publisher Project 5, click the Publisher Online Training link. When your browser displays the Microsoft Office Online Web page, click the Publisher link. Click one of the Publisher courses that covers one or more of the objectives listed at the beginning of the project on page PUB 274. Print the first page of the course before stepping through it.

12 Office Marketplace

Below Publisher Project 5, click the Office Marketplace link. When your browser displays the Microsoft Office Online Web page, click the Office Marketplace link. Click a topic that relates to Publisher. Print the first page.

Apply Your Knowledge

1 Creating a Monthly Statement

Instructions: Start Publisher. Open the publication, Apply 5-1, from the Data Disk. See the inside back cover for instructions for downloading the Data Disk or see your instructor for information about accessing the files required in this book. The publication is a monthly statement for a lawn care company (Figure 5-68). You will edit the text boxes, insert a decorative border, create a drop cap, and insert a coupon in the statement.

Perform the following tasks:

1. Click the top text box, press the F9 key, and then type `Evergreen Lawn Care` in the text box. Enter the address and telephone information as shown in Figure 5-68.
2. Double-click the picture and replace it using the Clip Art task pane. Search for the key-word, lawn, and then choose a picture similar to the one in Figure 5-68.
3. Click to position the insertion point before the word, Monthly. Click Format on the menu bar and then click Drop Cap. Choose an appropriate style from the Available Drop Caps list. Click the Custom Drop Cap tab and then type `2` in the Size of letter box.
4. Click the text box for Statement #, Date, and Customer ID. Press CTRL+A to select the entire frame. Click the 1" mark on the horizontal ruler to set a tab. Enter the system date at the tab stop, as shown in Figure 5-68.
5. Click the Mailing Address text box and type in your name and address.
6. Select the Type column in the table. Click Table on the menu bar and then click Delete Columns.

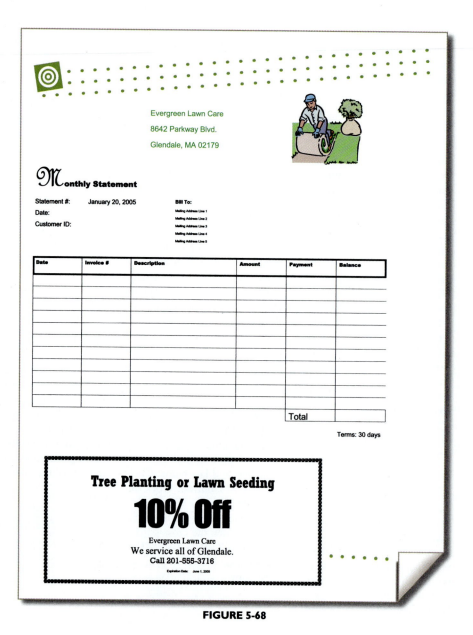

FIGURE 5-68

7. Insert a coupon in the lower portion of the statement. Change the text in the text boxes as necessary to read:

Tree Planting or Lawn Seeding

10% Off

Evergreen Lawn Care

We service all of Glendale.

Call 201-555-3716

Expiration Date: June 1, 2005

Click the border of the coupon so only the border is selected. Right-click the border and then click Format AutoShape. Choose an appropriate BorderArt for the coupon.

8. Click the Spelling button on the Standard toolbar to check spelling. Correct any spelling errors. Click Tools on the menu bar and then click Design Checker. Correct any design errors.

9. Save the publication with the file name, Apply 5-1 Lawn Care Statement, on your floppy disk. Print a copy.

1   Creating a Monthly Statement

Problem: Fredrick Russell owns and operates a candy store named The Fudge Factory. He has asked you to create a monthly statement he can use to send to retail outlets who order from his store. You decide to use a statement business form (Figure 5-69 on the next page).

Instructions:

1. Start Publisher. From the New Publication task pane, click Publications for Print. In the New from a design list, click Business Forms. When the list of available business forms is displayed, click Statement. Scroll as necessary and then click Radial Statement in the preview pane.
2. When the Business Form Options task pane is displayed, in the logo area, click None.
3. Use the Mistletoe color scheme and the Economy font scheme.
4. Click the top text box, press the F9 key, and then type The Fudge Factory in the text box.
5. Insert an appropriate graphic using the Clip Art task pane. Resize the graphic to fit to the right of the address text boxes.
6. Click the word, Statement, to select the text box. Click Format on the menu bar and then click Drop Cap on the Format menu. Choose an appropriate style from the Available Drop Caps list.
7. Click the text box for Statement #, Date, and Customer ID. Press CTRL+A to select the entire frame. Press the DELETE key.
8. Zoom in and then select each of the shapes filled with black. If necessary, ungroup and then select a color from the color scheme.

(continued)

In the Lab

Creating a Monthly Statement *(continued)*

9. Click the .75" mark on the Horizontal Ruler to set a tab. Type `Statement #:` and then press the TAB key. Press the ENTER key. Type `Date:` and then press the TAB key. Enter a system date and then press the ENTER key. Type `Customer ID:` and then press the TAB key.

10. Click the Mailing Address text box and type in your name and address.

11. Save the publication with the file name, Lab 5-1 Fudge Factory Statement, on your floppy disk. Print a copy.

2 Creating an Origami Box

Problem: A local youth organization has asked you to create party favors for their annual Blue and Gold Banquet. You would like to include foil-covered chocolates (in blue and gold, of course) at each place setting. Because you are on a tight budget, you decide to try your hand at designing a do-it-yourself gift box to hold the candies. Printing on heavy card stock paper, you use the ancient art of Origami paper folding to create two boxes, one slightly larger than the other for a top and bottom box set (Figure 5-70).

Instructions: Perform the following tasks:

1. Start Publisher. From the New Publications task pane, click Blank Publications and then zoom to Full page. Close the task pane.

2. Use the Insert Table button on the Objects toolbar to draw a table approximately six inches square. When the Create Table dialog box is displayed, create four rows and four columns, using the Default table format. Close the Create Table dialog box by clicking its OK button.

FIGURE 5-69

3. Click Table on the menu bar, point to Select, and then click Table. On the Formatting toolbar, click the Line/Border Style button, and then click More Lines in the list.

4. When the Format Table dialog box is displayed, if necessary, click the Colors and Lines tab. In the Presets area, click the third button (full grid), and then click the OK button.

5. Click Table on the menu bar and then click Cell Diagonals. When the Cell Diagonals dialog box is displayed, click Divide up. Click the OK button in the Cell Diagonals dialog box. Click outside the table to remove the selection.

6. Using the Line button on the Objects toolbar, draw seven

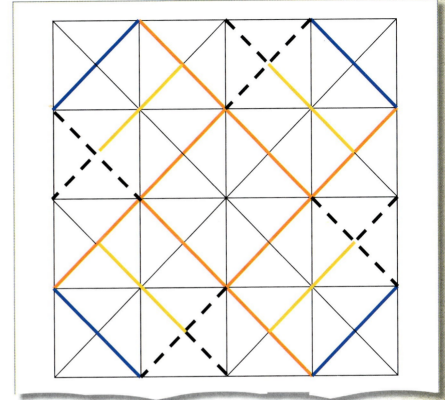

FIGURE 5-70

lines to dissect the table cells the opposite way from the diagonals. Holding down the SHIFT key while drawing the line ensures a straight 45-degree line.

7. If desired, you may format the lines for color and style or simply use the figure as a reference for folding and trimming in Step 8.
    a. To add color, click the line in the publication to select it. Click the Line button on the Objects toolbar and then click the Line Color button on the Formatting toolbar. Choose the appropriate color from the Line Color menu. Hold down the SHIFT key and draw the colored lines over the top of the black lines in the table as shown in Figure 5-70.
    b. To create dotted lines, click the line in the publication to select it. Click the Line button on the Objects toolbar and then click the Dash Style button on the Formatting toolbar. Choose an appropriate dotted line from the Dash Style menu. Hold down the SHIFT key and draw the dotted lines on top of the black lines in the table, as shown in Figure 5-70.

8. Save the publication as Lab 5-2 Origami Box on your floppy disk. Print the publication, and then using Figure 5-70 as a guide, trim the printout, and fold the bottom of the box set as follows:
    a. Cut around the edge of the table and on the dotted lines.
    b. Fold the orange lines first to form a box shell, keeping the tabs on the inside.
    c. Fold the blue lines inward.
    d. Fold the yellow lines third, working around from one corner of the box to the next.

9. Click Edit on the menu bar and then click Select All. Click the Group Objects button and then SHIFT-drag a corner handle until the box is approximately 1/5-inch larger. Print and assemble the top of the box set. (*Hint:* You may cheat and use a small piece of tape to hold down the "blue" fold if you like.)

3 Creating a Web Calendar with Graphics

Problem: You recently have been hired as the Webmaster's assistant for the city of Smithville, Missouri. The Parks and Recreation department wants to post a Web calendar of events for the month of June 2005. They would like a large calendar with some graphics and text. They have sent you the data, which is shown in Table 5-7.

Table 5-7 Parks and Recreation Calendar Data	
DATE	EVENT
June 2, 9, 16, 23, and 30	Synchronized Swimming
June 11	Shopping at the Plaza
June 13	Crafts for Kids
June 25	Soccer Sign-up

The Webmaster has asked you to include a navigation bar across the bottom with a link back to the home page. He will complete the Web address later. A sample of the Web calendar is illustrated in Figure 5-71.

June 2005

Sun	Mon	Tue	Wed	Thu	Fri	Sat
			1	2 Synchronized Swimming	3	4
5	6	7	8	9 Synchronized Swimming	10	11 Shopping at the Plaza
12	13 Crafts for Kids	14	15	16 Synchronized Swimming	17	18
19	20	21	22	23 Synchro-nized Swimming	24	25 Soccer Sign-up
26	27	28	29	30 Synchro-nized Swimming		

Parks and Recreation

FIGURE 5-71

In the Lab

Instructions: Perform the following tasks:

1. Start Publisher. When the New Publication task pane is displayed, click Blank Publications. In the list of blank publications, click Web Page. Select the Marine color scheme and the Basis font scheme.
2. Click the Design Gallery Object button on the Objects toolbar. When Publisher displays the Design Gallery dialog box, click Calendars in the Categories list. When the previews display, click the Pixel Calendar. Click the Insert Object button.
3. When Publisher displays the calendar in the workspace, move and resize the calendar as necessary so that it displays close to the top and left edges of the Web page layout.
4. Click the calendar's wizard button. When the Calendar Design task pane is displayed, click the Change date range button. Choose June 2005 in the Change Calendar Dates dialog box.
5. Insert the text from Table 5-7 into the appropriate cells using the following technique: Click after the number in the given cell. Click the Font Size box arrow and then click 10 in the Font Size list. Press the SPACEBAR and then type the text.
6. Using the Clip Art task pane, search for graphics with the keywords, swimming, bus, crafts, and soccer. Find graphics that are similar to the ones displayed in Figure 5-71. Resize and move the graphics as necessary.
7. Click the Design Gallery Object button on the Objects toolbar again. When Publisher displays the Design Gallery dialog box, click Navigation Bars in the Categories list. When the previews are displayed, click Capsule Navigation Bar in the Navigation Bars area. Click the Insert Object button.
8. When Publisher displays the Create Navigation Bar dialog box, click the OK button.
9. When the navigation bar is displayed in the page layout, drag the navigation bar to a place approximately centered below the calendar.
10. Select the text in the navigation bar. Type `Parks and Recreation` to replace the selected text.
11. Click the navigation bar's wizard button. When the Navigation Bar task pane is displayed, click Vertical in the Orientation area. Click Large buttons in the Apply a design area to select it. Close the Navigation Bar task pane.
12. Save the publication as a Publisher file, with the name Lab 5-3 Parks and Recreation Web Calendar.
13. Save the publication again. Use the Save as type box arrow to save it as a Single File Web Page with the same name.
14. Print a copy for your instructor.

Cases and Places

The difficulty of these case studies varies:
■ are the least difficult and ■■ are more difficult. The last exercise is a group exercise.

La Chareada Restaurant would like a coupon that advertises its buy one, get one free offer on
Create a blank publication with a custom size of 7 by 3 so the coupon will fit in a local mailing.
e margins to ½ inch. Use the Design Gallery to insert a coupon and resize it to fit in the margins.
border of the sun around the edge. Use appropriate font and color schemes.

he owner of We Are the Office Place, whose logo is a picture of pens and papers, is located at
E. Huron, Chicago, IL, 60609. He would like a purchase order template that his employees can
fill out orders for customers. Use the Bars Purchase Order and fill in the name and addresses of
ompany. Click in the appropriate text boxes to create easy-to-complete fields with tabs and a sys-
ate. Use a drop cap W in the company name.

Research laboratories at major teaching hospitals usually are funded not only by their research
s, but also by providing services to the hospital and associated physicians. The Flow Cytometry
t University Hospital faxes results to pathologists and transplant surgeons at the hospital and to
banks all over the city. They need a standardized fax cover sheet for their multipage lab reports.
a template, create a fax cover template they will print on pre-printed stationery. Leave two inches
top of the page to accommodate their masthead and format the objects using the tools and tech-
s you learned in this project. Use a system date, a drop cap, and tab stops in each data entry field
lab assistants can position text easily.

The Tire Garage needs a time card. The owner has just hired two extra mechanics and an office
ger because business is booming. Using a Weekly Record business form, select the time card table,
hen paste it into a blank publication. To change the orientation to Landscape, click Page Setup on
le menu and then click the Landscape option button. Create a text box below the table with the
s, Name and Date, and appropriate blank lines, for employees to sign and date their time cards.
multiple copies for the Tire Garage's employees.

Working Together   As a group, find a local not-for-profit agency that needs documents such as
es, order forms, or other publications on Publisher's list of business forms. Discuss with the
y manager the needs of the agency and the skills of your group. As a group, decide on consistent
, colors, logos, and styles. Individually, create different business publications for the agency. Bring
ublications to the group, discuss each one, and make recommendations for change. Edit the
ations and submit them to your instructor. Submit final copies to the agency.

Creating an E-Commerce Web Site

CASE PERSPECTIVE

Teresa Chen, owner of Only Cakes, now is ready to take her business to a new level via e-commerce. She wants you to construct a Web page that will allow customers to order cakes online with a user-friendly form that is easy for customers to complete.

You two agree that the usual customer information should be collected, as well as four other pieces of data: size of cake, flavor, icing, and additional instructions — a blank box where customers can request special decorations, lettering, and delivery times. The form should have one button to submit the order and another to reset the form if the customer wants to make changes before submission.

You suggest that Teresa include a return customer check box so she can verify the Publisher database created in Project 4 and option buttons for pick up or delivery. Additionally, because this page eventually will be uploaded to the Web, you decide to program a reminder message box; that way, if Teresa edits the page in the future, she will be reminded to upload the newest copy to the Web before she closes the publication. The two of you also agree that an attractive fill and subtle background sound will help catch and keep the attention of potential customers. Finally, Teresa wants a message to scroll across the bottom of the form reminding the user of the bakery's phone number.

As you read this project, you will learn how to use Publisher to create an e-commerce site that sends data to its owner, complete with text boxes, text areas, check boxes, option buttons, command buttons, and HTML code. Additionally, you will learn how to program a message box that is displayed when you close the publication.

Creating an E-Commerce Web Site

Objectives

You will have mastered the material in this project when you can:

- Create a Web page from scratch
- Start Publisher with a blank Web publication
- Make Web design choices
- Use a textured background
- Insert form controls
- Distribute objects
- Edit form control data names and set return values
- Define option button groups
- Add items to a list box
- Specify command button options
- Insert a picture hyperlink
- Add alternative text to a picture hyperlink
- Use VBA to create a message box
- Set the security level in Publisher

Introduction

Electronic commerce, or **e-commerce**, has established itself in the business world as an inexpensive and efficient way to increase visibility and, therefore, sales. Customers visit, browse, make purchases, and ask for assistance at a Web site, just as they would at a physical location.

An electronic form is used on a Web page to collect data from visitors. **Electronic forms** are used to request and collect information, comments, or survey data, and to conduct business transactions. An electronic form is made up of a collection of **form controls**, which are the individual buttons, boxes, and hyperlinks that let Web site visitors communicate with Web site owners. Electronic forms must include a submit button; otherwise Web site visitors cannot return their form data.

As e-commerce becomes more popular, desktop publishing theory must include both electronic and print publishing concepts. Publisher's Design Gallery contains many electronic mastheads, navigation bars, Web buttons, and forms, all designed to look good and load quickly on the Web. Additionally, the Form Control menu contains many features to assist in designing forms from scratch. Most desktop publishers use a combination of rapid form development techniques to tailor their Web site to suit their needs.

When you issue an instruction to Publisher by clicking a Web control button or a command, Publisher follows a prewritten, step-by-step set of instructions to accomplish the task. For example, when you click the Print button on the Standard toolbar, Publisher follows a precise set of steps to print your publication. In Publisher, this precise, step-by-step series of instructions is called a **procedure**. A procedure also is referred to as a **program** or **code**.

The process of writing a procedure is called **computer programming**. Every Publisher command on a menu and button on a toolbar has a corresponding procedure that executes when you click the command or button. **Execute** means that the computer carries out the step-by-step instructions. In a Windows environment, an event causes the instructions associated with a task to be executed. An **event** is an action such as clicking a button, clicking a command, dragging a scroll box, or right-clicking selected text.

Although Publisher has many toolbar buttons and menu commands, it does not include a command or button for every possible task. Thus, Microsoft has included with Publisher a powerful programming language called Visual Basic for Applications. The **Visual Basic for Applications** (**VBA**) programming language allows you to customize and extend the capabilities of Publisher.

Project Six — Creating an E-Commerce Web Site

To illustrate some of the Web form features of Microsoft Publisher, this project presents a series of steps to create an e-commerce site for the bakery named Only Cakes, as shown in Figure 6-1a. Additionally, it demonstrates the use of a VBA-generated message box to remind the editor of the publication to upload the most recent copy to the Web (Figure 6-1b).

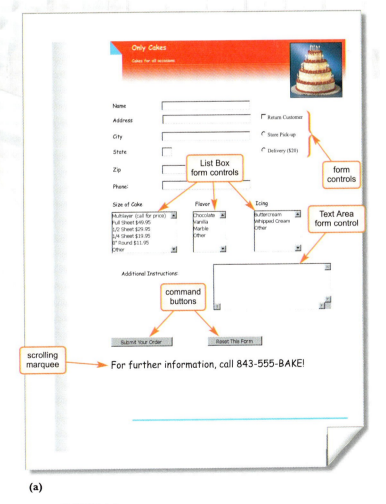

(b) **VBA** message box

(a)

FIGURE 6-1

More About

Publisher Web Pages

For more information about creating Web pages from scratch, visit the Publisher 2003 More About Web page (scsite.com/pub2003/more) and then click Publisher Web Pages.

Creating a Web Page from Scratch

In an effort to automate Only Cakes' ordering process, the company would like a Web page created from **scratch**, which means beginning with a blank page rather than a Web site wizard or template. When beginning with a blank Web page, desktop publishers set font and color schemes and then insert text and appropriate electronic form controls, as well as graphics and sounds. A variety of objects is available, including design sets with mastheads, color schemes, font schemes, backgrounds, and navigation bars.

Creating a Blank Web Page

Publisher provides a blank Web page for users who wish to start from scratch. The following steps show how to start Publisher and display a blank Web page.

To Start Publisher with a Blank Web Page

1 Click the Start button on the Windows taskbar, point to All Programs on the Start menu, point to Microsoft Office on the All Programs submenu, and then click Microsoft Office Publisher 2003 on the Microsoft Office submenu.

2 If the Publisher window is not maximized, double-click its title bar to maximize it.

3 If Publisher does not display the New Publication task pane, click View on the menu bar and then click Task Pane. If the Publication Designs task pane is displayed, click the Other Task Panes button on the task pane title bar, and then click New Publication.

4 If the Language bar is displayed, click its Minimize button.

5 In the New Publication task pane, click Blank Web Page in the New area.

The blank Web page layout is displayed in the workspace. Web page rulers display pixel measurements rather than inches, as shown in Figure 6-2.

Setting the Color and Font Schemes

The next steps show how to set the color and font schemes for the blank Web page.

To Set the Color and Font Schemes

1 Click Color Schemes in the Publication Designs task pane. If necessary, scroll to and then click Parrot in the Apply a color scheme list.

2 Click Font Schemes in the Color Schemes task pane. If necessary, scroll to and then click Casual in the Apply a font scheme list.

Making Web Design Choices in the Publication Designs Task Pane

The next series of steps shows how to choose designs, page content, page layout, and Web page options, such as keywords and sounds. One of the Web page options is to give the Web page a name. Because this order form is not the home page of Only Cakes, the name will be changed from the default value, index, to OrderForm.

To Make Web Design Choices

1

• **In the Publication Designs task pane, click Publication Designs.**

• **Scroll as necessary in the Apply a design list and then point to Marker.**

In addition to Publication Designs options, the Publication Designs task pane displays choices for Web Site Options, Page Content, Color Schemes, and Font Schemes (Figure 6-2).

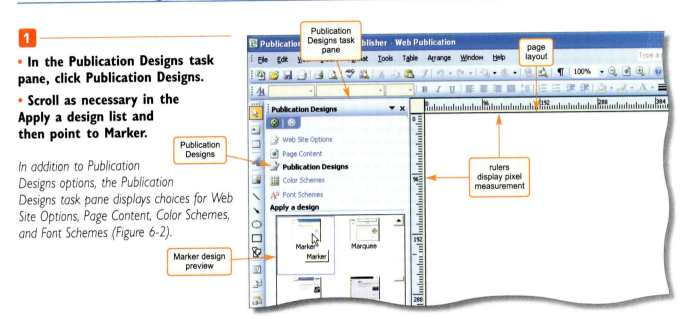

FIGURE 6-2

2

• **Click Marker in the Apply a design list.**

• **Click Page Content in the Publication Designs task pane.**

Publisher adds the Marker masthead to the page layout (Figure 6-3). The Page Content task pane also is displayed. Publisher may display an arrow at the bottom of the task pane, indicating that more choices are available.

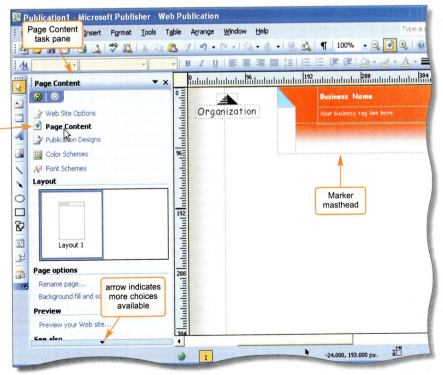

FIGURE 6-3

3

- **If necessary, click the arrow at the bottom of the Page Content task pane. Click More Web page options.**

- **When the Web Page Options dialog box is displayed, type** `Only Cakes Web Order Form` **in the Page title text box, and then press the TAB key twice.**

- **Type** `OrderForm` **in the File name text box and then press the TAB key.**

- **In the Description text box, type** `This Is the Only Cakes E-Commerce Web Site`, **and then press the TAB key.**

- **Type** `order cakes online Only Cakes Teresa Chen` **in the Keywords text box.**

Publisher displays the Web Page Options dialog box (Figure 6-4).

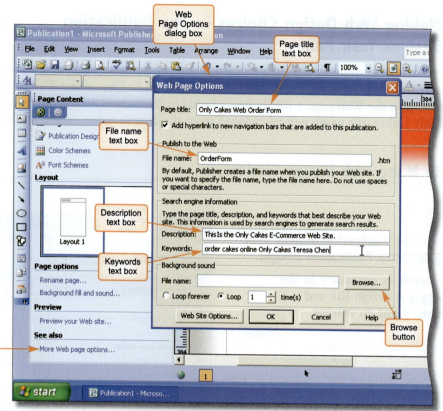

FIGURE 6-4

4

- **Click the Browse button.**

- **When the Background Sound dialog box is displayed, click the file named FINCL_01.MID, or another sound file located on your system.**

Publisher displays the sounds installed with Office 2003 (Figure 6-5). Your list may differ.

5

- **Click the Open button.**

- **When the Web Page Options dialog box again is displayed, click the OK button.**

The Web option changes for the Only Cakes Web order form are complete.

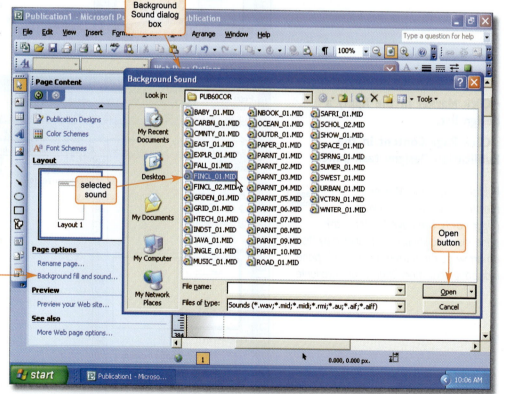

FIGURE 6-5

Recall that background sounds can loop continually while the visitor has the Web page open, or the sound can stop after one complete occurrence.

Textured Backgrounds

The same fill effects that you used for AutoShapes in previous projects can be used as a background for Web pages. Most Web design experts recommend a single color or texture for backgrounds to add interest, but not distract from the content.

The following steps illustrate choosing a textured background for the Web page.

More About

Sounds

For more information about using sound with Web pages, visit the Publisher 2003 More About Web page (scsite.com/pub2003/more) and then click Sounds.

To Insert a Textured Background

1

• **Click Background fill and sound in the Page options area in the Page Content task pane.**

The Background task pane is displayed (Figure 6-6). Colors from the color scheme display in the Apply a background area.

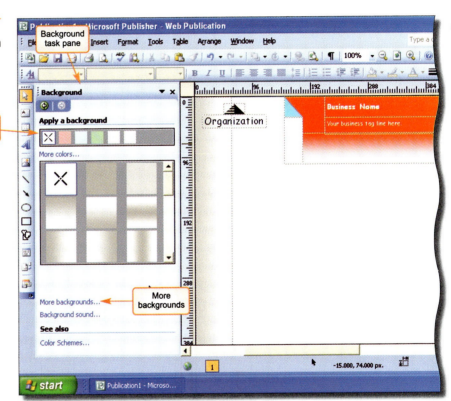

FIGURE 6-6

2

• **Click More backgrounds.**

• **When the Fill Effects dialog box is displayed, click the Texture tab and then click Blue tissue paper in the Texture area.**

As each texture is clicked, the name is displayed below the previews, and the fill effect is shown in the Sample area (Figure 6-7).

3

• **Click the OK button.**

• **Click the Close button in the Background task pane.**

Publisher adds the background texture to all white areas of the Web page that do not display design objects.

FIGURE 6-7

The next task is to delete the logo, as shown in the next step.

To Delete the Logo

1 **Right-click the logo. Click Delete Object on the shortcut menu.**

The next task is to apply the Secondary Business personal information set that will display Only Cakes' name and tag line, as shown in the following steps.

To Apply a Personal Information Set

1 **Click Edit on the menu bar and then click Personal Information.**

2 **When the Personal Information dialog box is displayed, click the Select a personal information set box arrow, and then click Secondary Business in the list.**

3 **Click the Update button.**

The Web page layout is displayed with the secondary business information and background texture (Figure 6-8). The logo is deleted.

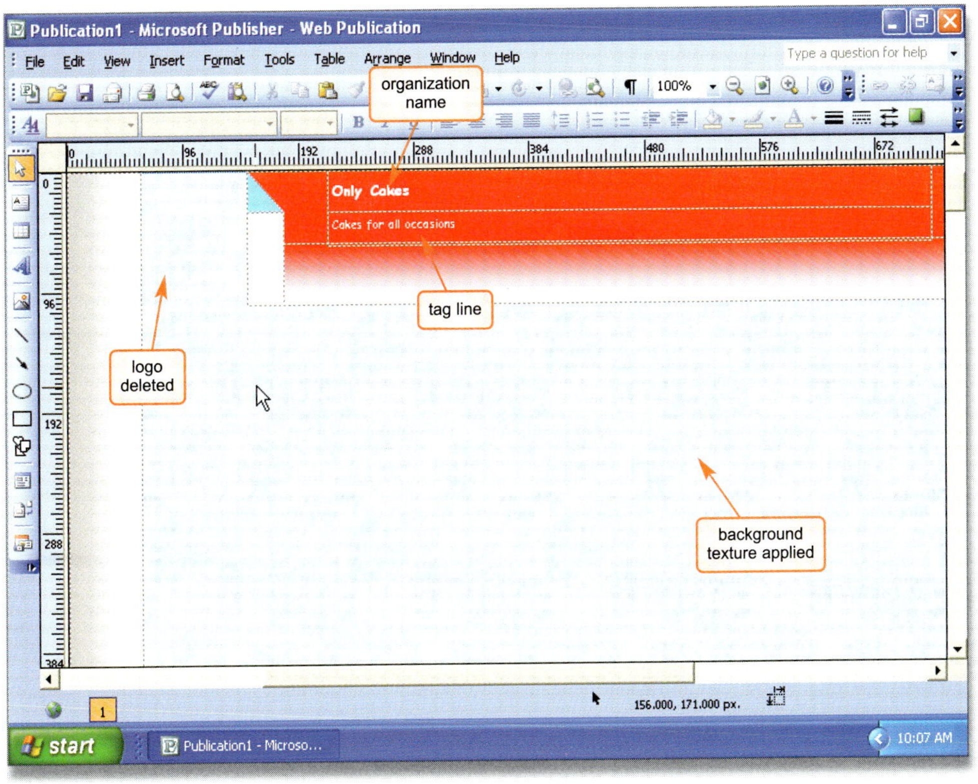

FIGURE 6-8

Inserting the Only Cakes Graphic

Before beginning to insert data collection objects in the Web page, Only Cakes wants to use the same picture on its Web page that it used on its letterhead. See pages PUB 229 through PUB 233 for the steps to retrieve the graphic of the cake, crop it, and add a border. Alternately, you can open the Only Cakes Letterhead and copy the graphic, as described in the following steps.

To Copy a Graphic from Another Publication

1 Click the Open button on the Standard toolbar. When the Open dialog box is displayed, click the Look in box arrow and then click 3½ Floppy (A:) in the Look in list. Double-click Only Cakes Letterhead.

2 Right-click the cake graphic and then click Copy on the shortcut menu.

3 Click the Close button on the Publisher title bar to exit the publication. If Publisher displays a dialog box that asks if you want to save the contents of the Clipboard, click the Yes button.

4 When the Web page again is displayed, right-click the page layout and then click Paste on the shortcut menu.

5 Drag the picture to the upper-right corner of the Web page.

The cake graphic is pasted in the Web page (Figure 6-9 on the next page).

More About

Web Graphics

For more information about graphics that download quickly over the Web, visit the Publisher 2003 More About Web page (scsite.com/pub2003/more) and then click Web Graphics.

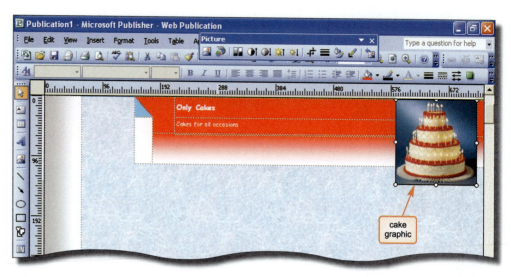

FIGURE 6-9

Microsoft Office
Publisher 2003

An **animated graphic** is a picture that displays animation when viewed in a Web browser. While too much animation may distract users, a subtle animated graphic may convey the Web site owner's message or style. To view possible animated graphics, in the Clip Art task pane, click the Results should be box arrow and then select only Movies.

Form Controls

Form controls are the individual boxes and buttons used by Web site visitors to enter data. The data from a form control is transmitted from the visitor to the site owner via a submit button. Publisher supports six types of form controls.

A **check box** is a square box that presents a yes/no choice. Selected, it displays a check mark or X. Several check boxes function as a group of related but independent choices. An **option button** is a round button that presents one choice. When it is selected, an option button circle is filled in. When grouped, option buttons function like multiple-choice questions. The difference between an option button and a check box is that users can select only one option button within a group, but any number of check boxes. Check boxes and option buttons both display a label you can edit. Furthermore, you can choose to display either control as selected or not selected at startup.

A **list box** presents a group of items in a list. Visitors can scroll to select from one or any number of choices in the list box. You determine the available choices and the number that may be selected when you set list box properties.

If you want Web visitors to type information in a text box, you insert a **text box**. Sensitive information, such as credit card information or passwords, can be displayed as asterisks or bullets. Textbox form controls are different from regular text box controls that display text entered during the design process. Textbox form controls are displayed as white boxes, with an insertion point for data entry by the Web user.

A **text area**, or multiline text box, provides a means of entering information by making available to the visitor a larger text box with multiple blank lines. Next to Textbox and Text Area form controls, it is advisable to include regular text boxes as instruction labels, to assist visitors in entering the correct information.

You must include a **submit command button** on every form. This button allows visitors to send you their form data. A **reset command button** is optional, but provides a way to clear form data and allow the Web visitor to start over. Command buttons can display any words in their visible labels, such as Send or Clear.

Form controls each have a logical **internal data label**, also called a **return data label**. This return data label references and identifies the visitor-supplied information when submitted to the Web site owner. For instance, a return data label with the word, Course#, could accompany a user-supplied course number in an e-mail submission. Without a return data label, a random number in the e-mail might be hard to decipher. You may assign return data labels, as well as other settings, by double-clicking the control.

Inserting and Distributing Labels

Some Publisher form controls do not include text to prompt the Web user for specific kinds of data entry. In those cases, it is appropriate to use a text box, placed close to the form control, as a label. A **label** is an instructive word or words, directing the user to enter suitable data. Because the Only Cakes Web order form will collect six pieces of individual information entered by the user, each one needs to be labeled to instruct and assist the user in filling out the form.

The following steps drag ruler guides to help align the labels that are inserted as text boxes. The text boxes will be aligned vertically using the Distribute command. **Distribute** means to make equal spaces between each selected object, whereas align means to line up the edges.

To Insert and Distribute Labels

1

• **Drag from the horizontal ruler to the 384 pixels measurement.**

• **Drag from the vertical ruler to the 142 pixels measurement.**

The ruler guides are displayed in the publication (Figure 6-10).

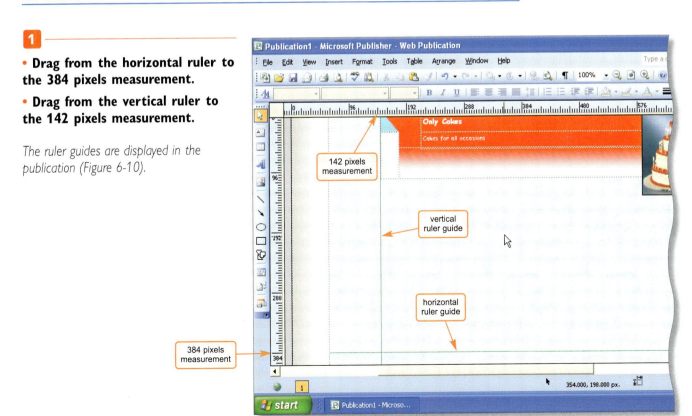

FIGURE 6-10

2

• **Click the Text Box button on the Objects toolbar and then drag a small text box from the vertical ruler guide just below the Web masthead.**

• **Click in the text box.**

• **Click the Font Size box on the Formatting toolbar and then type 10 as the new font size.**

• **In the text box, type** Name: **to insert the text.**

The text box is displayed in the publication (Figure 6-11).

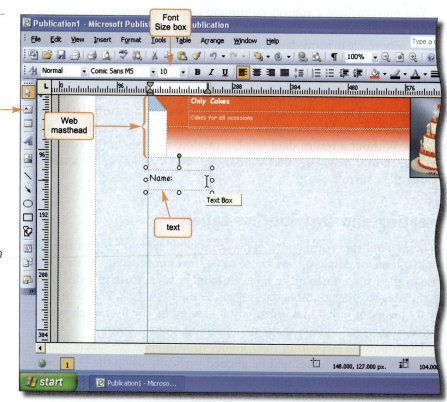

FIGURE 6-11

3

• **With the text box still selected, press CTRL+C to copy the text box.**

• **Click away from the text box, so it is not selected.**

• **Press CTRL+V to paste the text box. Drag the copy below the original, aligned with the ruler guide.**

• **Paste again to create a total of six text boxes.**

The six labels are aligned with the vertical ruler guide (Figure 6-12).

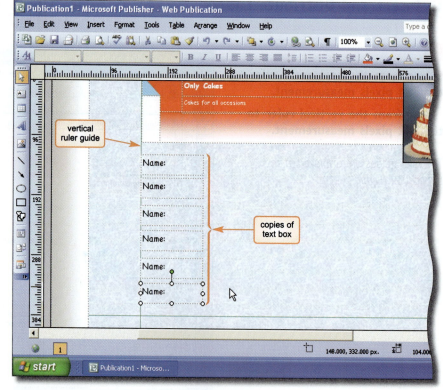

FIGURE 6-12

4

• SHIFT-click each of the text boxes so they all are selected.

• Click Arrange on the menu bar and then point to Align or Distribute.

Publisher displays the Arrange menu and the Align or Distribute submenu (Figure 6-13).

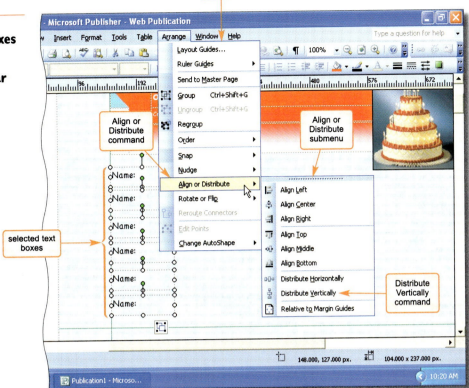

FIGURE 6-13

5

• Click Distribute Vertically.

Publisher distributes the text boxes (Figure 6-14).

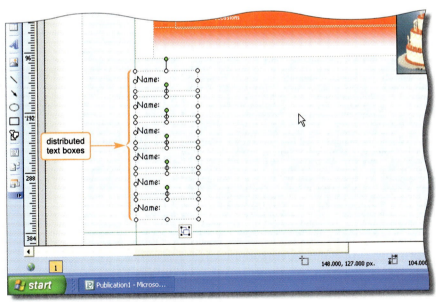

FIGURE 6-14

Other Ways

1. Right-click multiple selected objects, point to Align or Distribute on the shortcut menu, click Distribute Vertically

If you want to distribute objects throughout the length or width of the entire page, click Relative to Margin Guides on the Align or Distribute submenu (Figure 6-13), before clicking the appropriate distribute command.

The steps on the next page edit the text in each of the copied text box labels.

To Edit Text Box Labels

1 **Double-click the text in the second text box. Type** Address: **to replace the text.**

2 **One at a time, double-click each of the remaining text boxes and type the new label for each, as shown in Figure 6-15.**

The copies of the text boxes contain their new labels.

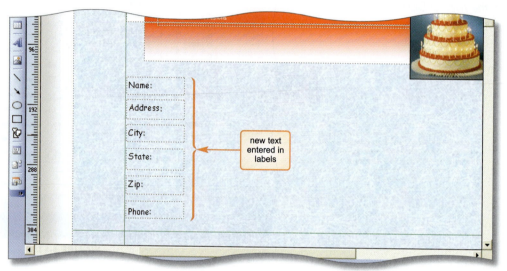

FIGURE 6-15

Textbox Form Controls

The Only Cakes Web order form contains six Textbox form controls to collect information from customers. In the following steps, you will see that you can help the user to enter information by placing Textbox form controls close to their labels and changing the size or width of the controls. Setting each Textbox form control's return data label will help the Web site owner identify the source of the data.

To Insert Textbox Form Controls

1

• **Click the Form Control button on the Objects toolbar.**

The choices on the Form Control menu are displayed (Figure 6-16).

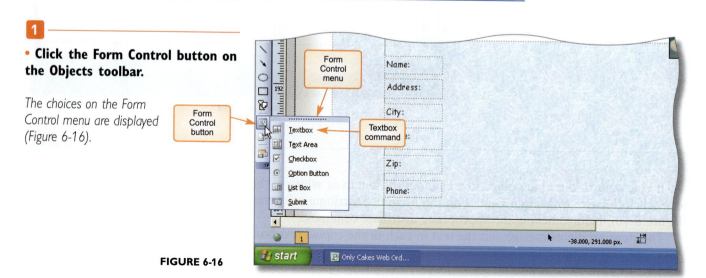

FIGURE 6-16

2

• **Click Textbox.**

Publisher places a Textbox form control in the publication (Figure 6-17).

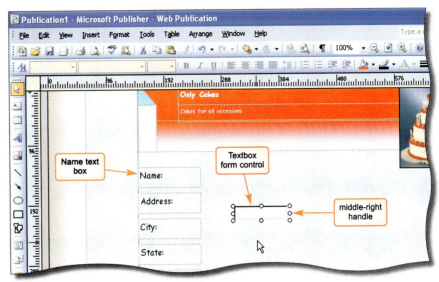

FIGURE 6-17

3

• **Drag the middle-right handle of the Textbox form control to create a box that is approximately two inches wide.**

• **Drag the Textbox form control to the right of the Name label.**

• **With the Textbox form control still selected, press CTRL+C to copy the control.**

• **Press CTRL+V five times to create five more Textbox form controls, dragging each copy to the right of a label.**

The six Textbox form controls are displayed (Figure 6-18).

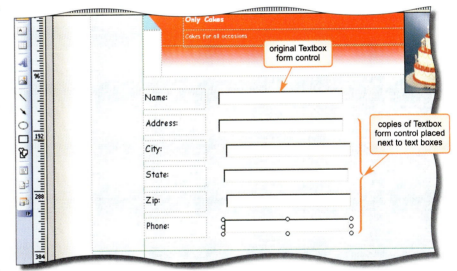

FIGURE 6-18

4

• **SHIFT-click each of the Textbox form controls so all six are selected.**

• **Click Arrange on the menu bar, point to Align or Distribute, and then click Distribute Vertically.**

• **Click Arrange on the menu bar again. Point to Align or Distribute and then click Align Left.**

The text boxes are aligned on the left and are distributed vertically (Figure 6-19).

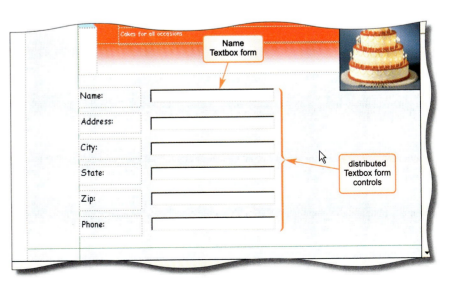

FIGURE 6-19

5

- Click in the publication to remove the selection from the six Textbox form controls and then click to select only the Textbox next to State.

- Drag the middle-right handle of the Textbox form control that corresponds to State, in order to make the Textbox narrower, as shown in Figure 6-20.

Users will enter the two-character code for their state.

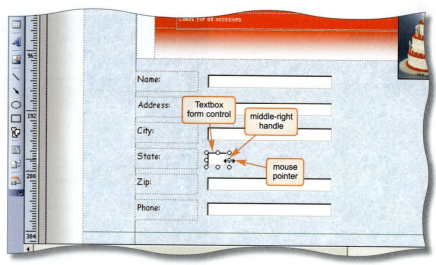

FIGURE 6-20

6

- Select the Textbox that corresponds to Zip and then drag the middle-right handle, in order to make the text box narrower.

- Select the Textbox that corresponds to Phone and then drag the middle-right handle, in order to make the Textbox narrower.

The user will enter a five- or nine-digit zip code and a typical telephone number with area code (Figure 6-21).

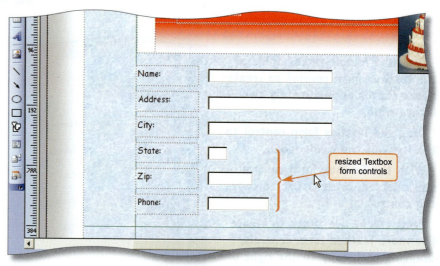

FIGURE 6-21

7

- Double-click the first Textbox form control.

- When the Text Box Properties dialog box is displayed, select any text in the Return data with this label Textbox and then type Name as the entry.

Publisher displays the Text Box Properties dialog box (Figure 6-22).

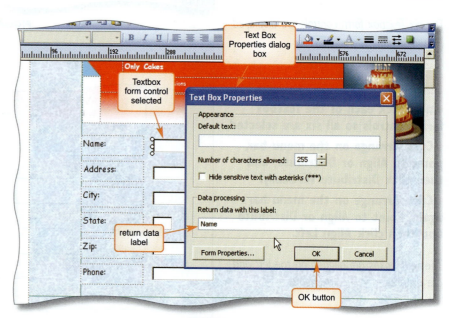

FIGURE 6-22

8

• **Click the OK button.**

• **Double-click the second Textbox form control.**

• **When the Text Box Properties dialog box is displayed, select any text in the Return data with this label text box and then type** Address **as the entry.**

The second form control will return data to the Web site owner with the label, Address (Figure 6-23).

9

• **Click the OK button.**

• **One at a time, double-click each of the remaining Textbox form controls. Enter the appropriate return data labels of City, State, Zip, and Phone.**

• **When the Text Box Properties dialog box is displayed for State, double-click the Number of characters allowed box to select the text and then type** 2 **as the new number.**

• **When the Text Box Properties dialog box is displayed for Zip, double-click the Number of characters allowed box to select the text and then type** 10 **for a possible zip code with hyphen.**

Each of the Textbox form controls now has a return data label.

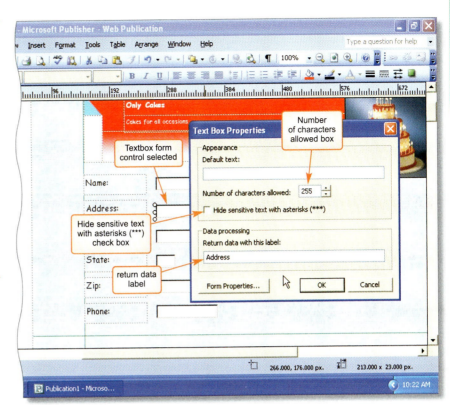

FIGURE 6-23

It is appropriate for some entries to be displayed as asterisks, such as passwords, credit card numbers, or social security numbers. To accomplish this, you can click the Hide sensitive text with asterisks check box (Figure 6-23). Additionally, Publisher can place default text in Textbox form controls, which might be useful for further instructions to the user.

Checkbox Form Controls

Publisher provides Checkbox form controls to allow users to submit yes and no responses without having to type the words into a text box. Unlike Textbox form controls, Checkbox form controls come with their own labels. When clicked, the Checkbox form control displays a check mark.

The steps on the next page show how to create a check box for customers to indicate that they are return customers.

> ### Other Ways
>
> 1. On Insert menu point to Form Control, click Textbox
> 2. In Voice Command mode, say "Form Control, Textbox"
> 3. In Voice Command mode, say "Insert, Form Control, Textbox"

To Insert Checkbox Form Controls

1

• **Click the Form Control button on the Objects toolbar.**

The Form Control menu is displayed (Figure 6-24).

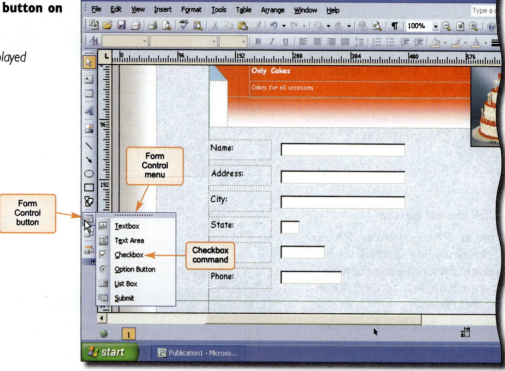

FIGURE 6-24

2

• **Click Checkbox.**

• **When Publisher displays the Checkbox form control, drag it to the right of the Address Textbox.**

Publisher displays the control with its square check box and label (Figure 6-25).

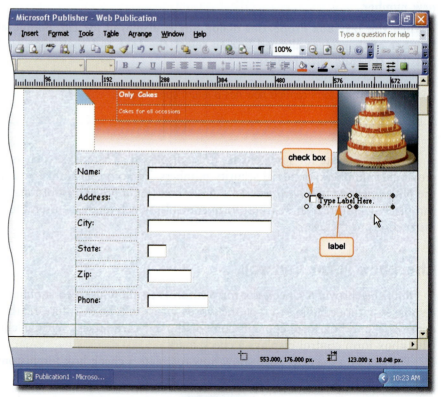

FIGURE 6-25

• **Click the label text in the Checkbox form control, and then type** Return Customer **to change the label.**

The new label text is displayed (Figure 6-26).

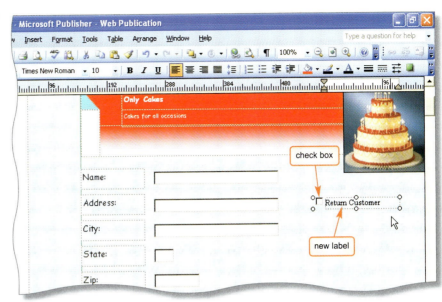

FIGURE 6-26

4

• **Double-click the check box in the Checkbox form control.**

• **When Publisher displays the Checkbox Properties dialog box, if necessary, click Not selected.**

• **Select any text in the Return data with this label text box and then type** Return_Customer **as the new text.**

• **Type** Yes **in the Checkbox value text box.**

Publisher displays the Checkbox Properties dialog box (Figure 6-27). The control will not display a check mark when users first see the form.

• **Click the OK button.**

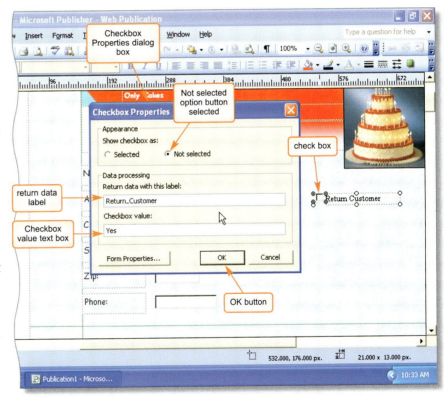

FIGURE 6-27

In Figure 6-27, the name of the data label was entered as Return_Customer, with no spaces. Some database programs will not accept spaces in field names; consequently, upon submission, Publisher forms that update databases might generate an error if a space were included. It is a good practice to omit spaces in data labels or replace them with an underscore character.

Other Ways

1. On Insert menu point to Form Control, click Checkbox
2. In Voice Command mode, say "Form Control, Checkbox"
3. In Voice Command mode, say "Insert, Form Control, Checkbox"

More About

Check Boxes and Option Buttons

Check boxes and option buttons are grouped objects in Publisher; that is, the physical box or button is grouped with an accompanying text box label. To ungroup or regroup them, press CTRL+SHIFT+G.

Form controls with labels are grouped objects in Publisher, consisting of a box or button that can be clicked and a label. Therefore, when editing the properties, you must double-click the box portion of the control rather than the label.

Option Button Form Controls

Publisher provides Option Button form controls to allow users to make one choice from a group of options. Like Checkbox form controls, Option Button form controls come with their own labels. When clicked, the Option Button form control displays a filled-in circle or bullet.

Recall that multiple Option Button form controls are grouped so users may select only one. For example, Only Cakes customers cannot request that their orders both be delivered and picked up. The Only Cakes Web order form will use option buttons to allow users to choose whether they will pick up their cakes or pay a delivery charge. The following steps show how to create two options buttons that will be used to indicate pick-up or delivery.

To Insert Option Button Form Controls

1

• **Click the Form Control button on the Objects toolbar, as shown in Figure 6-28.**

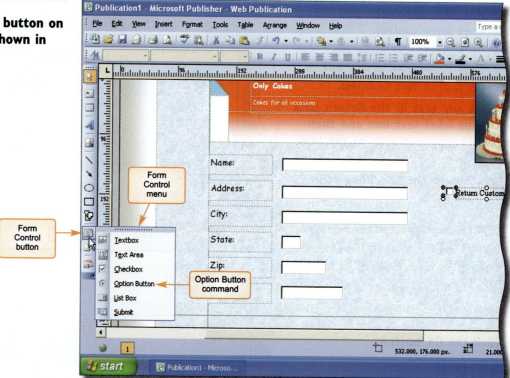

FIGURE 6-28

2

- **Click Option Button.**

- **When the Option Button form control is inserted in the publication, drag it to the right of the City Textbox, approximately aligned under the Return Customer check box.**

Publisher displays the Option Button form control with its round option button and a label (Figure 6-29).

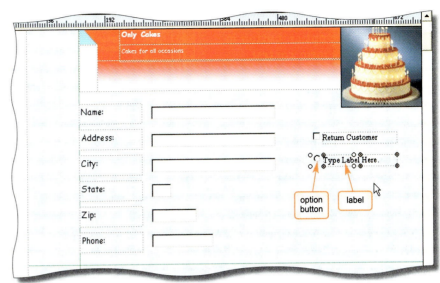

FIGURE 6-29

3

- **Click the label text and then type** Store Pick-Up **to replace the text.**

The new label text is entered (Figure 6-30).

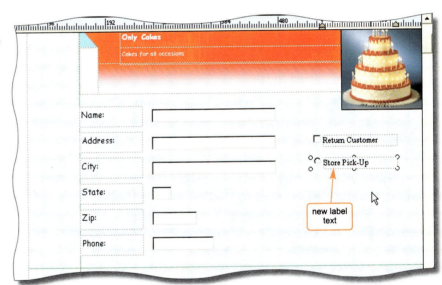

FIGURE 6-30

4

- **Click so the Store Pick-Up option button control is not selected.**

- **Click the Form Control button on the Objects toolbar again, and then click Option Button.**

- **When the Option Button form control is displayed, drag it to the right of the State Textbox, aligned under the Store Pick-Up option button.**

- **Click the label text and then type** Delivery ($20 Charge) **to replace the text.**

Publisher displays the new text in the second Option Button form control (Figure 6-31).

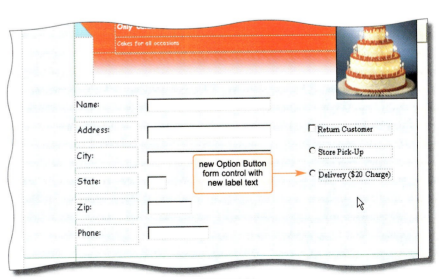

FIGURE 6-31

5

• **Double-click the option button in the Store Pick-Up form control.**

• **When Publisher displays the Option Button Properties dialog box, click Selected. Select any text that appears in the Return data with this label text box and then type** Service **as the new text. Select any text that appears in the Option button value text box, and then type** Store Pick-Up **as the new text.**

The Option Button Properties dialog box is displayed (Figure 6-32).

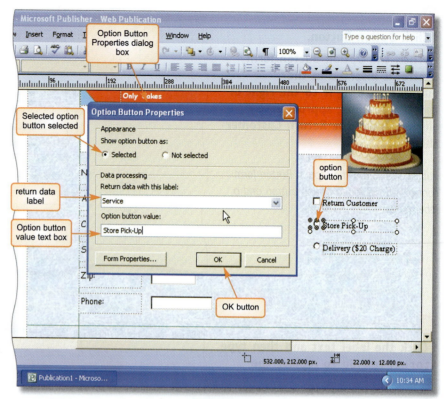

FIGURE 6-32

2

• **Click the OK button.**

• **Double-click the option button in the Delivery ($20 Charge) form control.**

• **When Publisher displays the Option Button Properties dialog box, if necessary, click Not selected to select it. Select any text in the Return data with this label text box and then type** Service **as the new text. Select any text in the Option button value text box and then type** Delivery **as the new text.**

The return data label for both option buttons is the same; the Option button value field will indicate which button was selected when the form is submitted (Figure 6-33).

7

• **Click the OK button.**

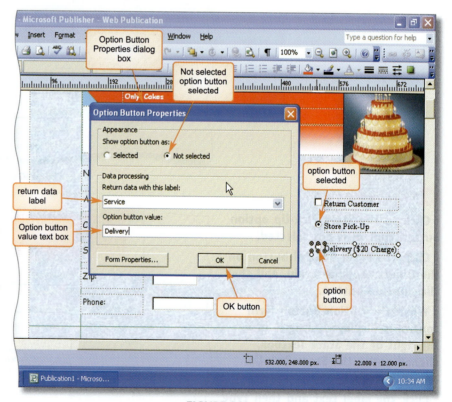

FIGURE 6-33

Other Ways

1. On Insert menu point to Form Control, click Option Button
2. In Voice Command mode, say "Form Control, Option Button"
3. In Voice Command mode, say "Insert, Form Control, Option Button"

In Figure 6-33, choosing the same return data label indicates grouping. Therefore, if you want more than one grouping in your Web site, you would use different return data labels for each group. For example, three options buttons for small, medium, or large, might contain a return data label of Size. On the same form three other option buttons, for red, blue, or green might contain a return data label of Color. Without the return label designation, users could select only one option button on the entire form, rather than one per group.

List Box Form Controls

A List Box form control offers users one or more specific choices. Designers use a list box rather than grouped option buttons when the choices are related closely, such as a list of quantities; when the list is long, such as a list of states; or when users may choose more than one from the list.

List boxes can be customized with item text, initial selections, and return values that can be updated and reordered easily.

The following steps create three text boxes used as labels for three list boxes.

To Create Labels for the List Box Form Controls

1 Scroll to the middle portion of the Web page, so the horizontal ruler guide is displayed toward the top of the screen.

2 On the Objects toolbar, click the Text Box button, and then drag to draw a text box from the corner of the vertical and horizontal ruler guides down and right.

3 Click the Font Size box on the Formatting toolbar and then type 10 to set the font size.

4 Click inside the text box and then type Size of Cake to enter the label.

5 Create two more text boxes just below the vertical ruler guide and enter Flavor and Icing as the respective labels.

6 SHIFT-click each of the three text boxes to select them all. Click Arrange on the menu bar, point to Align or Distribute, and then click Distribute Horizontally.

The three text box labels are entered (Figure 6-34).

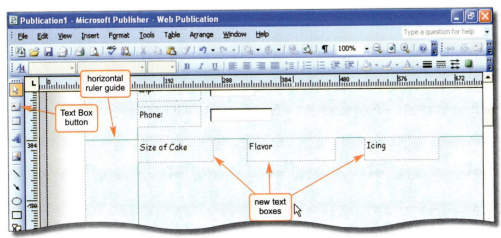

FIGURE 6-34

The Only Cakes Web order form will use list boxes to allow users to choose the size, flavor, and icing of their cakes. The next steps create three List Box form controls and set their return values.

To Insert List Box Form Controls

1

• **Click the Form Control button on the Objects toolbar.**

The Form Control menu is displayed (Figure 6-35).

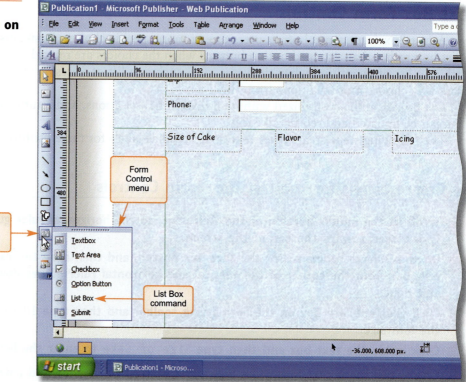

FIGURE 6-35

2

• **Click List Box.**

Publisher inserts a List Box form control in the publication (Figure 6-36).

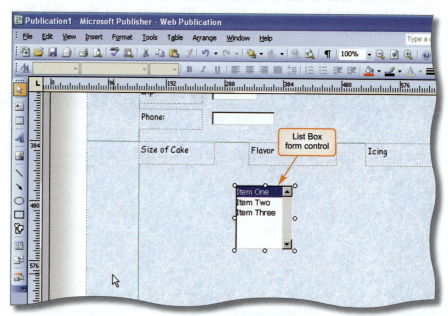

FIGURE 6-36

3

• Drag the List Box form control to a location below the Size of Cake text box.

• Double-click the List Box form control.

• When Publisher displays the List Box Properties dialog box, select the text in the Return data with this label text box and then type Size_of_Cake as the new text.

Publisher displays the List Box Properties dialog box (Figure 6-37). The three preset list items are displayed in the Appearance area, with Item One selected.

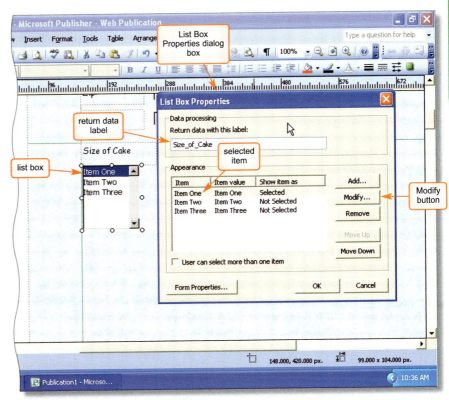

FIGURE 6-37

4

• Click the Modify button.

• When the Add/Modify List Box Item dialog box is displayed, type Multilayer (call for price) in the Item text box. If necessary, click Not selected to select it. If necessary, click the Item value is same as item text check box so it displays a check mark.

Publisher displays the Add/Modify List Box Item dialog box (Figure 6-38). Upon submission of the form, the return value will be the same as the item text.

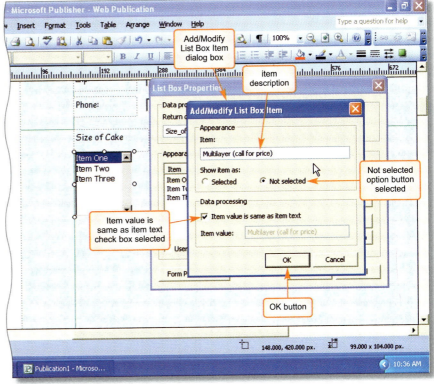

FIGURE 6-38

5

• **Click the OK button.**

• **When the List Box Properties dialog box is visible again, click Item Two in the Appearance area, and then click the Modify button.**

• **When the Add/Modify List Box Item dialog box is displayed, type** Full Sheet $49.95 **in the Item text box and select the other options, if necessary, as shown in Figure 6-39.**

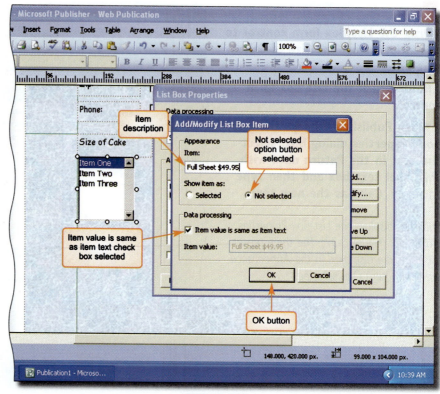

FIGURE 6-39

6

• **Click the OK button.**

• **Repeat the process for Item Three with the item text,** 1/2 Sheet $29.95.

• **Click the Add button in the List Box properties to add two more items:** 1/4 Sheet $19.95 **and** 8" Round $11.95.

The five items for the List Box form control are displayed in the List Box Properties dialog box (Figure 6-40). Your display may differ.

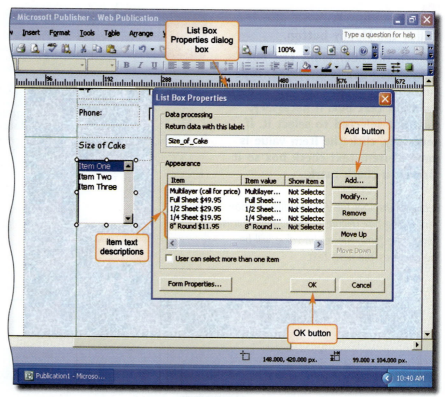

FIGURE 6-40

7

• **Click the OK button.**

Publisher displays the modified list box items in the form control (Figure 6-41).

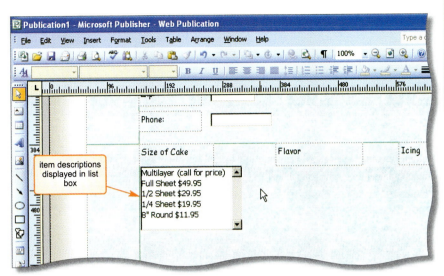

FIGURE 6-41

8

• **Repeat Steps 1 through 7 to create two more List Box form controls with the items that are displayed in Figure 6-42.**

• **Use the return data labels, Flavor and Icing.**

• **Drag the new list boxes so they are positioned approximately as shown in Figure 6-42.**

The Flavor and Icing list boxes are displayed (Figure 6-42).

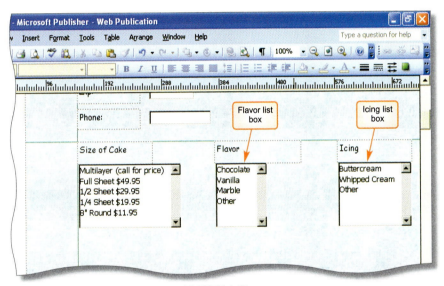

FIGURE 6-42

The Move Up and Move Down buttons in the List Box Properties dialog box, shown in Figure 6-40, can be used to reorder the items in the list box. Simply select the item in the Appearance area, and then click the appropriate button. The Remove button can be used to delete selected items from the list.

Text Area Form Controls

A Text Area form control allows users to enter multiple lines of text. On the Web, the scroll bar and scroll arrows become active when the text area begins to fill. The Only Cakes Web order form will use a text area to allow users to enter additional instructions about their order, such as specific lettering or designs.

The steps on the next page create a label and text area for the order form.

To Insert a Text Area Form Control

1

• **Click the Text Box button on the Objects toolbar and then drag to draw a text box below the Size of Cake list box.**

• **Click the Font Size box on the Formatting toolbar and type** 10 **as the new font size. In the text box, type** Additional Instructions: **to create a label.**

• **Click outside the text box so it no longer is selected.**

• **Click the Form Control button on the Objects toolbar.**

The text box label is entered (Figure 6-43). The Form Control menu also is displayed.

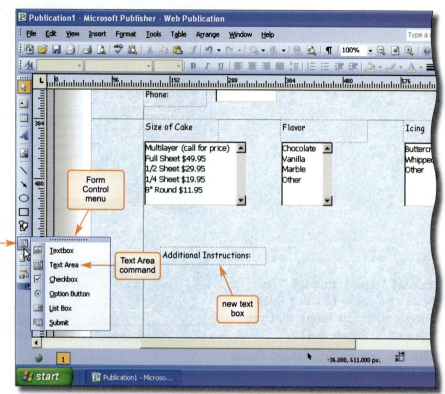

FIGURE 6-43

2

• **Click Text Area.**

• **Drag the Text Area form control to the right of the label and resize it, as shown in Figure 6-44.**

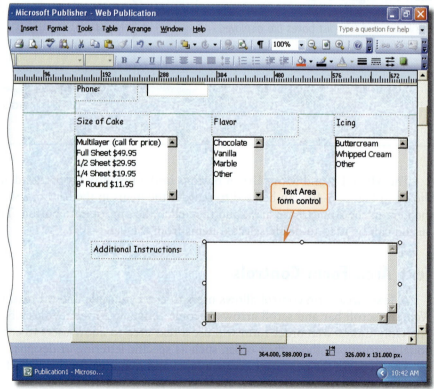

FIGURE 6-44

3

• **Double-click the Text Area form control.**

• **When Publisher displays the Text Area Properties dialog box, select any text in the Return data with this label text box and then type** Additional_Instructions **as the new text.**

Publisher displays the Text Area Properties dialog box (Figure 6-45). Any instructions entered by the user will be submitted with the return label, Additional_Instructions.

4

• **Click the OK button.**

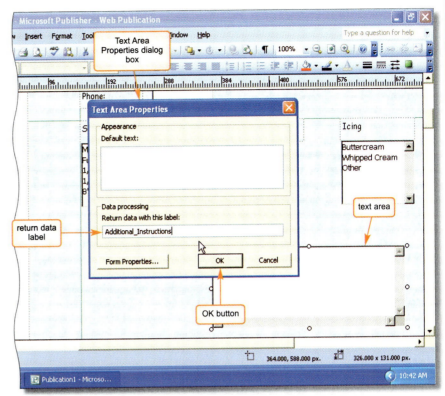

FIGURE 6-45

If you want some text to display automatically in the text area, you can type in the Default text text box in the Text Area Properties dialog box. For example, some Web site designers use text areas to ask for visitor feedback or comments by inserting the default text, Type your comments here, rather than creating an accompanying label.

Submit Button Form Controls

A Submit Button form control is clicked by the user to submit data from all controls on the form. Three kinds of submission are available: saving the data in a file on the Web server, sending the data via e-mail, and using a special program provided by the Internet Service Provider (ISP).

The owner of the Only Cakes Web order form wants the data sent to her via e-mail. She also wants a second button labeled Reset, which will allow users to clear previous entries. The Submit Button form control is a special kind of command button used to issue commands in a graphical user interface. You can tailor the button by changing its caption and its type or purpose. The two available types of command buttons in Publisher are Submit and Reset.

The steps on the next page show how to create two buttons and set the properties of the form to send data via e-mail.

Other Ways

1. On Insert menu point to Form Control, click Text Area
2. In Voice Command mode, say "Form Control, Text Area"
3. In Voice Command mode, say "Insert, Form Control, Text Area"

More About

The Reset Button

The Reset command button in Publisher automatically restores all fields back to their original or default values. Text boxes and text areas either are cleared or display their default text; check boxes and option buttons are reset; and list boxes display their default setting. If a choice originally was set to display selected, it will be selected again when the Reset button is clicked, no matter what choices were made by the user.

To Insert Submit Button Form Controls

1

• **Scroll down in the publication workspace so the Additional Instructions text area is displayed toward the top of the screen.**

• **Click the Form Control button on the Objects toolbar.**

The Form Control menu is displayed (Figure 6-46).

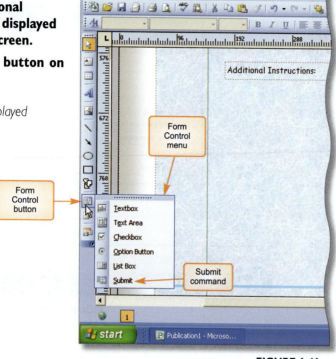
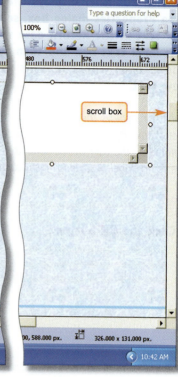

FIGURE 6-46

2

• **Click Submit.**

• **When the Command Button Properties dialog box is displayed, click Button text is same as button type so it no longer displays a check mark.**

• **Select the text in the Button text text box and then type** Submit Your Order **to change the caption.**

Publisher displays the Command Button Properties dialog box (Figure 6-47).

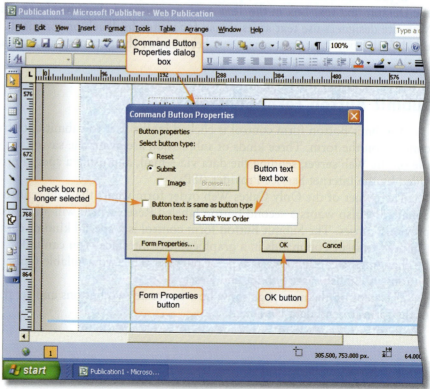

FIGURE 6-47

3

• **Click the Form Properties button.**

• **When Publisher displays the Form Properties dialog box, click Send data to me in e-mail to select it.**

• **Click in the Send data to this e-mail address box and then type** teresa@onlycakes.com **as the new address.**

• **Press the TAB key and then type** Web Site Order **in the Subject of e-mail text box.**

The data from the form will be sent via e-mail (Figure 6-48).

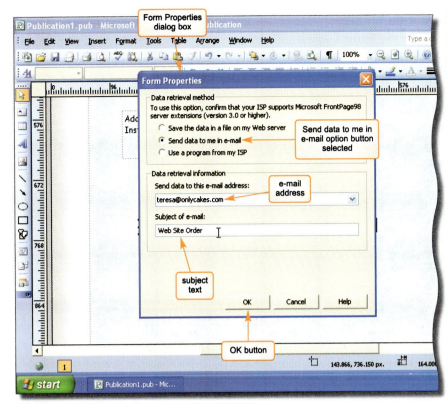

FIGURE 6-48

4

• **Click the OK button.**

• **When the Command Button Properties dialog box is visible again, click the OK button.**

• **When the button is inserted in the publication, drag it to a location below the Additional Instructions label, as shown in Figure 6-49.**

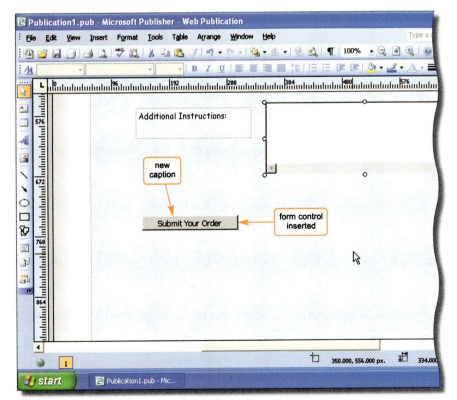

FIGURE 6-49

5

• **Click the Form Control button on the Objects toolbar and then click Submit.**

• **When the Command Button Properties dialog box is displayed, click Reset.**

• **Click Button text is same as button type to remove the check mark.**

• **Select any text in the Button text text box and then type** Reset This Form **to replace the text.**

The properties are set for the Reset button (Figure 6-50).

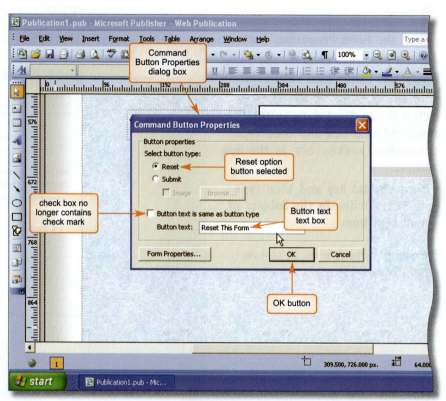

FIGURE 6-50

6

• **Click the OK button.**

• **When the button is inserted in the publication, drag it to the right of the Submit Your Order button, as shown in Figure 6-51.**

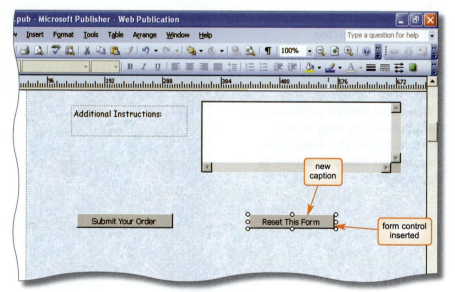

FIGURE 6-51

In order for the submit button to work properly on the Web, your Internet Service Provider (ISP) must support Microsoft FrontPage version 3.0 or later server extensions. If you are unsure whether your ISP supports the extensions, contact your ISP or ask your instructor for more information about your school's Web hosting policy and servers.

Now that the form controls are complete, it is a good time to save the publication, as shown in the following steps.

To Save the Publication

1 With a formatted floppy disk in drive A, click the Save button on the Standard toolbar.

2 With the default file name selected, type the file name `Only Cakes Web Order Form` in the File name text box. Do not press the ENTER key after typing the file name.

3 Click the Save in box arrow and then click 3½ Floppy (A:) in the Save in list.

4 Click the Save button in the Save As dialog box.

The file is saved on the floppy disk.

Picture Hyperlinks

To facilitate communication, electronic forms also may contain hyperlinks. Recall that text hyperlinks are colored and underlined text that you click to go to a file, an address, or another HTML page on the Web. A **picture hyperlink**, or **hot spot**, is a specific object containing a hyperlink, typically a graphic or picture. Users may click the picture hyperlink in the same way they click text hyperlinks.

When viewing a Web page with a browser, the mouse pointer changes to a hand when positioned on a text or picture hyperlink. The change in the mouse pointer icon is called a **mouse over event**. Events are an integral part of the object-oriented concepts used in Web technology. Even the click of a hyperlink or button is considered an event.

Screen readers that read Web pages for people with disabilities can identify picture hyperlinks that have alternative text. **Alternative text** is descriptive text that appears as an alternative to a graphic image on Web pages. Web browsers display alternative text when graphics are loading or when graphics are missing. Screen readers read the alternative text. Alternative text describes the picture or picture hyperlink when it cannot be seen.

Creating a Picture Hyperlink with Alternative Text

The steps on the next page show how to create a picture hyperlink for the Only Cakes graphic on the Web order form. Users of the form will be able to click the picture hyperlink to send an e-mail to the company. The alternative text will describe the hyperlink.

Q&A

Q: How do I automatically connect my data with a database?

A: Your Web server must have a special program or script to update a database from a Web submission. When clicked, the Use a program from my ISP option button in the Form Properties dialog box (Figure 6-48 on page PUB 359) allows you to specify the program and appropriate get or post method.

More About

Screen Readers

For more information about screen readers, visit the Publisher 2003 More About Web page (scsite.com/pub2003/more) and then click Screen Readers.

To Insert a Picture Hyperlink

1

• **Scroll to the top of the page layout.**

• **Right-click the picture of the cake or other graphic that you selected, and then click Hyperlink on the shortcut menu.**

• **When the Insert Hyperlink dialog box is displayed, click E-mail Address in the Link to bar.**

• **Type** teresa@onlycakes.com **in the E-mail address text box.**

• **Press the TAB key and then type** E-mail from the Web Site Order Form **in the Subject text box.**

The picture hyperlink directs users to the e-mail address of the company (Figure 6-52). The word mailto automatically is displayed.

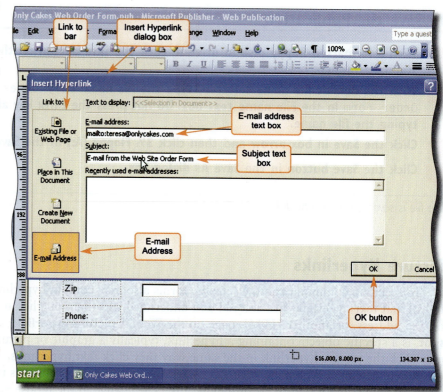

FIGURE 6-52

2

• **Click the OK button.**

The graphic is now a picture hyperlink that, when clicked, opens the user's e-mail message window. Pointing to the picture hyperlink now will display a hand mouse pointer and an e-mail ScreenTip with the e-mail address.

The following steps add alternative text to the graphic.

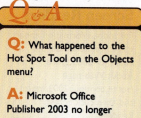

Q: What happened to the Hot Spot Tool on the Objects menu?

A: Microsoft Office Publisher 2003 no longer offers a Hot Spot Tool. The same effect can be obtained by using a picture hyperlink or text hyperlink. The mouse pointer displays a hand representing a hyperlink just as it did for hot spots.

To Add Alternative Text

1

• **Right-click the graphic. On the shortcut menu, click Format Picture.**

• **When the Format Picture dialog box is displayed, click the Web tab.**

• **Type** Click this graphic of a cake to e-mail the Only Cakes bakery. **in the Alternative text text box.**

The Web sheet of the Format Picture dialog box is displayed (Figure 6-53).

2

• **Click the OK button.**

The picture's alternative text is set.

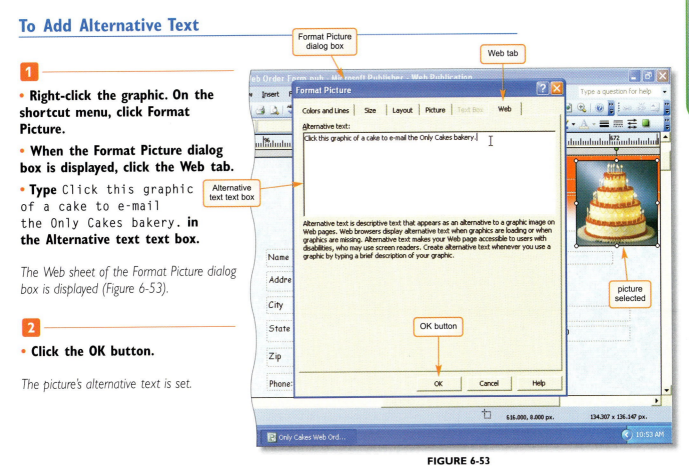

FIGURE 6-53

Alternative text or text descriptors also are displayed to users who have turned off graphics or to those who use text-only browsers.

HTML Code Fragments

An **HTML code fragment** is code that you add to your Web page to create features such as a counter, a scrolling marquee, or advanced data collection objects. Publisher does not supply HTML code fragments. You must have the correct HTML code to insert into the HTML Code Fragment object once it is inserted on the Web page.

Creating a Scrolling Marquee

The owner of the Only Cakes bakery wants a scrolling message to remind customers of the bakery's telephone number. Using HTML code, the following steps insert an HTML code fragment to create a scrolling marquee. A **scrolling marquee** is an animation technique that displays text that scrolls across the screen.

The HTML code and its purpose are listed in Table 6-1 on the next page.

Table 6-1   HTML Code

HTML CODE	PURPOSE
`<font face="Comic Sans MS, Arial, Helvetica">`	Sets font
`<p align="center"><b>`	Sets alignment and font style
`<font color="#FF0000" size="5">`	Sets font color and font size
`<marquee>For further information, call 843-555-BAKE!`	Sets text
`</marquee></font></b></p>`	Closes settings

The following steps insert an HTML code fragment to display a scrolling marquee across the bottom of the Only Cakes Web page.

To Insert an HTML Code Fragment

1

• **Click the HTML Code Fragment button on the Objects toolbar.**

• **When the Edit HTML Code Fragment dialog box is displayed, type the code that is displayed in the first column of Table 6-1.**

The HTML code is displayed (Figure 6-54).

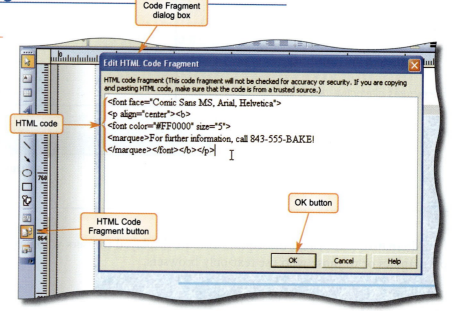

FIGURE 6-54

2

• **Click the OK button.**

• **Drag the HTML Code Fragment object below the two command buttons and resize, as shown in Figure 6-55.**

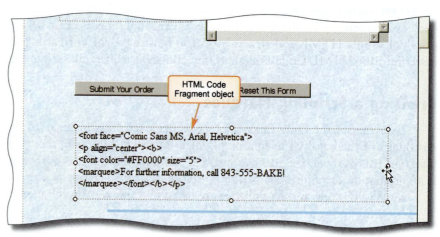

FIGURE 6-55

Other Ways

1. On Insert menu click HTML Code Fragment
2. In Voice command mode, say "Insert HTML Code Fragment"

Errors in HTML code fragments may cause performance or security problems for your Web site. Publisher does not verify HTML code fragments for accuracy or security. If you download code fragments from the Web, Microsoft Help warns users to make sure that the HTML is from a trusted source.

HTML code fragments appear as code in a frame on the Web page. The result of the HTML code appears when you preview or publish your Web page, as shown in the following steps. The text will scroll from the right side of the screen to the left, displaying in the width of the HTML Code Fragment box.

To Preview the Web Page

1 **Click the Web Page Preview button on the Standard toolbar. Point to the graphic and notice that the mouse pointer changes to a hand.**

2 **Scroll to the lower portion of the Web page.**

The HTML code fragment displays the scrolling marquee (Figure 6-56). If your system is connected to speakers, the background sound will play.

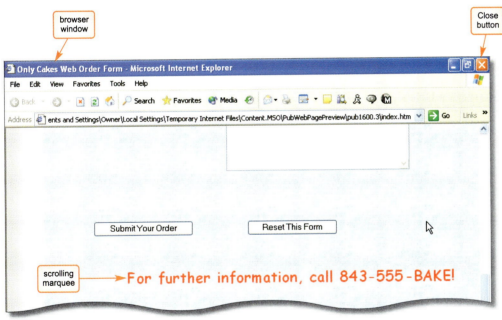

FIGURE 6-56

More About

HTML

For more information about HTML code, visit the Publisher 2003 More About Web page (scsite.com/pub2003/more) and then click HTML.

3 **Click the Close button on the browser title bar.**

It is possible to enter text, make choices, and click the Reset This Form button in the Web page preview; however, the Submit button will not work until the Web page is uploaded to an appropriate server.

If you do not see the scrolling text or if it is displayed incorrectly, there are several possible reasons. You may have made errors in typing the HTML code, or the HTML code fragment might overlap another object. Additionally, different browsers interpret HTML in different ways, with potentially different results. Do not add borders or BorderArt around HTML code fragments.

Eventually, this file will become part of the Only Cakes Web site created in an earlier project. When this page is added to that Web site, Publisher will offer choices to insert a navigation bar and link the page.

Visual Basic for Applications

Visual Basic for Application (VBA) is a powerful tool to program how Publisher and other applications perform while creating documents. In Publisher, VBA includes the ability to run macros, write procedures, and create new menus and buttons.

A **macro** is a procedure made up of VBA code. Recall that a procedure is a precise, step-by-step series of instructions. In some applications, you can create new macros by recording keystrokes of common tasks that you wish to automate. In Publisher, you can run macros recorded elsewhere or program the macros yourself.

Publisher has seven prenamed macros, called **document events**, which execute automatically when a certain event occurs. Table 6-2 lists the name and function of these document events.

Table 6-2	Document Events
MACRO NAME	**RUNS**
BeforeClose	Immediately before any open publication closes.
ShapesAdded	When one or more new shapes are added to a publication. This event occurs whether shapes are added manually or programmatically.
Undo	When a user undoes the last action performed.
Redo	When reversing the last action that was undone.
Open	When you open a publication containing the macro.
ShapesRemoved	When a shape is deleted from a publication.
WizardAfterChange	After the user chooses an option in the wizard pane that changes any of the following settings in the publication: page layout (page size, fold type, orientation, label product), print setup (paper size or print tiling), adding or deleting objects, adding or deleting pages, or object or page formatting (size, position, fill, border, background, default text, text formatting).

The name you use for an automatic macro depends on when you want certain actions to occur. In this project, when a Publisher user exits the Web Order Form publication, you want a message box to be displayed, reminding the user to upload the appropriate files to the Web. Thus, you will see how to create a BeforeClose macro using the Visual Basic Editor.

Using the Visual Basic Editor

The **Visual Basic Editor** is a full-screen editor, which allows you to enter a procedure by typing lines of VBA code as if you were using word processing software. VBA displays a **code window** in which you may choose document events and type code.

Because the code window is similar to a text box or word processor window, at the end of a line, you press the ENTER key or use the DOWN ARROW key to move to the next line. If you make a mistake in a code statement, you can use the ARROW keys and the DELETE or BACKSPACE keys to correct it. You also can move the insertion point to lines requiring corrections.

The following steps open the VBA coding window.

To Open the VBA Code Window

1

• **Click Tools on the menu bar and then point to Macro.**

The Tools menu and the Macro submenu are displayed (Figure 6-57).

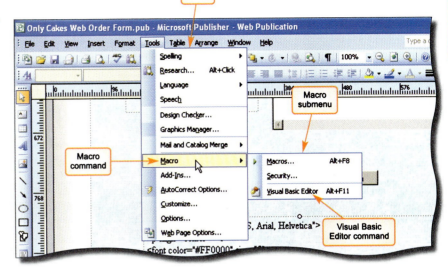

FIGURE 6-57

2

• **Click Visual Basic Editor.**

• **When the Microsoft Visual Basic window opens, if necessary, double-click the Microsoft Visual Basic title bar to maximize the window.**

• **If the Project window is not displayed, click View on the menu bar and then click Project Explorer.**

• **In the Project window, if a plus sign is displayed next to Project (Only Cakes Web Order Form), click the plus sign.**

• **If a plus sign is displayed next to Microsoft Office Publisher Objects, click the plus sign.**

• **Double-click ThisDocument.**

The code window is opened (Figure 6-58).

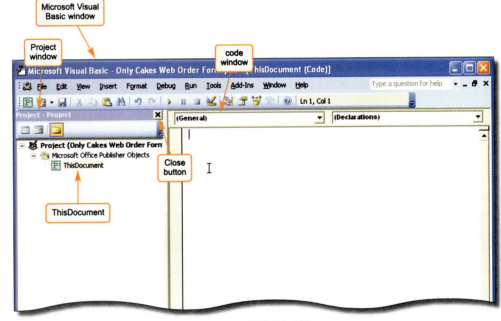

FIGURE 6-58

Other Ways

1. Press ALT+F11

The document event will apply only to the current publication. Other publications will not have access to the macro created in this publication.

More About

Message Boxes

VBA offers several intrinsic constant keywords to assist you with the buttons in message boxes, including vbOKOnly, vbOKCancel, vbYesNo, vbYesNoCancel, vbRetryCancel, and vbAbortRetryIgnore. To use these constant keywords, type a comma after the MsgBox prompt and then type the keyword.

Entering Code Statements and Comments

The BeforeClose event in the Only Cakes Web Order Form publication includes a code statement that calls a function called MsgBox. A **function** is a keyword, already programmed in VBA, which activates a procedure. The **MsgBox function** displays a message in a dialog box and then waits for the user to click a button. In its simplest forms, the code statement includes the function keyword, MsgBox, and the text that will be displayed in the message box enclosed in quotation marks. VBA programmers use a message box to display copyright information about a publication, remind users to save publications in a certain location, or let Web users know their submission was complete.

Adding comments before and within a procedure helps you remember the purpose of the macro and its code statements later. **Comments** begin with the keyword, Rem, or an apostrophe (') and are displayed in green in the code window. Comments have no effect on the execution of a procedure; they simply provide information about the procedure, such as its name and description.

The following steps show how to write a comment and code statement in the BeforeClose event. VBA provides beginning and ending code statements for document event procedures. It is common practice to indent comments and code within those statements.

To Program the BeforeClose Event

1

• **If the My Properties window is displayed, click its Close button. Click the Close button in the Project window title bar.**

• **Click the Object box arrow and then click Document in the list.**

• **Click the Procedure box arrow and then click BeforeClose in the list.**

The beginning and ending code statements for the procedures are entered (Figure 6-59). Publisher automatically displays the Open procedure, but it will have no effect on this publication.

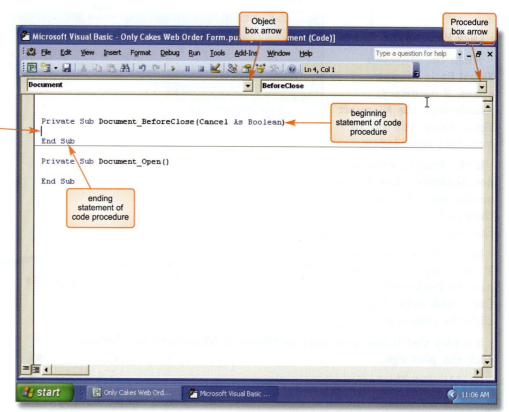

FIGURE 6-59

2

• **Press the TAB key. Type** 'When the publication closes, a reminder message box will be displayed. **and then press the** ENTER **key.**

• **Press the TAB key. Type** MsgBox "Remember to upload this file to the Web site." **to complete the code.**

The comment and code statement are entered (Figure 6-60). Pressing the TAB key indents the lines of code. The TAB key has no effect on how the code is executed; it merely aids in readability.

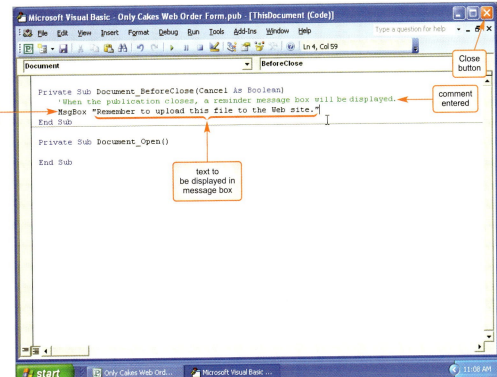

FIGURE 6-60

3

• **Click the Close button on the Microsoft Visual Basic title bar.**

The VBA window closes, and the publication is displayed again.

You can modify the procedure or event associated with any command on Publisher's menu bar or toolbar, and you can create custom toolbars, menu bars, and shortcut menus using VBA. VBA is a large programming language with an extensive Help library. To find out more about functions you can use in document events, type document events in the Type a question for help box on the right of the Microsoft Visual Basic menu bar.

Security Levels

A **computer virus** is a potentially damaging computer program designed to affect, or infect, your computer negatively by altering the way it works without your knowledge or permission. Currently, more than 80,000 known computer viruses exist, and an estimated six new viruses are discovered each day. The increased use of networks, the Internet, and e-mail has accelerated the spread of computer viruses.

To combat this evil, most computer users run antivirus programs that search for viruses and destroy them before they ever have a chance to infect the computer. Macros are a known carrier of viruses, because of the ease with which a person can write code for a macro. For this reason, you can reduce the chance your computer will be infected with a macro virus by setting a **security level** in Publisher. These security levels allow you to enable or disable macros. An **enabled macro** is a macro that Publisher will execute, and a **disabled macro** is a macro that is unavailable to Publisher.

More About

The VBA Editor

The VBA editor uses AutoComplete boxes as you type the code. When you type the beginning of a command, the VBA editor displays a prompt to help you construct the remainder of the command, complete with the type of data it expects, or a list of valid constant keywords from which you may choose.

Table 6-3 summarizes the four available security levels in Publisher.

Table 6-3 Publisher Security Levels	
SECURITY LEVEL	**CONDITION**
Very High	Publisher will execute only macros installed in trusted locations. All other signed and unsigned macros are disabled when the publication is opened.
High	Publisher will execute only macros that are digitally signed. All other macros are disabled when the publication is opened.
Medium	Upon opening a publication that contains macros from an unknown source, Publisher displays a dialog box asking if you wish to enable the macros.
Low	Publisher turns off macro virus protection. The publication is opened with all macros enabled, including those from unknown sources.

Setting Security Levels in Publisher

If Publisher security is set to very high or high and you attach a macro to a publication, Publisher will disable that macro when you open the publication. Because macros are created in this project, you should ensure that your security level is set to medium. Thus, each time you open this Publisher publication or any other document that contains a macro from an unknown source, Publisher displays a dialog box warning that a macro is attached and allows you to enable or disable the macros. If you are confident of the source (author) of the publication and macros, you should click the Enable button in the dialog box. If you are uncertain about the reliability of the source of the publication and macros, you should click the Disable button.

The following steps set Publisher's security level to medium.

To Set a Security Level in Publisher

1

• **Click Tools on the menu bar, point to Macro, and then click Security.**

• **When the Security dialog box is displayed, if necessary, click the Security Level tab.**

• **Click Medium.**

Publisher displays the Security dialog box (Figure 6-61). The Medium option button is selected.

2

• **Click the OK button.**

Publisher sets its security level to medium.

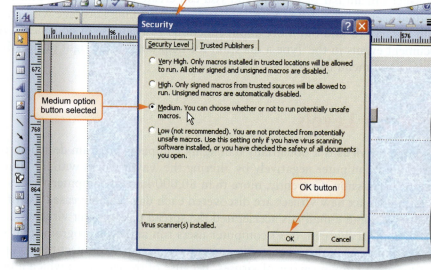

FIGURE 6-61

Other Ways

1. In Voice Command mode, say "Tools, Macro, Security, Medium, OK"

The next time you open a publication that contains a macro from an unauthorized source, Publisher will ask if you wish to enable or disable the macro with a dialog box similar to the one shown in Figure 6-62.

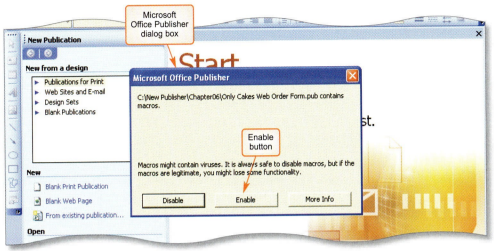

FIGURE 6-62

Checking and Saving the Publication

To complete the Web order form, the final tasks are to check for spelling and design errors, save the publication as both a Publisher publication and as a Web file, and then test the macro.

Checking for Spelling and Design Errors

Recall that Publisher's Design Checker scans the publication for overlapping errors and large graphics that may prevent the page from loading quickly on the Web.

The following steps show how to check for spelling errors, run the Design Checker, and save the publication with the same file name.

To Check the Publication and Save Again

1 Click the Spelling button on the Standard toolbar. If Publisher flags any words that are misspelled, fix them.

2 When Publisher asks to check the entire publication, click the Yes button.

3 Fix any other errors.

4 Click Tools on the menu bar and then click Design Checker. If the Design Checker identifies any errors, fix them as necessary.

5 Ignore any messages regarding the RGB mode or picture scaling.

6 Close the Design Checker task pane.

7 Click the Save button on the Standard toolbar.

The checked publication saves in the same location with the same file name.

More About

Digital Signatures

Several companies provide authenticated, certified digital signatures via the Web. When you attach a digital signature to a macro project, Publisher will display the digital signature when the user of the file is asked to enable macros.

Saving the Web Files

Saving the Web order form involves using Publisher's Publish to the Web command. Recall that this command saves the publication as a filtered Web page ready for uploading. The following steps show how to publish to the Web.

To Publish to the Web

1 Click File on the menu bar and then click Publish to the Web. If a Microsoft Publisher dialog box is displayed, reminding you about Web hosting services, click the OK button.

2 When the Save As dialog box is displayed, type OrderForm as the file name.

3 Click the Save button in the Save As dialog box. If a Microsoft Publisher dialog box is displayed, reminding you about filtered HTML, click the OK button.

The saved file is ready to send to the Web.

Talk to your instructor about making this Web site available to others on your network, intranet, or the World Wide Web (see Appendix C). The **server**, or hosting computer system, on which you store e-commerce Web pages must support Microsoft Front Page extensions, a common format for Web transactions.

After you have published to the Web, you should test your electronic form to make sure it functions as you intended and returns the form data to you. The following steps illustrate this procedure. To receive results, change the e-mail address to your own in the Form Properties dialog box (Figure 6-48 on page PUB 359).

To Check Form Controls for Accuracy

1. Use a browser to locate your Web site on the Web.
2. Enter information into several of the text boxes and click one of the option buttons.
3. Click the Reset This Form button.
4. Complete the electronic form. As you use the form, make sure the controls work as you intended.
5. Click the Submit Your Order button.
6. Verify that you received the data you entered. If you did not, contact your Internet service provider and ask about their ability to support Microsoft FrontPage server extensions, version 3.0 or above.
7. Check the data to make sure you understand the format in which the responses were returned to you.

Testing the Macro and Quitting Publisher

To test the automatic macro, you activate the event that causes the macro to execute. For example, the BeforeClose macro runs whenever you exit the Publisher publication. The following steps show the reminder message box that is displayed when the user quits Publisher.

To Test the Macro and Quit Publisher

1

• **Click the Close button on the Publisher title bar.**

The message box created by the macro is displayed (Figure 6-63).

2

• **Click the OK button in the message box.**

The Publisher window closes.

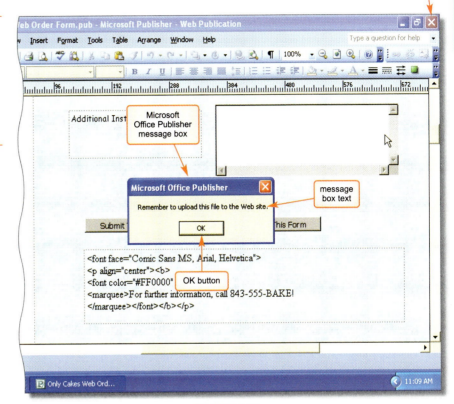

FIGURE 6-63

Project Summary

Project 6 introduced you to Web forms in Publisher. First, the project created a blank Web page and set Web page options, formatting, color and font schemes, and inserted a graphic. Next, form controls were inserted, edited, and aligned. You learned that each form control should have a unique name and a return value for submission purposes. Text boxes, text areas, check boxes, option buttons, list boxes, and command buttons were added to the interface. Then, a picture hyperlink with alternative text was created using the Only Cakes graphic. A scrolling marquee coded with HTML was displayed across the lower portion of the Web page. Finally, a message box was programmed in the publication itself, using Visual Basic for Applications. When the publication closes, the message box reminds users to upload the latest version of the Web page.

What You Should Know

Having completed this project, you should be able to perform the tasks below. The tasks are listed in the same order they were presented in this project. For a list of the buttons, menus, toolbars, and commands introduced in this project, see the Quick Reference Summary at the back of this book and refer to the Page Number column.

1. Start Publisher with a Blank Web Page   (PUB 332)
2. Set the Color and Font Schemes   (PUB 332)
3. Make Web Design Choices   (PUB 333)
4. Insert a Textured Background   (PUB 335)
5. Delete the Logo   (PUB 336)
6. Apply a Personal Information Set   (PUB 336)
7. Copy a Graphic from Another Publication (PUB 337)
8. Insert and Distribute Labels   (PUB 339)
9. Edit Text Box Labels   (PUB 342)
10. Insert Textbox Form Controls   (PUB 342)
11. Insert Checkbox Form Controls   (PUB 346)
12. Insert Option Button Form Controls (PUB 348)
13. Create Labels for the List Box Form Controls   (PUB 351)
14. Insert List Box Form Controls   (PUB 352)
15. Insert a Text Area Form Control   (PUB 356)
16. Insert Submit Button Form Controls (PUB 358)
17. Save the Publication   (PUB 361)
18. Insert a Picture Hyperlink   (PUB 362)
19. Add Alternative Text   (PUB 363)
20. Insert an HTML Code Fragment   (PUB 364)
21. Preview the Web Page   (PUB 365)
22. Open the VBA Code Window   (PUB 367)
23. Program the BeforeClose Event   (PUB 368)
24. Set a Security Level in Publisher   (PUB 370)
25. Check the Publication and Save Again (PUB 371)
26. Publish to the Web   (PUB 372)
27. Test the Macro and Quit Publisher   (PUB 373)

Learn It Online

Instructions: To complete the Learn It Online exercises, start your browser, click the Address bar, and then enter the Web address scsite.com/pub2003/learn. When the Publisher 2003 Learn It Online page is displayed, follow the instructions in the exercises below. Each exercise has instructions for printing your results, either for your own records or for submission to your instructor.

1 Project Reinforcement TF, MC, and SA

Below Publisher Project 6, click the Project Reinforcement link. Print the quiz by clicking Print on the File menu for each page. Answer each question.

2 Flash Cards

Below Publisher Project 6, click the Flash Cards link and read the instructions. Type 20 (or a number specified by your instructor) in the Number of playing cards text box, type your name in the Enter your Name text box, and then click the Flip Card button. When the flash card is displayed, read the question and then click the ANSWER box arrow to select an answer. Flip through Flash Cards. If your score is 15 (75%) correct or greater, click Print on the File menu to print your results. If your score is less than 15 (75%) correct, then redo this exercise by clicking the Replay button.

3 Practice Test

Below Publisher Project 6, click the Practice Test link. Answer each question, enter your first and last name at the bottom of the page, and then click the Grade Test button. When the graded practice test is displayed on your screen, click Print on the File menu to print a hard copy. Continue to take practice tests until you score 80% or better.

4 Who Wants To Be a Computer Genius?

Below Publisher Project 6, click the Computer Genius link. Read the instructions, enter your first and last name at the bottom of the page, and then click the PLAY button. When your score is displayed, click the PRINT RESULTS link to print a hard copy.

5 Wheel of Terms

Below Publisher Project 6, click the Wheel of Terms link. Read the instructions, and then enter your first and last name and your school name. Click the PLAY button. When your score is displayed, right-click the score and then click Print on the shortcut menu to print a hard copy.

6 Crossword Puzzle Challenge

Below Publisher Project 6, click the Crossword Puzzle Challenge link. Read the instructions, and then enter your first and last name. Click the SUBMIT button. Work the crossword puzzle. When you are finished, click the Submit button. When the crossword puzzle is redisplayed, click the Print Puzzle button to print a hard copy.

7 Tips and Tricks

Below Publisher Project 6, click the Tips and Tricks link. Click a topic that pertains to Project 6. Right-click the information and then click Print on the shortcut menu. Construct a brief example of what the information relates to in Publisher to confirm you understand how to use the tip or trick.

8 Newsgroups

Below Publisher Project 6, click the Newsgroups link. Click a topic that pertains to Project 6. Print three comments.

9 Expanding Your Horizons

Below Publisher Project 6, click the Articles for Microsoft Publisher link. Click a topic that pertains to Project 6. Print the information. Construct a brief example of what the information relates to in Publisher to confirm you understand the contents of the article.

10 Search Sleuth

Below Publisher Project 6, click the Search Sleuth link. To search for a term that pertains to this project, select a term below the Project 6 title and then use the Google search engine at google.com (or any major search engine) to display and print two Web pages that present information on the term.

11 Publisher Online Training

Below Publisher Project 6, click the Publisher Online Training link. When your browser displays the Microsoft Office Online Web page, click the Publisher link. Click one of the Publisher courses that covers one or more of the objectives listed at the beginning of the project on page PUB 330. Print the first page of the course before stepping through it.

12 Office Marketplace

Below Publisher Project 6, click the Office Marketplace link. When your browser displays the Microsoft Office Online Web page, click the Office Marketplace link. Click a topic that relates to Publisher. Print the first page.

Apply Your Knowledge

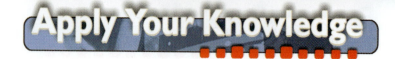

1 Working with Form Controls

Instructions: Start Publisher. Open the publication, Apply 6-1, on the Data Disk. See the inside back cover for instructions for downloading the Data Disk or see your instructor for information on accessing the files required in this book. The publication is a Web page order form for a swimming pool store. You are to insert a masthead, a graphic with a picture hyperlink and alternative text, and form controls as described below to create an electronic form. The completed form is shown in Figure 6-64.

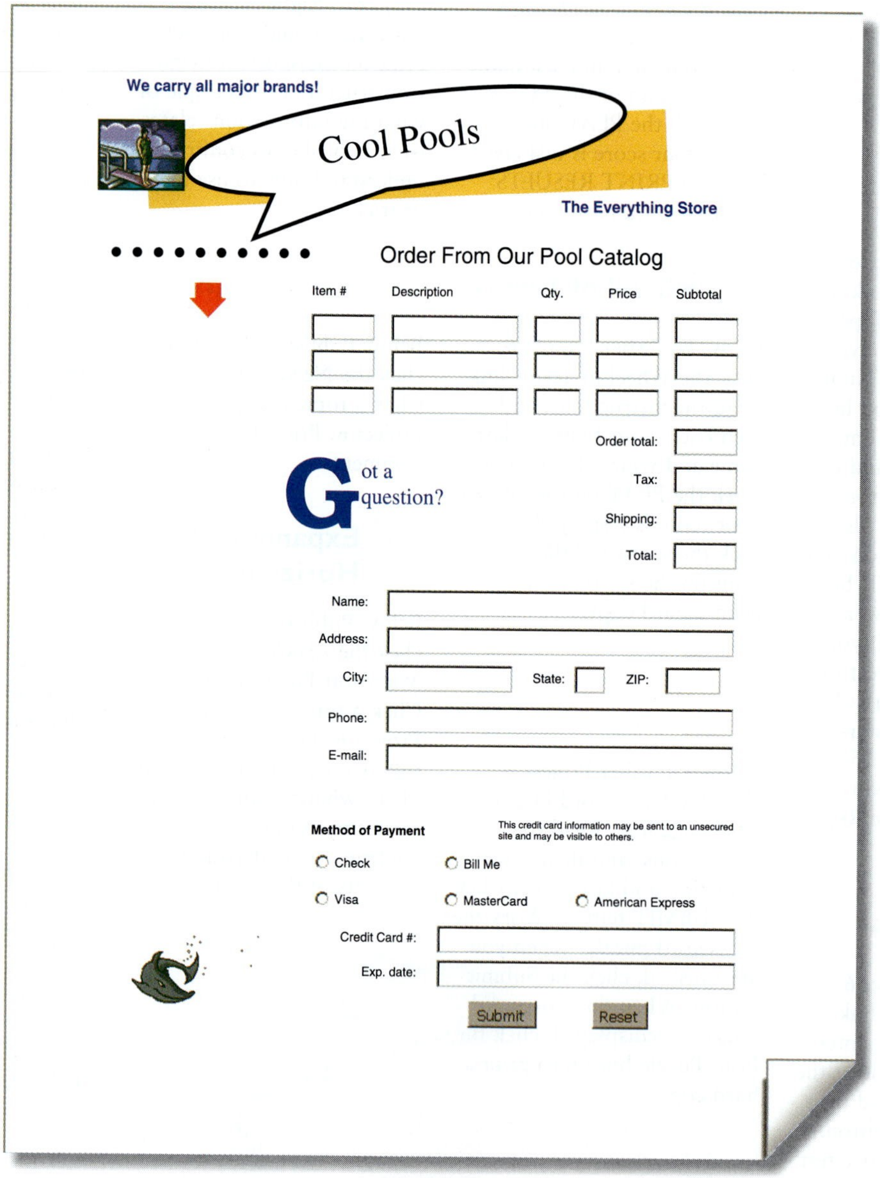

FIGURE 6-64

Apply Your Knowledge

Perform the following tasks:

1. With the Apply 6-1 publication, click the Design Gallery button on the Objects toolbar. Click Web Mastheads in the Categories list and then insert the Bubbles Masthead at the top of the publication. Triple-click each text box in the masthead individually, and edit the text to match Figure 6-64.

2. Ungroup the masthead by pressing CTRL+SHIFT+G. Delete the graphic. Use the Insert Clip Art task pane to insert a new graphic similar to the one in Figure 6-64. Insert another graphic of your choice lower on the page.

3 Right-click the graphic and then click Format Picture. On the Web tab, insert alternative text describing the picture. Do the same for the graphic in the lower portion of the page.

4. Select the graphic in the lower portion of the page and press CTRL+K to insert an e-mail hyperlink so that users who click the graphic can send an e-mail to webmaster@coolpools.com. Type Web Site Form Response as the subject of the e-mail.

5. Use the Align or Distribute command on the Arrange menu to align any controls that seem out of alignment.

6. Double-click the Credit Card # Textbox form control. When the Properties dialog box is displayed, click to select the check box that hides sensitive text with asterisks. Do the same for the expiration date.

7. Use the Form Control button on the Objects toolbar to insert a Submit button and a Reset button at the bottom of the page. Use the Align or Distribute command on the Arrange menu to align the two command buttons along their top edges. Double-click the Submit button and then click the Form Properties button. Have the data sent to the same e-mail address and use the same subject line as the picture hyperlink in Step 4.

8. Run the Design Checker. If errors occur, click the Explain button and follow the instructions to fix the error. If a dialog box is displayed asking you to check the publication for its ability to download quickly, click the Yes button.

9. Make sure you have a floppy disk with adequate free space in drive A. On the File menu, click Publish to the Web and select 3½ Floppy (A:) in the Save in list. Type Apply 6-1 Pool Order Form in the File name text box and then click the Save button in the Save as Web Page dialog box.

10. Click the Print button on the Standard toolbar. Turn in the printed copy to your instructor.

1 Creating a Web Order Form

Problem: The Textbook Connection is a bookstore located on a local college campus. They would like a Web order form for students to order textbooks online as shown in Figure 6-65. Data should be collected about the student including name, address, telephone number, and credit card information. Also include option buttons for delivery or pick-up and a text area where students can list their course numbers or the names of the books they wish to purchase.

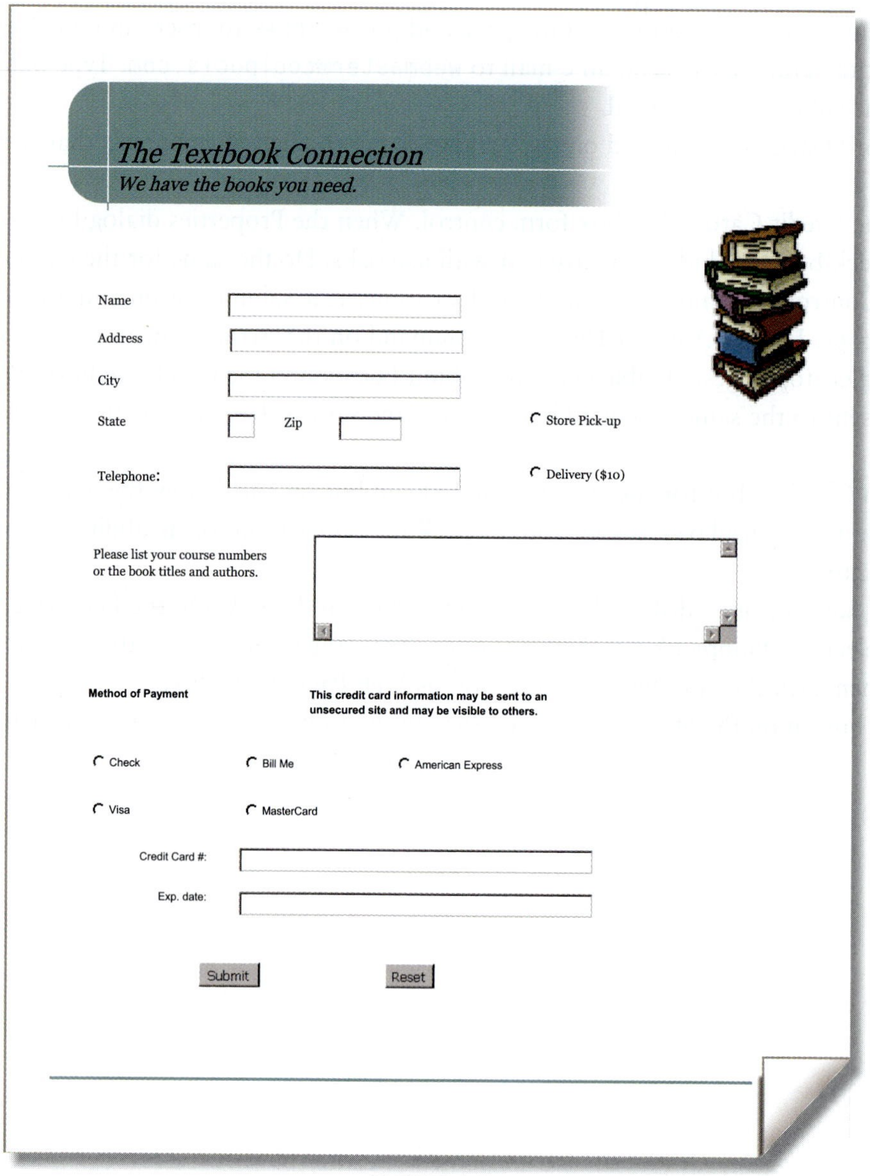

FIGURE 6-65

Instructions: Perform the following tasks with a computer:

1. Start Publisher with a blank Web publication.
2. In the Publications Design task pane, choose the Crisscross design.
3. Click Colors Schemes and then click Waterfall in the Apply a color scheme list.
4. Click Font Schemes and then click Impact in the Apply a font scheme list.
5. Click Page Content and then click Background fill and sound.
6. Click More backgrounds. When the Fill Effects dialog box is displayed, click the Texture tab and then select the Parchment texture.
7. In the masthead, click the text in the Organization Name Text Box and then type `The Textbook Connection` to replace the text.
8. Select the text in the Tag Line text box and then type `We have the books you need.` as the new tag line.
9. Right-click the logo and then click Delete Object on the shortcut menu. Click Insert on the menu bar and then click Picture. When the Clip Art task pane is displayed, type `book` in the Search box. Click the Results should be box arrow and remove check marks until only the Movies check box is selected. Click the Go button. Choose a graphic similar to the one shown in Figure 6-65.
10. In the upper half of the Web page, create text box labels for Name, Address, City, State, Zip, and Telephone. Position them as shown in Figure 6-65. Create a Textbox form control to accompany each of the labels. Resize the form controls and place them appropriately. One at a time, double-click each form control and set the return data label to be the same as the accompanying label. Align and distribute the controls as necessary.
11. To the right of the form controls and labels, create two option buttons. Change the label text on the first option button to read `Store Pick-up`. Change the label text on the second option button to `Delivery ($10)`. One at a time, double-click each option button and set the return data label to the word `Service`. Set the option button value to be the same as the accompanying label. Align and distribute the controls as necessary.
12. Below the previously inserted form controls, create a text box with the words `Please list your course numbers or the book titles and authors.` and then position and resize as necessary. Create a Text Area form control. Move it to the location shown in Figure 6-65 and resize as necessary. Double-click the text area, and set the return data label to `Book_Information`.
13. Below the previously inserted form controls, create a text box with the words, `Method of Payment`. Create another text box with the words, `This credit card information may be sent to an unsecured site and may be visible to others.`
14. Next, create five option buttons with the following labels:
    - Check
    - Bill Me
    - American Express
    - Visa
    - MasterCard

    One at a time, double-click each option button and set the return data label to the word `Payment`. Set the option button value to be the same as the accompanying label. Align and distribute the controls as necessary.

(continued)

Creating a Web Order Form *(continued)*

15. Create two more text boxes with the words, `Credit Card #:` and `Exp. date:`. Create accompanying Textbox form controls with return data labels that match the text boxes. Move, resize, align, and distribute to resemble Figure 6-65 on page PUB 378.
16. Finally, create a Submit button that sends data to your e-mail address, and a Reset button to clear the form.
17. Check the publication for spelling and design errors. Preview the publication using the Web Page Preview button on the Standard toolbar.
18. Save the publication with the file name, Lab 6-1, and then print a copy.
19. Publish the publication to the Web.

2 Creating a Web Page with Picture Hyperlinks and HTML Code Fragments

Problem: Your friend, Fred Jones, has asked you to make a family home page for him, as shown in Figure 6-66. He wants to include pictures of his wife and children, a background sound, and a scrolling marquee at the top. He has friends and co-workers who routinely use screen readers, so he also has asked you to include alternative text. The hyperlink information, alternative text, and caption are displayed in Table 6-4.

Table 6-4   Data for Picture Hyperlinks and Alternative Text

PICTURE	HYPERLINK INFORMATION	ALTERNATIVE TEXT	CAPTION
baby	http://www.jonesfamily.com/~deanna	This is a picture of baby Deanna. Click here to see more.	Click Deanna's picture to see more cute poses.
corn	http://www.jonesfamily.com/~paul	This is a picture of 5-year-old Paul in the cornfield. Click here to see more.	Paul can attest to last year's bumper crop. Click the picture to see more.
fish	helen@jonesfamily.com	This is a picture of Helen holding a fish. Click here to send her an e-mail.	Click the picture to send Helen your own fish stories.

Instructions: Perform the following tasks with a computer:

1. Start Publisher with a blank Web publication.
2. In the Publications Design task pane, click No Design.
3. Click Page Content and then click Background fill and sound. Click More backgrounds. In the Fill Effects dialog box, click the Texture tab, and then click Canvas.
4. Click the Other Task Panes button on the title bar of the task pane and then click Page Content. Scroll down and click More Web Page Options in the task pane. In the Web Page Options dialog box, type `The Jones Family Home Page` in the Page title box. Type `index` in the File name box. Type `This is the home page of the Jones family.` in the Description box. Type `Deanna, Paul, Helen, Fred Jones Des Moines Iowa` in the Keywords box.
5. Click the Browse button and then select the SWEST_01.MID sound file or other suitable sound on your system. Click the OK button to close the Web Page Options dialog box.

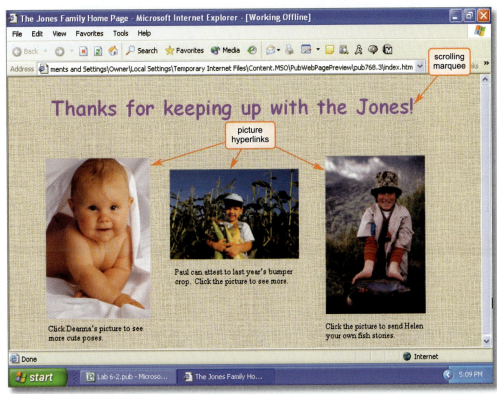

FIGURE 6-66

6. Click the HTML Code Fragment button on the Objects toolbar. When the Edit HTML Code Fragment window opens, type the following code:

```
<font face="Comic Sans MS, Arial, Helvetica">
<p align="left"><b>
<font color="#9933CC" size="6">
<marquee>Thanks for keeping up with the Jones!
</marquee></font></b></p>
```

7. Click the OK button and then drag the HTML Code Fragment object to the top of the page approximately ¼ inch from the top. Drag the left handle to approximately ½ inch from the left side of the page. Drag the right handle to approximately ½ inch from the right side of the page.

8. Click Insert on the menu bar point to Picture, and then click Clip Art. When the Clip Art task pane is displayed, type children in the Search box. Click the Results should be of type box arrow and then remove check marks until only Photographs is selected. Click the Go button. Select a picture of a baby similar to the one shown in Figure 6-66. Drag the picture to just below the HTML Code Fragment and align it on the left side.

9. Click the publication so the picture is not selected, and then scroll to select another picture in the Clip Art task pane, similar to the picture of the boy holding corn in Figure 6-66. Drag the picture to the center of the publication, approximately ½ inch below the HTML Code Fragment.

10. Click the publication so the picture is not selected, and then scroll to select another picture in the Clip Art task pane, similar to the picture of the fish in Figure 6-66. Drag the picture to the right side of the publication, directly below the HTML Code Fragment.

(continued)

Creating a Web Page with Picture Hyperlinks and HTML Code Fragments *(continued)*

11. One at a time, select each picture and press CTRL+K to create a picture hyperlink. Enter the information from Table 6-4 on page PUB 380.

12. One at a time, right-click each picture and then click Format Picture. Click the Web tab and then enter the alternative text from Table 6-4.

13. Check the publication for spelling and design errors. Preview the publication using the Web Page Preview button.

14. Save the publication with the file name, Lab 6-2, and then print a copy.

15. Publish the publication to the Web.

3 Adding VBA Procedures to a Publication

Problem: The Only Cakes bakery would like to add a copyright notice to one of its previous publications. The owner now has asked you to insert a copyright message box each time the publication is opened, as shown in Figure 6-67a. The message box should display the information icon that is represented in VBA by the code, vbInformation. The title bar of the message should contain the name of the business. Table 6-5 lists the code and its purpose to create a copyright message box.

Table 6-5 VBA Code for a Copyright Message Box	
VBA CODE	**PURPOSE**
'When the publication opens, a copyright message box will be displayed.	Comment
MsgBox "This publication is copyrighted by Only Cakes.", vbInformation, "Only Cakes Bakery"	Function to display message box prompt, icon, title bar caption

She also wants to warn any employees who edit the publication of accidental deletions (Figure 6-67b). Table 6-6 displays the code and its purpose to create a message box that will be displayed when an object in the publication is deleted.

Table 6-6 VBA Code for a Warning Message Box	
VBA CODE	**PURPOSE**
'When a user deletes an object in the publication, a confirmation message box will be displayed.	Comment
Dim intResponse As Integer	Declares a storage location for the user's response
intResponse = MsgBox("Do you really want to delete this object?", vbYesNo)	Function to display message box prompt and two command buttons
If intResponse = vbNo Then Publisher.ActiveDocument.Undo	Tests to see if the user clicked the No button and then calls the Undo button procedure

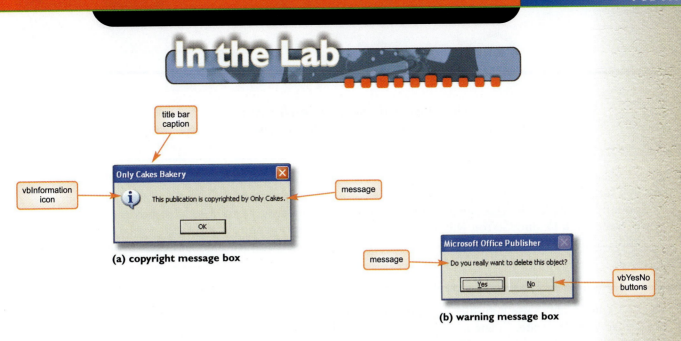

(a) copyright message box

(b) warning message box

FIGURE 6-67

Instructions: Perform the following tasks with a computer:

1. Start Publisher and open the Only Cakes Web Order Form or any of your previous publications.
2. Press ALT+F11 to open the Visual Basic Editor window.
3. If necessary, click the plus sign next to Project (Only Cakes Web Order Form) and then click the plus sign next to Microsoft Office Publisher Objects. Double-click ThisDocument.
4. Click the Close button on the Project window title bar.
5. Click the Object box arrow and then click Document in the list.
6. Click the Procedure box arrow and then click Open.
7. Enter the code from Table 6-5, pressing the TAB key at the beginning of each line.
8. Click the Procedure box arrow and then click ShapesRemoved.
9. Enter the code from Table 6-6, pressing the TAB key at the beginning of each line.
10. Click File on the menu bar and then click Print. Retrieve the printout and check your code for accuracy.
11. Click the Close button in the Microsoft Visual Basic window.
12. Click Tools on the menu bar, point to Macro, and then click Security. When the Security dialog box is displayed, if necessary, click Medium to select it, and then click the OK button.
13. Save the publication with the file name, Lab 6-3. Test the two macro events by quitting Publisher and reopening the publication. When the Microsoft Office Publisher dialog box is displayed warning you of possible macro viruses, click the Enable button. When Publisher displays the information dialog box, click the OK button.
14. Delete an object in the publication. When Publisher displays the message box, click the No button.

Cases and Places

The difficulty of these case studies varies: ■ are the least difficult and ■■ are more difficult. The last exercise is a group exercise.

1 ■ Casey's Model Train Shop is looking to increase its business with online sales. Casey has asked you for help. He would like you to design a Web order form for out-of-town customers. Use grouped option buttons for diesel or steam engines and freight or passenger cars. Use a list box for train sizes of N-Scale, HO, O, and G. You will need to create Textbox form controls and labels for customer name, address, telephone, and credit card number. Make sure the credit card number displays with asterisks.

2 ■ You decide to use Publisher to create form controls to collect information about people who have visited your Web site. Create a Web page with a background texture of your choice; a scrolling marquee that reads, Welcome to My Home Page; and a graphic with alternative text. Include Textbox form controls for the visitor's name and e-mail address. Make sure to set the return data labels for the text boxes. Include a submit button that sends data to you in an e-mail and a reset button.

3 ■■ Choose any publication you previously have created from scratch and add a message box when the publication opens. Use Visual Basic for Applications to program a MsgBox function for the Open document event. Code the message box to say, This publication was created by, and then insert your name. Be sure to include a comment in the code.

4 ■■ Craig Doakes is the city planner for Greendale. A new city growth plan has been announced, and pro- and anti-plan groups have flooded his office with responses. Craig wants an online form that people can fill out and submit with their views on specific topics. Specifically, Craig wants sets of grouped option buttons so once a choice is made on one topic the others are closed, thus giving a clear-cut response. Create a set named Schools that includes options to use existing schools, expand existing schools, or build new schools. Create a set named Economics that includes options to build new strip malls, build individual businesses, or no new buildings. Create a set named Parks that includes an option to build new parks, expand existing parks, or no expansion of parks. Make sure to use appropriate data return labels. Include a Submit button.

5 ■■ **Working Together** Microsoft Publisher is a popular solution to desktop publishing needs. Other software is available, however, for preparing everything from greeting cards to book publication film. Several products exist for desktop publishing, such as QuarkXPress, Adobe Acrobat, and Print Shop; and products such as Microsoft FrontPage and Macromedia Director create interactive kiosks and Web pages. Surf the Internet for pages that display a creation product logo. Compare Publisher's Web form controls to those of some other popular Web creation products and then use Publisher to write a report about your findings. Include a table that lists popular controls as columns and the products as rows.

MICROSOFT
Office Publisher 2003

Linking a Publisher Publication to an Excel Worksheet

CASE PERSPECTIVE

Quinton Emery, director of sales and marketing for Jacob's Jackets, Ltd., sends out a memo to all sales staff showing the latest quarterly report of sales for the company. He currently uses Publisher to produce the memo and then attaches a table of the quarterly figures that he creates in Excel. The wording in the memo remains constant while the table of sales and returns changes each quarter.

Quinton recently heard of the object linking and embedding (OLE) capabilities of Microsoft Office 2003. He wants to use it to create the basic memo, first using Publisher to create the memo form (Figure 1a on the next page), and then linking the quarterly earnings from an Excel worksheet (Figure 1b). Each quarter, he envisions distributing the publication with the updated worksheet (Figure 1c). Once the link is established, he can update the worksheet, then print the report or send it electronically as an attachment.

As Quinton's technical assistant, he has asked you to handle the details of linking the Excel quarterly report to the Publisher sales memo. Quinton will send you the individual files. You then can experiment with differences in linking and embedding. You suggest to Quinton that he also might want to consider publishing the report on the company's intranet.

As you read this Special Feature, you will learn how to use object linking and embedding (OLE) — a powerful tool to incorporate many types of documents within your Publisher publications. You will learn how to import an Excel worksheet into a Publisher publication as a link so it updates each time the publication is opened. Then you will learn how to import a worksheet as a one-time embedded object. Additionally, you will learn how to edit the embedded or linked portion of the publication. Finally, you will learn how to print a publication that uses OLE.

Objectives

You will have mastered the material in this project when you can:
- Understand object linking and embedding (OLE)
- Link an Excel worksheet to a Publisher publication
- Print and save a publication containing a linked worksheet
- Edit a linked worksheet
- Embed an Excel worksheet in a Publisher publication
- Edit an embedded worksheet
- Save a publication containing an embedded worksheet

Introduction

With Microsoft Office 2003, you can incorporate parts of files or entire files called objects from one application into another application. In Project 2, you learned how to import a text file from Microsoft Word into Publisher. This project shows how to copy a worksheet created in Excel into a Publisher publication. In this case, the worksheet in Excel is called the **source document** (copied from), and the publication in Publisher is called the **destination document** (copied to). Figure 1a on the next page shows the Publisher publication before OLE. Figure 1b shows the Excel worksheet source document. The publication with the copied worksheet is displayed in Figure 1c.

Copying specific objects between applications can be accomplished in one of three ways: (1) copy and paste, (2) copy and embed, and (3) copy and link. All of the Microsoft Office 2003 applications allow you to use these three methods to copy objects between applications. The first method uses the Copy and Paste buttons on the Standard toolbar. The latter two use the Paste Special command on the Edit menu with **object linking and embedding** (**OLE**).

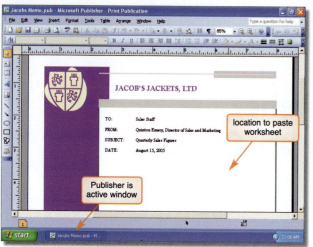

(a) Publisher publication

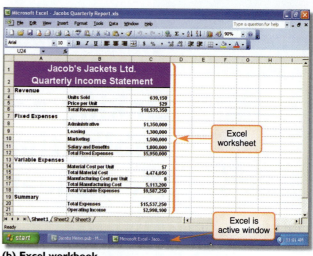

(b) Excel workbook

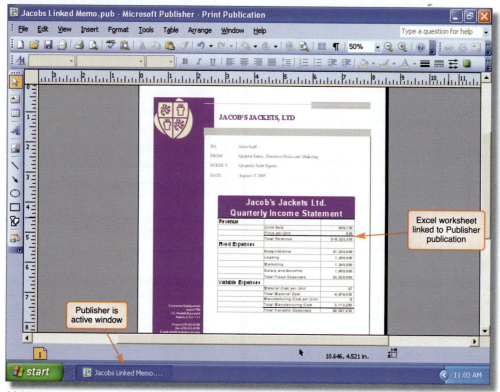

(c) Linked memo

FIGURE 1

You would use copy and paste when you want a static, or unchanging, copy of an object in two different documents. For example, a pie chart of last year's sales probably is not going to change; thus, if you paste it into a Publisher brochure about the company's sales history, it will look the same each time you open the publication. Copy and paste is easy to do across applications.

You would use the copy and embed method when you want the ability to edit the object in its destination location. For example, if someone sends you a table of figures that you would like to use in an expense report created with Publisher, you can embed it into Publisher, retaining the ability to edit some of the numbers and recalculate the totals. When you edit an embedded object, the source application software allows you to use its features; however, when you save the file, the changes are reflected in the destination publication only.

You would use the copy and link method over the other two methods when an object is likely to change and you want to make sure the object reflects the changes in both the source and destination documents. For example, suppose you link a portion or all of an Excel worksheet to a Publisher investment statement and update the worksheet quarterly in Excel. With linked documents, any time you open the investment statement in Publisher, the latest update of the worksheet will be displayed as part of the investment statement; in other words, you always have the latest data. You also might use the copy and link method when the copied object is large, such as a video clip or sound clip, because only one copy of the object is stored on disk when you link.

Table 1 summarizes the differences between the three methods.

Table 1 Copying between Applications	
METHOD	**CHARACTERISTICS**
Copy and paste	Source publication becomes part of destination publication. Object can be edited, but the editing features are limited to those in the destination application. An Excel worksheet becomes a Publisher table. If changes are made to values in the Publisher table, any original Excel formulas are not recalculated. Publisher objects become pictures when pasted into Excel worksheets.
Copy and embed	Source publication becomes part of the destination publication. Object can be edited in destination application using source-editing features. Excel worksheet remains a worksheet in Publisher. If changes are made to values on the worksheet within Publisher, Excel formulas will be recalculated, but the changes are not updated in the Excel worksheet in the workbook on disk. If you use Excel to change values on the worksheet, the changes will not show in the Publisher publication the next time you open it.
Copy and link	Source publication does not become part of destination publication even though it is displayed. Rather, a link is established between the two publications so that when you open the Publisher publication, the worksheet is displayed as part of it. When you attempt to edit a linked worksheet in Publisher, the system activates Excel. If you change the worksheet in Excel, the changes will show in the Publisher publication the next time you open it. When copying from Publisher to Excel, a link becomes an icon on the worksheet.

Moving objects from Publisher into other applications deserves special consideration. Text boxes paste, embed, and link in a manner similar to Microsoft Word documents; that is, they are treated as text. Tables paste, embed, and link in a manner similar to Microsoft Excel worksheets. Other objects paste as pictures or link as icons. The embed option typically is not available when moving grouped objects from Publisher into another application.

Most Office applications also provide a method for copying entire files from one application to another. On the Insert menu, the Object command gives you the same linking or embedding options as discussed above, but extends the connection to a wider array of file types.

Linking an Excel Worksheet to a Publisher Publication

The following pages discuss how to link an Excel worksheet to a Publisher publication so that the publication updates automatically after the worksheet is edited. Both of the files you will use in this project, the Publisher publication (Jacobs Memo.pub) and the Excel workbook (Jacobs Quarterly Report.xls), are on the Data Disk. If you did not download the Data Disk, see the inside back cover for instructions for downloading the Data Disk or see your instructor.

Starting Publisher and Excel

The first step in linking the Excel worksheet to the Publisher publication is to open both the publication in Publisher and the workbook in Excel, as shown in the following steps.

To Start Publisher and Excel

1

• **Insert the Data Disk in drive A. Click the Start button on the Windows taskbar, point to All Programs on the Start menu, point to Microsoft Office on the All Programs submenu, and then click Microsoft Office Publisher 2003 on the Microsoft Office submenu.**

• **Click the Open button on the Standard toolbar.**

• **When the Open Publication dialog box is displayed, if necessary, click 3½ Floppy (A:) in the Look in list. Double-click the Integration Feature folder.**

• **Double-click the file name, Jacobs Memo.**

Publisher starts and the Jacobs Memo is displayed in Whole Page view (Figure 2).

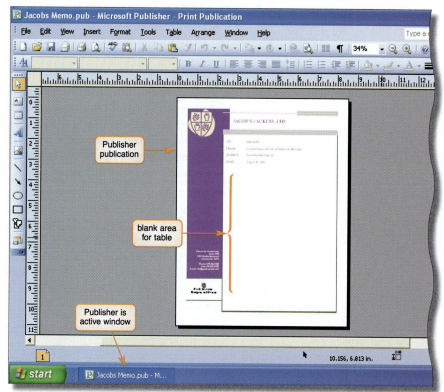

FIGURE 2

2

- Click the Start button on the Windows taskbar, point to All Programs on the Start menu, point to Microsoft Office on the All Programs submenu, and then click Microsoft Office Excel 2003 on the Microsoft Office submenu.

- Click the Open button on the Standard toolbar.

- When the Open dialog box is displayed, if necessary, click 3½ Floppy (A:) in the Look in list.

- Double-click the Integration Feature folder. Double-click the file name, Jacobs Quarterly Report.

Excel starts and the Jacobs Quarterly Report workbook is displayed (Figure 3). At this point, Publisher is inactive, but still is in main memory. Excel now is the active window, as shown on the taskbar.

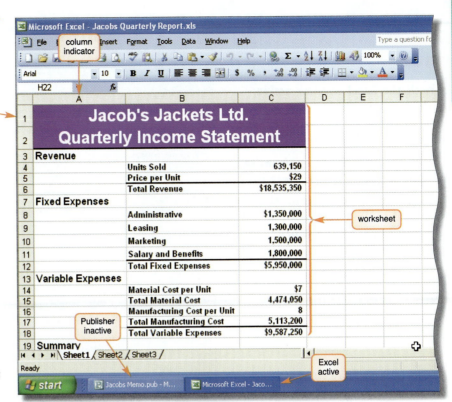

FIGURE 3

Other Ways

1. In Explorer window, double-click file name

With both Publisher and Excel in main memory, you can switch between the applications by clicking the appropriate button on the taskbar. The next step saves the worksheet with a new name in preparation for linking.

To Save the Worksheet with a New File Name

1 Click the Microsoft Excel button on the taskbar. With your floppy disk in drive A, click File on the menu bar and then click Save As. If necessary, click the Save in box arrow and then click 3½ Floppy (A:) in the list. Type the file name Jacobs Updated Quarterly Report in the File name box. Click the Save button in the Save As dialog box.

Publisher saves the worksheet on your floppy disk with the file name, Jacobs Updated Quarterly Report.

Linking an Excel Worksheet

Linking means pasting a copy of a source document into a destination document, establishing a permanent link. When linked objects are edited, changes affect both documents.

The Jacobs Quarterly Report needs to be linked with the Jacobs Memo. With both applications running, the next step in this Special Feature is to link the Excel worksheet to the Publisher publication. The Excel cell references in the steps on the next page represent the intersection of the column (indicated by a capital letter) and the row (indicated by a number).

To Link an Excel Worksheet to a Publisher Publication

1

• **With the Excel window active, click the Zoom box on the Standard toolbar, type** 90 **as the entry, and then press the ENTER key.**

• **Drag through the range from cell A1 through cell C21 to select it.**

• **Click the Copy button on the Standard toolbar to place the selected range on the Office Clipboard.**

Excel displays a marquee around the range of cells A1 through C21 (Figure 4).

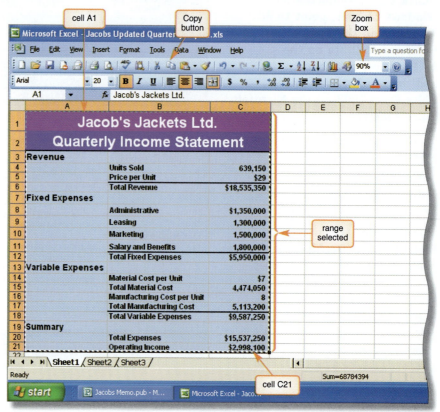

FIGURE 4

2

• **Click the Jacobs Memo button on the taskbar to activate the Publisher window.**

• **Click Edit on the menu bar.**

The Jacobs Memo publication and the Edit menu are displayed on the screen (Figure 5).

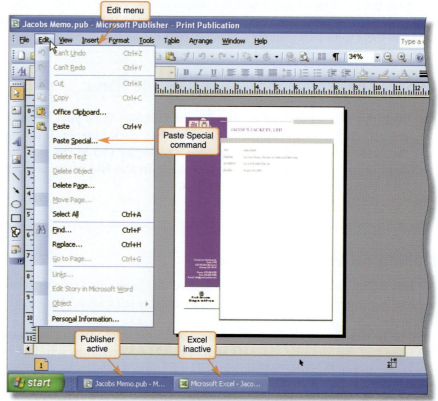

FIGURE 5

Publisher Integration Feature

3

- **Click Paste Special.**

- **When the Paste Special dialog box is displayed, click Paste Link. If necessary, click Microsoft Excel Worksheet Object Link in the As box.**

The Paste Special dialog box is displayed (Figure 6).

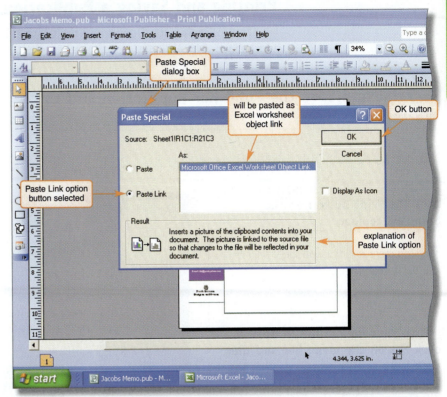

FIGURE 6

4

- **Click the OK button.**

- **If necessary, when the table is inserted, drag it to an open space in the publication.**

- **Click the Zoom In button on the Standard toolbar twice to increase the magnification.**

The range of cells A1 through C21 of the worksheet is displayed in the Publisher publication (Figure 7).

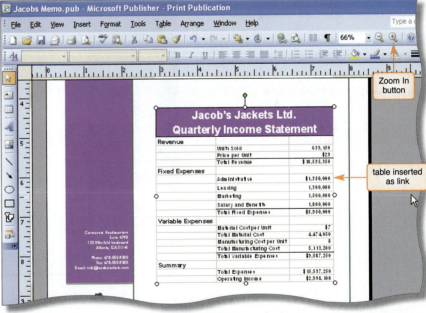

FIGURE 7

The Excel worksheet now is linked to the Publisher publication. If you save the Publisher publication and reopen it, the worksheet will be displayed just as it is in Figure 7. If you want to delete the worksheet, select it and then press the DELETE key.

Other Ways

1. On Insert menu click Object, click Create from File, click Link, browse to file, click OK

Printing and Saving a Publication with a Linked Worksheet

The following steps print and then save the Publisher publication with the linked worksheet.

To Print and Save the Publisher Publication and the Linked Worksheet

1

• **With the Publisher window active, click the Print button on the Standard toolbar.**

The statement and the worksheet print as one publication (Figure 8).

2

• **With your floppy disk in drive A, click File on the menu bar and then click Save As. If necessary, click the Save in box arrow and then click 3½ Floppy (A:) in the list. Type the file name** Jacobs Linked Memo **in the File name box. Click the Save button in the Save As dialog box.**

Publisher saves the publication on your floppy disk with the file name, Jacobs Linked Memo.

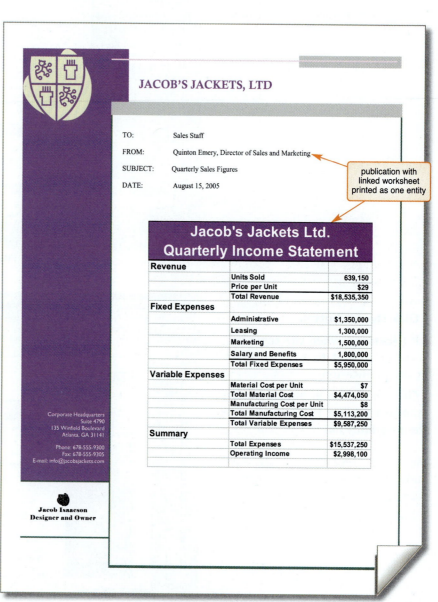

publication with linked worksheet printed as one entity

FIGURE 8

If you exit both applications and reopen Jacobs Linked Memo, the worksheet will be displayed in the publication even though Excel is not running. Because Publisher supports object linking and embedding (OLE), it can display the linked portion of the Excel worksheet without Excel running.

The next section illustrates what happens when you edit the linked worksheet while Publisher is active.

Editing a Linked Worksheet

You can edit any of the cells on the worksheet while it is displayed as part of the Publisher publication. To edit the worksheet in Publisher, double-click it. If Excel is running in main memory, the system will switch to it and display the linked workbook and its worksheet. If Excel is not running, the system will start Excel automatically and display the linked workbook. The following steps show how to edit the units sold (cell C4) from 639,150 to 684,123.

To Edit a Linked Worksheet

1

• **With the Publisher window and the Jacobs Linked Memo publication active, double-click the worksheet table.**

• **When the Excel window becomes active, double-click the worksheet's title bar to maximize the window.**

Windows switches from Publisher to Excel and displays the workbook, Jacobs Updated Quarterly Report.

2

• **Click cell C4 and then type** 684123 **as the new value for units sold. Click the Enter box (designated with a green check mark) in the formula bar.**

Excel recalculates all formulas in the worksheet (Figure 9).

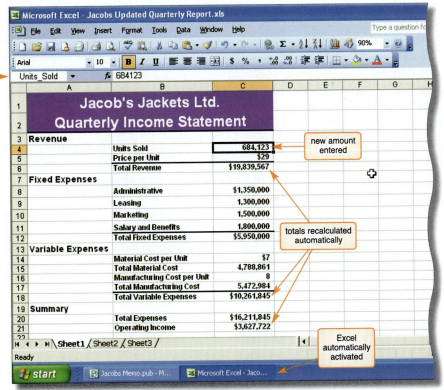

FIGURE 9

3

• **Click the Close button on the Excel window's title bar. When the Excel dialog box is displayed asking if you want to save the changes, click the Yes button.**

The Publisher window becomes active (Figure 10). The amount for units sold, which was 639,150, now is 684,123. New totals for Total Revenue, Variable Expenses, and the Summary are displayed.

4

• **On the File menu, click Close. When Publisher displays a dialog box asking if you wish to save the updates, click the Yes button.**

The Publisher file closes, but Publisher remains open and the New Publication task pane is displayed.

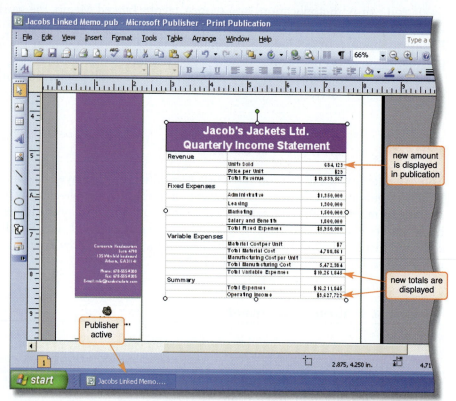

FIGURE 10

As you can see from the previous steps, you double-click a linked object when you want to edit it. Windows will activate the application and display the workbook or document from which the object originated. You then can edit the object and return to the destination application. Any changes made to the object will be displayed in the destination publication. While editing the object in the source application, you cannot edit it in the destination publication.

The edited changes to the linked worksheet became permanent when the Excel file was saved. The next time you open the publication, Publisher will verify that you wish to update the link to the Excel worksheet, thereby presenting the most current data.

Embedding an Excel Worksheet in a Publisher Publication

Embedding means using a copy of a source document in a destination document without establishing a permanent link. Embedded objects can be edited; however, changes do not affect the source document. For example, if a business embeds an Excel worksheet into their Publisher electronic newsletter that contains a what-if template, users viewing the publication in Publisher could enter their personal data into the embedded table and calculate totals. Those users would not need access to the original Excel worksheet.

Opening the Publication for Embedding

The following steps show how to open the Jacobs memo publication again, in preparation for embedding the Jacobs Quarterly Report worksheet.

To Open a Publisher Publication

1 In Publisher, click the Open button on the Standard toolbar.

2 When the Open Publication dialog box is displayed, click the Look in box arrow and then click 3½ Floppy (A:) in the list. Double-click the Integration Feature folder.

3 Double-click the file named, Jacobs Memo.

Publisher opens the memo.

Embedding an Excel Worksheet

The next steps illustrate how to embed, rather than link, the quarterly report Excel worksheet.

To Embed an Excel Worksheet in a Publisher Publication

1

• **Click Insert on the menu bar and then click Object.**

• **When the Insert Object dialog box is displayed, click Create from File.**

• **Click the Browse button.**

• **When Publisher displays the Browse dialog box, if necessary, click the Look in box arrow and then click 3½ Floppy (A:) in the list. Double-click the Integration Feature folder and then click the Jacobs Quarterly Report. Click the Open button.**

• **When the Insert Object dialog box again is displayed, do not click the Link check box.**

Publisher displays the Insert Object dialog box (Figure 11).

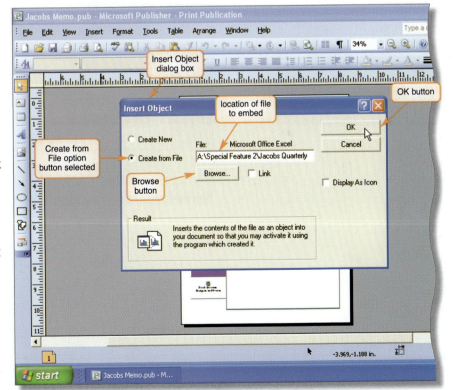

FIGURE 11

2

• **Click the OK button.**

• **When Publisher displays the worksheet in the publication, drag it to an open space in the publication.**

Publisher embeds the worksheet object.

Other Ways

1. Copy worksheet cells, paste in Publisher, do not click Link check box

Editing an Embedded Worksheet

Double-clicking most embedded objects does not start the source application; rather, a small subset of the source application — usually a toolbar or few buttons — is displayed in the destination application. The toolbar and buttons allow you to make minor edits to the object. Editing the object in Publisher does not change any saved files in the source application.

The following steps show how to edit the embedded quarterly report worksheet for Jacobs Jackets, Ltd.

To Edit an Embedded Worksheet

1

• **Click the Zoom In button on the Standard toolbar twice to increase the magnification.**

• **Double-click the embedded worksheet.**

Publisher displays the worksheet with scroll capabilities and row and column buttons (Figure 12). A formula bar is displayed in the Publisher toolbar area. Excel buttons for AutoSum, sorting, and charting appear on Publisher's Standard toolbar.

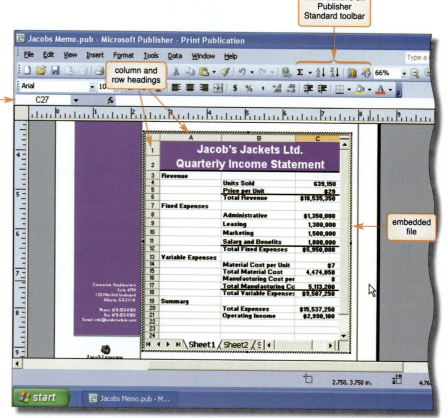

FIGURE 12

2

• **Double-click the cell containing price per unit figure (cell C5). In the formula bar, change the value 29 to 30.**

• **Click the Enter box in the formula bar.**

The end result of raising the price is displayed in the Total Revenue, as all cells are recalculated (Figure 13). The original worksheet, saved on disk, will not change.

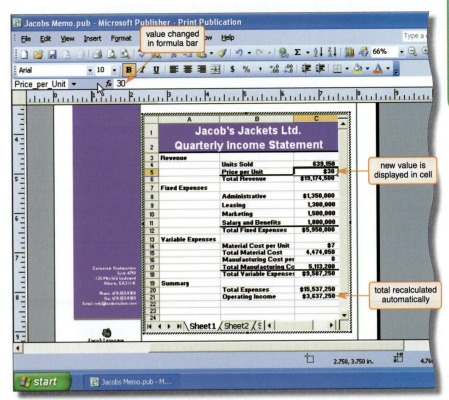

FIGURE 13

Other Ways

1. On Edit menu point to Microsoft Office Excel Worksheet Object, click Edit

When you edit an embedded object, you do not have to have the source application installed on your system. This is a tremendous advantage for Web-based publications, as users have the ability to do what-if calculations without installing Excel.

Saving a Publication with an Embedded Worksheet

The next steps save the Publisher publication containing the embedded worksheet with the file name, Jacobs Embedded Memo.

To Save a Publisher Publication with an Embedded File and Quit Publisher

1 **With your floppy disk in drive A, click File on the menu bar and then click Save As. When the Save As dialog box is displayed, type the file name Jacobs Embedded Memo in the File name box. Click the Save button in the Save As dialog box.**

2 **Click the Close button on the title bar.**

Only the Publisher publication is saved.

If you exit Publisher and re-open Jacobs Embedded Memo, the worksheet will be displayed in the publication even though Excel is not running. Because Publisher supports Object Linking and Embedding (OLE), it can display the embedded portion of the Excel worksheet without Excel running.

Special Feature Summary

This Special Feature introduced you to object linking and embedding (OLE). OLE allows you to bring together data and information that has been created using different applications. When you link an object to a publication and save it, only a link to the object is saved with the publication. You edit a linked object by double-clicking it. The system activates the application and opens the file in which the object was created. If you change any part of the object and then return to the destination publication, the updated object will display. When you embed an object in a publication, the changes you make to that object appear only in the publication. Double-clicking an embedded object causes a subset of editing commands from the destination application to display in Publisher.

What You Should Know

Having completed this project, you should be able to perform the tasks below. The tasks are listed in the same order they were presented in this project. For a list of the buttons, menus, toolbars, and commands introduced in this project, see the Quick Reference Summary at the back of this book, and refer to the Page Number column.

1. Start Publisher and Excel   (PUB 388)
2. Save the Worksheet with a New File Name (PUB 389)
3. Link an Excel Worksheet to a Publisher Publication   (PUB 390)
4. Print and Save the Publisher Publication and the Linked Worksheet   (PUB 392)
5. Edit a Linked Worksheet   (PUB 393)
6. Open a Publisher Publication   (PUB 395)
7. Embed an Excel Worksheet in a Publisher Publication   (PUB 395)
8. Edit an Embedded Worksheet   (PUB 396)
9. Save a Publisher Publication with an Embedded File and Quit Publisher   (PUB 397)

1 Linking an Investment Statement to a Report

Problem: Mildred Newhart is Director of Personnel Resources for Natural Life. She sends out a memo (Figure 14a) to all employees in the retirement program showing changes in fund balance reserves for the previous quarter. You have been asked to simplify her task by linking the balance sheet (Figure 14b) to the quarterly report memo.

Instructions: Perform the following tasks:

1. One at a time, open the publication Natural Life Memo and the workbook Natural Life Quarterly Reserves on the Data Disk.
2. In preparation for linking, use the Save As command on the File menu to save the Publisher publication with the file name Natural Life Linked Memo on your floppy disk. Save the Excel worksheet with the file name Natural Life Updated Quarterly Reserves on your floppy disk.

In the Lab

3. With the Excel workbook active, copy the range A3 through D21 from the Excel workbook.

4. Click the Publisher button on the taskbar. Use the Paste Special command on the Edit menu to link the copied range to the bottom of the Natural Life Linked Memo publication. Resize as necessary to fit the linked worksheet into the open space in the memo.

5. Print the publication.

6. Double-click the linked worksheet and use the keyboard to increase the Member contributions value from 52,451,478 to 53,135,246.

7. Close the Excel window. If Excel asks if you want to save the worksheet, click the Yes button.

8. Click the Publisher button on the taskbar again to activate Publisher, and print the publication with the new values. Close the publication and the workbook.

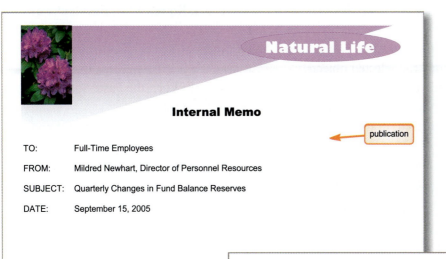

Natural Life

Internal Memo

publication

TO: Full-Time Employees

FROM: Mildred Newhart, Director of Personnel Resources

SUBJECT: Quarterly Changes in Fund Balance Reserves

DATE: September 15, 2005

(b) Excel workbook

| NATURAL LIFE CHANGES IN FUND BALANCE RESERVES | | | |
| For the Quarter Ending September 30, 2005 | | | |
	Refundable Member's Reserve	Employer's Reserve	Future Benefit Increase Reserve
Balance -- June 30, 2005	$ 395,990,517	$ 3,699,639,034	$ 746,019,685
Distribute of Revenue and Expenses			
Member contributions	52,451,478		
Employer contributions		46,890,892	
Earnings on investments		588,132,626	
Pension benefits		-145,302,173	
Refunds to terminated members	-3,480,194	-1,833,401	
Administrative expenses		-616,109	
Distribution of Transfers			
Excess investment for future benefits		-72,225,529	72,225,529
Earnings on excess		-91,835,023	91,835,023
Amount utilized by benefit increases		47,639,499	-47,639,499
Net transfers	298,995	359,437	
Balances transferred due to retirement	-26,413,782	26,413,782	
Balance -- September 30, 2005	$ 418,847,014	$ 4,097,263,035	$ 862,440,738

worksheet

(a) Publisher publication

FIGURE 14

2 Pasting a Publication into a Workbook

Problem: Mildred Newhart now has asked you to paste the Publisher publication into the Excel workbook, rather than linking the Excel workbook to the Publisher publication as was done in Exercise 1.

Instructions: Perform the following tasks:

1. One at a time, open the publication Natural Life Memo and the workbook Natural Life Quarterly Reserves on the Data Disk.
2. With the Excel window active, drag through the row numbers 1 through 20 on the left border of the worksheet to select all 20 rows. Click Insert on the menu bar and then click Rows. When the blank rows display, click cell A1.
3. Click the Publisher button on the taskbar. Click Select All on the Edit menu. Click the Copy button on Publisher's Standard toolbar to copy the selected objects.
4. Click the Excel button on the taskbar. On the Edit menu, click Paste Special. When the Paste Special dialog box is displayed, click Picture (Enhanced Metafile), and then click the OK button.
5. When the publication object is displayed, drag the picture to the upper-left corner of the worksheet and resize as necessary.
6. Save the workbook with the file name, Lab I-2 Quarterly Reserves with Memo. Print a copy. Quit Excel. Quit Publisher without saving the publication or the Clipboard contents.

3 Embedding a Worksheet

Problem: Mildred Newhart now has asked you to embed the Excel workbook into the Publisher publication, rather than linking it as you did before.

Instructions: Perform the following tasks:

1. One at a time, open the publication Natural Life Memo and the workbook Natural Life Quarterly Reserves on the Data Disk.
2. With the Excel workbook active, copy the range A3 through D21 from the Excel workbook.
3. Click the Publisher button on the taskbar. On the Edit menu, click Paste Special. When the Paste Special dialog box is displayed, click the Paste option button to embed the worksheet rather than link it. Click Microsoft Office Excel Worksheet Object in the As box. Click the OK button.
4. When the worksheet range is displayed as a table in the publication, double-click it. Notice that Excel is not linked or activated. Rather, row and column borders are displayed around the table.
5. Look at the toolbars. The Standard toolbar now displays some buttons unique to Excel. Below the Standard toolbar is an Excel Formula bar. Point to each button on the toolbars and, as their ScreenTips are displayed, make a list of their names on a piece of paper. Turn the list in to your instructor.
6. Save the publication as Lab I-3 Natural Life Embedded Report and then quit Publisher and quit Excel.

Appendix A

Microsoft Publisher Help System

Using the Publisher Help System

This appendix shows you how to use the Microsoft Publisher Help system. At any time while you are using Publisher, you can interact with its Help system and display information on any Publisher topic. It is a complete reference manual at your fingertips.

As shown in Figure A-1, five methods for accessing the Publisher Help system are available:

1. Microsoft Office Publisher Help button on the Standard toolbar
2. Microsoft Office Publisher Help command on the Help menu
3. Function key F1 on the keyboard
4. Type a question for help box on the menu bar
5. Office Assistant

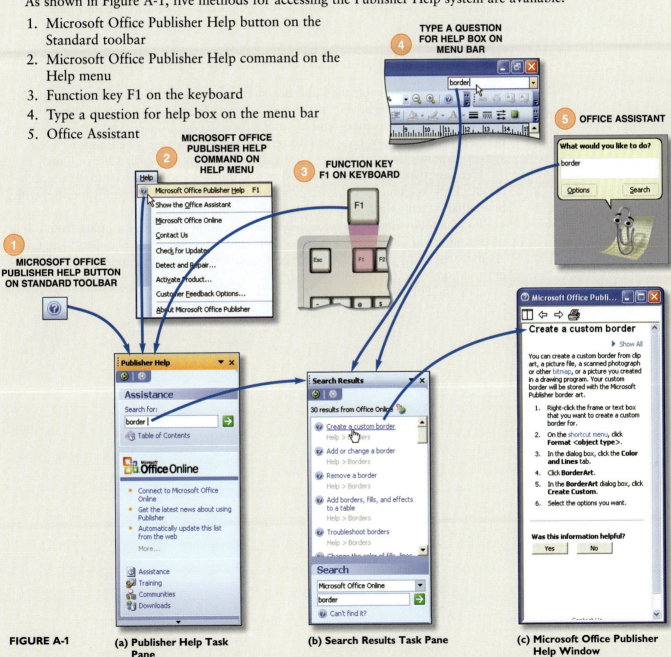

FIGURE A-1

(a) Publisher Help Task Pane

(b) Search Results Task Pane

(c) Microsoft Office Publisher Help Window

All five methods result in the Publisher Help system displaying a task pane on the left side of the Publisher window. The first three methods cause the **Publisher Help task pane** to display (Figure A-1a on the previous page). This task pane includes a Search for text box in which you can enter a word or phrase on which you want help. Once you enter the word or phrase, the Publisher Help system displays the Search Results task pane (Figure A-1b on the previous page). With the Search Results task pane displayed, you can select specific Help topics.

As shown in Figure A-1, methods 4 and 5 bypass the Publisher Help task pane and immediately display the **Search Results task pane** (Figure A-1b) with a list of links that pertain to the selected topic. Thus, the ultimate result of any of the five methods for accessing the Publisher Help system is the Search Results task pane. Once the Publisher Help system displays this task pane, you can choose links that relate to the word or phrase for which you searched. In Figure A-1, for example, border was the search topic. Clicking the Create a custom border link resulted in the Publisher Help system displaying the **Microsoft Office Publisher Help window** with information about creating custom borders (Figure A-1c on the previous page).

Navigating the Publisher Help System

The quickest way to enter the Publisher Help system is through the Type a question for help box on the right side of the menu bar at the top of the screen. Here you can type words, such as format, replace, or file formats; or you can type phrases, such as preview a Web page, or how do I do remove text formatting. The Publisher Help system responds by displaying the Search Results task pane with a list of links.

Here are two tips regarding the words or phrases you enter to initiate a search: (1) check the spelling of the word or phrase; and (2) keep your search specific, with fewer than seven words, to return the most accurate results.

For the following example, assume that you want to remove a bullet from a line of text, and you do not know how to do it. The likely keyword is bullets. The following steps show how to use the Type a question for help box to obtain useful information by entering the keyword, bullets. The steps also show you how to navigate the Publisher Help system.

To Obtain Help Using the Type a Question for Help Box

1

• **Click the Type a question for help box on the right side of the menu bar, type** bullets **and then press the ENTER key.**

The Publisher Help system displays the Search Results task pane on the left side of the window. The Search Results task pane includes eight resulting links (Figure A-2). If you do not find what you are looking for, you can modify or refine the search in the Search area at the bottom of the Search Results task pane. The results returned in your Search Results task pane may be different.

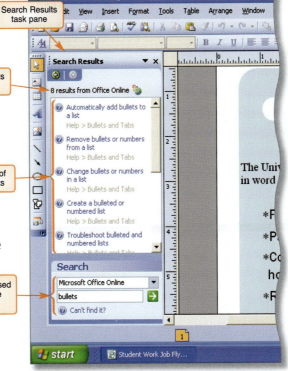

FIGURE A-2

2

• **In the list of links in the Search Results task pane, click the Remove bullets or numbers from a list link.**

• **When the Publisher Help system opens the Microsoft Office Publisher Help window, click its Auto Tile button in the upper-left corner of the window, if necessary, to tile the windows.**

The Publisher Help system opens the Microsoft Office Publisher Help window with the desired information about removing bullets from a list (Figure A-3). Your Help window may be displayed in a different part of the screen. With the Microsoft Office Publisher Help window and Microsoft Publisher window tiled, you can read the information in one window and complete the task in the other window.

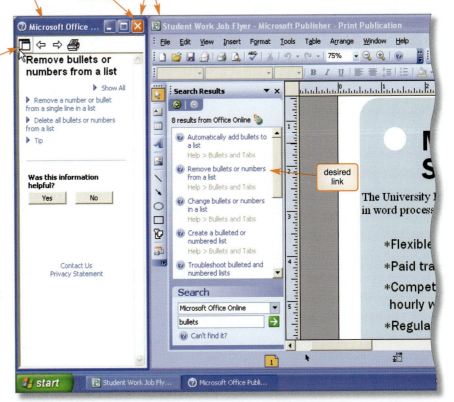

FIGURE A-3

3

- **Double-click the Microsoft Office Publisher Help window title bar.**

- **Click the Show All link in the upper-right corner of the window.**

- **After reviewing the information, click the Hide All link that replaced the Show All link.**

The Microsoft Office Publisher Help window is maximized so it fills the entire screen (Figure A-4). If you are connected to the Internet, you can give Microsoft your opinion as to whether the information was helpful by clicking the Yes or No button at the bottom of the page. The Show All link expands the coverage of information, and the Hide All link condenses the information displayed on the topic in the Publisher Help window.

4

- **Click the Restore Down button on the right side of the Microsoft Office Publisher Help window title bar to return to the tiled state shown in Figure A-3 on the previous page.**

- **Click the Close button on the Microsoft Office Publisher Help window title bar.**

The Microsoft Office Publisher Help window closes, and the Publisher window is active.

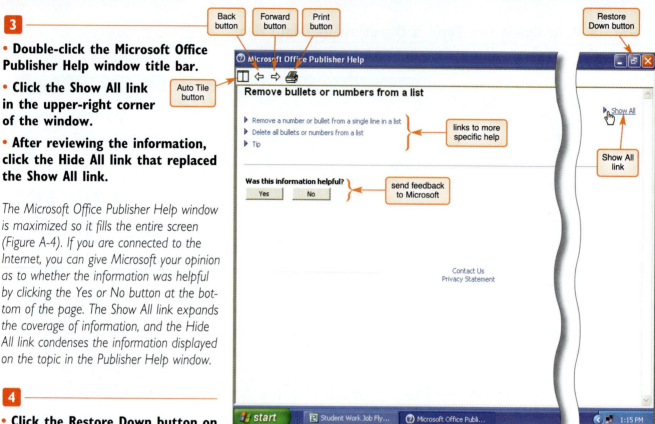

FIGURE A-4

Use the four buttons in the upper-left corner of the Microsoft Office Publisher Help window (Figure A-4) to tile or untile, navigate through the Help system, or print the contents of the window. As you click links in the Search Results task pane, the Publisher Help system displays new pages of information. The Publisher Help system remembers the links you visited and allows you to redisplay the pages visited during a session by clicking the Back and Forward buttons (Figures A-3 and A-4).

If none of the links presents the information you want, you can refine the search by entering another word or phrase in the Search area in the Search Results task pane (Figure A-3). If you have access to the Web, then the scope is global for the initial search. **Global** means all the categories listed in the Search box of the Search area in Figure A-5 are searched. Alternately, you can restrict the scope to **Offline Help**, for example, which results in a search of related links only on your hard disk.

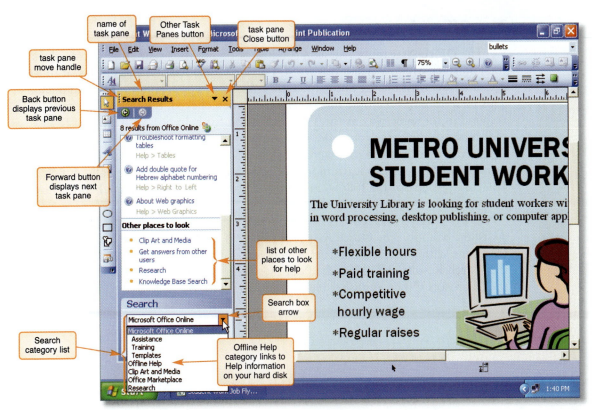

FIGURE A-5

Figure A-5 shows several additional features of the Search Results task pane with which you should be familiar. The buttons immediately below the name of the task pane allow you to navigate between task panes. The Other Task Panes button and the Close button on the Search Results task pane title bar let you change task panes and close the active task pane. You can drag the move handle to reposition the task pane on the screen.

In the lower portion of the Search Results list is a set of links to other places to look for help.

As you enter questions and terms in the Type a question for help box, the Publisher Help system adds them to its list. Thus, if you click the Type a question for help box arrow, a list of previously used words and phrases are displayed (Figure A-6).

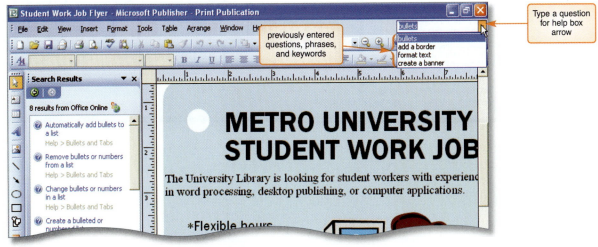

FIGURE A-6

The Office Assistant

The **Office Assistant** is an icon (middle of Figure A-7) that Publisher displays in the Publisher window while you work. For the Office Assistant to display, it must be activated by invoking the Show the Office Assistant command on the Help menu. This Help tool has multiple functions. First, when clicked, the Office Assistant will respond in the same way as the Type a question for help box with a list of topics that relate to the entry you make in the text box of the Office Assistant balloon. The entry can be in the form of a word or phrase as if you were talking to a person. For example, if you want to learn more about creating a banner, in the balloon text box, you can type any of the following words or phrases: banner, create a banner, how do I create a banner, or anything similar.

In the example in Figure A-7, the phrase, create a banner, is entered in the Office Assistant balloon. The Office Assistant responds by displaying the Search Results task pane with a list of links from which you can choose. Once you click a link in the Search Results task pane, the Publisher Help system displays the information in the Microsoft Office Publisher Help window (Figure A-7).

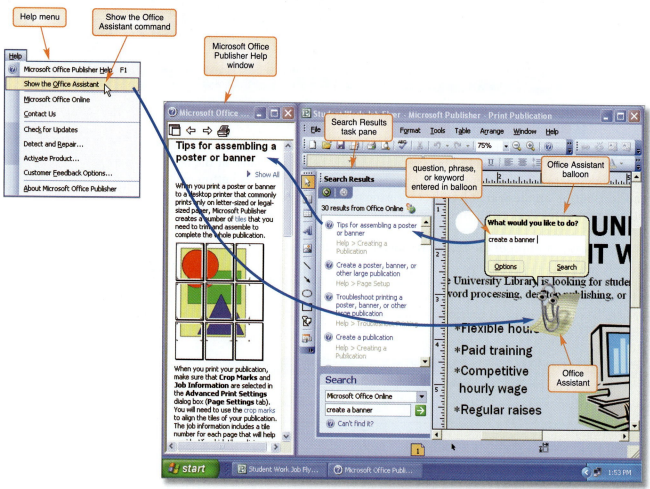

FIGURE A-7

Second, during a session, the Office Assistant monitors your work and accumulates tips on how you might increase your productivity and efficiency. The accumulation of tips must be enabled. You enable the accumulation of tips by right-clicking the Office Assistant, clicking Options on the shortcut menu, and then selecting the types of tips you want accumulated. You can view the tips at any time. The accumulated tips display when you activate the Office Assistant balloon. Also, if at anytime you see a lightbulb above the Office Assistant, click it to display the most recent tip. If the Office Assistant is hidden, the lightbulb shows on the Microsoft Publisher Help button on the Standard toolbar.

You hide the Office Assistant by clicking the Hide the Office Assistant command on the Help menu or by right-clicking the Office Assistant and then clicking Hide on the shortcut menu. The Hide the Office Assistant command shows on the Help menu only when the Office Assistant is active in the Publisher window. If the Office Assistant begins showing up on your screen without you instructing it to show, then right-click the Office Assistant, click Options on the shortcut menu, click the Use the Office Assistant check box to remove the check mark, and then click the OK button.

Third, if the Office Assistant is active in the Publisher window, Publisher displays all program and system messages in the Office Assistant balloon.

You may or may not want the Office Assistant to display on the screen at all times. As indicated earlier, you can hide it and then show it later through the Help menu. For more information about the Office Assistant, type `office assistant` in the Type a question for help box and then click the links in the Search Results task pane.

Help Buttons in Dialog Boxes and Subsystem Windows

As you invoke commands that display dialog boxes or other windows and task panes, you will see buttons and links that offer helpful information. Figure A-8 shows the types of Help buttons and links you will see as you work with Publisher.

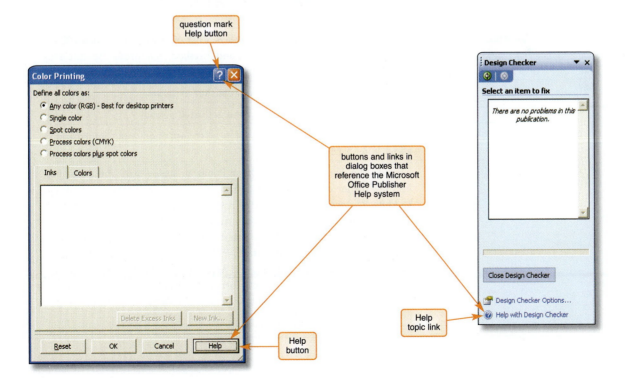

FIGURE A-8

Other Help Commands on the Help Menu

Thus far, this appendix has discussed the first two commands on the Help menu: (1) the Microsoft Office Publisher Help command (Figure A-1 on page APP 1) and (2) the Show the Office Assistant command (Figure A-7 on page APP 6). Several additional commands are available on the Help menu as shown in Figure A-9. Table A-1 summarizes these commands.

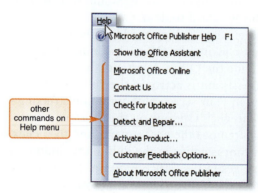

FIGURE A-9

Table A-1 Summary of Other Commands on the Help Menu	
COMMAND ON HELP MENU	**FUNCTION**
Microsoft Office Online	Activates your browser, which displays the Microsoft Office Online Home page. The Microsoft Office Online Home page contains links that can improve your Office productivity.
Contact Us	Activates your browser, which displays Microsoft contact information and a list of useful links.
Check for Updates	Activates your browser, which displays a list of updates to Office 2003. These updates can be downloaded and installed to improve the efficiency of Office or to fix an error in one or more of the Office applications.
Detect and Repair	Detects and repairs errors in the Publisher program.
Activate Product	Activates Publisher if it has not been activated already.
Customer Feedback Options	Gives or denies Microsoft permission to collect anonymous information about your hardware.
About Microsoft Office Publisher	Displays the About Microsoft Office Publisher dialog box. The dialog box lists the owner of the software and the product identification. You need to know the product identification if you call Microsoft for assistance. The three buttons below the OK button are the System Info button, the Tech Support button, and the Disabled Items button. The System Info button displays system information, including hardware resources, components, software environment, and applications. The Tech Support button displays technical assistance information. The Disabled Items button displays a list of disabled items that prevent Publisher from functioning properly.

Use Help

1 Using the Type a Question for Help Box

Instructions: Perform the following tasks using the Publisher Help system.

1. Use the Type a question for help box on the menu bar to obtain help on creating tables.
2. Click Create a table in the list of links in the Search Results task pane. Tile the windows, if necessary. Double-click the Microsoft Office Publisher Help window title bar to maximize it. Click the Show All button. Read and print the information. At the top of the printout, write down the number of links the Publisher Help system found.
3. One at a time, click two additional links in the Search Results task pane and print the information. Hand in the printouts to your instructor. Use the Back and Forward buttons to return to the original page.
4. Use the Type a question for help box to search for information on alignment. Click the Align or distribute objects link in the Search Results task pane. When the Microsoft Office Publisher Help window is displayed, maximize the window. Read and print the information. One at a time, click the links on the page and print the information for any new page that displays. Close the Microsoft Office Publisher Help window.
5. For each of the following words and phrases, click one link in the Search Results task pane, click the Show All link, and then print the page: text, date, curves, print resolution, shadows, 3-D effects, and create a logo.

2 Expanding on the Publisher Help System Basics

Instructions: Use the Publisher Help system to understand the topics better and answer the questions listed below. Answer the questions on your own paper, or hand in the printed Help information to your instructor.

1. Show the Office Assistant. Right-click the Office Assistant and then click Animate! on the shortcut menu. Repeat invoking the Animate! command to see various animations. Right-click the Office Assistant, click Options on the shortcut menu, click the Reset my tips button, and then click the OK button. When you see a lightbulb above the Office Assistant, it indicates that the Office Assistant has a tip to share with you. Click the lightbulb to display the tip.
2. Use the Office Assistant to find help on undoing tasks. Print the Help information for three links in the Search Results task pane. Close the Microsoft Office Publisher Help window. Hand in the printouts to your instructor. Hide the Office Assistant.
3. Press the F1 key. Search for information on Help. Click the first two links in the Search Results task pane. Read and print the information for both.
4. One at a time, invoke the first three commands in Table A-1. Print each page. Click two links on one of the pages and print the information. Hand in the printouts to your instructor.
5. Click About Microsoft Office Publisher on the Help menu. Click the Tech Support button and print the resulting page. Click the System Info button. If necessary, click the plus sign next to Components in the System Summary pane to expand its contents. Below the Components category, click CD-ROM. Click File on the menu bar and then click Print. Click Display in the list. Print the information. Hand in the printouts to your instructor.

Appendix B

Speech and Handwriting Recognition and Speech Playback

Introduction

This appendix discusses the Office capability that allows users to create and modify publications using its alternative input technologies available through **text services**. Office provides a variety of text services, which enable you to speak commands and enter text in an application. The most common text service is the keyboard. Other text services include speech recognition and handwriting recognition.

The Language Bar

The **Language bar** allows you to use text services in the Office applications. You can utilize the Language bar in one of three states: (1) in a restored state as a floating toolbar in the Publisher window (Figure B-1a or Figure B-1b if Text Labels are enabled); (2) in a minimized state docked next to the notification area on the Windows taskbar (Figure B-1c); or (3) hidden (temporarily closed and out of the way). If the Language bar is hidden, you can activate it by right-clicking the Windows taskbar, pointing to Toolbars on the shortcut menu (Figure B-1d), and then clicking Language bar on the Toolbars submenu. If you want to close the Language bar, right-click the Language bar and then click Close the Language bar on the shortcut menu (Figure B-1e).

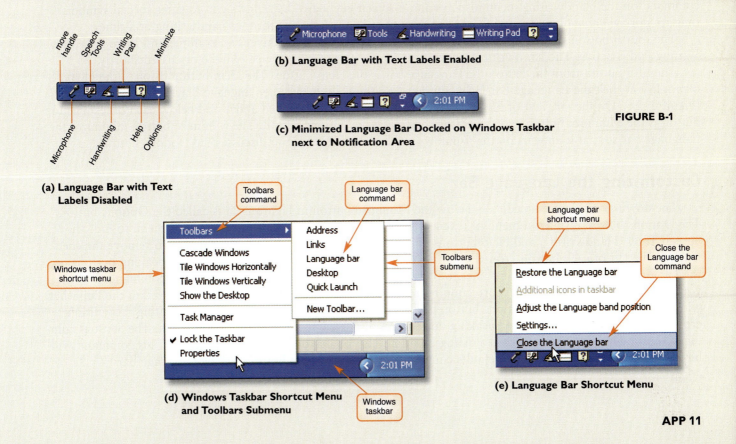

(a) Language Bar with Text Labels Disabled

(b) Language Bar with Text Labels Enabled

(c) Minimized Language Bar Docked on Windows Taskbar next to Notification Area

(d) Windows Taskbar Shortcut Menu and Toolbars Submenu

(e) Language Bar Shortcut Menu

FIGURE B-1

When Windows was installed on your computer, the installer specified a default language. For example, most users in the United States select English (United States) as the default language. You can add more than 90 additional languages and varying dialects such as Basque, English (Zimbabwe), French (France), French (Canada), German (Germany), German (Austria), and Swahili. With multiple languages available, you can switch from one language to another while working in Publisher. If you change the language or dialect, then text services may change the functions of the keys on the keyboard, adjust speech recognition, and alter handwriting recognition. If a second language is activated, then a Language icon appears immediately to the right of the move handle on the Language bar and the language name is displayed on the Publisher status bar. This appendix assumes that English (United States) is the only language installed. Thus, the Language icon does not appear in the examples in Figure B-1 on the previous page.

Buttons on the Language Bar

The Language bar shown in Figure B-2a contains seven buttons. The number of buttons on your Language bar may be different. These buttons are used to select the language, customize the Language bar, control the microphone, control handwriting, and obtain help.

The first button on the left is the Microphone button, which enables and disables the microphone. When the microphone is enabled, text services adds two buttons and a balloon to the Language bar (Figure B-2b). These additional buttons and the balloon will be discussed shortly.

The second button from the left is the Speech Tools button. The Speech Tools button displays a menu of commands (Figure B-2c) that allow you to scan the current document looking for words to add to the speech recognition dictionary; hide or show the balloon on the Language bar; train the Speech Recognition service so that it can interpret your voice better; add and delete specific words to and from its dictionary, such as names and other words not understood easily; and change the user profile so more than one person can use the microphone on the same computer.

The third button from the left on the Language bar is the Handwriting button. The Handwriting button displays the Handwriting menu (Figure B-2d), which lets you choose the Writing Pad (Figure B-2e), Write Anywhere (Figure B-2f), or the on-screen Standard keyboard (Figure B-2g). The On-Screen Symbol Keyboard command on the Handwriting menu displays an on-screen keyboard that allows you to enter special symbols that are not available on a standard keyboard. You can choose only one form of handwriting at a time.

The fourth button indicates which one of the handwriting forms is active. For example, in Figure B-2a, the Writing Pad is active. The handwriting recognition capabilities of text services will be discussed shortly.

The fifth button from the left on the Language bar is the Help button. The Help button displays the Help menu. If you click the Language Bar Help command on the Help menu, the Language Bar Help window appears (Figure B-2h). On the far right of the Language bar are two buttons stacked above and below each other. The top button is the Minimize button and the bottom button is the Options button. The Minimize button minimizes the Language bar so that it appears on the Windows taskbar. The next section discusses the Options button.

Customizing the Language Bar

The down arrow icon immediately below the Minimize button in Figure B-2a is called the Options button. The Options button displays a menu of text services options (Figure B-2i). You can use this menu to hide the Speech Tools, Handwriting, and Help buttons on the Language bar by clicking their names to remove the check mark to the left of each button. You also can show the Correction, Speak Text, and Pause Speaking buttons on the Language bar by clicking their names to place a check mark to the left of the respective command. When you select text and then click the Correction button, a list of correction alternatives is displayed in the Publisher window. You can use the Corrections button to correct both speech recognition and handwriting recognition errors. The Speak Text and Pause Speaking buttons are discussed at the end of this Appendix. The Settings command on the Options menu displays a dialog box that lets you customize the Language bar. This command will be discussed shortly. The Restore Defaults command redisplays hidden buttons on the Language bar.

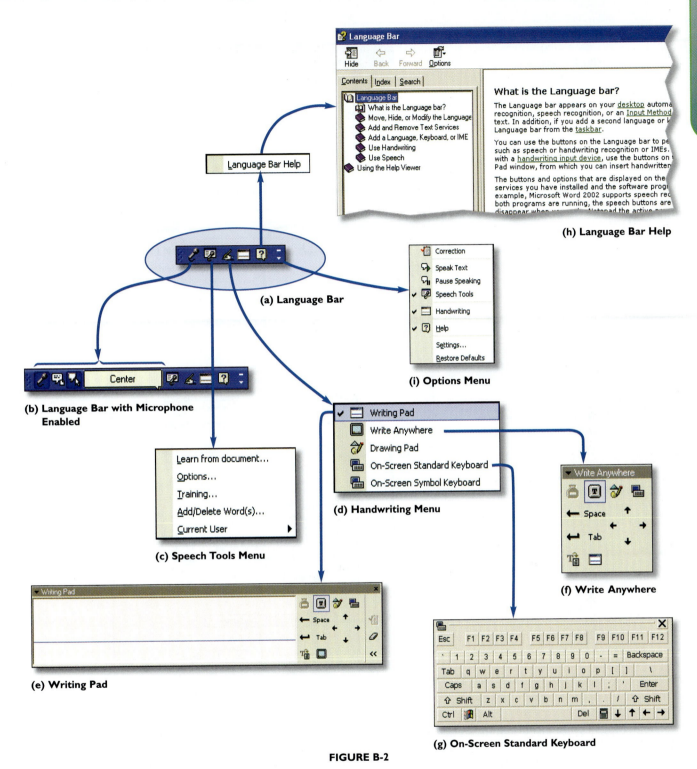

FIGURE B-2

(h) Language Bar Help

(a) Language Bar

(b) Language Bar with Microphone Enabled

(i) Options Menu

(c) Speech Tools Menu

(d) Handwriting Menu

(f) Write Anywhere

(e) Writing Pad

(g) On-Screen Standard Keyboard

If you right-click the Language bar, a shortcut menu appears (Figure B-3a on the next page). This shortcut menu lets you further customize the Language bar. The Minimize command on the shortcut menu docks the Language bar on the Windows taskbar. The Transparency command in Figure B-3a toggles the Language bar between being solid and transparent. You can see through a transparent Language bar (Figure B-3b). The Text Labels command toggles on text labels on the Language bar (Figure B-3c) and off (Figure B-3b). The Vertical command displays the Language bar vertically on the screen (Figure B-3d).

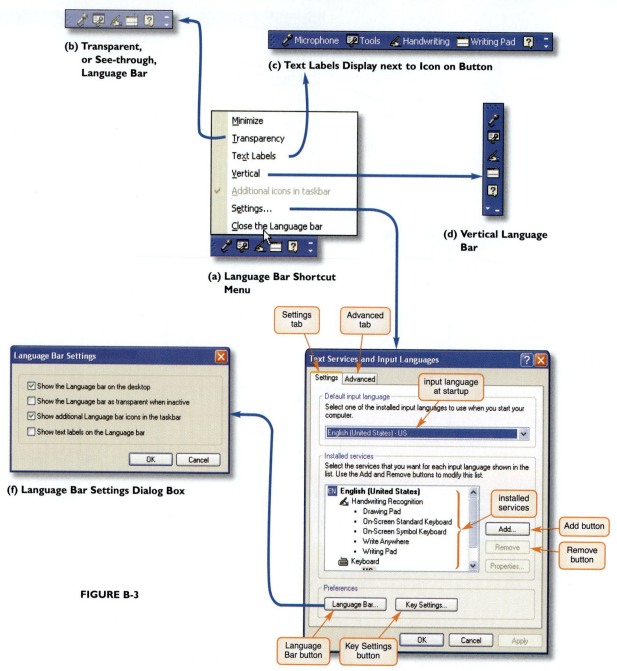

(b) Transparent, or See-through, Language Bar

(c) Text Labels Display next to Icon on Button

(d) Vertical Language Bar

(a) Language Bar Shortcut Menu

(f) Language Bar Settings Dialog Box

FIGURE B-3

(e) Text Services and Input Languages Dialog Box

The Settings command in Figure B-3a displays the Text Services and Input Languages dialog box (Figure B-3e). The Text Services and Input Languages dialog box allows you to add additonal languages, add and remove text services, modify keys on the keyboard, modify the Language bar, and extend support of advanced text services to all programs, including Notepad and other programs that normally do not support text services (through the Advanced tab). If you want to remove any one of the services in the Installed services list, select the service, and then click the Remove button. If you want to add a service, click the Add button. The Key Settings button allows you to modify the keyboard. If you click the Language Bar button in the Text Services and Input Languages dialog box, the Language Bar Settings dialog box appears (Figure B-3f). This dialog box contains Language bar options, some of which are the same as the commands on the Language bar shortcut menu shown in Figure B-3a.

The Close the Language bar command on the shortcut menu shown in Figure B-3a closes or hides the Language bar. If you close the Language bar and want to redisplay it, see Figure B-1d on page APP 11.

Speech Recognition

The **Speech Recognition service** available with Office enables your computer to recognize human speech through a microphone. The microphone has two modes: dictation and voice command (Figure B-4). You switch between the two modes by clicking the Dictation button and the Voice Command button on the Language bar. These buttons appear only when you turn on Speech Recognition by clicking the Microphone button on the Language bar (Figure B-5a on the next page). If you are using the Microphone button for the very first time in Publisher, it will require that you check your microphone settings and step through voice training before activating the Speech Recognition service.

The Dictation button places the microphone in Dictation mode. In **Dictation mode**, whatever you speak is entered as text in the active text box. The Voice Command button places the microphone in Voice Command mode. In **Voice Command mode**, whatever you speak is interpreted as a command. If you want to turn off the microphone, click the Microphone button on the Language bar or in Voice Command mode say, "Mic off" (pronounced mike off). It is important to remember that minimizing the Language bar does not turn off the microphone.

(a) Enter Text in Dictation Mode

(b) Enter Commands in Voice Command Mode

FIGURE B-4

The Language bar speech message balloon shown in Figure B-5b displays messages that may offer help or hints. In Voice Command mode, the name of the last recognized command you said appears. If you use the mouse or keyboard instead of the microphone, a message will appear in the Language bar speech message balloon indicating the word you could say. In Dictation mode, the message, Dictating, usually appears. The Speech Recognition service, however, will display messages to inform you that you are talking too soft, too loud, too fast, or to ask you to repeat what you said by displaying, What was that?

Getting Started with Speech Recognition

For the microphone to function properly, you should follow these steps:

1. Make sure your computer meets the minimum requirements.
2. Start Publisher. Activate Speech Recognition by clicking Tools on the menu bar and then clicking Speech.
3. Set up and position your microphone, preferably a close-talk headset with gain adjustment support.
4. Train Speech Recognition.

The following sections describe these steps in more detail.

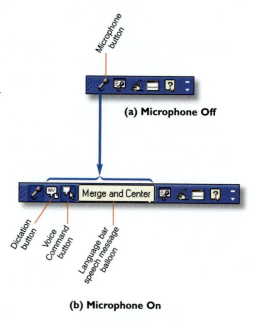

(a) Microphone Off

(b) Microphone On

FIGURE B-5

SPEECH RECOGNITION SYSTEM REQUIREMENTS   For Speech Recognition to work on your computer, it needs the following:

1. Microsoft Windows 98 or later or Microsoft Windows NT 4.0 or later
2. At least 128 MB RAM
3. 400 MHz or faster processor
4. Microphone and sound card

SETUP AND POSITION YOUR MICROPHONE   Set up your microphone as follows:

1. Connect your microphone to the sound card in the back of the computer.
2. Position the microphone approximately one inch out from and to the side of your mouth. Position it so you are not breathing into it.
3. On the Language bar, with the Microphone button on, click the Speech Tools button and then click Options on the Speech Tools menu (Figure B-6a).
4. When text services displays the Speech input settings dialog box (Figure B-6b), click the Advanced Speech button. When text services displays the Speech Properties dialog box (Figure B-6c), click the Speech Recognition tab.
5. Click the Configure Microphone button. Follow the Microphone Wizard directions as shown in Figures B-6d, B-6e, and B-6f. The Next button will remain dimmed in Figure B-6e until the volume meter consistently stays in the green area.
6. If someone else installed Speech Recognition, click the New button in the Speech Properties dialog box and enter your name. Click the Train Profile button and step through the Voice Training dialog box. The Voice Training dialog box will require that you enter your gender and age group. It then will step you through voice training.

You can adjust the microphone further by clicking the Settings button in the Speech Properties dialog box (Figure B-6c). The Settings button displays the Recognition Profile Settings dialog box that allows you to adjust the pronunciation sensitivity and accuracy versus recognition response time.

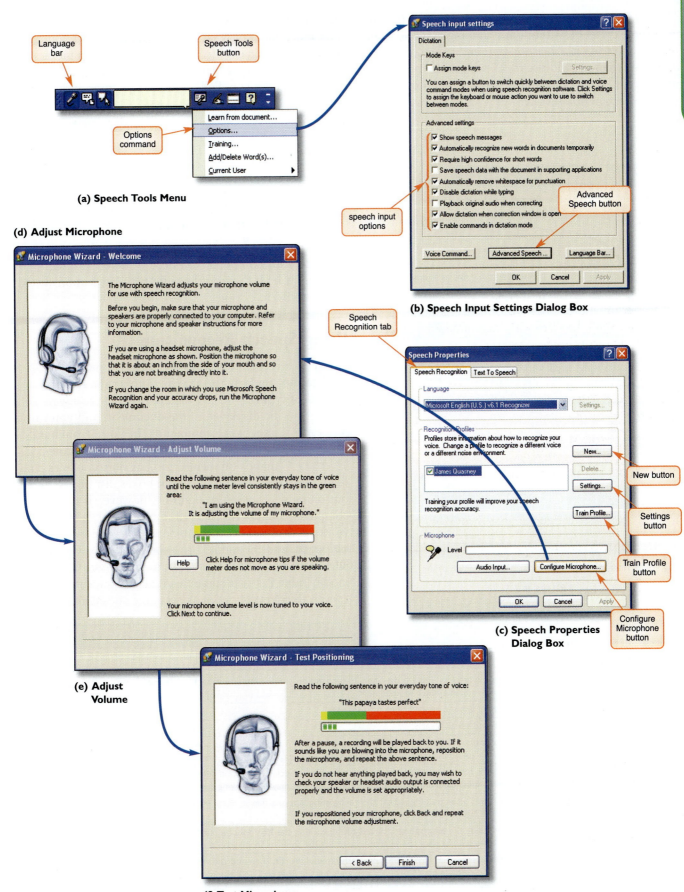

(a) Speech Tools Menu

(b) Speech Input Settings Dialog Box

(c) Speech Properties Dialog Box

(d) Adjust Microphone

(e) Adjust Volume

(f) Test Microphone

FIGURE B-6

TRAIN THE SPEECH RECOGNITION SERVICE The Speech Recognition service will understand most commands and some dictation without any training at all. It will recognize much more of what you speak, however, if you take the time to train it. After one training session, it will recognize 85 to 90 percent of your words. As you do more training, accuracy will rise to 95 percent. If you feel that too many mistakes are being made, then continue to train the service. The more training you do, the more accurately it will work for you. Follow these steps to train the Speech Recognition service:

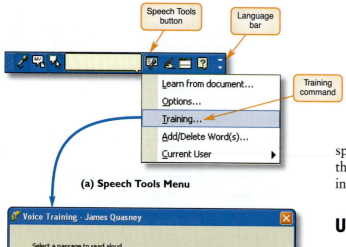

(a) Speech Tools Menu

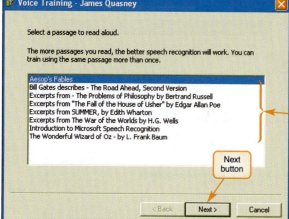

(b) Voice Training Dialog Box

FIGURE B-7

1. Click the Speech Tools button on the Language bar and then click Training (Figure B-7a).
2. When the Voice Training dialog box appears (Figure B-7b), click one of the sessions and then click the Next button.
3. Complete the training session, which should take less than 15 minutes.

If you are serious about using a microphone to speak to your computer, you need to take the time to go through at least three of the eight training sessions listed in Figure B-7b.

Using Speech Recognition

Speech recognition lets you enter text into a publication similarly to speaking into a tape recorder. Instead of typing, you can dictate text that you want to be displayed in the document, and you can issue voice commands. In Voice Command mode, you can speak menu names, commands on menus, toolbar button names, and dialog box option buttons, check boxes, list boxes, and button names. Speech recognition, however, is not a completely hands-free form of input. Speech recognition works best if you use a combination of your voice, the keyboard, and the mouse. You soon will discover that Dictation mode is far less accurate than Voice Command mode. Table B-1 lists some tips that will improve the Speech Recognition service's accuracy considerably.

Table B-1	Tips to Improve Speech Recognition
NUMBER	**TIP**
1	The microphone hears everything. Though the Speech Recognition service filters out background noise, it is recommended that you work in a quiet environment.
2	Try not to move the microphone around once it is adjusted.
3	Speak in a steady tone and speak clearly.
4	In Dictation mode, do not pause between words. A phrase is easier to interpret than a word. Sounding out syllables in a word will make it more difficult for the Speech Recognition service to interpret what you are saying.
5	If you speak too loudly or too softly, it makes it difficult for the Speech Recognition service to interpret what you said. Check the Language bar speech message balloon for an indication that you may be speaking too loudly or too softly.
6	If you experience problems after training, adjust the recognition options that control accuracy and rejection by clicking the Settings button shown in Figure B-6c on the previous page.
7	When you are finished using the microphone, turn it off by clicking the Microphone button on the Language bar or in Voice Command mode, say "Mic off." Leaving the microphone on is the same as leaning on the keyboard.
8	If the Speech Recognition service is having difficulty with unusual words, then add the words to its dictionary by using the Learn from document and Add/Delete Word(s) commands on the Speech Tools menu (Figure B-8a). The last names of individuals and the names of companies are good examples of the types of words you should add to the dictionary.
9	Training will improve accuracy; practice will improve confidence.

The last command on the Speech Tools menu is the Current User command (Figure B-8a). The Current User command is useful for multiple users who share a computer. It allows them to configure their own individual profiles, and then switch between users as they use the computer.

For additional information about the Speech Recognition service, enter speech recognition in the Type a question for help box on the menu bar.

Handwriting Recognition

Using the Office **Handwriting Recognition service**, you can enter text and numbers into Publisher by writing instead of typing. You can write using a special handwriting device that connects to your computer or you can write on the screen using your mouse. Four basic methods of handwriting are available by clicking the Handwriting button on the Language bar: Writing Pad; Write Anywhere; Drawing Pad; and On-Screen Keyboard. Although the on-screen keyboard does not involve handwriting recognition, it is part of the Handwriting menu and, therefore, will be discussed in this section.

If your Language bar does not include the Handwriting button, then for installation instructions, enter install handwriting recognition in the Type a question for help box on the menu bar.

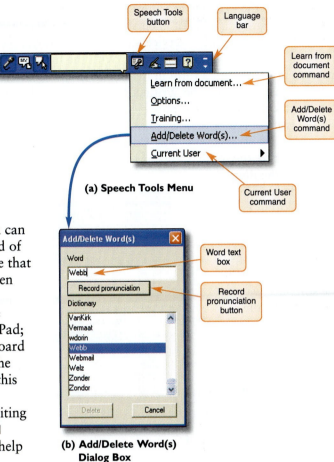

(a) Speech Tools Menu

(b) Add/Delete Word(s) Dialog Box

FIGURE B-8

Writing Pad

To display the Writing Pad, click the Handwriting button on the Language bar and then click Writing Pad (Figure B-9). The **Writing Pad** resembles a notepad with one or more lines on which you can use freehand to print or write in cursive. With the Text button enabled, you can form letters on the line by dragging the mouse. To the right of the notepad is a rectangular toolbar. Use the buttons on this toolbar to adjust the Writing Pad, insert spaces and tabs, and perform other handwriting activities.

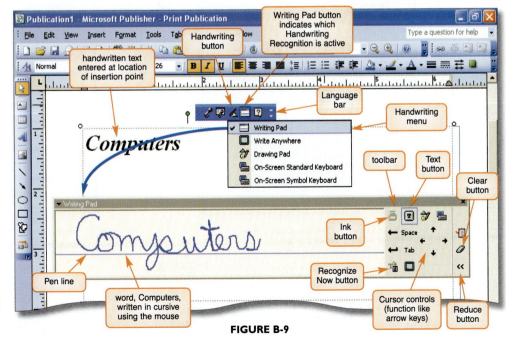

FIGURE B-9

Consider the example in Figure B-9 on the previous page. With a text box selected in the publication, the word, Computers, is written in cursive on the **Pen line** in the Writing Pad. As soon as the word is complete, the Handwriting Recognition service automatically converts the handwriting to typed characters and inserts the text at the location of the insertion point. With the Ink button enabled, instead of the Text button, the text is inserted in handwritten form in the document.

You can customize the Writing Pad by clicking the Options button on the left side of the Writing Pad title bar and then clicking the Options command (Figure B-10a). Invoking the Options command causes the Handwriting Options dialog box to be displayed. The Handwriting Options dialog box contains two sheets: Common and Writing Pad. The Common sheet lets you change the pen color and pen width, adjust recognition, and customize the toolbar area of the Writing Pad. The Writing Pad sheet allows you to change the background color and the number of lines that are displayed in the Writing Pad. Both sheets contain a Restore Default button to restore the settings to what they were when the software was installed initially.

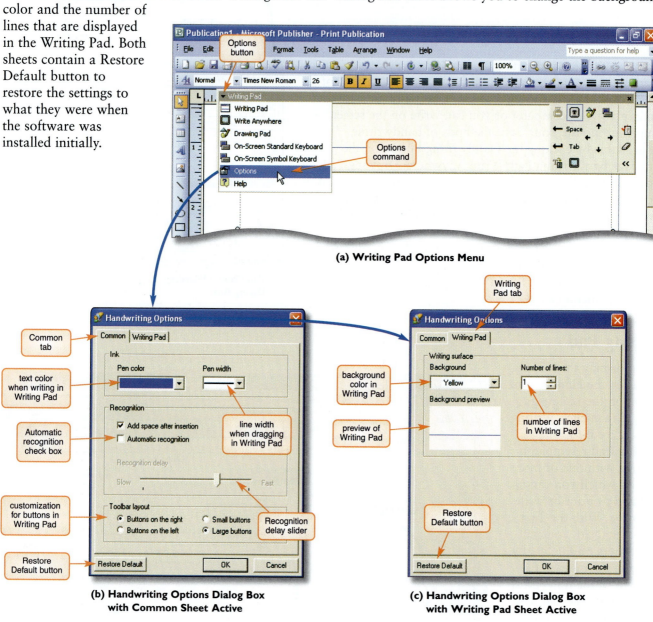

(a) Writing Pad Options Menu

(b) Handwriting Options Dialog Box with Common Sheet Active

(c) Handwriting Options Dialog Box with Writing Pad Sheet Active

FIGURE B-10

When you first start using the Writing Pad, you may want to remove the check mark from the Automatic recognition check box in the Common sheet in the Handwriting Options dialog box (Figure B-10b). With the check mark removed, the Handwriting Recognition service will not interpret what you write in the Writing Pad until you click the Recognize Now button on the toolbar (Figure B-9 on the previous page). This allows you to pause and adjust your writing.

The best way to learn how to use the Writing Pad is to practice with it. Also, for more information, enter handwriting recognition in the Type a question for help box on the menu bar.

Write Anywhere

Rather than use Writing Pad, you can write anywhere on the screen by invoking the Write Anywhere command on the Handwriting menu (Figure B-11) that displays when you click the Handwriting button on the Language bar. In this case, the entire window is your writing pad.

In Figure B-11, the word, Budget, is written in cursive using the mouse button. Shortly after the word is written, the Handwriting Recognition service interprets it, assigns it to the active text box, and erases what was written.

It is recommended that when you first start using the Write Anywhere service, you remove the check mark from the Automatic recognition check box in the Common sheet in the Handwriting Options dialog box (Figure B-10b). With the check mark removed, the Handwriting Recognition service will not interpret what you write on the screen until you click the Recognize Now button on the toolbar (Figure B-11).

Write Anywhere is more difficult to use than the Writing Pad, because when you click the mouse button, Publisher may interpret the action as an object rather than starting to write. For this reason, it is recommended that you use the Writing Pad.

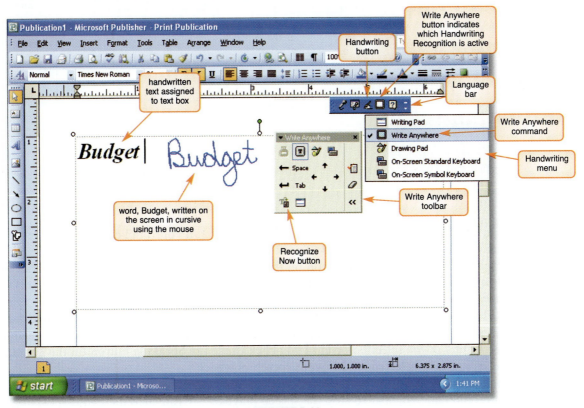

FIGURE B-11

On-Screen Keyboard

The On-Screen Standard Keyboard command on the Handwriting menu (Figure B-12) displays an on-screen keyboard. The **on-screen keyboard** lets you enter data at the location of the insertion point by using your mouse to click the keys. The on-screen keyboard is similar to the type found on handheld computers or PDAs.

The On-Screen Symbol Keyboard command on the Handwriting menu displays a special on-screen keyboard that allows you to enter symbols that are not on your keyboard, as well as Unicode characters. **Unicode characters** use a coding scheme capable of representing all the world's current languages.

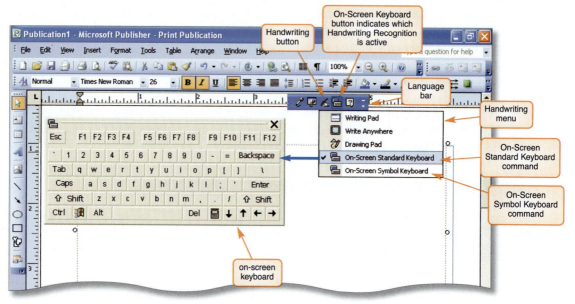

FIGURE B-12

Speech Playback

Using **speech playback**, you can have your computer read back the text in your publication's text boxes. Publisher provides two buttons for speech playback: Speak Text and Pause Speaking. To show the Speak Text button on the Language bar, click the Options button on the Language bar (Figure B-13) and then click Speak Text on the Options menu. Similarly, click the Options button on the Language bar and then click Pause Speaking on the Options menu to show the Pause Speaking button on the Language bar.

To use speech playback, select the text you want the computer to start reading back in the publication and then click the Speak Text button on the Language bar (Figure B-13). The computer reads from the beginning of the selected text, until the end of the selection or until you click the Pause Speaking button on the Language bar. After the computer reads back the selected text, it stops speech playback.

When you click the Speak Text button on the Language bar, it changes to a Stop Speaking button. Click the Stop Speaking button on the Language bar to stop the speech playback. If you click the Pause Speaking button on the Language bar to stop speech playback, the Pause Speaking button changes to a Resume Speaking button that you click when you want the computer to continue reading the document from the location at which it stopped reading.

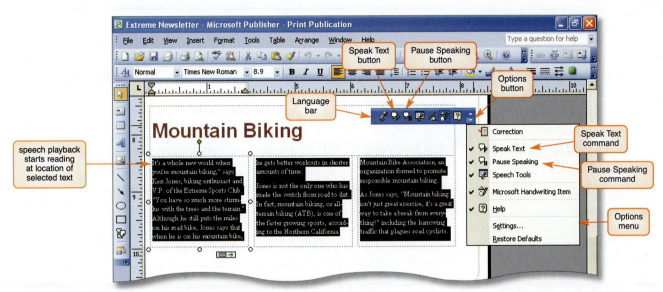

speech playback starts reading at location of selected text

FIGURE B-13

Customizing Speech Playback

You can customize speech playback through the Speech Properties dialog box. With the Microphone button off, click the Speech Tools button on the Language bar and then click Options on the Speech Tools menu (Figure B-2c on page APP 13). When text services displays the Speech Properties dialog box, click the Text To Speech tab (Figure B-14). The Text To Speech sheet has two areas: Voice selection and Voice speed. The Voice selection area lets you choose between two male voices and one female voice. You can click the Preview Voice button to hear a sample of the voice. The Voice speed area contains a slider. Drag the slider to slow down or speed up the pace of the speaking voice.

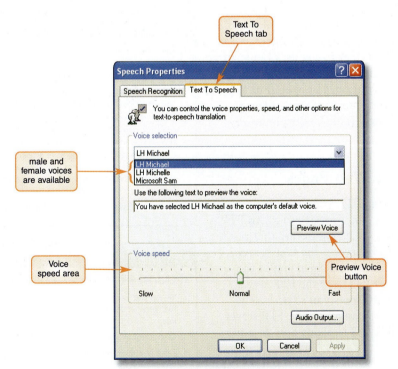

FIGURE B-14

Appendix C

Publishing Office Web Pages to a Web Server

With the Office applications, you use the Save as Web Page command on the File menu to save the Web page to a Web server using one of two techniques: Web folders or File Transfer Protocol. A **Web folder** is an Office shortcut to a Web server. **File Transfer Protocol** (**FTP**) is an Internet standard that allows computers to exchange files with other computers on the Internet.

You should contact your network system administrator or technical support staff at your ISP to determine if their Web server supports Web folders, FTP, or both, and to obtain necessary permissions to access the Web server. If you decide to publish Web pages using a Web folder, you must have the Office Server Extensions (OSE) installed on your computer.

Using Web Folders to Publish Office Web Pages

When publishing to a Web folder, someone first must create the Web folder before you can save to it. If you are granted permission to create a Web folder, you must obtain the URL of the Web server, a user name, and possibly a password that allows you to access the Web server. You also must decide on a name for the Web folder. Table C-1 explains how to create a Web folder.

Office adds the name of the Web folder to the list of current Web folders. You can save to this folder, open files in the folder, rename the folder, or perform any operations you would to a folder on your hard disk. You can use your Office program or Windows Explorer to access this folder. Table C-2 explains how to save to a Web folder.

Using FTP to Publish Office Web Pages

When publishing a Web page using FTP, you first must add the FTP location to your computer before you can save to it. An FTP location, also called an **FTP site**, is a collection of files that reside on an FTP server. In this case, the FTP server is the Web server.

To add an FTP location, you must obtain the name of the FTP site, which usually is the address (URL) of the FTP server, and a user name and a password that allows you to access the FTP server. You save and open the Web pages on the FTP server using the name of the FTP site. Table C-3 explains how to add an FTP site.

Office adds the name of the FTP site to the FTP locations list in the Save As and Open dialog boxes. You can open and save files using this list. Table C-4 explains how to save to an FTP location.

Table C-1 Creating a Web Folder

1. Click File on the menu bar and then click Save As (or Open).
2. When the Save As dialog box (or Open dialog box) appears, click My Network Places on the My Places bar, and then click the Create New Folder button on the toolbar.
3. When the Add Network Place Wizard dialog box appears, click the Next button. If necessary, click Choose another network location. Click the Next button. Click the View some examples link, type the Internet or network address, and then click the Next button. Click Log on anonymously to deselect the check box, type your user name in the User name text box, and then click the Next button. Enter the name you want to call this network place and then click the Next button. Click the Finish button.

Table C-2 Saving to a Web Folder

1. Click File on the menu bar and then click Save As.
2. When the Save As dialog box appears, type the Web page file name in the File name text box. Do not press the ENTER key.
3. Click My Network Places on the My Places bar.
4. Double-click the Web folder name in the Save in list.
5. If the Enter Network Password dialog box appears, type the user name and password in the respective text boxes and then click the OK button.
6. Click the Save button in the Save As dialog box.

Table C-3 Adding an FTP Location

1. Click File on the menu bar and then click Save As (or Open).
2. In the Save As dialog box, click the Save in box arrow and then click Add/Modify FTP Locations in the Save in list; or in the Open dialog box, click the Look in box arrow and then click Add/Modify FTP Locations in the Look in list.
3. When the Add/Modify FTP Locations dialog box appears, type the name of the FTP site in the Name of FTP site text box. If the site allows anonymous logon, click Anonymous in the Log on as area; if you have a user name for the site, click User in the Log on as area and then enter the user name. Enter the password in the Password text box. Click the OK button.
4. Close the Save As or the Open dialog box.

Table C-4 Saving to an FTP Location

1. Click File on the menu bar and then click Save As.
2. When the Save As dialog box appears, type the Web page file name in the File name text box. Do not press the ENTER key.
3. Click the Save in box arrow and then click FTP Locations.
4. Double-click the name of the FTP site to which you wish to save.
5. When the FTP Log On dialog box appears, enter your user name and password and then click the OK button.
6. Click the Save button in the Save As dialog box.

Appendix D

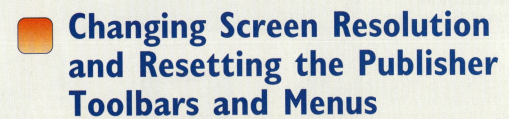

Changing Screen Resolution and Resetting the Publisher Toolbars and Menus

Changing Screen Resolution

The **screen resolution** indicates the number of pixels (dots) that your system uses to display the letters, numbers, graphics, and background you see on your screen. The screen resolution usually is stated as the product of two numbers, such as 800 × 600. An 800 × 600 screen resolution results in a display of 800 distinct pixels on each of 600 lines, or about 480,000 pixels. The figures in this book were created using a screen resolution of 800 × 600.

The screen resolutions most commonly used today are 800 × 600 and 1024 × 768, although some Office specialists operate their computers at a much higher screen resolution, such as 2048 × 1536. The following steps show how to change the screen resolution from 1024 × 768 to 800 × 600.

To Change the Screen Resolution

1

• **If necessary, minimize all applications so that the Windows desktop appears.**

• **Right-click the Windows desktop.**

Windows displays the Windows desktop shortcut menu (Figure D-1).

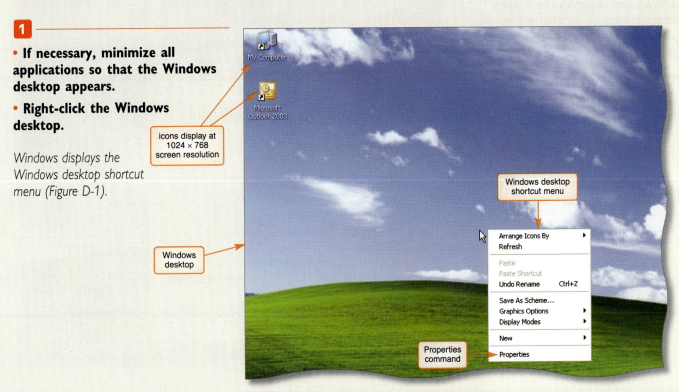

icons display at 1024 × 768 screen resolution

Windows desktop shortcut menu

Windows desktop

Properties command

FIGURE D-1

2

• **Click Properties on the shortcut menu.**

• **When Windows displays the Display Properties dialog box, click the Settings tab.**

Windows displays the Settings sheet in the Display Properties dialog box (Figure D-2). The Settings sheet shows a preview of the Windows desktop using the current screen resolution (1024 × 768). The Settings sheet also shows the screen resolution and the color quality settings.

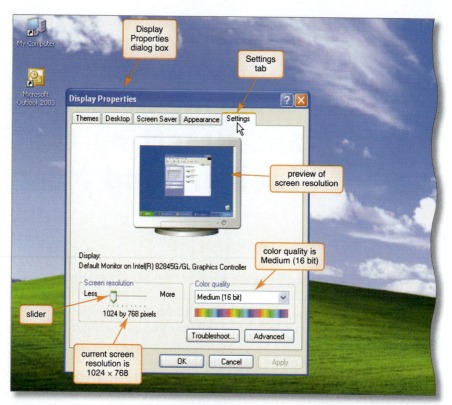

FIGURE D-2

3

• **Drag the slider in the Screen resolution area to the left so that the screen resolution changes to 800 × 600.**

The screen resolution in the Screen resolution area changes to 800 × 600 (Figure D-3). The Settings sheet shows a preview of the Windows desktop using the new screen resolution (800 × 600).

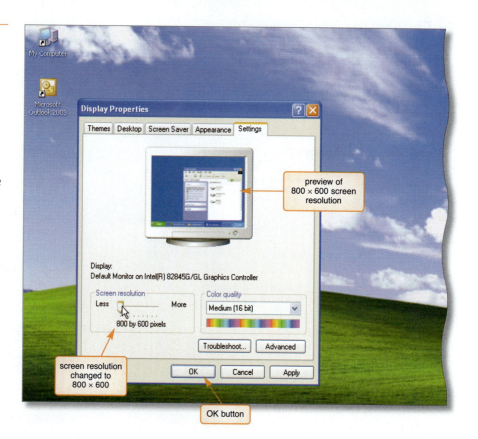

FIGURE D-3

4

• **Click the OK button.**

• **If Windows displays the Monitor Settings dialog box, click the Yes button.**

Windows changes the screen resolution from 1024 x 768 to 800 x 600 (Figure D-4).

icons display at 800 × 600 screen resolution

FIGURE D-4

As shown in the previous steps, as you decrease the screen resolution, Windows displays less information on your screen, but the information increases in size. The icons are slightly larger in Figure D-4 than they are in previous figures. The reverse also is true: as you increase the screen resolution, Windows displays more information on your screen, but the information decreases in size.

Resetting the Publisher Toolbars and Menus

Publisher customization capabilities allow you to create custom toolbars by adding and deleting buttons and to personalize menus based on their usage. Each time you start Publisher, the toolbars and menus display using the same settings as the last time you used it. The figures in this book were created with the Publisher toolbars and menus set to the original, or installation, settings.

Resetting the Standard and Formatting Toolbars

The steps on the next page show how to reset the Standard and Formatting toolbars.

To Reset the Standard and Formatting Toolbars

1

• **If necessary, start Publisher for your system as described in Project 1.**

• **Click the Toolbar Options button on the Standard toolbar and then point to Add or Remove Buttons on the Toolbar Options menu.**

Publisher displays the Toolbar Options menu and the Add or Remove Buttons submenu (Figure D-5).

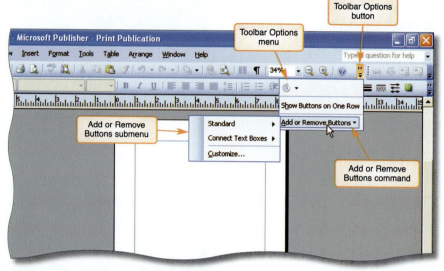

FIGURE D-5

2

• **Point to Standard on the Add or Remove Buttons submenu.**

• **When the Standard submenu displays, scroll down and then point to Reset Toolbar.**

Publisher displays the Standard submenu, which lists the buttons and boxes that can be displayed on the Standard toolbar (Figure D-6). To remove a button from the Standard toolbar, click a button name with a check mark to the left of the name to remove the check mark.

3

• **Click Reset Toolbar.**

• **If Publisher displays the Microsoft Publisher dialog box, click Yes.**

Publisher resets the Standard toolbar to its original settings.

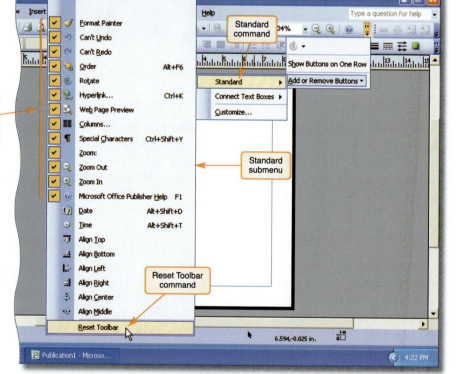

FIGURE D-6

4

• **Reset the Formatting toolbar by following Steps 1 through 3 and replacing any reference to the Standard toolbar with the Formatting toolbar.**

Not only can you use the Standard submenu shown in Figure D-6 to reset the Standard toolbar to its original settings, but you also can use it to customize the Standard toolbar by adding and deleting buttons. To add or delete buttons, click the button name on the Standard submenu to add or remove the check mark. Buttons with a check mark to the left currently are displayed on the Standard toolbar; buttons without a check mark are not displayed on the Standard toolbar. You can complete the same tasks for the Formatting toolbar, using the Formatting submenu to add or delete buttons on the Formatting toolbar.

Resetting the Publisher Menus

The following steps show how to reset the Publisher menus to their original settings.

To Reset the Publisher Menus

1

• **Click the Toolbar Options button on the Standard toolbar and then point to Add or Remove Buttons on the Toolbar Options menu.**

The Toolbar Options menu and the Add or Remove Buttons submenu are displayed (Figure D-7).

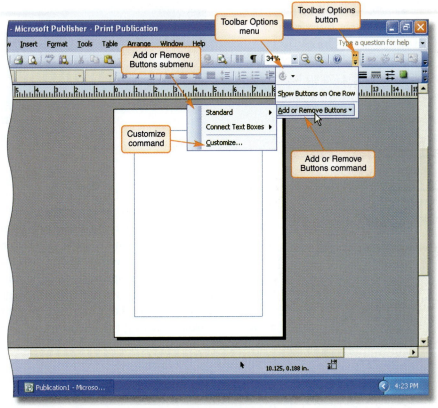

FIGURE D-7

2

• **Click Customize on the Add or Remove Buttons submenu. When Publisher displays the Customize dialog box, click the Options tab.**

Publisher displays the Customize dialog box (Figure D-8). The Customize dialog box contains three sheets used for customizing the Publisher toolbars and menus.

3

• **Click the Reset menu and toolbar usage data button. When Publisher displays the Microsoft Publisher dialog box, click the Yes button.**

• **Click the Close button in the Customize dialog box.**

Publisher resets the menus to the original settings.

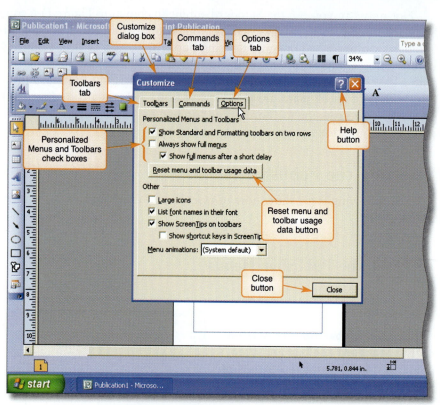

FIGURE D-8

Other Ways

1. On View menu point to Toolbars, click Customize on Toolbars submenu, click Options tab, click Reset menu and toolbar usage data button, click Yes button, click Close button
2. Right-click toolbar, click Customize on shortcut menu, click Options tab, click Reset menu and toolbar usage data button, click Yes button, click Close button
3. In Voice Command mode, say "View, Toolbars, Customize, Options, Reset menu and toolbar usage data, Yes, Close"

Using the Options sheet in the Customize dialog box, as shown in Figure D-8 on the previous page, you can select options to personalize menus and toolbars. For example, you can place or remove a check mark that instructs Publisher to display the Standard and Formatting toolbars on two rows. You also can select whether Publisher always displays full menus or displays short menus followed by full menus, after a short delay. Other options available on the Options sheet include settings to instruct Publisher to display toolbars with large icons; to use the appropriate font to display font names in the Font list; and to display a ScreenTip when a user points to a toolbar button. Clicking the Help button on the title bar in the Customize dialog box displays the Microsoft Office Publisher Help window with more information about each of the customize features.

Using the Commands sheet in the Customize dialog box, you can add buttons to toolbars and commands to menus. Recall that the menu bar at the top of the Publisher window is a special toolbar. To add buttons to a toolbar, click a category name in the Categories list and then drag the command name in the Commands list to a toolbar. To add commands to a menu, click a category name in the Categories list, drag the command name in the Commands list to a menu name on the menu bar, and then, when the menu is displayed, drag the command to the desired location in the list of menu commands.

Using the Toolbars sheet in the Customize dialog box, you can add new toolbars and reset existing toolbars and the menu. To add a new toolbar, click the New button, enter a toolbar name in the New Toolbar dialog box, and then click the OK button. Once the new toolbar is created, you can use the Command sheet to add or remove buttons, as you would with any other toolbar. If you add one or more buttons to an existing toolbar and want to reset the toolbar to its original settings, click the toolbar name in the Toolbars list so a check mark displays to the left of the name and then click the Reset button. If you add commands to one or more menus and want to reset the menus to their default settings, click Menu Bar in the Toolbars list so a check mark displays to the left of the name and then click the Reset button. When you have finished, click the Close button to close the Customize dialog box.

Index

MICROSOFT
Office Publisher 2003

Quick Reference Summary

In Microsoft Office Publisher 2003, you can accomplish a task in a number of ways. The following table provides a quick reference to each task presented in this textbook. The first column identifies the task. The second column indicates the page number on which the task is discussed in the book. The subsequent four columns list the different ways the task in column one can be carried out. Besides using the mouse or keyboard, you can invoke the commands listed in the MOUSE, MENU BAR, and SHORTCUT MENU columns using Voice commands.

Microsoft Office Publisher 2003 Quick Reference Summary

TASK	PAGE NUMBER	MOUSE	MENU BAR	SHORTCUT MENU	KEYBOARD SHORTCUT
Add Border	PUB 233	Line/Border Style button on Formatting toolbar	Format | <object>	Format <object>	ALT+O | E
Address List	PUB 250		Tools | Mail and Catalog Merge | Create Address List		ALT+T | G
Align Objects	PUB 166		Arrange | Align or Distribute	Align or Distribute	ALT+R | A
Alternate Text	PUB 336	Format Picture button on Formatting toolbar	Format | Picture	Format Picture	ALT+O | E
Attention Getters	PUB 90	Design Gallery Object button on Objects toolbar	Insert | Design Gallery Object | Attention Getters		ALT+I | D
AutoFit Text	PUB 31		Format | AutoFit Text	Change Text | AutoFit Text	ALT+O | X
Automatic Page Numbering	PUB 111	Insert Page Number button on Header and Footer toolbar	Insert | Page Numbers		ALT+I | U
AutoShapes	PUB 158	AutoShapes button on Objects toolbar	Arrange | Change AutoShape		ALT+R | C
Backgrounds	PUB 335		Format | Background		ALT+O | K
Bold	PUB 145	Bold button on Formatting toolbar	Format | Font	Change Text | Font	CTRL+B
BorderArt	PUB 293	Line/Border Style button on Formatting toolbar	Format | <object>	Format <object>	ALT+O | E
Bullets	PUB 23	Bullets button on Formatting toolbar	Format | Indents and Lists	Change Text | Bullets and Numbering	ALT+F | B
Cell Diagonals	PUB 312		Table | Cell Diagonals	Change Table | Cell Diagonals	ALT+A | C
Center	PUB 161	Center button on Formatting toolbar	Arrange | Align or Distribute	Change Text | Font	CTRL+E
Change Calendar Date	PUB 315	Change date range button on Calendar Options task pane			
Change Pages	PUB 73	Page icon on status bar	Edit | Go to Page		CTRL+G or F5
Column Guides	PUB 300		Arrange | Layout Guides		ALT+R | L
Copy and Paste	PUB 109	Copy button and Paste button on Standard toolbar	Edit | Copy; Edit | Paste	Copy; Paste	CTRL+C; CTRL+V
Convert to Web Site	PUB 51		File | Convert to Web Publication		

Microsoft Office Publisher 2003 Quick Reference Summary *(continued)*

TASK	PAGE NUMBER	MOUSE	MENU BAR	SHORTCUT MENU	KEYBOARD SHORTCUT
Create Shadowed Text Box	PUB 302	Shadow Style button on Formatting toolbar			
Crop Picture	PUB 321	Crop button on Picture toolbar	Format | Picture, Picture sheet	Format Picture | Picture	ALT+O | E
Custom Color Schemes	PUB 136	Color Schemes button on Formatting toolbar	Format | Color Schemes		ALT+O | C
Delete Objects	PUB 26	Cut button on Standard toolbar	Edit | Delete Object	Delete Object	DELETE
Delete Pages	PUB 73		Edit | Delete Page	Delete Page	ALT+E | A
Design Checker	PUB 48		Tools | Design Checker		ALT+T | K
Distribute Objects	PUB 339		Arrange | Align or Distribute	Align or Distribute	ALT+R | A
Drop Cap	PUB 284		Format | Drop Cap	Change Text | Drop Cap	ALT+O | D
Edit a Story in Microsoft Word	PUB 86		Edit | Edit Story in Microsoft Word		ALT+E | W
Edit Embedded Worksheet	PUB 396	Double-click worksheet	Edit | Microsoft Office Excel Worksheet Object | Edit	Microsoft Office Excel Worksheet Object | Edit	ALT+E | O | E
Edit Graphics	PUB 36	Double-click graphic	Format | Picture	Format Picture	ALT+O | E
Edit Linked Worksheet	PUB 393	Double-click worksheet	Edit | Microsoft Office Excel Worksheet Object | Edit	Microsoft Office Excel Worksheet Object | Edit	ALT+E | O | E
Edit Personal Information Set	PUB 218		Edit | Personal Information		ALT+E | N
Edit Style	PUB 92	Style box on Formatting toolbar	Format | Styles and Formatting		ALT+O | S
Embed Excel Worksheet	PUB 395		Insert | Object		ALT+I | O
Fill Effects	PUB 221	Fill Color button on Formatting toolbar	Format | <object>	Format <object>	ALT+O | E
Font	PUB 11	Font box on Formatting toolbar	Format | Font	Change Text | Font	CTRL+SHIFT+F
Font Color	PUB 136	Font Color button on Formatting toolbar	Format | Font	Change Text | Font	ALT+O | F
Font Effect	PUB 148	Font button on Formatting toolbar	Format | Font	Change Text | Font	ALT+O | F
Font Size	PUB 145	Font Size box on Formatting toolbar	Format | Font	Change Text | Font	CTRL+SHIFT+P
Form Controls	PUB 338	Form Control button on Objects toolbar	Insert | Form Control		ALT+I | F
Format Painter	PUB 239	Format Painter button on Standard toolbar			CTRL+SHIFT+C; CTRL+SHIFT+V
Forms	PUB 133	Design Gallery Object button on Objects toolbar	Insert | Design Gallery Object | Reply Forms		ALT+I | D
Group	PUB 167	Group button	Arrange | Group	Group	CTRL+SHIFT+G
Help	PUB 54 and Appendix A	Microsoft Office Publisher Help button on Standard toolbar	Help | Microsoft Office Publisher Help		F1
HTML Code Fragment	PUB 364	HTML Code Fragment button on Objects toolbar	Insert | HTML Code Fragment		ALT+I | H
Import Text	PUB 78	Drag and drop text	Insert | Text File	Change Text | Text File	ALT+I | E
Insert Date	PUB 242		Insert | Date and Time		ALT+I | T
Insert Field Codes	PUB 254		Tools | Mail and Catalog Merge | Insert Field		
Insert Graphic	PUB 229	Picture Frame button on Objects toolbar	Insert | Picture		ALT+I | P

Microsoft Office Publisher 2003 Quick Reference Summary

TASK	PAGE NUMBER	MOUSE	MENU BAR	SHORTCUT MENU	KEYBOARD SHORTCUT
Insert Hyperlink	PUB 47	Insert Hyperlink button on Standard toolbar	Insert | Hyperlink	Hyperlink	CTRL+K
Insert Pages	PUB 75		Insert | Page		CTRL+SHIFT+N
Insert Personal Information Component	PUB 225		Insert | Personal Information		ALT+I | R
Insert Tab	PUB 287	Double-click ruler	Format | Tabs	Change Text | Tabs	ALT+O | T
Kerning	PUB 236	Kerning box on Measurement toolbar	Format | Character Spacing	Change Text | Character Spacing	CTRL+SHIFT+[; CTRL+SHIFT+]
Language Bar	APP 11	Language indicator button in tray status area			
Layout Guides	PUB 213		Tools | Layout Guides		ALT+R | D
Line Color	PUB 224	Line Color button on Formatting toolbar	Format | <object>	Format <object>	ALT+O | E
Line Spacing	PUB 150	Line Spacing button on Formatting toolbar	Format | Paragraph	Change Text | Paragraph	ALT+O | P
Link Excel Worksheet	PUB 390		Edit | Paste Special		ALT+E | S
Master Page	PUB 111		View | Master Page		CTRL+M
Mastheads	PUB 75	Design Gallery Object button on Objects toolbar	Insert | Design Gallery Object | Mastheads		ALT+I | D
Merge Cells	PUB 241		Table | Merge Cells	Change Table | Merge Cells	ALT+A | M
Move	PUB 39	Point to border and drag	Edit | Cut; Edit | Paste	Cut; Paste	CTRL+X; CTRL+V
Navigation Bar	PUB 318	Design Gallery Object button on Objects toolbar	Insert | Navigation Bar		ALT+I | N
New Publication	PUB 8	New button on Standard toolbar	File | New		CTRL+N
Open Publication	PUB 43	Open button on Standard toolbar	File | Open		CTRL+O
OverFlow Text	PUB 89		Format | AutoFit Text	Change Text | AutoFit Text	ALT+O | X
Pack and Go	PUB 175		File | Pack and Go		ALT+F | K
Photographs	PUB 154	Picture Frame button on Objects toolbar	Insert | Picture | From File	Change Picture | From File	ALT+I | P | F
Picture Hyperlink	PUB 362	Insert Hyperlink button on Standard toolbar	Insert | Hyperlink	Hyperlink	CTRL+K
Position Objects	PUB 236	Double-click Object Size box on status bar	Format | <object>	Format <object>	ALT+O | E
Preview Publication	PUB 171	Print Preview button on Standard toolbar	File | Print Preview		ALT+F | V
Print Publication	PUB 41	Print button on Standard toolbar	File | Print		CTRL+P
Publish to the Web	PUB 52		File | Publish to the Web		ALT+F | T
Pull Quotes	PUB 105	Design Gallery Object button on Objects toolbar	Insert | Design Gallery Object | Pull Quotes		ALT+I | D
Quit Publisher	PUB 56	Close button on title bar	File | Exit		ALT+F4
Recolor Graphic	PUB 234	Format Picture button on Picture toolbar	Format | Picture	Format Picture	ALT+O | E
Resize Graphic	PUB 39	Drag sizing handle	Format | Picture | Size	Format Picture | Size	ALT+O | E | S
Rotate Object	PUB 238	Free Rotate button on Standard toolbar	Arrange | Rotate or Flip	Format <object> | Size tab	ALT+R | P

Microsoft Office Publisher 2003 Quick Reference Summary *(continued)*

TASK	PAGE NUMBER	MOUSE	MENU BAR	SHORTCUT MENU	KEYBOARD SHORTCUT
Ruler Guides	PUB 215	Drag ruler	Arrange | Ruler Guides		ALT+R | D
Save Publication – New Name	PUB 33		File | Save As		ALT+F | A
Save Publication – Same Name	PUB 41	Save button on Standard toolbar	File | Save		CTRL+S
Select All Text	PUB 30		Edit | Select All		CTRL+A
Send a Publication via E-Mail	PUB 205	Send This Page as Message button on Standard toolbar	File | Send E-Mail		ALT+F | D
Set Margins	PUB 214		Arrange | Layout Guides		ALT+R | L
Set Security Level	PUB 370		Tools | Macro | Security		ALT+T | M | S
Shortcut Menu	PUB 27	Right-click object			SHIFT+F10
Sidebars	PUB 99	Design Gallery Object button on Objects toolbar	Insert | Design Gallery Object | Sidebars		ALT+I | D
Smart Tags	PUB 106	Click Smart Tag button	Tools | AutoCorrect Options		ALT+T | A
Special Characters	PUB 199	Special Characters button on Standard toolbar			
Spell Check	PUB 114	Spelling button on Standard toolbar	Tools | Spelling	Proofing Tools | Spelling	F7
Task Pane	PUB 8		View | Task Pane		CTRL+F1
Tear-offs	PUB 23	Design Gallery Object button on Objects toolbar	Insert | Design Gallery Object | Phone Tear-Offs		ALT+I | D
Text Boxes	PUB 22	Text Box button on Objects toolbar	Insert | Text Box		ALT+I | X
Texture	PUB 335	Fill Color button on Formatting toolbar	Format | Background		ALT+O | K
Toolbar, Dock	PUB 20	Drag toolbar to dock			
Toolbar, Reset	APP 28	Toolbar Options button, Add or Remove Buttons, Customize, Toolbars tab	View | Toolbars | Customize | Toolbars |	Customize | Toolbars tab	ALT+V | T | C | B
Toolbar, Show Entire	PUB 9	Double-click move handle			
Toolbar, Show or Hide	PUB 9	Right-click toolbar, click toolbar name	View | Toolbars	Toolbars	ALT+V | T
Tracking	PUB 235	Tracking box on Measurement toolbar	Format | Character Spacing	Change Text | Character Spacing	ALT+O | R
Transparent Objects	PUB 186	Set Transparent Color button on Picture toolbar	Format | <object>	Format <object>	CTRL+T
Undo	PUB 28	Undo button on Standard toolbar	Edit | Undo	Undo	CTRL+Z
Ungroup	PUB 168	Ungroup button	Arrange | Ungroup	Ungroup	CTRL+SHIFT+G
VBA Window	PUB 367		Tools | Macro | Visual Basic Editor		ALT+F11
Web Page Options	PUB 262	Page Content button on Standard toolbar | More Web page options	Tools | Web Page Options		ALT+T | E
Web Page Preview	PUB 53	Web Page Preview button on Standard toolbar	File | Web Page Preview		ALT+F | B
WordArt	PUB 94	Insert WordArt button on Objects toolbar	Insert | Picture | WordArt		ALT+I | P | W
Zoom	PUB 22	Zoom box on Standard toolbar	View | Zoom	Zoom	F9